C000108967

Mike is a retired geology lecturer and STEM coordinator with a passion for history and a love of old military aircraft. Having grown up living close to RAF Biggin Hill, which is known as 'the Home of the Battle of Britain,' stories of this momentous air battle fascinated him.

Facing the Abyss: Two Decisive Battles for Britain was inspired by watching the film *Elizabeth the Golden Age* in 2007. Mike was struck by similarities between the fight against the Spanish Armada and the Battle of Britain. In 2008, he commenced a journey of research to discover whether these perceived views were indeed true.

To Macey

Mike Leddra

FACING THE ABYSS

TWO DECISIVE BATTLES FOR BRITAIN

AUSTIN MACAULEY PUBLISHERS™

LONDON • CAMBRIDGE • NEW YORK • SHARJAH

Copyright © Mike Leddra (2019)

All rights reserved. No part of this publication may be reproduced, distributed, or transmitted in any form or by any means, including photocopying, recording, or other electronic or mechanical methods, without the prior written permission of the publisher, except in the case of brief quotations embodied in critical reviews and certain other non-commercial uses permitted by copyright law. For permission requests, write to the publisher.

Any person who commits any unauthorized act in relation to this publication may be liable to criminal prosecution and civil claims for damages.

Ordering Information:
Quantity sales: special discounts are available on quantity purchases by corporations, associations, and others. For details, contact the publisher at the address below.

Publisher's Cataloging-in-Publication data
Leddra, Mike
Facing the Abyss: Two Decisive Battles for Britain

ISBN 9781641828277 (Paperback)
ISBN 9781641828284 (Hardback)
ISBN 9781645366195 (ePub e-book)

The main category of the book — HISTORY / Europe / Great Britain / General

Library of Congress Control Number: 2019934485

www.austinmacauley.com/us

First Published (2019)
Austin Macauley Publishers LLC
40 Wall Street, 28th Floor
New York, NY 10005
USA

mail-usa@austinmacauley.com
+1 (646) 5125767

My many thanks go to Gordon Handley and Bob Dickson, who provided me with helpful feedback in the writing of this book. I would also like to thank year six pupils at Bournmoor Primary School and their teachers, especially Danielle and Laura, for allowing me to 'try-out' many of the stories included in this book.

I have read so many informative books prior to and during the writing of this book, particularly about the Battle of Britain, but have only included the ones from which I have included quotes. Many of the personal memoirs are truly inspirational and deserve to be read by many more people.

Finally, I would like to thank my wife, Ann, who supported and encouraged me to finish the book.

Introduction

There have been a few occasions in the past where other nations or peoples have threatened to invade us. However, there have only been three times when we have faced a real threat of imminent invasion, the prevention of which depended on a famous battle, namely the defeat of the Spanish Armada in 1588, the Battle of Trafalgar in 1805, and the Battle of Britain in 1940. These, together with the Battle of Waterloo in 1815, are generally considered to be the greatest battles in our history. Two of these great battles were against Napoleon's forces in the 19th century; the first was Vice Admiral Nelson's Battle of Trafalgar, which was fought on Monday, 21 October 1805. This took place 48 miles (77km) off the Spanish Atlantic coast almost halfway between the port of Cadiz and Gibraltar. The second, the Battle of Waterloo, which was purely a land battle, was led by the Duke of Wellington and occurred on Sunday, 18 June 1815, 11 miles (18km) south of Brussels.

Clearly, both of these crucial Napoleonic battles were fought well away from home soil, whereas, only the defeat of the Spanish Armada in the summer of 1588 and the defeat of the Luftwaffe during the Battle of Britain in the summer of 1940 were witnessed by people at home. Watching these first-hand, or hearing about them happening on your doorstep, helped bring home the seriousness of the situation and allowed people to see what their armed forces were doing to defend them. It also allowed them to feel as though they were playing a direct part in both battles and of course, many were either actively or passively involved. For example, the crowds on the Isle of Portland on Tuesday, 2 August 1588, were able to shout encouragement to Frobisher and his men. People threw food to the English ships, and some of the noblemen even joined ships to be able to take part in the battle. In 1940, even more of the public were in the frontline, not just during the Blitz but during all of the daytime and night-time air-raids that ranged across much of the country. Those in the south and east of the country, in particular, witnessed first-hand the many air battles taking place over their heads, while others across the country listened to the BBC radio broadcasts and news. They saw aircraft from both sides shot down and were able to offer help whenever possible. It would be fair to say that during both battles, there was a feeling of collective responsibility, a feeling of all being in it together, a feeling which was also engendered by stirring speeches made by two famous leaders and orators, namely Queen Elizabeth I and Winston Churchill, that have gone down in the annals of history.

On both occasions, our island position was a key factor in our success; the fact that an invading army had to cross the 24 miles (38km) between us and the continent has often proved to be more difficult than expected. As David Thomas explains in his book, *The Illustrated Armada Handbook:*

'Curiously, Parma's [the commander of the Spanish invasion army in the Netherlands in 1588] invasion plan foreshadowed the appreciations of Napoleon and Hitler for their own assaults on England centuries later. It is interesting to observe that all of the plans foundered on insufficient consideration being given to the question of command of the sea. Parma, Napoleon, and Hitler, military geniuses of their eras, gravely overestimated the ability of the military to cross the Channel with relative ease.'

For Philip of Spain's and Hitler's invasions to be successful, the Spanish had to neutralize the English Navy in 1588 and the Luftwaffe had to gain air superiority over the Royal Air Force in 1940. On both occasions, the introduction of new equipment on this side of the Channel led to the adoption of new tactics which, to a large extent, set the pattern for following confrontations. Our ability to re-supply, re-arm, and re-deploy forces from home bases was a great advantage and helped significantly in both battles against what were perceived as overwhelming odds.

We will see that Parma appears to have had grave doubts that he could transport his army across the English Channel without the support and success of the Armada, and the German Navy in 1940 felt that they were in no position to support or mount an invasion fleet without the success of the Luftwaffe. Even if both the Armada and the Luftwaffe had been successful in their missions, the other commanders still harbored significant doubts about their own forces. In 1805, Napoleon faced similar problems; the combined naval forces of Spain and France were close to a match for the Royal Navy in numbers of ships that would face each other (thirty-three verses twenty-seven), but his invasion ships were generally unseaworthy and his army was suffering from similar difficulties to those faced by Parma. Alan Schom explains in his book, *Trafalgar: Countdown to Battle 1803–1805*, that the

Battle of Trafalgar was the 'culmination of an intense 29-month campaign waged by the Royal Navy to prevent a French invasion.' It is interesting to note that during the Seven Years' War (1756–1763), in spite of a twenty-month close blockade by the Royal Navy, the French were gathering their land and sea forces in preparation for an earlier invasion of England. Their plans were scuppered by another naval battle, which is sometimes referred to as 'the other Trafalgar,' namely the Battle of Quiberon Bay. In his book, *The Battle of Quiberon Bay, 1759: Admiral Hawke and the Defeat of the French Invasion,* Nicholas Tracy describes how in the midst of a severe gale and raging seas on 20 November 1759, Hawke 'was able to seize the opportunity to destroy the [French] Brest fleet in the most dramatic sea battle in the age of sail.'

Both Trafalgar and Quiberon Bay were single naval battles fought on single days, whereas neither the defeat of the Armada nor the Battle of Britain can be regarded as a single event even though they had pivotal days within them, namely 8 August 1588 and 15 September 1940. Both could be described as more of a running conflict that ebbed and flowed during which our commanders reacted by modifying their tactics, either to changing conditions or to the tactical changes made by the enemy.

On both occasions, Britain effectively stood alone, and defeat in either battle would have had a significant outcome not just for this country but for much of Europe (during the Battle of Waterloo, Wellington's army fought alongside a Prussian army).

The English Navy at the time of the Armada had a core of largely professional sailors, some of whom had somewhat dubious backgrounds and many of them were related to each other in some way (see Table 1). Most of their main fighting ships were specifically designed for the role they were about to undertake, and they were built and supported by dedicated naval dockyards. Even so, a significant proportion of the ships' crew were inexperienced, and, when the two fleets met off the coast of Fowey, Cornwall, on 30 July 1588, it was the first time that the English Navy had sailed with such a large force. Therefore, it lacked the training or experience of operating so many ships together as a single force.

People who may have heard of 'the Few'—pilots of the Battle of Britain—may never have realized the tremendous support given by other services and civilians engaged in war work, often facing situations as dangerous as those faced by the pilots.

Since its formation on April Fool's Day 1918, the Royal Air Force (RAF) instigated an extremely well-developed training regime for all of its pilots and ground crew, so that when it came to the Battle of Britain, the service had a first-class pedigree and a first-class support system behind it.

One of the most important aspects that relate to both battles is that they were led by men, Francis Howard in 1588 and Hugh Dowding in 1940, who knew the ins and outs of every part of their commands. The main fighting force in both the English Navy in 1588 and Fighter Command 1940 comprised of ships and aircraft that were suited for home defense.

The newly designed ships of the Elizabethan English fleet did not have the space to be able to carry provisions, cannonballs, and gunpowder for extended periods at sea. The early Hurricanes and Spitfires of Fighter Command did not have the fuel capacity to take the fight to the enemy far beyond the Channel, but then, at that time, following the evacuation at Dunkirk, they were not required to do so.

The defeat of the Armada signaled the demise of the Spanish as a major naval power and the beginning of the ascendancy of the Royal Navy—or more correctly, the Navy Royal as it was known at the time—when Britain began to 'rule the waves.' This 'rule' finds no better culmination than Nelson's victory at Trafalgar and his famous signals to his fleet that 'England expects that every man to do his duty' followed by 'Engage the enemy more closely.' As Thomas writes of the defeat of the Armada:

> '...it was to take years, even a generation or more, to appreciate the real magnitude of the English victory. It was a watershed in the story of England, the birth of a new patriotism, and the beginning of a new belief in the Navy, a belief that was to grow in intensity in future centuries. Although tested time and time again in the furnace of battle, the Navy was never to be found wanting.'

That was until World War Two when the use of air power effectively took the Navy's crown away because the RAF were required to maintain air superiority over the south and east of the country, where ships had proved to be far too vulnerable to Luftwaffe attacks. Even so, we will see that the Navy continued to play a significant role in both defensive and offensive capabilities of this country. The mere presence of the capital ships of Royal Navy, albeit not in the proposed invasion area, was sufficient to influence German planning.

In Air Marshal Sir Denis Crowley-Milling's foreword to Richard Townshend Bickers book, *The Battle of Britain: The Greatest Battle in the History of Air Warfare*, published to mark the 50th anniversary of the Battle of Britain, he writes:

'...let us consider for a moment, fifty years on, how different history would have been had the German air force gained that vital air superiority over Britain—so necessary before there could be any thought of the invasion that Goering had boasted could be launched within a matter of weeks, with forces moving across the Channel unmolested by air attack to achieve final occupation. First there would have been no American intervention and support in arms or men, no massive bombing offensive against Germany, and no base from which to launch a second front. Hitler's war machine would have been largely committed to the defeat of Russia and under these circumstances it could well have been successful. Also, having no disruption in their nuclear research and development work, it is conceivable that Germany would have had the atomic bomb within a few years, thus strengthening her position as the master of Europe. Britain could well have been an occupied country to this day.'

He adds that

'1940 was the year that air power truly came of age. The success of all campaigns that followed depended heavily upon gaining and sustaining air superiority.'

In his book *RAF Biggin Hill: The Other Side of the Bump*, Peter Osborne observes that

'During the four years of the Great War, as is common in most conflicts, great strides were taken to improve how men could obliterate men more efficiently. It is also observed that great wars begin with weapons and tactics of the last major conflict.'

We will see that this observation applies to the Spanish, and that lessons learnt by the English whilst fighting the Spanish Navy in 1588 resulted in its naval superiority until 1940 when new tactics were needed to defend the British Isles. 1940 signaled the beginning of a new era in which air power and air superiority were vital components of most modern warfare. This still exists today where conflicts involve aircraft or increasingly remote-controlled drones conduct war at arm's length. Having said that, as Alfred Price highlights in *The Battle of Britain,* (edited by Kenneth Munson and John Taylor),

'...the notion that Fighter Command was all that stood in the way of a successful German invasion in 1940 is deeply rooted in British folklore;

but folklore is a poor substitute for historical analysis. The truth is that given the size, the state of equipment and the level of training of the RAF, even without Fighter Command, and of the Royal Navy and the British Army, coupled with the resolute political leadership of Winston Churchill and fortified by the advanced knowledge of German intentions through deciphered signals, an invasion could not possibly have succeeded.'

It is said that knowledge is a great power, and knowing your enemies' plans is one of the most important aspects of war. This was equally true for the Spanish Armada and their army in the Low Countries.

Francis Walsingham's network of spies and double agents meant that he knew some, but not all, of the Spanish plans and who, in this country, was likely to support them. The Spanish vastly underestimated the resolve of the British people to fight, even if it meant Catholics defending a Protestant Queen. German High Command made the same mistake in 1940 when they thought that the British public would force the government to accept Hitler's peace terms.

Walsingham is famous as a spymaster, who although had an extensive spy network at home, but the quality of his spies and the information they were able to glean on the continent may not have lived up to this reputation. It is often said that in 1940, the Germans sent over a 'flood' of spies. In fact, everyone was paranoid about the existence of spies; a paranoia which, it appears, was less than justified in the early days of World War Two. Trying to find out what the Germans were planning was essential, and probably the most well-known method of information gathering was the *Enigma* code breaking system at Bletchley Park. However, within the same geographical area—around Leighton Buzzard—were numerous other integrated listening, communication, and spy systems. Although Bletchley Park is rightfully famous for breaking the *Enigma* codes, it depended on a myriad of dedicated women and men across the country and indeed, across the world, who listened and copied down all enemy communications as part of the *Y-Service*. Nor must the work of the deception organizations be forgotten, people who set up fake airfields and other fake target sites—known as '*Q*' and '*K*' sites— and diversionary fires etc. in order to draw German bombers away from their intended targets.

It is interesting to note that in recent years, some authors have partially dismissed both battles by suggesting that neither Philip II nor Hitler really wanted to or had any intention of invading Britain. This may or may not be true, but it must be remembered that this does not diminish the importance of both battles, and, even if, on both occasions, the governments on this side of the Channel were receiving information that supported these as possibilities, they could not afford to let their guard down for a single minute.

In his book, *The Spanish Armada,* Roger Whiting suggests that the Armada was really just posturing by Philip II to force Elizabeth I to negotiate a peace treaty. If this is true, he and Philip III, who succeeded him in 1598, put a great deal of their country's money, resources, and people's lives at risk to do so—acts from which the Spanish never fully recovered. In fact, the Armada of 1588, the great 'Enterprise of England' as the invasion of England was known, was only the first of five Armadas that the two Philips sent. The second sailed with one hundred and forty ships on 29 October 1596 with the intension of landing an invasion force in Ireland. This Armada was hit by a severe storm while it was sailing off Cape Finisterre on the coast of Portugal and lost thirty-eight ships and 5,000 men; it also bankrupted Philip II. The third Armada in October/November 1597 was intended to land an army of 6,000–8,000 soldiers at either Falmouth on the south coast of Cornwall or Milford Haven in South Wales. Having set sail with another one hundred and forty ships and 13–14,000 men on 18 October, this too was stopped a few miles south of the Lizard by a large storm which lasted for three days and battered, and scattered the ships. Some of the ships managed to land troops on both shores where they held out for two days. The Spanish lost twenty-eight ships, and more than 1,500 men were killed or taken prisoner. This Armada nearly bankrupted the king again. What made this Armada so disconcerting was that at the time no one had any idea that it was on its way. Some of the men and ships involved in this Armada had taken part in the Battle of Cornwall two years earlier when between 2–4 August four galleys landed troops on the southern Cornish coast, where they set fire to the towns of Mousehole, Paul, Newlyn, and Penzance. The fourth Armada (sometimes referred to as the Invisible Armada), comprising six galleys, was dispatched by Philip III in the summer of 1599. This fleet was not headed for England but was sent with reinforcements to Calais. The fifth Armada, in 1601, landed troops in Ireland. Even then, this final Armada was affected by the weather. Even before it reached the Irish coast, a storm dispersed the fleet, leading to nine ships turning back. Weather conditions also meant that the other twenty-eight ships, carrying around 3,300 men landed their troops in two different places on the southwest coast of County Cork, about 65km apart. Des Ekin's book *The Last Armada—Queen Elizabeth, Juan del Aguila, and Hugh O'Neill: The Story of the 100-Day Spanish Invasion* relates the story of their endeavors. (It is also worth looking out for John Wilkinson's historic novel, *The Pirate and the Prophecy...of the Keigwins of Mousehole and the Spanish Raid on Cornwall*.)

In his book, *Dunkirk the Necessary Myth*, Nicholas Harman puts the situation in 1940 clearly in to context when he says that:

'In Europe in 1940 the stakes were terribly high. The penalty for permanent failure by the Allies does not bear thinking about. Whatever the motive and whatever the conduct of the British, they were at least on the right side, against the right enemy of the giant power whose part in the defeat of Hitler was in the end to be decisive, the Russians were at the time passively entwined in alliance with the Nazis. The Americans were worried...about their own domestic future.'

It is thought that Hitler did not consider Britain to be Germany's natural enemy and that the British people would settle for peace so that he could concentrate on turning his armed forces towards Russia, who he regarded as his and Europe's real enemy. Equally, he did not want have to fight on two fronts. Even if this is true, he still sent a significant proportion of his air force against us in the summer of 1940 to try to take Britain out of the equation.

The problem with perception, therefore, is that it depends on which side of the conflict you perceive the threat to be. In both 1588 and 1940, people in this country had no reason to think that either the launching of the Armada or the Luftwaffe gave any impression that the threat was just posturing. In both cases, the entire country, not just those in charge, thought that the threat of invasion was real and imminent. As Geoffrey Moorhouse states in his book *Great Harry's Navy*, when talking about the build-up of navy to face the Spanish in 1588:

'The Spaniards may have regarded this above all as a punitive expedition, but for the defenders it was nothing less than a national emergency. That is why [as we shall see] so much was put into it by private shipowners, municipalities, and corporations as well as by the monarch.'

When you think you are under threat, you do not sit back and wait to see what might or might not happen. Equally, when an enemy is on your doorstep with a large force, most people would not turn around and say, "It's OK, they don't really mean it"; they would defend themselves as best they could. Therefore, on this side of the Channel, people viewed things differently. In 1588, each county had to call to arms ordinary men to defend the country against the threat of invasion. If the Spanish landed, the Trained

Bands and men of the General Muster were instructed to destroy everything that might be of any use and burn all crops as they retreated.

In 1940, the same thing happened again with the establishment of the Home Guard who made thousands of Molotov Cocktails and homemade explosives to fight against invading troops and tanks. They dug up fields, put anything they could find in open areas to defend against gliders, were ready to blow up bridges, destroy anything that might be useful to the Germans, and if necessary, they too were to burn all the crops if they had to retreat.

History has shown that these two battles played a fundamental part in making England, the rest of the UK, and most of Europe what it is today. But why as a geologist and geographer should I write a history book, comparing the Spanish Armada and the Battle of Britain? Geology and, therefore, geography, and history are strongly related and, in fact, each subject area has had a strong influence on the other, and I think they should be studied together.

The geology and the landscape of the UK and the coasts of France, the Low Countries, Portugal, and Spain played an important part in both sets of invasion plans. The Spanish needed deep-water harbors on the Spanish and Portuguese coasts in which to assemble the Armada, and another one on the French or Low Countries coast in which they could bring the Armada and Parma's army together for the invasion. They also needed one on the English coast in which they could land the army and then be able to use it as a base from which they could defend the invasion barges against the Navy Royal.

The nature of the coastline and the sea played an important part in the day-to-day tactics of the Navy Royal, whose primary aim was to deprive the Armada of its ability to secure a deep-water harbor or a landing site, as it progressed up the English Channel. In 1940, the Germans faced similar restrictions; they too required deep-water ports for the assembly of their invasion barges on the French, Belgium, and Dutch coasts, and deep-water ports on the southern or eastern coasts of England from which they could disembark the majority of their troops and equipment.

One of the other important geographical aspects of both battles was the weather. The British are supposed to be notorious for their obsession with the weather; we use it as an introduction to many conversations, and we often complain about it. Because it is so variable, it frequently affects our lives far more than we realize.

The weather played a critical part in both battles. The unseasonable weather during 1587 and 1588 disrupted the sailing of the Armada, controlled the timing and nature of individual battles during the Armada's journey up the English Channel, and ultimately led to the destruction of many of its ships. It was intimate knowledge of the weather, wind, and local tidal and sea conditions along the coast that gave the English mariners a distinct advantage in 1588. Conversely, it was a lack of knowledge of the Scottish and Irish coasts and sea conditions, particularly around the north of Scotland and Ireland that led to the destruction of the Armada during its attempt at the long journey home.

During the Battle of Britain, the weather gave Fighter Command crucial periods of respite in which it was able to rebuild and re-supply it squadrons and airfields in Southern England. It also deprived the Luftwaffe of their 'four clear days' in which they were supposed to drive Fighter Command from the skies.

My interest in geography and history, however, goes much further back than just an academic interest. As children, our summer holidays were always to either the Isle of Wight, the Dorset or Devon coasts. As a geologist, I have been on countless field trips to the Dorset and Cornish coastlines where my ex-colleagues and I have taught students over many years. In fact, when I told a couple of the other geologists that I was going to write this book, one of them said, "I hope you are going to include all the stories you used to tell us about the Spanish Armada when we were on the Isle of Portland."

"Yes, Richard, Andy and Iain, I have!"

Although I am a geologist, my obsession (as my family would say) are old airplanes. I have loved old airplanes for as long as I can remember—a passion inherited from my dad. I was bought up in Orpington, Kent, I was just a stone's throw from RAF Biggin Hill, the airfield that is known as the 'Home of the Battle of Britain.' I can still remember going to my first airshow at Biggin Hill at the age of four, and I have been hooked ever since. In fact, the family always complain that they cannot go anywhere without Dad having sorted out where there are some old aircraft to photograph beforehand. I was fortunate enough to be able to attend the air display commemorating the 75th anniversary of the 'Hardest Day' on 18 August 2015 at Biggin Hill, whose motto was the 'Strongest Link' referring to the ring of Fighter Command airfields around London. Standing on the airfield, you can look across to London and clearly see the skyscrapers at Canary Wharf in what was, in 1940, one of the Luftwaffe's main targets—the London Docks. As you stand there, you can visualize the people on the airfield as it was being attacked, but also picture them looking out towards the docks as they were being bombed, and appreciate what it must have meant to all of them—civilians and military personnel—as they tried to repulse the Luftwaffe. I remember my dad telling stories of seeing Heinkel bombers flying past his home in Mottingham in Southeast London, "so low you could see into the cockpits," or the aftermath, "when one of their bombs destroyed the house next door and half of ours."

If I were to look at all the books that I have on my bookshelves, the majority of which are obviously geology related, the largest number on a single subject are the ones about the Battle of Britain. So much has been written and rewritten about this crucial battle, but in my opinion, it is still a relatively unknown and a relatively unappreciated part of our history for the majority of the British public.

It is very easy in a book like this to try to shoehorn direct comparisons to emphasize a point or to bring out a similarity that does not exist; therefore, since I started writing this in 2008, I have tried to be very careful not to make links where none exist. This is especially important given that there are over three hundred and fifty years between the two events, which could almost be regarded as being 'two worlds apart.' However, I think you will see, there really are significant similarities between these two important episodes in British history.

You will see that I have divided the book in to two parts, one covering the defeat of the Armada, the other covering the Battle of Britain. I have used the same chapter titles in each part to draw out their similarities.

In Chapter 1, we will see that the English Navy in the 1500s went through major changes, as the country began to challenge Spanish and Portuguese dominance of the seas. Queen Elizabeth I saw maritime trade and unofficial pirating as a way of getting her hands on money because the country was in a state of near bankruptcy. At the same time, John Hawkins introduced significant changes to the design of our ships, doing away with large fore and after castles, reducing the width of the Queen's ships, making them sleeker, 'race-built' vessels that were far more maneuverable. This went hand-in-hand with the major changes William Wynter introduced to the ship's guns and gun carriages, which enabled our ships to attack enemy ships from a far greater distance, and fire and reload our cannons faster and more efficiently. This allowed the English ships to mount a completely different form of attack to that used by the Spanish.

Following the formation of the Royal Air Force in 1918, from the combination of the navy's Royal Navy Air Service and army's Royal Flying Corps, it too struggled under financial constraints during the 1920s and 1930s. Under the driving force of Hugh Dowding, Fighter Command introduced new monoplane aircraft, powered by a new generation of aero engines, armed with more guns. He was also instrumental in building the infrastructure to support, direct, and control his aircraft, using new technology, such as radar, information integration and filtering, and the group and sector station system. As Sinclair McKay comments in his book *The Secret Life of Fighter Command: The Men and Women who beat the Luftwaffe:*

> '...this cat's cradle network of intelligence—the bluff old Observer Corpse men, the dedicated and intelligent women, and the eager young civilian scientists looking after the brand new radar technology—had been painstakingly devised by a commander who was misunderstood and treated with cold contempt by his superiors.'

Dowding had seen and was fundamentally involved in turning flying from 'a rare miracle of daring and aeronautic skill to a new, modern branch of warfare.' The Battle of Britain, the first modern, large-scale air battle, involved far more than just the fighter pilots—the Few. It relied on support, supply, intelligence, and control systems manned by service and civilian personnel across the country.

In Chapter 2, we turn our attentions to the situation on the continent where European politics, alliances, and power play drew us into inevitable conflicts. This was compounded by two super-powers: Spain, under the rule of King Philip II, and Germany, under Hitler's rule, who both viewed the English-British as troublesome irritants who would not keep their nose out of what they were trying to achieve. We will see that Spain's pattern of marine warfare was set through long-term conflicts with the Turks; and Germans relied on Blitzkrieg 'lightning war' where aircraft and land forces working together had successfully swept across Western Europe.

Chapter 3 looks at the preparations made by Spain and Germany to invade us, and our response to them. Both had large, well-equipped armies on the continent, ready to mount an invasion, but neither had the marine capabilities to transport and protect their soldiers and their equipment if they tried to cross the Channel. We will see how effective or ineffective spies, spying networks, and sources of intelligence were in the lead up to the battles. This chapter also includes the withdrawal of our army from the continent on both occasions, leaving the home forces in a completely inadequate state to repel an invasion.

In Chapter 4, we look at the actions taken to prevent an invasion. Before the Armada sailed, Francis Drake caused havoc and destruction along the coasts of Spain and Portugal, actions that led to crucial (from the English point of view) and disastrous (from the Spanish point of view) delays in the build-up of forces and resources needed by the Armada. We will also see the actions in 1940 of the Royal Navy, and the often nearly suicidal bombing campaigns of Bomber and Coastal Command, all of which combined to attack the build-up of German ships and barges day after day and night after night. This action, together with both commands' attacks on Luftwaffe bases and war supply infrastructures, also meant that Hitler had to continuously postpone the invasion until ultimately the opportunity was missed.

In the next chapter (Chapter 5), we turn to the battles themselves and look at the opening rounds. Francis Howard, in charge of the Navy Royal and the leaders of the Fleet were able to marshal their ships and use their captains' local knowledge to keep their ships in control of the fighting with their primary aim of preventing the Spanish reaching a deep-water harbor at high tide. During the opening rounds of the Battle of Britain, we see how Dowding's years of careful planning together with his Air Vice Marshal, Keith Parks, and his other group commanders marshaling the fighter aircraft, irrespective of the Luftwaffe tactics, which meant that they too never lost control of the battle, although on several occasions, as we will see, it came close to it.

Chapter 6 covers the most crucial period of both battles when both forces were being put under increasing pressure, and resources were being stretched to the limits. This covers the Armada's arrival at Calais, the night of the fire ships, and Goering's continuous changing tactics, which helped snatch defeat from the arms of victory.

Chapter 7 covers the action on the Big Day in both battles. On the afternoon of 8 August in 1588, we see that, for the first time, all of Howard's ships are ready to face the Armada and that through their actions they spread panic through the Spanish ships. On 15 September 1940, all of Dowding's aircraft, including the Duxford Big Wing, come together—a sight that spread fear through the Luftwaffe's pilots and aircrew.

Although neither the sea battle of 8 August nor the air battle of 15 September were a knockout blow, they both led to the enemy effectively giving up the fight. Hence in Chapter 8, we see both adversaries licking wounds and changing their tactics, with the abandonment of a possible invasion. Although both opponents had lost their opportunity to mount an invasion, we see that on this side of the Channel those in charge could not drop their guard. The country stayed on full alert, not being sure that an invasion had been prevented. Consequently, on Thursday, 18 August 1588, as the battered Spanish ships sailed up the North Sea and around the tip of Scotland, Queen Elizabeth gave her stirring speech to the army assembled at Tilbury. In 1940, for six weeks after 15 September, Fighter Command continued to engage enemy aircraft.

Chapter 9, 'They Think It's All Over,' describes the Armada's attempts to get home with their tattered ships and crews while suffering tragic losses in the seas around Scotland and along the Irish coast. We also see the Luftwaffe's gradual run down of their air campaign against fighter Command, as Hitler starts to turn his attention eastwards.

Chapter 10, 'Scapegoats in the Aftermath,' looks at the repercussions of Howard's 'failure to destroy the Armada' and the treatment of his sailors in a cash-strapped England. We also see the 'meeting of shame' that followed the Battle of Britain when the knives came out against Huge Dowding and Keith Park. Both historic battles ended in a rather disgraceful way in which, 'national heroes' played their parts. We see that Drake rather than Howard was given the glory at home for the defeat of the Armada, and that Medina Sidonia rather than Parma took the blame for the failure of the Armada and the invasion—something that stayed with him until he died. We also see that the actions of Bader and Leigh-Mallory, backed by senior RAF officers with their own agendas, behaved disgracefully towards Dowding and Park, even before the Battle of Britain had officially ended.

Finally, there is an old saying that history keeps repeating itself. It is important to view the future with one eye on the past and learn from it. However, one of the problems with history is that it is always being rewritten, revamped, or reinterpreted. Sometimes, the beauty of hindsight allows us to view situations in a significantly different way to which they were viewed at the time. It is therefore important that, with any books that cover historical events, the writer and reader do not lose sight of the context in which the events occurred. We continuously see that new information is discovered, or released, particularly with regard to more recent history, which allows us to re-evaluate historic events and to be able to understand how the people involved reacted and have some appreciation of why they did what they did. However, it is always important to remember that this information was not necessarily known or appreciated by all those involved at the time.

Part 1. 1588:
The Spanish Armada

Chapter 1
Fundamental Changes

Being an island nation, the British people have always had a close association with the sea. It divides us from our neighbors and enemies in equal measure. It provides a barrier that we have been able to hide behind when we need or want to, but it also proves to be a barrier which has to be overcome if we want to be part of Europe. During the Second World War, Britain was regarded as the 'aircraft carrier of Europe.' Prior to 1588, it was recognized as Garrett Mattingly puts it in his book *The Defeat of the Spanish Armada*, that:

> '...the English had become conscious that they were guarded by the sea and the sea was theirs to guard.'

To this end, following the conclusion of the Hundred Years War, Henry VIII spent a significant amount of money building up the navy; a process that Elizabeth I continued, which meant that by the time that Philip II launched the Armada in 1588, the Spanish faced one of the most powerful navies in the world. Prior to this, the Spanish and Portugal navies had had a long history of Mediterranean and worldwide maritime operations, which the English Navy did not. Why then should the smaller English Navy hold such a position?

This is partly down to history and partially down to organization. The Spanish had been fighting the Turks and Moors in the Mediterranean during which they gained significant experience in ramming, boarding, and over-powering their enemy's ships. To enable them to do this, they had to be able to smash the enemy's masts, sails, and upper woodwork before they could come alongside to allow their soldiers to board the oppositions ships. Their ships were armed with cannons, which did not need to be rapidly reloaded and which fired large objects over a relatively short distance, so that they could inflict substantial damage to the superstructures of their enemies' ships. To facilitate the boarding process, they built large fore and aft castles on the upper decks of their ships, which gave their soldiers the advantage of height and some degree of protection. They were, therefore, effectively used as floating army forts. This primary military function meant that they had to carry as many soldiers as possible and this led to the ships being built as wide as possible to hold the soldiers, their equipment, and provisions. This basic shape also allowed the ships to be relatively stable, which facilitated the boarding process.

As the sea conditions in the Mediterranean were relatively calm, they were also generally built with thinner hulls and mast positions further forward, compared with ships that were required to sail in the Atlantic or Pacific oceans, or even the North Sea. They were also built on experience from pervious battles in which galleys—oar-powered ships—were regarded as the fleet's most heavily armed ships. These were incredibly maneuverable in light winds where sails were less effective. They were also used to ram the opposition. A later development of the galley was the galleass, some of which sailed with the Armada. These were large ships powered by both sails and oars, thus, they were a type of halfway house between galleys and galleons. These vessels could use their sails when conditions allowed; but if the wind dropped or was blowing from the wrong direction, the oars could be used to bring the galleass in to battle. However, in rough seas, they were liable to flood, as water poured in through the ports in their hulls that were used for the oars.

The Armada comprised ships that were, therefore, primarily built to carry troops effectively to fight a land battle at sea, and it is, therefore, interesting to note that when the Armada was first proposed, its composition included a significant number of galleys and galleasses.

So did the English Navy follow the same format? In short, the answer is no. The English Navy had been going through a major period of shipbuilding under Henry VIII which ironically was also encouraged by Philip II when he married Mary Tudor. In doing so, they had produced their own version of the galleon, the heavy fighting ship, which was a combination of ships that had the seaworthiness of Atlantic merchantmen and the fighting capacity of Mediterranean galley. Henry VIII also changed the way in which naval ships were built, manned, and maintained, which would result not just in the Royal Navy we have today but also in the navies of every other country around the world. How did he achieve this? Arthur Herman's book, *To Rule the Waves*, provides a very good insight in to how and why he did it:

'Henry VIII was no different then to other European rulers, or his medieval predecessors. But his determination to spend money to get the navy he wanted did have important unforeseen consequences.

'First, he expanded the number of royal ships from 12 to 84. To build and service them, he had new shipyards constructed on the Thames at Deptford, Erith and Woolwich, just above and below his palace at Greenwich so that he could visit the docks himself... Henry also built new ship facilities at Portsmouth where King John had first built a dock in the 13th century and which was an important assembly point for fleets of the "Navy Royal." But the real headquarters of Henry's navy was Deptford. By the time of his death, more than six hundred shipwrights and laborers were working there or at Woolwich and Portsmouth... Warehouses, docks, building yards, and workshops sprang up in abundance.'

He also established the Navy Board, which oversaw and controlled his navy, something that, at the time, no other navy in the world had. This enabled it to be managed and developed in an organized manner, which gave it a distinct advantage over other naval forces.

Incidentally, the name Royal Navy did not come into being until England and Scotland were united under James I (James VI of Scotland). Interestingly, Herman points out that the navy was the first to use the Union Jack in 1606, which comprised only the cross of St. George on top of the cross of St. Andrew, decades before it was adopted as the national flag.

Most of us know or have heard of the *Mary Rose*, Henry VIII's flagship, now preserved at Portsmouth, which sank in 1545, as it went out to meet a French invasion fleet. Although she was built sometime between 1509 and 1511 as a 600-ton (609 tonnes) ship, she was rebuilt in 1536 to be a prototype 700-ton (711 tonnes) galleon able to carry heavy guns. During this rebuild, they reduced the height of her castles, beginning the changes in design that would separate the ships of the Navy Royal (as the Royal Navy was originally known following its creation by Henry after his coronation in 1509) from all other fighting ships at the time. As she sailed out to meet the French in front of the rest of the English fleet on the evening of 19 July 1545, she turned to present her broadside guns to the enemy and a gust of wind tilted her over. Because her lower gun deck ports, which were only 16 inches (0.4m) above the waterline, were open, water flooded in and she sank.

Her redesign and rebuild were the initial steps in the modernization of the English fleet that was designed to fight a different type of battle in a different way. She had been rebuilt to carry heavier guns that could be used to smash into the hulls of the opposition from a distance rather that the traditional close quarters fighting. These new guns were also mounted on a new type of gun carriage which meant that they could be moved more easily than the previous guns, reloaded faster, and could be more accurately aimed at enemy ships. This process of improvement continued throughout the following thirty years, resulting in the galleons of Elizabeth's navy, which faced the Spanish in 1588.

Geoffrey Moorhouse in his book *Great Harry's Navy: How Henry VIII Gave England Sea Power*, explains that, 'The year 1545 best marks the birth of the English naval power; it is the year that most clearly displays the transition from oars to sails…[however] modern experts put their money…on 1546 because that was when the most significant administrative strides were made,' as outlined above. These also included the Lord Treasurer giving, on advice from the Lord Admiral, an annual budget, which the Admiral could 'use as he thought fit.'

When Queen Elizabeth I came to power, she inherited a navy which had a well-organized, well-run system of development, care, and maintenance, but which, as we shall see, she could ill afford to expand. As Hugh Bicheno notes in his book *Elizabeth's Sea Dogs*, their superior naval administration enabled the English to 'mobilise in a month the resources it took Philip a year to assemble.' Soon after starting her reign, the Queen asked William Wynter to conduct a complete review of the state of her navy. This included not only the condition of her ships but also the cost of maintaining and manning them together with the function and provision of her royal dockyards. He reported that twenty-one of her ships were in a sound condition, whilst ten were in need of urgent and major repair; but once repairs had been made, they would only be useful for a limited time. A further three were beyond economic repair and use. He also said that there were at least forty-five merchant ships which could be easily modified for use as fighting ships in as little as two months if required. It must be remember that the working life of a wooden ship at the time was in the order of twenty-five years before it needed a substantial rebuild. Therefore, as Moorhouse comments, although the Queen had fewer ships than Henry VIII, they were in better condition. She made up most of the shortfall by having further twenty-five ships built before her navy faced the Spanish in 1588.

During her reign, a number of other important and influential people would also have a profound effect on the Navy Royal. One of these was Dr. John Dee, a mathematician, who taught many key English mariners navigation and was also the Queen's astrologer. He was the person who introduced the concept and term 'British Empire' at a time when we were really just a small, isolated island trying to survive. As far as our story goes, though, one of his most important pieces of work was the publication in 1578, of his 'A Petty Navy Royal' in which, as Ronald points out, he changed the countries perception of its relationship with the sea. This comprised a 13-point plan designed to develop a fully provisioned and manned navy, comprising seventy-five ships capable of mounting patrols around our coastline. As Herman reports, Dee spent a great deal of time while looking for links between King Arthur and lands abroad. He argued that Arthur had ruled most of Europe after the collapse of the Roman Empire, and set out extend to Arthur's legendary rule to include anywhere that he could find a British link, including North America, which would invalidate any Spanish and Papal claims to that country.

This precept would also allow the English to develop a foreign policy and defend itself without the cost of an expensive standing army, which was crippling Philip II. As Herman observes, 'defense of Elizabeth's realm against Spain would depend on her navy—frankly and simply because she had nothing else.'

This new-found 'legitimacy' gave Elizabeth and her merchant adventurers, privateers and pirates 'permission' that allowed them to trade, colonize, and exploit the America's and challenge Spain's authority on the high seas. With this strategy, she was able to use her pirates to attack Spain's treasure ships, which bought Philip's wealth across the Atlantic from the mines in Peru and Chile. This would help reduce his ability to wage war on her and the Low Countries without having to use her own money to finance them. It also gave her the opportunity to officially deny any knowledge or accountability for their actions, whilst still gaining from their exploits. Her mariners were able to build their own ships that the Queen could call on in times of need, again at their own expense. It would also enable her Navy Royal to call on very experienced seamen and armed, seaworthy ships when necessary. In her book, *The Pirate Queen: Queen Elizabeth I, Her Pirate Adventurers, and the Dawn of Empire,* Susan Ronald describes it like this:

'…from an English point of view, any acts of piracy, trade or war were the basic ingredients needed for survival against the great Catholic powers. English adventurers were "admired and feared by all"… In England, these men were the new "Robin Hoods" seeking to redress the previous years of bloody Catholic cruelty under Mary [Tudor] and dreaming of rich prizes to distribute among their friends… It was these adventurers, pirates, merchants who Elizabeth used to finance the transition of England from a poor backwater island into a world player.'

To encourage her men to go to sea, the Queen introduced fish days on a Wednesday as well as the Friday's of tradition, that increased the demand for fish which ensured that not only more men went to sea in fishing boats, but that they also went further afield.

As Hugh Bicheno points, because the English were playing a war of attrition against Spanish and Portuguese shipping, they were designing and building 'well-armed, agile, small-to-medium sized ships whose guns further reduced the relatively limited space available for stores and cargo—an excellent short-range warship.' This lack of storage capacity would affect the English fleet's ability to stay at sea for prolonged periods and would also inhibit its fighting capabilities during a sustained period of engagement. It also meant that Elizabeth could not keep her ships at sea, which would have been hugely expensive, even if she wanted or had been able to afford to do so. Bicheno goes on to explain that the nature of fighting that the English had adopted, i.e., corsairs/privateers/semi-legitimate pirates meant that it affected their tactical ability to use their superior firepower because you could not make any money from a ship that you had sunk.

This may go some way to explaining why, during the running battle against the Armada, so few Spanish ships were sunk by English firepower.

Most of the famous mariners came from the West Country, and many of them were related in some way. As Herman relates, they tended to be suspicious of strangers and banded together as fellow countrymen and, to some extent, equal partners. Having members of your family and friends sailing with you also kept the financial rewards in-house.

Add this to Ronald's observations that this resulted in a navy manned by ordinary men, who if they survived service at sea, could move up into the higher echelons of society. An even better reason for keeping it in the family. Not all of the famous sailors of the time came from the West Country, Martin Frobisher came from Yorkshire, and Thomas Fenner came from Sussex. Many of these men played a crucial role in expanding English influence and income, often through very dubious actions. One of the most famous amongst them was Francis Drake. It is not my intention to include many of his exploits here, as you can find them in so many books, but his influence on the disposition of the English fleet when it came to meet the Armada is crucial. One other thing that he can be rightly credited with was another foundation of the Royal Navy—the unit of command. As Herman explains, the captain of a ship held all authority and power over everyone no matter what their rank or title, and over everything on board his ship.

This was a principle that the Spanish could have done with adopting in their navy. Interestingly, much has been written about Drake, most of it highly complementary, so I thought it was worth adding a few of Bicheno's comments. He says that Drake did not take himself too seriously, but was 'sly, casually cruel, no more honest than he had to be, boastful and inclined to swagger.' In sum, he was a "wide boy" from who you would be ill-advised to buy a used galleon.' He notes that Elizabeth referred to him as 'my pirate.' He also says that although history has portrayed him as a great military commander, 'this does not hold up to even casual skeptical scrutiny. The evidence is clear that his secretive and idiosyncratic style of leadership was only effective at the single-ship or small flotilla level.'

Two other men were to have a significant influence on the state of the navy when it sailed to meet the Spanish in 1588. The introduction of changes to ship design and armament have primarily been attributed to John Hawkins and William Wynter (see above and below). Although in 1574, Francis Drake had a ship, the *Pelican*, built to his own design which was longer and sleeker than traditional ships. It was this ship that Walter Raleigh later renamed the *Golden Hind* after Christopher Hatton whose family crest featured a hind.

John Hawkins was one of the band of privateers who, at one time appears to have been working as a double agent for both Philip II and Sir Francis Walsingham, the Queen's spymaster and Secretary of State. In 1562, Hawkins set out on the first of his voyages to the New World in which he transported English cloth and other goods to West Africa where he picked up five hundred slaves, most of which were prisoners that he bought from different local chiefs. He then transported them to Spanish colonies in the Caribbean where he traded them for sugar, pearls, and other goods, which he then bought back to England. This trade made him a very wealthy man. In 1568, on one of his voyages he, together with Sir Francis Drake (who was one of his cousins) managed to escape from an attack whilst in a port in Mexico where most of their crews were killed. Unlike many of his contemporaries, Hawkins was known as the 'most respectable of pirates,' he mixed pirating with legitimate trade. During his slave trade voyages, he was known for his care of the slaves on board his ships, which presumably may have been based on the fact that the better the conditions on board the better the chances that he could ensure that more slaves survived the journey and hence made more money for his backers. His experiences provided him with the expertise to look at, and conduct a different type of naval warfare, battles in which boarding was not the principal use of warships. In 1577, Hawkins became Treasurer of the Navy after the death of his father-in-law Benjamin Gonson, who was probably the most important person on the Navy Board during the establishment of Henry VIII's Navy Royal. This role put Hawkins in charge of rebuilding and repairing the navy's ships.

Eventually, he was able to build new ships to his own design, which were even longer and sleeker than the *Pelican*. He continued to redesign the Queen's ships, generally with a length to width ration of 3:1; some were to have an even larger length/width ratio than this. This made them faster and significantly more maneuverable but less stable than traditional designs such as those used by the Spanish. They would be able to carry more guns and make better use of the wind by being able to sail when the wind was blowing in a wider range of directions compared with the direction in which the ship was traveling than traditionally designed vessels. In fact, they could still sail forward in winds that were blowing at 45° to the direction of the ship. He also reduced their draught, i.e., made them shallower in the water and introduced the idea of adding horsehair between the double planking of the hull below the water line, a practice which as Moorhouse says continued until the 18th century when hulls started to be clad with sheets of copper. These reductions in width and draught meant, however, that the ships had less storage space available for supplies and arms, a problem that, as we shall see, would lead to the English ships requiring constant resupplying of both.

Other changes included replacing traditional plunger pumps with more efficient, chain-driven ones. He continued to reduce the size of the fore and aft castles, a process known as razing them, which resulted in raze or race-built ships. The deck between the fore and aft castles was covered, providing additional protection for the crew and enabling ships to carry even more guns. Hawkins set about building all new ships and rebuilding older ships to the new design.

Were these changes all down to Hawkins as most books suggest? The answer is really, no. Although Hawkins had an overall design, each ship was effectively different. Designing each ship was in the hands of individual shipwrights, such as Peter Pett and Matthew Baker. This meant that, in reality, each ship was a slightly different design rather than one of a 'class' of ships, i.e., ships built to the same design, a concept that was not developed until the next century. In fact, Matthew Baker was the first person to become a Royal Master Shipwright who was paid a salary for the post. Pett was later joined by Richard Bull. Baker was also the first shipbuilder to use blueprints which meant that ships could be constructed to the same design.

One of the penalties of reducing the draught and streamlining the ships was that it decreased stability. This was to have an effect during the coming battle when the lower gun decks on some of the English ships could not be used because of fear of flooding due to the weather conditions and the swaying of the ships. To counteract this tendency, other shipwrights, such as

Richard Chapman began to reduce the length-breadth ration to less than 3:1 but still kept it significantly higher than pervious designs.

Sir William Wynter—who was both a rival to, enemy of, and collaborator with Sir John Hawkins—made an equally important contribution to the development of the Queen's navy, which enabled it to face the Armada with confidence. He tried to have the gravel ballast in all the ships replaced with stone to reduce disease. He also had ships' galleys moved to reduce the risk of fire. However, such ideas were often resisted by sailors who were notoriously suspicious of change. Wynter's most significant input lies in redesigning the armament of Hawkins race-built ships. Wynter had led a squadron of ships to attack Spanish and French reinforcements sent by Philip II to Smerwick in County Kerry to support troops that had been dispatched to invade Ireland. During this campaign, Wynter's ships managed to completely destroy the castle in which the troops were stationed, using just their shipboard guns.

In 1549, he became Surveyor of the Navy and issued a new set of fighting instructions which indicate that, at the time, he still thought that ships should primarily be used in the traditional sense as floating fortresses. In 1557, he became the Master of Ordnance for the navy; and two years later, he led a squadron of ships to Ireland to relieve troops faced by an invasion force of Spanish and Italian soldiers. He also led an English fleet to prevent Francis de Guise's attempts to secure Mary Stuart's claim to the Scottish throne. During this campaign, he managed to catch the French navy on its way to Scotland and forced it back to the Low Countries. He then sailed into Leith, to isolate and defeat the French army. This action ultimately led to Mary, Queen of Scots, and her husband, Francis II, abandoning their claim to the English throne. In fact, in 1560, following Mary de Guise's death and the subsequent Treaty of Edinburgh, French troops left Britain forever. He spent over three months at sea on this campaign during which he managed to keep his ships in good repair and continuously supplied from the Queen's dockyards on the Thames. Wynter was considered 'the best sea officer for a generation' and, prior to engaging the Armada, he was the only person with experience in leading an English Navy fleet in to battle.

He oversaw the gradual replacement of bronze and brass guns with ones cast in iron. He also moved away from large cannons which fired 50lb (22.7kg) shot, and demi-cannons which fired 30lb (13.6kg) shot, to culverins and demi-culverins, firing 18lb (8.2kg) and 9lb (4kg) shot. These guns were smaller, more maneuverable, and easier to handle without a significant loss of either firepower or accuracy.

At the time, the best cannons were being made in Venice, the Low Countries, and England, particularly in the Forest of Dean, Kent, and Sussex. Although the finest cannons were made of bronze, which made them more flexible, durable, and reliable, they were very expensive (which England could ill afford) and were made on the continent. Fortunately, in 1543, during the reign of Henry VIII, it was found that iron from the Weald of Kent and Sussex proved to be very good for making cannons. Using iron reduced cost and reliance on foreign imports and helped us to develop a home-grown industry, using blast furnaces, that ultimately led to the industrial revolution.

So more out of necessity than anything else, the English developed and made most of their own cannons, whilst the Spanish and Portuguese bought theirs from Germany and the Low Counties. Consequently, they became dependent on countries which were predominantly anti-Catholic; yet one more reason why Philip was determined to hold on to and subdue the Low Countries. It also prevented the Spanish from developing their own gun-making industries.

The casting of cannons was a specialized job, and the English used cannons made in a single, vertical casting which meant that the thickest metal was around the rear-end of the cannon where the force of the ignition process would be greatest. Generally, English cannons were also cast with thicker barrels to reduce the possibility of them blowing up. A number of the Spanish cannons still comprised of strips of iron, hammer-welded together to form a barrel and held together with ropes or strong metal rings. The Spanish also suffered from shortage of copper and good quality iron with which to make their cannons; they also lacked foundrymen capable of casting them. Subsequently, many of their cannons were cast with their bores off-center, which meant that the barrels were subject to unequal pressure and heat when fired. The English were able to use higher quality iron, and, with their skilled foundrymen, were able to cast smaller, stronger, higher quality cannons with more consistent bores. The Spanish were also at a disadvantage when it came to their cannonballs. A significant shortage of cannonballs meant that they had to produce them quickly; and in order to produce them, they tended to cool them down too quickly after casting them, causing them to be so brittle that they often broke up in the cannons or on impact with their targets. This lack of care and accuracy in cannonball production had other consequences. The larger the space between the diameter of a cannonball and the bore of the cannon, the less efficient the cannon becomes. This is because more of the explosive power of the gunpowder is lost. The larger the gap (known as windage) between the bore of the cannon and the cannonball, the more likely it is that the cannonball will bounce around in the cannon when being fired, leading to a reduction in velocity and a loss of accuracy.

Spanish problems did not end there. There was also a difference in the quality of the gunpowder used by both sides. The Spanish used a higher quality, fine-grained 'corn' powder, which was more explosive, whilst the English only had cheaper, coarser 'serpentine' powder, which was less effective. Unfortunately, the higher pressures and temperatures generated by the better quality Spanish powder resulted in a number of cannons exploding when fired and a higher possibility that the cannonballs would shatter in the cannons when fired.

Wynter also continued with the changes initiated during the time of Henry VIII and featured on the Mary Rose. Her smaller cannons were mounted on four-wheeled gun carriages as opposed to the large two-wheeled ones used on the Spanish ships, which followed the design of land-based gun carriages. This change made moving, aiming, cleaning, and reloading the English muzzle (front) loaded cannons far easier which in turn led to the English being able to maintain a higher rate of fire. With the Spanish reliance on close-quarter fighting and boarding of enemy ships, they did not need to rely on being able to reload the heavy cannons, which were difficult to handle especially in the cramped space on board ship. Hanson points out that unlike the Navy Royal, the Spanish did not use specialist gun crews. They called down soldiers from the upper decks, usually six or more to each cannon, to haul them in, clean them down, reload, maneuver, aim, and secure them to the ship's hull before they could be fired again. At this point, the soldiers would return to their stations, and a gunner would fire the cannon; the whole process would then have to be repeated. This meant that the Spanish usually only managed to fire each cannon two or three times during a battle that might last all day. The English on the other hand employed dedicated, highly regarded gun crews who worked as a unit, which together with their smaller four-wheeled gun carriages, could fire a greater volume of shot in a shorter period of time. Sometimes, being able to reload in as little as two minutes. They were only limited by the amount of powder and shots they could store, and the need to let each cannon cool down before it could be fired again to prevent them from igniting the powder before they were ready to be fired.

It is clear, therefore, that there were significant differences between how the Spanish and English thought ships should be used in battle, and this affected not only how they were to be used during the forthcoming battle but also the entire philosophy of their design, operation, and nature of the crews onboard each fleet.

Charles Howard, the second Lord of Effingham and the first Earl of Nottingham, was appointed as Admiral of the Fleet in 1585; he had been an admiral since 1570. (The word admiral comes from the Arabic phrase which means prince of the seas.) He was the fourth member of his family to hold the post. A position which he gained because of his social rank rather than military experience: he and his wife were related to the Queen and most of the great families in England. He had previously been the English Ambassador to France (see chapter 2) where he witnessed and appears to have been greatly affected by the conflict and power struggles in that country. In 1569, when he was General of the Horse, he was involved in subduing the catholic northern rising in the North of England. At the time of the Armada, he was fifty-two years old.

Although he did not have the military and particularly the naval background to command the fleet, he did take a great deal of interest in all aspects of its ships, men, and their provisions—a quality that was to prove important. As Hanson informs us, because of his diligent duty, in making sure that he knew how all of his ships and men worked, he was able to engender a high morale in his crews that led to increased efficiency that also resulted in increasing its effectiveness as a fighting force. He continued this level of interest with regard to all the ships under his command. He also took advice from, and supported, more experienced sailors, in particular Drake, Hawkins, and Frobisher.

Howard was keen to make sure that the fleet was in the best possible condition to face the Armada when it came. He was continuously sending letters and requests for ammunition, food, water, and other supplies needed to allow the fleet to operate to the best of its ability. Thomas includes an example of his desire to make sure that his ships were in the best possible state when he went to inspect the ships of the Eastern Squadron as they were moored in the Medway. Thomas records that he 'crawled into fore peaks and bilges—and other places not meant for admirals to check' after which he is reported to have said that 'I have been aboard every ship.'

One of the main advantages of having someone with Howard's noble background in charge of the fleet was his closeness to and influence with those in power, as this would give him a better chance of securing the provisions his ships. Although there were five lords in the English fleet, most of his ships captains had gained their position through merit.

As we will see later, this is significantly different from the situation in the Armada where rank and title was everything.

So Howard was fortunate to be in charge of a very experienced group of commanders, sailing in first-class, generally modern, or modernized ships in seas they were extremely familiar with. He also had a pool of specialized gunners and gun crews who were held in high status onboard the English ship, a situation which was almost the opposite of that in the Armada.

In December 1587, when Howard took command of the fleet, the Navy Royal element comprised thirty-four ships and pinnaces, of which four, the *Triumph, Elizabeth Jonas, White Bear* and *Victory* were regarded as the 'four great ships.' Of these four, the first three were the largest and oldest of the Queen's ships, and therefore, they did not conform to Hawkins design philosophy; meaning that they still had large castles and were broader than the other ships.

In addition to these, there were fourteen other navy ships which made up the core of the fighting ships; they were the *Ark Royal, Rainbow, Golden Lion, Vanguard, Revenge, Antelope, Dreadnought, Elizabeth Bonaventure, Mary Rose, Nonpareil, Hope, Swiftsure, Foresight,* and *Swallow*.

Prior to engaging the Armada, these thirty-four Queen's ships were divided in to two fleets, with fourteen ships based in and around the Thames to provide a force that could defend London and the east and southeast ports (known as the Narrow Seas Fleet). They were also designated with the task of covering any moves by Parma to bring his invasion fleet across the Channel. The other twenty were stationed with Howard in Plymouth to cover the southwest approaches and a possible invasion of southern Ireland. They were also tasked with preventing the Armada, securing any of the south coast harbors. But why position the largest proportion of the fleet in the southwest where the Channel is at its widest when it would have been more effective to concentrate resources in the southeast where the Armada would have been caught with less maneuvering space? As the prevailing winds in the Channel are primarily westerlies, i.e., they blow from west to east, this meant that a Plymouth-based fleet would be able to sail and maneuver behind and with the wind, to engage and fight the Armada rather than against it.

As we have seen, the Navy Royal was an established organization compared with that of the army (hence, it is still known as the Senior Service), which meant that it had its own dockyards at Chatham, Deptford, Woolwich, and Plymouth in which ships were built and maintained. By this time, Deptford was no longer used for large-scale shipbuilding and, when in the Thames, most of the ships were moored further down the river around the Medway where most ship repairs were also undertaken. Portsmouth was only used as a summer base. These shipyards employed master shipwrights, such as Pett and Baker (see above) who were more able to look after and, if necessary, modify their ships because they had originally been responsible for building them. As McDermott notes in his book, *England and the Spanish*

Armada: The Necessary Quarrel, having an established system meant that it could expand when necessary. The structural changes introduced by Lord Trenchard when he took over command of the Royal Air Force in 1918 enabled it to do the same in the build up to the Second World War. The same could not be said for the supply system on which the operational side of the navy depended. As we have seen, the navy could also call on a pool of sailors with significant experience as privateers and sometime pirates who were well-versed in handling ships in the Atlantic Ocean and North Sea. These could be used to command either the Queen's ships or the armed merchant ships in which they had gained so much experience not only in sailing but fighting; ships that could be hired at the Queen's expense or levied for service when needed.

When it came to challenging the Armada, although the navy's well-established systems meant all ships could be ready in a short period, Howard faced a number of problems caused by the governments supply system, which were compounded by the fact that the majority of the fleet had been collected together at Plymouth. It appears that virtually all of the country's supply of gunpowder and cannonballs were stored in the Tower of London, and they had to be transported from there to the ships wherever they were stationed or if they were at sea. Presumably, this was a precaution designed to prevent such equipment falling in to the wrong hands. It meant that any requests for supplies for the largest proportion of the fleet had to be transported from London all the way to Plymouth, which could take days to achieve and which, during the running battle in the Channel meant that the fleet was often short of ammunition. To add to his problems, food was only supplied on a month-by-month basis, and each month's supply was only ordered the month before. To complicate matters even further, it could take up to two months to gather each month's food supplies together. This meant that as the size of the naval force increased, there was no guarantee that the next month's supplies would be sufficient to meet the fleet's requirements. Howard, along with most of his commanders, was concerned that the Armada might arrive towards the end of a month when the fleet would not have sufficient food and water to fight, which would effectively put the English ships out of action between 26 June to 2 July and 24 to 29 July. He also adds that if the Spaniards had arrived off Plymouth during either of those periods, the English ships would not have been able to chase after or engage them because they would have been stuck in port. In fact, when the Armada was sighted off the Cornish coast, the fleet in Plymouth was still in the process of loading provisions that had just arrived. There was a suspicion amongst those in charge of the fleet that the Spanish knew about the system of supplying the fleet's provisions and would take advantage of the situation, Whiting says, 'Howard felt the Armada was pursuing some dark plot to delay to the point when the English ran out of food and would be obliged to stand their fleet down.'

After continuous badgering, Howard managed to convince those holding the purse strings in London to supply three month's supplies at a time. The problem with this change of strategy was that the people in charge of supplies had a great deal of difficulty accessing such large quantities of food and beer in the local area, given that transportation, particularly over land was difficult. This was compounded by the fact that Howard and Drake were to use the fleet in a way that had not been seen before. On Drake's advice, and with ships that were more capable than ever of sailing in adverse weather conditions, they intended to be at sea irrespective of the prevailing weather.

One of the unintended advantages these continuous financial constraints imposed on the Navy Royal compared with the Armada meant that they could not be continuously at sea. These restrictions also meant that by remaining in harbor, most of their crews were effectively on piecework at best and were, therefore, not paid, but the ships were under a program of continuous care and maintenance. Therefore, they were being kept in the best possible condition. One of the other benefits of keeping the ships in harbor and the crews onshore was the avoidance of widespread ship-borne diseases which, because of their poor diet and poor living conditions onboard, could quickly kill or disable large proportions of ships' crews. Paraphrasing Ronald's observations, as a result of the financial situation the Queen and the nation were in, she could not afford to permanently provision and man her ships, perversely, this worked in our favor.

At this point, it is worth thinking about why anyone would want to join the navy. Bicheno gives us a possible answer when we explains that:

'…only abject misery can explain how anyone would volunteers to crew the queen's ships. Although in theory, sailors serving in the Royal Navy in 1588 were paid 7s 6d per month, in practice they were paid late or not at all and had little prospect of spoil. The only certain payment was in kind: accommodation on board was better than sleeping on the street or in dosshouses, and while the food and drink was usually rank and sometimes poisonous, the alternative might be starvation.'

Not much of a choice then.

Before we turn to the Armada itself, let's look at those who commanded the Queen's ships. It is interesting to note, not only who the principal characters were but also the others that made up the majority of the commanders of the navy's ships. As you will see from the table below, many of them were directly or closely related to each other.

Table 1. The 18 principal ships of the Navy Royal employed in the defeat of the Spanish Armada.

Ship	Year of build or modification	Tons (tonnes)	Commander	Relationship
Triumph	1561	1,100 (1117)	Sir Martin Frobisher	
Elizabeth Jonas	1559	900 (914)	Sir Robert Southwell	Charles Howard's son-in-law
White Bear	1563	1,000 (1016)	Lord Sheffield	Charles Howard's nephew
Victory	b1559, m1586	800 (813)	Sir John Hawkins	Drake's cousin
Ark Royal	1587	800 (813)	Lord Charles Howard	
Rainbow	1586	500 (508)	Lord Henry Seymour	Step son of Howard's sister
Golden Lion	b1557, m1582	500 (508)	Lord Thomas Howard	Charles Howard's cousin
Vanguard	1586	500 (508)	Sir William Wynter	
Revenge	1577	500 (508)	Sir Francis Drake	John Hawkins cousin
Antelope	b1546, m1581	400 (406)	Sir Henry Palmer	
Dreadnaught	1573	400 (406)	Sir George Beeston	
Elizabeth Bonaventure	b1576, m1581	600 (609)	Earl of Cumberland	
Mary Rose	1556	600 (609)	Edward Fenton	John Hawkins brother-in-law
Nonpareil	b1556, m1584	500 (508)	Thomas Fenner	Edward Fenner's brother
Hope	b1559, m1584	600	Robert	

		(609)	Crosse	
Swiftsure	1573	400 (406)	Edward Fenner	Thomas Fenner's brother
Foresight	1570	300 (304)	Christopher Baker	
Swallow	b1544. m1573	360 (365)	Sir Richard Hawkins	John Hawkins son
Note: b= built; m = modified.				

Lord Howard also had Sir Richard Leveson and Sir Edward Holy, both of whom were his son-in-laws on the *Ark Royal* with him whilst his son, William Howard was on the *White Bear*. In addition, he supplied seven of his own ships for the fleet, each of which was commanded by a relative or close associate. It is also worth mentioning that not only was John Hawkins a cousin of Drakes but he was originally his captain, and his brother William Hawkins was the Mayor of Plymouth.

Table 2. The smaller Queen's ships employed in the defeat of the Spanish Armada.

Ship	Year of build	Tons (tonnes)
Aid	1562	250 (254)
Bull	1570	200 (203)
Tiger	1570	200 (203)
Tramontana	1586	150 (152)
Scout	1577	120 (121)
Achates	1573	100 (101)
Charles	1586	70 (71)
Moon	1586	60 (61)
Advice	1586	50 (51)
Merlin	1579	50 (51)
Spy	1586	50 (51)
Sun	1586	40 (41)
Cygnet	1585	30 (30)
Brigandine	1583	90 (91)
George, Hoy	????	100 (101)

The English fleet, including the armed merchantmen and supply ships totally one hundred and ninety-four ships (some sources quote this as one hundred and ninety-seven).

Table 3. The larger merchant ships employed in the defeat of the Spanish Armada.

Ship	Tons (tonnes)	Captain
Galleon Leicester	400 (406)	George Fenner
Merchant Royal	400 (406)	Robert Flicke
Edward Bonaventure	300 (304)	James Lancaster
Roebuck	300 (304)	Jacob Whiddon
Golden Noble	250 (254)	Adam Seager
Griffin	200 (203)	William Hawikins
Minion	200 (203)	William Wynter
Bark Talbot	200 (203)	Henry Whyte
Thomas Drake	200 (203)	Henry Spindlelow
Spark	200 (203)	William Spark
Hopewell	200 (203)	John Marchant
Galleon Dudley	250 (254)	James Erisey
Virgin God Save Her	200 (203)	John Grenville
Hope Hawkins	200 (203)	John Rivers
Hercules	300 (304)	George Barne
Toby	250 (254)	Robert Barrett
Mayflower	200 (203)	Edward Bancks
Minion	200 (203)	John Dale
Ascension	200 (203)	John Bacon
Primrose	200 (203)	Robert Bringborne
Margaret and John	200 (203)	John Fisher
Tiger	200 (203)	William Caesar
Red Lion	200 (203)	Jervis Wilde
Centurion	250 (254)	Samuel Foxcraft
Susan Parnell	220 (254)	Nicholas George
Violet	220 (254)	Martin Hawkes
George Bonaventure	200 (203)	Eleazer Hickman

Howard had nineteen fighting ships with him at Plymouth together with forty-six well-armed merchantmen and forty smaller ships, and Seymour had fifteen fighting ships plus a number of smaller ships in his Narrow Sea fleet. Many of the merchantmen that formed an important component of the fleet were captained (and crewed) by men with considerable sailing and fighting experience. This meant that they were probably more battle-hardened than the navy's own ships that were largely kept in port and only used for short term operations. Another consequence of this was that when Howard and the English fleet sailed out to meet the Armada, they had almost no previous experience of sailing and fighting in a large formation and had had virtually no time to practice or develop the new fighting techniques for which the navy's ships had been designed. As noted previously, William Wynter was the only commander who had had any extensive experience of commanding a fleet at sea, and he was with Seymour, based in the Thames, patrolling the Narrow Seas to prevent Parma form making a channel dash.

When the Spanish began to spread their wings and conquer the New Worlds of North and South America, their ships met little, if any, resistance and, therefore, required no armed support. When privateers and pirates began to attack their treasure fleets, they had to start either arming their merchantmen, which reduced their capacity to carry valuable goods, or send warships to escort them. The English on the other hand had built up a navy, which was required to defend us against the French, Spanish, and Dutch in the rougher conditions of the North Sea and eastern side of the Atlantic. As their sailors—which included naval, merchantmen, privateers, and pirates—continued to sail into even more adverse waters, the English sailors had to adapt the tactics and their ships to achieve their goals. Remember, Spanish fighting ships were primarily designed for wars with the Ottoman Empire in the Mediterranean, hence their principal men-of-war were galleys.

The size of the Spanish Empire gave them access to significant military resources, including ships. It is interesting to note that when the Armada sailed it had sailors and soldiers from Lisbon, but as Hanson noted, it comprised a collection of ships from all over Europe, crewed by an equally diverse range of crews all talking different languages. In contrast, the English forces on land and sea were almost entirely composed of Englishmen. Hanson also informs us that on the Spanish ships, the ships' captain and crew were under the command of a soldier, even if he was of a lower rank that the captain. This is because the Spaniards viewed the ships and their crews as merely transports for bringing soldiers in to combat against other ships or as a means of transportation, and they designed and operated their ships to meet these requirements. The English on the other hand had begun to view the navy as its main attack and defense force in which sailors were the primary crew, and the ships and their armament were designed to fight and destroy ships from a distance. The marines, their onboard soldiers, were used as a secondary force if necessary; they, therefore, designed their ships appropriately—this resulted in two completely different approaches to naval warfare. This emphasizes the difference between the Spanish and English approach to the use of ships and crews, it would be like a wrestler fighting a boxer, one gets close and personal whilst the other jabs at arm's length until his opponent is sufficiently weakened to enable him to come in close to deal a knockout blow.

In 1583, when Philip II asked Albaro de Bazan, the Marquis of Santa Cruz, to put together the Armada, Santa Cruz decided that he would require a force of five hundred and fifty-six ships. This fleet would include one hundred and eighty galleons, forty galleys, six galleasses, and forty hulks—ships usually stripped of all armament, sails, masts, and rigging, which could carry most of the provisions required for the enterprise. The Armada would sail with 30,000 sailors and 65,000 soldiers. He thought that the task of assembling and sailing the Armada to the Netherlands to meet Parma's army and then carry them to England would take approximately eight months, and therefore, it would have to be able to transport all of the provisions, armaments, and equipment required for that period of time to complete the task. This would cost the equivalent of three and a half years' profit from Spain's New World territories; a proposal that Philip thought was a totally unrealistic proposition.

It would appear that Philip thought that the Armada's main function would be to enable Parma's army to cross the Channel either aboard its ships or to support and protect Parma's ships, and that it was to avoid, if possible, engaging the Navy Royal. Some commentators have suggested that he was only using the Armada as a show of force and had no intention of invading England. If this were true, such a huge undertaking in gathering together all the men, equipment, provisions, and ships, let alone the cost of the enterprise seems rather extreme given the effect that its defeat had on Spain. Whatever its eventual size the Armada was to be, at that time, it would be the most powerful fleet that had ever assembled. The crippling costs involved in assembling and maintaining such a large force, together with funding Parma's army, meant that it must have been more than just a show of force.

Although plans for the Armada were initiated as early as 1580, nothing much happened with regard to assembling it until 1587 when Santa Cruiz took command. Although he was a brilliant military commander, it appears that his talents did not extend to being able to assemble and equip his fleet (see below). By February 1588, preparations seemed to be advanced, and Philip II was eager to dispatch the fleet as soon as possible to prevent the French from interfering with his plans for the Low Countries. Santa Cruz had assembled a fleet of a hundred and four ships which included twenty-eight galleons, eight of which had been redeployed from protecting New World convoys, and ships acquired when Spain annexed Portugal in 1580. The fleet also included four galleys and four galleasses, which, as we have seen, were fighting vessels designed for the relatively gentle conditions found in the Mediterranean. These would be extremely vulnerable to being swamped by the sea conditions found in the Atlantic and North Sea. There were also 23 hulks which were to be used to transport all of additional provisions and equipment for the voyage and invasion, and thirty-four pinnaces which could be used to send messages ahead of and between ships in the Armada, and also transport officers between ships. This represented a significantly smaller but more realistic and more affordable fleet than the one originally proposed by Santa Cruz.

Just as Philip was pressing him to sail in February 1588, Santa Cruz died. The situation took a further turn for worse when his Vice Admiral the Duke of Paliano also died two weeks later. The king, therefore, had to find a replacement quickly if the Armada was to be able to sail in 1588, so he turned to his cousin Don Alonso de Guzmán El Bueno, the Duke of Medina Sidonia. Unfortunately, Medina Sidonia, who had significant military experience, including, as we shall see later, facing Drake on-shore at Cadiz, did not consider himself up to the job. However, Philip did not give him a choice; he needed someone in charge who had the social rank, this means that no one in the Spanish hierarchical dominated military system could question his authority. Therefore, because, as Hanson puts it, of his 'unimpeachable lineage' over all the nobles and officers in the fleet, no one could be upset by his promotion. Reluctantly, Medina Sidonia accepted the post.

Philip also instigated a significant change to the composition of his Council of War, the committee that decided the general policies of war. Traditionally, this comprised members of aristocratic families who were on the Council of State. It appears that, following the aggressive reaction in Portugal to Spain's takeover, Philip added two experienced military commanders to the Council of War. These were Andres de Prada, who was put in charge of the land forces, and Andres de Alva, who was to oversee the navy. The remaining four members of the council included only one person from the Council of State and two members of the aristocracy. This Council of War had overall authority over military action but delegated responsibility for operational decisions to smaller committees called Juntas. Unfortunately, although this may have been the purpose of his command structure, Philip still effectively made all of the important plans and decisions, a situation, which proved to be disastrous for the whole enterprise.

On his arrival in Lisbon, where the Armada was assembling, Medina Sidonia found absolute chaos; fortunately, this is where his administrative skills came to the fore. Although many of the most important ships required for the Armada were there, their provisions and armament appeared to have been distributed amongst the ships according to the social rank or seniority of their commanders rather than according to function or size. This meant that some ships had cannons they could not use while others were almost devoid of any useful armaments.

This position played to Medina Sidonia's strength; he was a very good organizer, a bit of a paper-pusher. In fact, one of his first actions was to generate forms, which could be used to order supplies and equipment. He also bought together some of his most experienced commanders, including an Italian naval gunnery expert, to sort out what was needed. One of their primary concerns was the shortage of large cannons. Even when he managed to redistribute the cannons and ammunitions, he had amongst his fighting ships, status still played an important role. Mattingly provides a vivid description of the situation which faced him, which he describes as 'frozen chaos.' It had only been a week since Santa Cruz had died, but in that short period of time, crews had been boarded without any money, equipment, and in some cases, the clothes or food required for the mission. He found that there had been an uncontrolled grab by each captain, to get hold of anything they could. Unfortunately, even though more experienced officers could see what was happening, no one had the authority to stop it.

From this, it is obvious why Philip chose Medina Sidonia to take command. However, even with Medina Sidonia's organizational abilities and his unquestionable status, Hanson says that rank still played a significant role in which commanders and, therefore, which ships received the most armaments. It meant that some of the best fighting ships were not equipped with the cannons that they required, and because gunpowder and cannonballs were distributed on the basis of which ships had the most cannons, many of what would be the main fighting ships were under-provisioned.

One of the problems that has already been noted was the often-poor quality of the Spanish cannonballs. It appears that many were made in a hurry to make up for the shortfall found by Medina Sidonia. He had also been promised more cannons by foundries in Spain and Portugal, but these failed to materialize in the numbers required. Hanson explains that they were sourcing cannons from all over Europe, including England, where an iron foundry in Sussex supplied hundreds, and a merchant from Bristol supplied nine shiploads of culverins that had been cast in the Forest of Dean, as well as powder, muskets, and shot. They also got hold of cannons from Holland, but even with those and others taken from foreign ships that had been impounded in Spanish and Portuguese harbors it meant that the Armada was still grossly under-armed when it sailed.

The Armada faced even more problems with regard to the food, water, and wine required for the journey. With such a concentration of ships in Lisbon harbor, Medina Sidonia faced similar problems to that of the English. This was compounded by the order that all crews should be kept on board to prevent desertion. The problem with this was that the crews began to eat and drink their way through provisions designed for the trip and, because of the appalling conditions on board all ships at the time, a significant proportion of the crews went down with ship-borne diseases.

This situation had been largely generated by Drake and his voyage the previous spring. Having ventured in to Cadiz harbor, he encountered as many as sixty ships, of which he claimed to have sunk thirty (including one of Santa Cruz's own galleons) and captured six ships (the Spanish record that only twenty-four were destroyed). Many of these were either destined to join the Armada or were to be used to carry supplies for it. Following this raid, he then sailed back along the coast and spent a further six weeks, destroying or capturing an additional one hundred smaller ships. In response to these actions, Philip was so concerned that Drake's ships might catch some of the other ships, which were supposed to be sailing for Lisbon, that he kept most of them in their harbors. To compound his problems still further, he also had to divert some of his best warships to protect the convoy termed the 'Flota' which was due to come back from America in case Drake tried to intercept it. Santa Cruz, who was in Lisbon harbor, was unable to sail to face Drake because, although he was in command of the Portuguese galleons, which were considered to be some of the best ships in the world, he had no guns or ammunition and nowhere near enough soldiers and sailor to be able to put to sea to challenge Drake. All of these problems had prevented the Armada sailing in 1587, which was fortunate because the Navy Royal would not have been in a fit state to fight it.

By April 1588, the situation had improved, but as Mattingly points out, there were so many problems that it was impossible to sort them all out. This meant that the longer the Spanish fleet stayed in harbor, the more they used up their precious supplies. By May, many of the provisions that had been packed into caskets the previous October had become inedible and could not easily be replaced. Disease was also a significant problem, this together

47

desertion continuously reduced the fleet's manpower, so much so that by November 1587, Santa Cruz could not find enough experienced crew to man the ships, and this problem had become a critical situation by the following April.

Another problem the Armada faced was a lack of good quality barrels in which they could store their provisions. Following his raid on Cadiz (see Chapter 4), Drake then attacked a number of castles around Cape St. Vincent on the southwest coast of Portugal, where his land parties destroyed large quantities of seasoned wood destined to be made into barrels for the Armada. This action resulted in the Armada's provisions being stored in 'green wood' barrels, which turned their wine sour, allowed their food to rot and their water to leak. The results of these attacks would ultimately prove devastating for the survival of the Armada's crew and ships during the enterprise, and as they tried to make their way home through the North Sea, around Scotland and Ireland. As Mattingly and others state, when Drake burnt the barrel staves, he did more damage to the Armada than setting fire to the ships at Cadiz.

On top of all of these problems, Medina Sidonia had to contend with the Spanish system of command. As we have seen, their ships and the sea captains were under the command of army officers. This may not have been such a bad situation if those officers had obtained their commands through military exploits, experience, and merit. Unfortunately, the Spanish system did not work in that way. To compound the problems, many of them bought their servants and a large proportion of the household goods with them. Many of the soldiers on board, not only the wealthy, carried significant qualities of gold and jewels with them. In fact, it was common practice to sew much of this on to their uniforms, a practice, which was to have dire consequences when the fighting started and ships began to sink. It is estimated that there were over 1,000 gentleman adventurers who sailed with the Armada. Once on board their ships, they had their servant erect screens on the decks to give them privacy and separate them from the rest of the ship's crew. So not only did their presence, in positions of authority for which they had no experience, caused problems, but the huge amounts of personal possessions they bought with them and the partitions they had built to keep them apart, reduced the fighting capacity of the ships and provided numerous hazards when English cannonballs would lead to the decks, being showered with shards of flying wood. In response, Medina Sidonia ordered that everything that had been erected between the decks should be taken down to enable the ships crews to move freely.

By April 1588, Medina Sidonia had managed to assemble a substantial fleet, consisting of:

- Ten Portuguese galleons under his command.
- Ten Biscayan galleons commanded by John Martines de Ricalde.
- Ten galleons from Guipuzcoa in the Basque Province of Northern Spain, under the command of Michael de Orquendo.
- Ten galleons from Italy and the Levant Islands under Martine de Vertendona.
- Fourteen galleons from Castile, which included four galleons from the 'Indian Guard' (ships designed to protect trade in the West Indies), were under Diego Flores de Valdez.
- Eleven galleons from Andalusia commanded by Pedro de Valdez.
- Four galleasses commanded by Hugo de Moncada.
- Four Portuguese galleys led by Diego de Mendoza (although these did not sail with the Armada).
- Twenty Flemish hulks under the command of John Lopez de Medina.

Table 4. The principle Spanish and Portuguese fighting ships of the Spanish Armada.

Ship	Tons (tonnes)	Commander	
San Martin	1,000 (1,016)	Marolin de Juan	
San Juan de Portugal	1,050 (1,066)	Juan Martinez de Recalde	
San Marcos	790 (802)	Marquis de Penafiel	
San Felipe	800 (813)	Don Francisco de Toledo	
San Luis	830 (843)	Don Agustin Mexia	Portuguese Squadron with Medina Sidonia
Sam Mateo	750 (762)	Don Diego Pimentel	
Santiago	520 (528)	Antonio de Pereira	
San Francisco de Florencia	961 (976)	Gaspar de Sosa	
San Cistobal	352 (357)		
San Bernardo	352 (357)		
San Cristobal	700 (711)	Gregorio de las Alas	
San Juan de Castilla	750 (762)	Marcos de Aramburu	
San Pedro	530 (538)	Don Francisco de Cuellar	
San Juan	530 (538)	Don Diego Enriquez	
San Juan Bautista	650 (660)	Fernando Horra	Castilian Squadron with Diego Flores de Valdes
Santiago el Mayor	530 (538)		
San Felipe y Santiago	530 (538)		
La Asuncion	530 (538)		
N. S. de Begona	750 (762)	Juan Gutierre de Garibay	

San Medel y Celedon	530 (538)		
Santa Ana	250 (254)		
N. S. de Begona	750 (762)		
La Trinidad	872 (885)		
La Santa Catalina	882 (896)		
Santa Ana	768 (780)	Juan Perez de Mucio or Nicolas de Isla	
El Gran Grin	1,160 (1,178)	Don Pedro de Mendoza	
Santiago	666 (676)		
La Manuela	520 (528)		Biscayan Squadron with Juan Martinez de Recalde
La Maria Juan	665 (675)	Pedro de Ugarte	
Concepcion de Juan del Cano	418 (424)	Juan del Cano	
La Concepcion de Zubelzu	468 (475)		
La Magdalena	530 (538)		
San Juan	350 (538)		
S. M. de Monte-Mayor	707 (718)		
N. S. del Rosario	1,150 (1,168)	Don Pedro de Valdes	
San Francisco	915 (929)		
San Juan Bautista	810 (822)		
San Juan de Gargarin	569 (578)	Tome Cano	Andalusian Squadron with Don Pedro de Valdes
La Concepcion	862 (875)		
Duquesa Santa Ana	900 (914)	Don Pedro Mares	
Santa Catalina	730 (741)		
Santa Maria de Juncal	730 (741)		
La Trinidad	650 (660)		
San Bartolome	976 (991)		

Santa Ana	1,200 (1,219)	Migel de Oquendo	
Santa Maria de la Rosa	945 (960)	Martin de Villafranca	
San Salvador	958 (973)	Don Pedro Priego	
San Esteban	736 (747)	Don Filipe de Cordoba	
Santa Marta	548 (556)		Guipuzcoa Squadron with Migel de Oquendo
Santa Barbara	525 (533)		
San Buenaventura	379 (385)		
La Maria San Juan	291 (295)		
Santa Cruz	680 (690)		
Doncella	500 (508)		
La Regazona	1,249 (1,269)	Don Martin de Bertendona	
La Lavia	728 (739)	Don Diego Enriquez	
La Rata Encoronada	820 (833)	Don Alonso de Leyva	
San Juan de Sicilia	800 (813)	Don Diego Tellez Enriquez	
La Trinidad Valencera	1,100 (1,117)	Don Alonso de Luzon	
La Anunciada	703 (714)	O. Iveglia	Levantine Squadron with Don Martin de Bertendona
La Juliana	860 (873)	Don de Aranada	
San Bautista de la Esperanza	300 (304)		
San Nicolas Prodaneli	834 (847)	Maria Prodaneli	
Santa Maria de Vison	666 (676)	Juan de Bartolo	
La Trinidad de Scala	900 (914)		
San Lorenzo	600 (609)		Galleasses of Naples with Juan Gomez de Medina
Patrona Zuniga	600 (609)	Captain Peuchio	
Girona	600 (609)	Captain Fabrico	

		Spinola	
Napoltana	600 (609)		
Note: there are sometimes inconsistencies in the names of the commanders of Spanish ships given by different authors.			

These fighting ships were divided in to different squadrons, with the ten Portuguese galleons forming one of the two main battle squadrons, and the ten Castilian and four Indian Guard galleons forming the other. The four galleasses were also considered to be first-line fighting ships. The others, which were divided in to four additional squadrons formed the second line of attack.

These ships comprised the backbone of the Armada, whilst four of its commanders, Ricalde, Orquendo, Flores de Valdez, and Pedro de Valdez, together with Don Diego de Maldonado, Captain Marolin de Juan, and an Italian expert on naval gunnery formed Medina Sidonia's Council of War. So although Medina Sidonia lacked naval experience himself, he had pulled together and took advice from men of great experience.

When the Armada was ready to sail in May, Medina Sidonia had managed to gather the arms required for the soldiers on board his ships. He also managed to increase the number of cannonballs available from thirty to fifty per cannon and had also doubled the amount of gunpowder available to his ships.

The last problem he and his commanders could have faced was a lack of maps of the English coastline. Maps were one of the most valuable assets any maritime nation could have. For example, the Portuguese, who as master mariners had undertaken most of the great voyages of exploration thought their value was such that if a ship was captured the captain would try to destroy their maps rather than let them fall in to enemy hands. Sailing in European waters was slightly better, as Whiting explains:

'…until a few years before it [the Armada] sailed, safe navigation had been restricted to inshore pilotage called "caping," that is, following the coast from cape to cape, using navigation books called rutters. These books covered the route the Armada was to take as it was a regular trade route. But they gave distances only in kennings, the distance at which a sailor could be expected to recognise, or ken, the coast. The Straits of Dover were given as one ken, while the west end of the Channel was five kens.'

In other words, it is quite possible that the Armada had relatively accurate maps of the English coast at the time the Armada sailed, whereas the Navy Royal did not. As was the normal custom, even with these maps, the Armada was to sail close to the English coast; Philip II had told them to keep away from the French and Flemish coasts because of their shallow water and sand banks. Although they may not have appreciated their importance when they left Lisbon, the Spanish maps of the North Sea, Scotland, and especially the west coast of Ireland were very poor, a situation that was to have dire consequences later on in their voyage.

Although the English may not have had copies of these maps at the time, most of the ships captains had years of experience, sailing our coastal waters. The North Sea and its coasts would therefore have been well-known to many of them, for example as a result of the huge amounts of coal that was being shipped from the Northumberland and Durham coalfields via Newcastle upon Tyne not just to the rest of England but across the North Sea, as well as other European trade. This gave the Navy Royal and its hired merchantmen a distinct advantage over the Armada.

Chapter 2

European Matters

Before we follow the course of the Armada after it sailed from Lisbon, let us have a look at the wider picture, and the reasons why Philip felt so compelled to assemble and send forth such a large undertaking. The Armada sailed on the back of the usual complicated European politics. Henry VIII had bought the English economy to its knees through wars with the 'eternal enemy,' France. When he died in 1547, he left three potential heirs to his throne: Mary I (Mary Tudor), daughter of Catherine of Aragon, Henry's first wife; Elizabeth I, daughter of Henry's second wife, Anne Boleyn; and Edward VI, son of his third and favorite wife, Jane Seymour.

Catherine of Aragon was the daughter of King Ferdinand and Queen Isabella of Spain and a cousin of Charles V, Emperor of the Holy Roman Empire. Catherine had originally been married to Henry's brother Arthur until he died in 1502, and it appears that Henry married her to maintain his alliance with Spain and help him with his wars against France. After twenty years of marriage, he became infatuated with Anne Boleyn, an English maid-in-waiting to Catherine. When the Pope did not grant him a divorce, he set up his own church, the Church of England, to enable the divorce to proceed. This caused a major rift with the Pope, his catholic followers, and in particular, the Spanish royal family all of which would not recognize the validity of the divorce.

Following his marriage to Anne Boleyn, she gave birth to their daughter, Elizabeth, who would always live under the shadow of her birthright; she would be regarded across Europe as the 'Bastard Queen.' Her position would be further compounded by her support of her father's church, which also made her a heretic in the eyes of the Catholic Church.

Henry married Jane Seymour, an English maid-in-waiting to Anne Boleyn eleven days after Anne had been beheaded. Jane gave him what he yearned for most dearly, a male heir, who became Edward VI; but she died twelve days after giving birth.

The other principal player in the succession argument was Mary Queen of Scots, daughter of James V of Scotland and Mary of Guise. James V was the son of James IV and Margaret Tudor, Henry VIII's eldest sister.

The first to take the throne in 1547 was Edward VI who continued his father's reformation of the church. Following his death in 1553, Mary I (Mary Tudor) took to the throne. She was half-Spanish and, as a devout Catholic, instigated her counter-reformation in order that the church and the people should come back to 'the one true faith.' Her brutal persecution and burning of English heretics led to her being remembered as 'Bloody Mary.' Her reputation was not helped by her marriage to King Philip II of Spain in 1554, an act which the vast majority of English people, both catholic and protestant, regarded as a disaster. As James McDermott puts it:

'…although the match had been gestating for some months and was commonly spoken of (and argued about) at Court, news of it came as a thunderbolt to most Englishmen. Almost overnight, the entire nation seemed to unite in outraged, fearful protest, even if the marriage's implications for the nation's spiritual identity concerned only a tiny minority.'

The English, then, far more than now, were highly suspicious of foreigners and suspected that Philip's motives for the marriage was to bring England under the authority of Spain. The English government set up a commission to make sure that his rights and powers were limited both in their extent and duration, he would lose all claims to the throne on Mary's death. The English people were petrified that with Philip on the throne, the Spanish Inquisition would be bought to the country to help root out heretics (non-Catholics). In fact, there is evidence that Philip tried hard to calm down the actions of his wife! It would appear that one of Philip's primary motives for marrying Mary was to prevent any chance of an English alliance with France. He persuaded her to declare war on France in 1557, which led to defeat and the loss of Calais, a town and harbor which, as far as the English were concerned, was as English as any other town in England. This was a loss that further added to Mary's negative publicity, and a loss which the English would come to regret at the time of the Armada. On the positive side, one of Mary's significant acts during her reign that would have a direct impact on the Armada was her drive to rebuild the Navy Royal. This was partially driven by her husband and his desire to keep the French in check. Mary I died on 17 November 1558.

Before we look at Elizabeth's reign, we need to establish the wider political situation in Europe. There were a number of different 'powerhouses' across Europe; including Spain, which was the largest and was headed by Philip II. Philip had inherited the throne when his father, Charles V, the Holy Roman Emperor abdicated. On abdication, he made Philip's brother, Ferdinand, Emperor and gave Philip control of all of his possessions outside of the Holy Roman Empire. These included all of Spain's possessions on the other side of the Atlantic Ocean. As we have already seen, Philip, who regarded himself as the defender of Catholicism, controlled a vast empire which had access to the enormous wealth of the Americas; a wealth he not only wanted but which he had to safe guard in order to support his empire. Portugal, the other worldwide empire at the time, was also Catholic. Switzerland and Germany were two of the significant protestant nations within the Holy Roman Empire under Charles V, and the other significant protestant 'country' was the Low Countries, which, in reality, were a loose confederation of states known as the Seventeen. France, the other great nation, was divided between Protestants (20%) and Catholics (80%) with two great families: the Guises who were catholic, and the Huguenot Bourbon's who were Protestants, battling it out for control through their numerous religious wars.

The central person in this battle was Catherine de Medici, who was born in Italy and orphaned two weeks after her birth when her mother died; her father died shortly afterwards. Catherine was a niece of the Pope. In 1533, at the age of fourteen, she was married to King Henry II of France; and, although he spent most of his time with his mistress, they produced nine children, five boys and four girls, seven of whom survived. Three became Kings of France; Francis II, Charles IX, and Henry III. She tried to marry one of her a daughters, Margaret, to Philip II but he refused, and she was eventually married to Henry of Navarre, a protestant who later became King Henry IV of France. She succeeded in marrying another of her daughters, Elizabeth, to Philip to become Queen Elizabeth of Spain. After Catherine's husband, Henry II died following a jousting accident, her son, Francis, became king. Unfortunately, he was only ten years old at the time, so his mother took on the role as Regent. In 1559, at the age of fifteen, he ascended to the throne as Francis II but only ruled for sixteen months before he died in 1560. As far as our story is concerned, his primary influence was his marriage to Mary Stuart in 1558 when she was fifteen. Mary, the only surviving, legitimate heir of King James V of Scotland, had already been crowned Queen of Scotland in Stirling Castle in December 1542 when she was six days old. At the age of five, she was betrothed to Francis and sent to

France to become a ward of Catherine's to be bought up in the French Court. Following Mary Tudor's death, Mary Stuart and Francis II declared themselves King and Queen of France, Scotland, England, and Ireland. This link to France was a major concern to Philip II, who, even though Mary Stuart was a Catholic, did not want a French person on the throne of England. In order to remove the French influence following Francis II death, Philip II tried to persuade Mary Stuart to marry his semi-insane son Don Carlos, but she refused. Philip's illegitimate half-brother, Don Juan of Austria also wanted to marry her, but he died 1578.

It is said that each of Catherine's sons were fairly weak and feeble-minded, not really fit to take on the role of kingship. This meant that Catherine had to protect them and their interests; in fact, it is said that she put her son's needs above that of her country. As we have seen, she was in an unfortunate position, as there were two powerful families, one Catholic and the other Protestant, who were battling it out for influence and control. To try to counterbalance both sides, she often supported one side or the other; a role which helped to lead to the wars of religion, the St. Bartholomew's Day massacre, the Day of the Barricades, and the establishment of the Catholic Holy League led by Henry of Guise, one of Mary Stuart's uncles. One of Mary's aunties, Mary of Guise, was also the Queen Dowager of Scotland. The brutality exhibited during this power struggle led Elizabeth I and Walsingham in particular, who, at the time, was the English Ambassador to France and a passionate Protestant, to consider that similar atrocities would cross the Channel if Catholic forces managed to take over England. As Robert Hutchinson in his book *Elizabeth's Spy Master: Francis Walsingham and the Secret War that Saved England* vividly describes:

'For Walsingham, and indeed for Elizabeth's government, the French massacre was a stunning, horrific reminder of the brutal, genocidal anti-Protestant Spanish campaign in the Low Countries and a warning of what might follow in England if the realm was ever returned to Catholicism.'

Walsingham realized that Britain was now almost surrounded by enemies just waiting to pounce.

Following the death of Francis II, Charles IX ascended to the throne of France, but as he was too young to take up the role so yet again Catherine became Regent. Charles sent an army to the Low Countries, which was under Spanish control, but it was defeated. He was also involved in the St. Bartholomew's Day massacre, when approximately 6,000 Huguenots (Protestants) in, and around, Paris were killed. A massacre which was triggered by an attempt on his life whilst he was at the wedding of his sister Margaret and Henry of Navarre. The massacre also led Queen Elizabeth I to put aside the peace treaty of 1579, which had been negotiated by the Duke of Alencon, Catherine's youngest son, and also helped strengthen the protestant rebels in the Low Countries under William of Orange. To counter this, it should be pointed out that the peace treaty between France and England led to the formation of the Catholic Holy League. The massacre was also followed by an attempted *coup d'etat* against Charles IX led by the Duke of Alencon and Henry of Navarre, who was arrested, but later, escaped and went to join the Huguenots.

Charles IX died on 30 May 1574 and Catherine's third son, Henry III, became king.

These power struggles that dominated European politics when Elizabeth came to the throne just added to her already weak and vulnerable position. Susan Ronald outlines the situation thus:

'No one in England was more acutely aware of the precariousness of her position than Elizabeth herself. For her Catholic population, Mary Queen of Scots held a better claim to the throne as the great-granddaughter of Henry VII. The maternal uncle of Mary Queen of Scots, the powerful French Guise family, ruled Scotland by virtue of the Queen Mother's regency in the name of the French crown, and the complaint among privy councillors was that Henry II, the French king, was "bestriding the realm, having one foot in Calais and the other in Scotland." This simple fact made urgency for a religious settlement that could be acceptable to both English Protestants and Catholics essential.'

She also comments that:

'At the time, England was by and large rightly regarded as a military and economic backwater by both the French and the Spanish, and there were ample reasons for this perception.'

We were weak, and the Queen knew it. Added to this was the problem that the main focus for her entire reign was securing her own and her country's security when she was surrounded, literally, on all sides by Catholic countries. When you consider that she had to achieve this when the country was in a state of continuous 'near bankruptcy,' you can begin to understand some of the motives and methods she employed in handling of her neighbors, friends, and enemies, which do not forget were primarily male. Remember that she lived in a very male-dominated society in which many thought it was impossible for a woman to run a country. She would have to gain both hers and her country's security through minimal cost, and as much political maneuvering and manipulation as possible.

Elizabeth I, who was therefore in no position militarily or financially to threaten France, renewed the Anglo-French peace treaty that included the eventual return of Calais. The loss of Calais deprived England of being able to control shipping from both sides of the Narrow Seas (the English Channel) at the same time. The renewed peace between Spain's two main rivals, England and France, was a major problem as far as Philip II was concerned. It could also lead to further problems with his control of the Low Countries in which England might support French intervention. Such an alliance would also cause problems with his supply and merchant ships in the Channel. Philip was also concerned that if Mary Stuart were to take over the throne of England an even stronger Anglo-French alliance would follow. He therefore wanted, if possible, to maintain his own peace treaty with Elizabeth to keep her in power, which she needed as much as he did.

Having looked at the situation in France, let us turn our attentions to the Low Countries. Spain considered the Low Countries to be theirs, and they were determined to stop both France and England interfering with that claim. The Spanish Hapsburg royal house had inherited the Low Counties through marriage and, even though they were held together in a loose federation—the Seventeen Provinces—their taxes provided an important source of income for Philip once he was crowned King Philip II of Spain in 1556.

In 1559, he appointed his half-sister, Margaret of Parma, to be his Regent in the Low Countries with her husband the Duke of Alba, in order to fight against heresy and Dutch anarchy against Spanish rule. To achieve this, Alba and his wife instigated a reign of terror partly to subdue the population but also to remove or reconvert the mainly Protestant population back to Catholicism. In 1568, Elizabeth impounded four Spanish ships that were carrying money to Alba. In retaliation, Philip closed all the Low Countries ports to English ships. This was an important blow to Elizabeth I who, as we have seen inherited a very weak economy, as she gained most of the country's finances through the moneylenders in Antwerp and through the cloth trade, which was also centered on the same city. To counter this, Elizabeth put an embargo on all Spanish ships. Philip had already closed Spanish ports to English ships in retaliation to continued interference by, as far as he was concerned, crown sponsored pirates. This had a dramatic effect on the many Anglo-Spanish merchants who had operated successfully out of Spanish ports for years, but it was also an action, which significantly hurt

Spanish trade. Spanish trade was also severely harmed by the actions of the Dutch 'Sea Beggars,' a group of minor nobles who provided naval support for William of Orange's invasion of the Low Countries in 1572. These were said to be former fishermen from the provinces of Friesburg, Holland, and Zeeland, who, until Elizabeth kicked them out from English ports in 1572 as part of an attempted peace treaty with Spain, worked with English 'freebooters' to effectively bring Spanish trade and supplies to the Low Countries to a halt. Their actions reduced Alba's money supply to a trickle. The 'Sea Beggars' used 'flyboats' which were small, shallow-draught, highly maneuverable boats designed to operate in the shallow waters, creeks, and amongst the sandbanks that existed along the Dutch coast. These were boats which the Spanish had little power against, in fact, having been ejected from English ports, such as Dover by Elizabeth. In an attempt to smooth over relations with the Spanish, they captured Brill and Flushing from Spanish control. The loss of these two deep-water ports, the only ones in the Low Countries, would be a significant blow to Parma (see below) and the Enterprise in 1588.

In 1576, Philip sent Don Juan of Austria to the Low Countries to become his new regent; and two years later, he sent his cousin, Alexander Farnese, the Duke of Parma to try to repair the damage done by Margaret and Alba and to fight against William of Orange, who had successfully secured much of the Seventeen Provinces. William, who was also known as William the Silent, was subsequently assassinated in 1584.

Parma was the most experienced military leader in Spain, and probably in Europe, with a string of victories under his belt. He set about reorganizing, re-equipping, and strengthening the army, which included Germans, Flemings, Walloons, Italians, Burgundians, and English exiles. His aim was to try to reunite the Seventeen Provinces and princedoms to bring stability to the area, secure Spain's control, and prevent English and French interference. In 1585, Elizabeth formed an alliance with the Dutch rebels, suspended trade with Spanish traders in the Low Countries, and sent an army under the leadership of the Earl of Leicester to help their fight against Parma. Although Leicester was a particular inept leader, this caused enough concern to Parma that as late as March 1588, he was still urging Philip to conclude a peace treaty in the Low Countries so that his plans for meeting up with the Armada and invading England could proceed. Philip viewed things slightly differently. As far as he was concerned, he could not conquer the Low Countries until he had conquered England, given England's support for the protestant cause in the Low Countries and, therefore, he saw the Enterprise as his main priority.

Following the death of King Henry of Portugal in January 1580, after only two years in power, Philip II was able to claim his throne because he was half-Portuguese, through his mother Isabella, and his marriage to Maria the daughter of Henry's brother, John III. As a counter to this, the English backed Don Antonio of Avis, who was the illegitimate nephew of King Henry, but Philip won the day and was crowned. This allowed Philip to bring the Portuguese empire, which effectively claimed the other half of the known world not 'owned' by Spain, and his Spanish empire together under his control. The combination of the Portuguese and Spanish Navies also provided him with one of the strongest fleets in the world, which was six times larger than the English Navy Royal. It also gave him control of a significantly longer European coastline; in particular, it gave him access to the great harbor at Lisbon, the harbor from which the Armada would eventually sail.

With all of his problems in Europe, for a long time, Philip could not afford to start another conflict with England, but with the increased English support of the Low Countries and the apparent official backing of its uncontrollable pirates in the Atlantic Ocean, it meant that he was running out of both options and patience. Even so, he still considered France to be the greatest threat to Spain's European assets. Even though he and Elizabeth I were cousins, one of his greatest desires was to have a catholic on the throne of England in order to continue the counter-reformation work of Mary Tudor. The problem was that the principle catholic alternative, Mary Queen of Scots, was effectively French. He, therefore, decided that following a successful invasion of England, rather than have a French catholic as Queen, he would put his daughter Isabella on the throne—an idea that, as we shall see later, upset Parma.

Philip's problems did not end there. With English and other nations' pirates operating off the coast of the Americas—intercepting his ships, disrupting his trade, and stealing his treasure ships—he had to do something. When Drake and the others first started operating in those waters the Spanish treasures ships, principally those that made up the *Flota*, the treasure convoy, which sailed twice a year back to Spain, was virtually unprotected. The *Flota* comprised two separate *flotillas*, one bringing gold, silver, and other valuables from Mexico, and the other from Peru via Panama. The two fleets generally joined together at Havana before sailing back to Spain. The Spanish saw the actions of English pirates as an intrusion on their rightful ownership of the Americas and the seas between there and Europe. The English, the Queen, and the Privy Council saw it as legitimate revenge for Philip cutting off access to the money markets in Antwerp which was really the country's only legitimate source of finance. The Queen received a third of the value of all of the declared treasure bought back to England (much of the treasure often disappear before it had to be declared). The two sides were, therefore, effectively engaged in a trade war; the stakes were high and there could only be one winner, but who would it be?

In 1560, Philip declared himself bankrupt. This had an enormous effect on the banking system in Antwerp where both he and Elizabeth obtained most of their loans. It meant that he became even more dependent on the *Flota* to provide his financial support. Without this money, he would not be able to pay for his army in the Low Countries.

In 1562, the Queen gave John Hawkins permission to start slave trading with the Spanish settlements in America, a trade that they had been undertaking for at least fifty years. Philip saw this as yet another act of aggression even though Hawkins, at least to begin with, was engaged in legitimate trade as part of the free trade envisaged by John Dee. At the same time, the French gave Newhaven (*Le Harve*) to the English as part of an understanding that they would help fight against a possible invasion of Northern France by Parma's army and to stop Spanish ships reaching the Low Countries, thus cutting off his lines of supply. To compound the situation, the English also bought a huge supply of weapons and gunpowder from the continent as part of its re-armament against a possible attack by either Spain or France. Philip responded to this and other problems by banning all English ships from the continent and impounded those in Spanish ports; as we have seen, in retaliation, the Queen banned Spanish ships from English ports.

Things took a further turn for the worst in 1586 when four ships taking money to the Low Countries were chased by French ships during storm into Falmouth, Plymouth, and Southampton. The Queen found out that the money on board was a lone from an Italian merchant banker to Philip to pay his troops; a loan that had an interest rate of 10% attached to it. The Queen managed to convince the banker that she was a better bet for getting his money back than Philip, so the loan was transferred to her, and the money was transported to the Tower of London. (The same Italian had invested money in Hawkins second slave voyage.) The problem that Philip now faced was that many of his soldiers in the Low Countries were mercenaries, who—although were some of the best and toughest soldiers in the world—mainly fought for money, and they had not been paid for several months—without pay they could well walk away. In retaliation to losing his financial lifeline, Alba, who was in charge of the army at the time, seized all English property in the Low Countries. Ronald therefore suggests that sending the Armada was a matter of self-defense and national pride. Philip also viewed it as an economic necessity. His financial troubles were further compounded by his decision to stop the *Flota* from sailing because Drake was at sea.

Although Philip desperately needed the money the *Flota* would provide, to pay for the Armada and Parma's forces in the Low Countries, he could not afford to expose it to the possibility to being attacked by Drakes ships. Therefore, in 1585, the Pope promised to give Philip 1.8 million crowns a year for five years to get rid of the 'heretic queen.' However, although the Pope had also promised him 1,000,000 ducats once he had conquered England, he really needed the money in advance to pay for his increasing commitments. One of the conditions placed on Philip by the Pope for release of this payment was that before he could have the money, he was obliged to give every detail of his planned 'Enterprise of England' to the College of Cardinals, and as Bicheno comments, this was akin to 'posting it on the internet today.' Therefore, everyone, including the English, knew what the plan was.

Philip was also still involved in an on-going conflict with the Turkish Ottoman Empire in the Eastern Mediterranean which, as we have seen in the previous chapter, was the conflict which 'colored' the make-up of the Spanish fleet and its fighting tactics. In 1559, Spain also started a war against the Ottoman Empire for control of the Western Mediterranean, which was ended by a truce in 1577. But in 1588, an Anglo-Ottoman defense alliance was established which Elizabeth hoped would provide diversionary attacks on Spanish Mediterranean interests and cause Philip to either delay the launch of the Armada or at least force him to keep some of his fighting ships in home ports. In fact, he did. He kept the galley's back, which had already been discounted as being unsuitable for the Armada.

Chapter 3
Preparing for Invasion

Intelligence information of a potential enemy's thoughts and actions has always been one of the most important aspects of war. As we will see later when we look at the opening phases of the Second World War, this was crucial to Britain's survival. During Queen Elizabeth's reign this was equally true. We have seen that Elizabeth had inherited a nation that was almost bankrupt which meant that she did not have the resources necessary to cover all her options. Without friends on the continent and with enemies on every side, she had to, as Mattingly puts it, rely on her own wits.

This probably dictated, as much as her natural hesitancy and desire for peace, her efforts to play politics with the nations around her. Consequently, she had to have the best sources of information available; and fortunately, Sir Francis Walsingham, her Principal Secretary of State, had a vast system of spies. In his book, Hutchinson describes Walsingham's spy network thus:

'Walsingham's clandestine activities combined the roles fulfilled in modern British society by the Secret Intelligence Service (better known as MI6), the Security Service (or MI5) and the Special Branch of the Police. He was concerned not only with gathering and analysing vital military and diplomatic intelligence, but also with entrapping and ruthlessly destroying those subversives plotting the downfall of Elizabeth's government. At its peak, his extensive espionage network is said to have numbered fifty-three spies and eighteen agents in foreign courts, as well as a host of informers within the English realm itself, some of them turncoats, others from the detritus of Tudor society.'

Although Hutchison presents a very positive view of this network, which undoubtedly worked extremely well when it came to English-based plots and intrigues, particularly with regard to the plots involving the safety of the Queen, it appears to have been patchy at best when it came to information about the Armada. He does add that during the buildup of the Armada Walsingham was 'desperately short of reliable information.' In fact, he had managed to get a spy in Santa Cruz's household just before he died.

However, Mattingly counters this generally positive view when he describes Walsingham's spy network as:

> '…this impressive system of counter-espionage in England dwindles on inspection to a few underpaid agents of varying ability whose efforts were supplemented by causal informers and correlated by a single clerk who also handled much of Walsingham's ordinary correspondence—a system hardly larger or more efficient, except for the intelligence of its direction and the zeal of its volunteer aids, than that which every first-rate ambassador was expected to maintain.'

Not all of Walsingham's spies proved reliable, as Hanson explains, even after the Dutch captured and interrogated the nephew of one of the Vatican's cardinals who told them the details of the Armada, its timetable and destination, Walsingham ignored this information for several months because Sir Edward Stafford, the ambassador in Paris, had said they were false. Walsingham did not know that Stafford was supplying the English with false information while telling the Spanish the English plans. He even continued to pass on false information to the English after the Armada had actually sailed.

Walsingham is famous for the work of his spies with regard to the many Catholic intrigues and plots to assassinate Queen Elizabeth and put Mary Queen of Scots on the throne. These included the Throckmorton and Babington conspiracies, with the latter leading to the conviction and execution of Mary Queen of Scots on 8 February 1587. Prior to this, Walsingham had tried to persuade Mary's gaoler at Fortheringay Castle, Sir Amais Paulet, to murder her—he refused. One of his most reliable spies was a Dutchman named Mynheer Wychegerde, a merchant who appears to have sold goods to anyone who wanted to buy them, including the Spanish in the Low Countries. This trade allowed him to move relatively freely, and it was during one of his trips that he compiled accurate information on the disposition and size Parma's army, a figure which was significantly less than any other estimate—including that or the Earl of Leicester—that Walsingham's other sources had provided. Wychegerde was also able to report that although the army was significantly smaller than had be previously reported, it was a well-trained, highly experienced, and highly disciplined force.

Walsingham had other important spies, including Sir Anthony Standen, who was an agent in the Grand Duke of Tuscany's court. In 1586, Standen reported that Santa Cruz had proposed assembling a fleet of two hundred and six warships and 60,000 men together with two hundred invasion barges, which would sail directly from Spain to England. Fortunately, the cost of this plan made it prohibitive, but Santa Cruz and Philip used it as the basis for the plan for the Armada.

News and information were critical to the Queen, Walsingham, and the preparation of the Navy Royal. A lack of finances and the effects of Spanish actions on the Queen's ability to raise funds abroad meant that she could not keep the navy is a state of readiness for any significant periods of time. She therefore could not afford to keep her ships crewed and waiting in port even though Walsingham's spy network kept reporting contradictory information about the Armada's imminent departure. Therefore, most of the English ships lay in harbor with only a skeleton crew, often without provisions, their guns, and sometimes without masts or sails. However, as we have seen, the efficiency of naval dockyards was such that all the Queen's ships could be brought to readiness within a fortnight if necessary. This proved to be important on a number of occasions. Throughout 1587, Walsingham often received information that the Armada was either ready to set sail or had sailed. For example, in March 1587, Sir Edward Stafford, the double agent in Paris, sent information which said that the Armada would be ready sail within two weeks. This, when confirmed by other sources led to a mobilization of the Navy Royal. Stafford said that the aim of the Armada, which comprised one hundred and seventy-one ships and 18,000 men, was to defeat the English Navy, land the army, and march on London. In July, Sir Thomas Leighton in Guernsey reported that a force of a hundred ships and 15,000 men had assembled in Lisbon and would be ready sail within a month. In the middle of September, he reported that the Armada had set sail, but in late September, Walsingham received conflicting information from Stafford that ships were still assembling in Lisbon. In December, Walsingham received intelligence that the Armada had set sail from Lisbon. Although the information was incorrect, it did fit with Philip's original plans. Within a fortnight of receiving the information, the Navy Royal was fully equipped and ready to sail. When the information proved to be wrong, the Queen had the navy stood-down immediately to save money.

Throughout this period, Queen and country were in a continuous state of nervousness. She banned any ships from leaving harbor in case they were needed, which had a direct effect on Walter Raleigh's attempts to establish and support his fledgling settlements on the coast of North America.

It appears that the Queen was still desperately trying to avoid a war with Spain, which she could not afford, whilst Walsingham, and most of the navy, were itching to start one. Everyone was convinced that one of the Armadas' primary aims was to secure a deep-water harbor on the southern or eastern coast of England, which could be used as a bridgehead for the invasion fleet. With much of the coast being either beaches or cliffs, the number of havens available to the Spanish fleet was limited, and it would be one of the navy's primary objectives to prevent the Armada from reaching them. If the Navy Royal could be bought to a state of readiness within fourteen days, how prepared was the army to face the combined invasion force of the soldiers on board the Armada and Parma's army waiting in the Low Countries?

There was one other piece of information that Elizabeth, Philip, and a significant number of people throughout Britain and Europe also had on their minds, information that even today some people might interpret as potentially disastrous. Hanson outlines the reasons for these concerns, because according to some people's reading of the book of Revelation, 1588 and 1593 were the 5550th and 5555th years since creation. There had also been seven great cycles since the time of Christ, and the sixth cycle ended the year after Martin Luther started his great split in the Catholic Church. The next cycle was expected to end in 1588, when there would be a solar and two lunar eclipses. This was supposed to signify the time when the seventh seal would be opened, Christ would beat Satan and the Last Judgment would begin. This would also be accompanied by a series of natural disasters and a royal crown would fall. Therefore, it may not have been unreasonable to think, with all the upheavals in Europe, people were debating, watching, and waiting on tenterhooks in anticipation as the year began to see who would rise and who would fall.

Dr. Dee, the famous English astrologer, had prepared the Queen's horoscope which showed that the second eclipse would coincide with the start of her ruling sign and was only twelve days before her birthday. Although almanacs were printed in England, they avoided the issue. To print anything that might hint at trouble for the Queen would have been treated as high treason, which was punishable by death. It appears that, to quell discussion in the country, the Privy Council, probably through Walsingham's censorship regime, put pressure on printers not to print such information even though other almanacs were widely available across Europe that contained prophesies of doom and disaster. Everyone expected the coming battle to be a make or break situation for one side or the other, and both tried to decide which would be the winner; it may be no coincidence that desertions for the

Armada increased following the turn of the year—hence Philips insistence on keeping everybody onboard.

Given these prophesies of unusual weather, it was not unreasonable for people to be worried. From 1560 to 1600, the weather throughout Europe was significantly colder and stormier than today. The cold weather led to a slump in wine production, which resulted in people in Austria switching from drinking wine to drinking beer. It also led to poor harvests and poor summers, resulting in famines and large price rises for basic foods. It is also reported that the severe weather, particularly in 1587 and 1588 was partially blamed on Witchcraft. Northern Europe was in the coldest phase of a period known as the Little Ice Age, which lasted from 1315 to 1850. The incidents of storms increased by 85% during the second half of the 16th century, and the number of severe storms increased by 400% with almost hurricane strength winds. As we shall see in later chapters as we follow the running battles up the English Channel, in to the North Sea, and out in to the Atlantic, the weather played a crucial part in the entire episode.

The weather was also probably worse than people could remember, which tended to agree with conditions mentioned in these prophesies. Therefore, is it really surprising that everyone was nervous about the outcome of the approaching battle?

Delays caused by having to protect and then delay the *Flota* which was bringing gold, silver, and other valuable goods back from the America's from the threat of attack by Englishmen, such as Sir Francis Drake, in the summer of 1587, combined with the death of Santa Cruz on 9 February 1588 meant that the invasion of England had to be postponed. The death of Santa Cruz and the loss of money from the delayed *Flota* gained unexpected but extremely valuable time in which the English could better prepare their defenses.

Following the death of Mary Queen of Scots, orders were sent out to the Lord Lieutenants of each of the coast-bound counties to call the General Muster of the levies and their Trained Bands. Prior to this, the provision of land forces had been haphazard and inadequate. The cost of providing solders and any form of defense fell on each county. This had the advantage of removing the cost from the treasury, but it resulted in the distinct disadvantage of putting the burden on local landowners and others who paid tax and who were reluctant to pay any more than was necessary. Delays in training and re-equipping the army and improving coastal defenses were down to money. War and the preparations for war are a costly business. Much of England's meagre financial resources were being poured in to the Low Countries to support Leicester and his troops and his Dutch counterparts with little success. To make things worse, the trade embargo's and the loss of the Low Countries markets and financial system, together with generally poor weather, meant that England, whose income was never particularly great, was being gripped by recession. To help deal with the situation and avoid war, the Queen wanted a peace treaty with Parma and Philip.

Unlike many of its European neighbors, England had no professional, standing army apart from those stationed along the Scottish border, or Ireland and the Low Countries, each of which were only employed for the period necessary to meet each threat. Each county was required to call the muster of its men between the ages of sixteen and sixty with whatever weapons they had available for the occasional training day. Within the General Muster, each county had a smaller group of better-trained men who were referred to as the Trained Bands. It was these Trained Bands who would form the core of any defensive army. To achieve this, they were required to train together ten days a year, but few managed to achieve this. Many of the Trained Bands and musters were far stronger on paper than on the ground and corruption was wide spread. It was common practice for their leaders to keep dead men on their books so that they could continue to claim money for them. This meant that the number of men available to defend the country was significantly less than the government expected. Provision of horses and weapons also largely fell on local communities, with neighboring musters and Trained Bands sharing both when it came to their training days. To add to the problems, the funding and provision of local defenses, signal beacons, and any other defensive requirements were also to be paid for out of local funds. This inevitably meant that much of the country was poorly defended. In fact, Hutchinson makes an interesting observation when he comments that 'compared to these Elizabethan militia the raw but enthusiastic Local Defence Volunteers of the German invasion scare of the 1940s appear a finely honed military force.' He goes on to say that 'as in the dark days of 1940, when Britain faced the prospect of a Nazi invasion, it was realised in 1587 that, rather than attempting to defend every inch of the coastline, it would be better to concentrate forces to stand and fight at the most dangerous landing places.'

In October 1587, the Privy Council sent out orders demanding that regular training should be put in place to meet the threat of invasion. Measures were introduced to increase the size of the Trained Bands and provide them with more up-to-date equipment. Troops were also brought back from the Low Countries to help boost the home defenses, particularly around London. As McDermott reports, this had an immediate impact, as the numbers of soldiers and equipment increased from 28,900 trained foot, three hundred and seventy-one lancers and 2,114 light horse, supported by thirty-six pieces of ordnance in March, to 45,000 men, which comprised 41,000 foot and 4,000 horse-mounted soldiers, in June.

At the time, the English still tended to rely on long bows, as their chosen weapon whilst armies on the continent were using firearms. Longbows could still provide a faster rate of fire than muskets and were more accurate over longer distances. However, as Hanson records, only three hundred of the 1,800 men mustered in Surrey had bows and of the 1,700 men from Kent only six hundred had bows. Only four hundred of the 1,000 men sent to defend London were armed and most of the people across the southern and southwest counties had only their farming implements to defend themselves with. He also reports that most of the men that had muskets or arquebuses did not have gunpowder, shots, or matches to fire them; but if they did, they would be charged for every shot they fired. He also adds that, on paper, there were around 10,000 soldiers in London to protect the Queen, 2,500 cavalry and 27,000 troops to defend the south coast and another 12,500 that would be able to form up at Tilbury. These numbers may have been over optimistic, as he also points out that theoretically there were 6,000 men available to defend Cornwall, but, given that it was harvest time, as many as half of these may have refused to leave their fields.

To compound these problems, there would also be serious problems involved with movement of troops and equipment around the country due to the limited number of larger carts available. This meant that even if men could be bought to bear at particular places along the coast to meet Spanish forces, their equipment may not arrive in time. Hanson informs us that often the equipment the Trained Bands possessed was notional, as it was continuously being reduced when men were sent to fight in Holland or traded on the black market.

As for coastal defenses, the Isle of Wight was one of the principal possible landing sites; however, Hanson reports that it only had four mounted cannons and one day's worth of gunpowder. He adds that the Tower of London had been stripped of all of its cannons to further equip coastal fortifications and the navy, and they had even resorted to buying or borrowing cannons from private individuals. Other defenses designed to slow down Spanish forces once they had landed included the provision to knock down bridges, flood roads, use herds of animals to slow them down, and take away or destroy any usable carts and wagons. They also planned to set fire to crops. However, in spite of all of these delaying tactics, the truth was that many key harbors and fortifications were manned by old men and that much of the coastline lay effectively undefended and open to invasion. As reported by Robert Hutchinson in chapter three, *"Ramparts of Earth and Manure,"* in his book *The Spanish Armada*, a document had been produced that recorded the places of potential danger with regard to invasion. These included Milford Haven, Falmouth, Helford, Plymouth, Torbay, Portsmouth, and the Isle of Wight. It also included a survey of all beaches along the English Channel and identified likely landing areas for Parma's troops as The Downs, Margate, the Thames Estuary, Harwich, Yarmouth, Hull, and Scotland. Unaware that Parma planned to land in Kent, Elizabeth's advisors decided that the most likely landing sites would be in Essex, hence they set up their main defensive forces at Tilbury.

Given the state of the land forces it is hardly surprising that the Queen, Government, and indeed the entire country felt that even though they tried to strengthen the defenses, it was the ships of the Navy Royal that would provide the countries only real hope of being able to defeat the Spanish. The view of the situation across the continent was equally pessimistic; they expected any invasion to be 'a rout' when the ad-hoc English Trained Bands met Parma's battle-hardened, professional soldiers.

If the Spanish could break through or defeat the Navy Royal, there would be little realistic defense against them. With the Navy Royal unable to be at sea for any length of time in readiness to meet the Armada, it meant that intelligence from Walsinghams' spies was critical and being able to dissipate that news quickly so that defenses could be mounted was essential. The old signal system originally instigated by Henry VIII in 1545 to warn against the French was bought back in to use as the best method of passing on that news.

The chain of beacons that had long been used as an early warning system to signal the approach of enemy forces was renewed with additional beacons added where necessary. They were located approximately 15 miles (24km) apart. According to Hutchinson, Devon, and Kent each had forty-three beacons, Essex had twenty-six, Norfolk had sixteen, and Sussex and Hampshire had twenty-four each. This provided a network that covered the coast from Land's End to the Scottish borders at Berwick-upon-Tweed. Each beacon was provided with wood, pitch, and matches along with teams of watchers who were paid to provide an around the clock lookout for the Armada. Although the beacons are probably the most well-known feature of the early warning system, small boats were used to constantly patrol the numerous waterways, creeks, and marshes with such effect that the presence of any suspicious ships would soon be noticed.

The beacons are not the same as those we still see scattered around the coast today. Each beacon comprised three baskets, the lighting of which indicated different levels of alert. If one of the baskets were lit, it meant that the Armada had been spotted; by setting fire to two of the baskets, it indicated that the local militia were to assemble at prearranged locations and if all three were ignited, it meant that the Spanish had landed. On the face of it, this seems to be a very efficient system that allowed news and instructions to pass quickly along the coast however, numerous false alarms reduced its effectiveness. The premise for their construction was that they could provide news to London of any landing on the south coast within an hour. Many books report that this was used as a very efficient and fast way of alerting the whole country to the presence of the Armada; Susan Ronalds is typical,

'At first sight of the Spaniards, the order to light the first beacon would be given from a salvo let off at Plymouth, and it would take under fifteen minutes for the torchlight warnings to carry the news to court [in London].'

Moorhouse extends this slightly when he writes that:

'...when the enemy was sighted, beacons were lit the length of England, from the coast of Devon right up to the Scottish border, each one ignited as soon as flames from the one before it became visible. The news travelled all the way within an hour or two.'

This is the image we have from films etc., but the reality may have been somewhat different. After a number of false alarms, it was important to make sure that when the signal system was used to announce the arrival of the Armada is was not ignored. So before we look at how successful it was, let's have a look at how it was set up, manned, and operated. A small hut, often poorly built, was provided by each beacon, which was designed without somewhere to sit so that the men operating the beacon could not sit down and fall asleep. They were always manned by two people so that one could stay on lookout whilst the other went to tell the local magistrate or someone else in authority. The system worked, thus, on sighting the Armada, one person would set off to find the person with the authority to light the beacon. That person would have to come to the beacon to confirm the sighting before it could be set alight. Once this was observed from an adjacent beacon (remember they about 15 miles, 24km, apart), the process would be repeated. It might even mean bringing the same official to that beacon as well! This may seem to be an inefficient system, as it could up to three hours from leaving the beacon to returning with the person in authority, but the authorities had to try, as much as possible, to avoid any false alarms, especially as everyone expected the Spanish to arrive at any moment. This meant, as Hanson reports, that due to the positioning of the beacons on cliffs and open country away from villages and towns, the delay in lighting each beacon might be hours rather than minutes, and it took days for the message to spread out across the country so that pinnaces bringing the news by sea and horse-back messengers managed to take the news to London faster than the beacon chain. This meant that had the Armada made a swift landing, the Spanish might well have arrived at about the same time that news of the Armada reached the local Justice of the Peace.

This provides an interesting image of the message traveling slower that the Armada. It should be remembered that, unlike all the films or programs which show sailing ships cutting through the sea, the Armada, when it arrived off the English coast, and for most of its passage up the English Channel, was traveling at less than 4mph (6.4kph). In other words, at best, it was sailing at walking speed. In fact, there are reports that on many occasions people walked along the cliffs and beaches keeping up with the Armada and progress of the battles, as they made their stately way up the Channel.

As we saw in the first chapter, the Navy Royal, the Queen's ships, comprised thirty-four ships. Of these, only ten were capable of carrying a significant number of guns and would therefore comprise the main battle fleet, these were the *Ark Royal, Revenge, Dreadnought, Non Pareil, Golden Lion, Vanguard, Rainbow, Foresight, Antelope,* and *Swiftsure.* Of these, the *Rainbow* and *Vanguard* were relatively shallow-draft ships which were not suitable for operations in the open seas of the southwest approaches or the North Sea. They had been built to sail in the shallower seas close to shore or in areas with offshore sandbanks and shoals. We have also seen that four of the other capital ships, the *Triumph, Elizabeth Jonas, White Bear,* and *Victory*, were of an older design. To make things worse, all of these, apart from the *Victory*, were in need of some degree of repair in the winter of 1587–1588. This meant that if the Armada were to have sailed during this period, as Philip wanted, the defense of England would have fallen on as few as twenty-nine ships.

In October 1587, Frobisher set sail with a fleet of nine ships including the *Foresight* and *Rainbow*, to patrol the Narrow Seas in response to the perceived threat of Spanish support for Scotland from forces in the Low Countries. By the time that they returned, it was felt that all of these ships were in need of repair. Fortunately, due to the efficiency and effectiveness of the Royal Dockyards, by early December, all repairs were completed and the fleet was back up to full strength. When not at sea, the Navy Royal was either berthed in the docks at Woolwich and Deptford on the Thames or moored at

Chatham. Although this move was primarily financially driven, it had the added benefit that the crews were not held on ship for unnecessarily long periods of time, and it reduced wear and tear damage which occurred whilst ships were at sea.

Lord Admiral Charles Howard took overall command of the Royal ships in December 1587 and immediately set in motion processes and dispositions designed to bring the navy to state of readiness to enable it to respond to any threat.

By January 1588, the Queen's ships had been joined by twenty-three privately owned vessels paid for by the Queen, many of which were sent to strengthen Drakes six ships based in Plymouth. Drake had been sent to cover the Western Approaches and intercept any attempt by the Spanish to reach Scotland or, more probably, Ireland. Sir Henry Seymour's Narrow Sea's Fleet, comprising some thirty ships with William Wynter as his Vice Admiral were given the responsibility of patrolling the eastern Channel to prevent any moves by Parma. Howards task, with sixteen ships based at Queensborough closer to the mouth of the Thames, was be able to provide support to either of the other fleets if required. In spite of all of this activity, by the start of 1588, Howard still only had between fifty-five and sixty ships to engage the Armada if it appeared in the English Channel.

This shows just how crucial the delays caused by the death of Santa Cruz in February 1588 and the appointment of Medina Sidonia, who gallantly pulled the situation around, were to the assembly of the English fleet.

By March 1588, Howard was able to advise the Queen and the Privy Council that all but four of the 'great ships' were in position and ready to sail at relatively short notice. During the same month, more ships were added to boost English forces, which were supplied by, and paid for, by different people. These included eight ships, provided by the Grenville family that went to support Drake at Plymouth. The Queen had also sent out a levy on forty English ports and towns requiring them to supply forty-nine ships and twenty pinnaces, again at their own expense. Many were reluctant to do so and pleaded poverty, others supplied ships, which were in extremely poor condition and were positioned with Seymour's Narrow Sea Fleet to be used for reconnaissance or re-supply duties. On 1 March, Howard set sail to patrol off the coast of the France and Low Countries; he had returned to harbor by 10 March.

By the middle of May, the entire English fleet, except for the ships stationed with Drake in Plymouth, were at Margate. By now, Seymour's fleet comprised twenty-nine ships, and Howard had thirty-eight ships plus a number of pinnances under his command. In total, Howard had one hundred and eighty-seven ships available to him, which carried 15,410 men, but not all of these were deemed suitable for active service. Drake argued that his and Howard's central fleet should be concentrated in Plymouth to be able to meet the Armada with most of the Queen's ships. In response, Howard sailed with thirty ships (twenty belonged to the Navy Royal) for Plymouth on 21 May. Some books say that this was Drake's suggestion, others say that it was Howard's idea. When Howard arrived on 23 May, Drake bought his entire fleet out to meet him. By June 1588, Drake's fleet had swelled to between thirty and forty ships. With a fleet of this size, he argued that he should be allowed to sail for Lisbon to try to catch the Armada in harbor, but, with conflicting news and a significant degree of uncertainty as to the whereabouts of the enemy, the request was turned down. Why? There was a significant possibility that he could sail and, if the Armada had already sailed, he would miss it and be at sea with a significant part of the main battle fleet.

On 4 June, Seymour was once again at sea while following a rumor that Parma's forces were beginning to assemble at the coast in preparation for invasion.

With Howard in command, Drake as his Vice Admiral and John Hawkins as his Rear Admiral, Howard had the majority of the navy under his control. Following a Council of War, which by then was taking place almost every day, it was decided to put to sea to try to find the Armada. Fortunately, adverse weather conditions kept the ships in harbor for almost a month during which time they started to run out of food. As we saw in chapter 1, supplying food to such a large fleet had been something that the supply network had not faced before, and with limited local supplies and generally poor roads, rationing and disease started to affect the sailors and soldiers on board. Howard tried to offset a potentially disastrous situation by dispersing as many of his men as possible in the local area. He could not afford to risk losing a significant proportion of his fighting men, including many of his most experienced leaders, by keeping them onboard. Fortunately, after much complaining supplies finally arrived on 23 June.

This allowed Howard to set sail on 27 June to patrol between the Isles of Scilly and the French coast. When conditions permitted, he was able to use his ships as a screen with Hawkins, and his twenty ships stationed near the Isles of Scilly to cover any attempts by the Spanish to reach Ireland. Howard's twenty ships covering the center of the Western Approaches, and Drake's twenty ships positioned off the French coast. Following two weeks of searching, Howard received news that the ships of the Armada had been scattered by a storm and were now located in various Portuguese and Spanish harbors. This storm apparently did not affect the Queen's ships and caused only minor damage to the English merchant ships. Howard decided to take the entire fleet south to find them, but after two days at sea, the wind changed direction and forced them northwards. By 22 July, the day the Armada finally set sail yet again, the English ships were back in Plymouth.

Even though the Duke of Parma was an acknowledged master soldier, he went to great lengths to persuade Queen Elizabeth I that the peace treaty she wanted was possible. It is quite probable that at first he really preferred peace. However, by the time the English sent over a group of commissioners to Bourbourg to negotiate a peace deal, he was determined to only continue the process for as long as possible to delay and deceive the English. Furthermore, he had been told by Philip that there could be no possible peace with England. As we have seen, although Elizabeth wanted to avoid war, it did not stop her preparing her forces as much as she could with her limited resources. So if England was preparing for war, what were the Spanish doing on the other side of the Channel?

For Parma to be able to mount a successful invasion of England, one of his overwhelming requirements was securing a deep-water harbor on the Dutch coast, which would be safe against attacks from the Dutch 'Sea Beggars,' the English fleet or the French. Parma had no illusions about the difficulty of the task, which he was being asked to achieve. He considered that surprise was one of his best and most important weapons, but with the protracted and very visible build-up of the Armada, this was not possible. He also insisted that, given the number of ships belonging to both the Dutch and English that could put to sea to intercept his invasion barges, one of his principal requirements was that a Channel crossing had to be secured by the Armada before he could set sail with his troops. He also wanted the Armada to dock on the Dutch coast and help transport his troops across the Channel. Philip had other ideas; he wanted the Armada to sail straight for the English coast, probably to Margate or Dover, where it was to await Parma's arrival.

In 1585, Parma attacked and successfully captured the city of Antwerp. He then intended to march to Ostend to secure the coast but was prevented from doing so by Philip, who did not want him to do anything that would upset negotiations with the English. This resulted in a year's delay during which his army's potential was largely wasted, and as a result, Parma's view of the entire Enterprise continued to deteriorate.

In June 1587, he attacked the town and captured the port of Sluys, a deep-water harbor linked by a series of canals to Antwerp where the majority of his troops were stationed. He then built an additional 15 miles (24.1km) of canals, linking Sluys to Nieuport, that would enable him to move his troops from Antwerp to Dunkirk where he was assembling his invasion barges without interference from the 'Sea Beggars.' His next target was to be the deep-water port of Flushing, but Philip also stopped him from capturing it whilst peace negotiations continued.

In September, Parma's forces were boosted by a large contingent of reinforcements from Italy. These men took his force to a total of approximately 30,000 soldiers, the largest number he would achieve, and significantly more than he would have available by the time the Armada was ready to sail.

Parma had two hundred boats at Sluys, with another seventy at Dunkirk, and more being built in Dutch shipyards. He had also collected 20,000 barrels at Gravelines, which he intended to use as floating piers to allow his troops to disembark on the beach when they reached the English coast.

Parma faced two different threats to any attempts to launch his invasion fleet. The first, and most immediate, were the Dutch 'Sea Beggars.' They kept most of their four hundred fast inshore ships out of sight in order to entice him out to sea. Unfortunately, their tactics were negated by the second threat, Seymour and his Narrow Seas Fleet, which kept appearing off the coast. It would seem that although the Queen and Howard trusted the Dutch, their apparent lack of presence or action meant that Howard could not afford to bring Seymour's ships down to join him and the other ships at stationed at Plymouth.

Delays, bad weather, poor living conditions, and inadequate provisions, compounded by a lack of pay and a significant level of desertion reduced Parma's army from 30,000 to 17,000 over the winter. Although replacements were on their way, most of them were new, poorly trained, Italian, and German recruits, who, by the time they arrived, were in an equally poor condition. Replacements were barely keeping pace with the losses. By March 1588, with the launch of the Armada expected at any time, his army comprised 8,000 Germans and Walloons, 4,000 Spaniards, 3,000 Italians, 1,000 English, and 1,000 Burgundians. Parma also felt that he would need a force equivalent in size to the one he was supposed to send across the Channel to quell the increasing instability in the Low Countries.

His invasion barges were also of dubious quality. As Hanson reports, most of the barges were between 60–70 feet (18.2–21.3m) long and 15–20 feet (4.5–6.1m) wide with a draught of no more than three feet (0.9m). They had a single deck, which allowed each barge to carry four hundred soldiers. They had no sails or masts with which to sail them and no armament which could be used to defend them against the Dutch or English. These flat-bottomed boats would have been very unstable in any sea conditions, and a number sank or were damaged during a practice embarkation.

So Parma was in an unenviable position; he did not have the number of troops he needed to maintain stability in the Low Countries as well as meet his commitments to the invasion of England. He had insufficient ships to protect his invasion force, no secure deep-water harbor in which to join up with the Armada, and invasion barges that were un-seaworthy in all but the most calm of conditions. He also dispersed his troops so that the Dutch and English would find it harder to predict what his intensions were. Unfortunately, this meant that if and when the Armada finally arrived off the coast, it would take him quite a long time to gather his troops together. It is apparent that he had decided even before the Armada set sail that it was a waste of time; he had lost the vital element of surprise and could not possibly get his troops across the Channel in the boats he had to hand, especially with the Dutch 'Sea Beggars' and English ships patrolling off the coast. On top of that, he was also extremely disappointed that Philip, who was after all his uncle, was not going to make him regent in England.

In chapter 2, we saw the disposition of the Armada as it continued its preparations in Lisbon. Philip was eager for it to sail as soon as possible but, even though he had a Council of War to hand, his direct control of the Enterprise had led to and would continue to have disastrous consequences on the entire exercise. As Whiting explains, Philip saw the Armada as a means of transporting Parma's troops across the Channel and then protecting his supply lines rather than taking on the English fleet. This would involve a high level of communication between Medina Sidonia and Parma, but Philip was solely in charge of planning, coordinating, and negotiating with each of them. This meant that they could never have met to discuss what was being proposed, nor could they keep up with his continuous changes of mind, which meant that neither really knew what the other was supposed to do.

We have seen that the Armada's primary role was to act as a floating army designed to support Parma's army. If they came into contact with the English ships, their primary aim would be close-quarter fighting and boarding. Hutchinson records that of the one hundred and twenty-nine ships that sailed with the Armada, only thirty-five were major warships and a further thirty-eight comprised armed merchantmen or cargo ships. It also had two hospital ships with eighty-five staff, including five doctors and five physicians. Armament-wise it carried 2,485 cannons, 123,790 cannonballs, and 5,175 quintals (517,500kg) of gunpowder. There were 7,000 harquebuses (a type of matchlock gun), 1,000 muskets, 6,170 hand grenades, and 11,128 pikes. As the ships were to seize a landing site, they also carried twenty siege cannons and over 19,000 soldiers, 15,000 of which formed five heavy infantry brigades but only 10,000 of these were considered to be experienced soldiers. The remaining troops were lightly armed soldiers who were to move ahead to reconnoiter and clear the way for the infantry. Many of the soldiers were carried on the ships of the Levantine squadron, which, as Whiting describes, meant that they were designed to be used as fortified invasion transport ships because there were only 7,700 sailors on board of which only one hundred sixty-seven were gunners.

Chapter 1 included a list of the ships that had gathered at Lisbon in preparation to sail with the Armada, it also included the names of the squadron commanders, the men on whom the safe sailing, maneuvering and disposition of such a large number of ships were to depend. Even though they had faced significant difficulties in gathering the fleet together as well as providing all the equipment and provisions required for such an enormous undertaking, once at sea, their job would be further hampered by the huge diversity in the types and seaworthiness of the ships under their command.

With Philip's growing irritation at the delays and his continuous demands that it sail as soon as possible, the Armada was as ready as it was ever going to be to sail in April 1588. The unseasonable weather conditions that had kept the fleet holed up in Lisbon for weeks finally allowed the one hundred and thirty ships to set sail at last on 9 May 1588 for the 'Enterprise of England.'

Chapter 4

Attack Is the Best Form of Defense

Before we look at the opening phase of both battles, which were primarily defensive actions, it is important to include the offensive actions of Sir Francis Drake that had been briefly mentioned in the previous chapters. These had a profound effect on the build-up of the Armada and how its ships commanders reacted later on in the coming battle when they had reached Gravelines. In the second part of this book, which looks at the Battle of Britain, it will become clear that the offensive actions of Bomber Command during the opening months of the Second World War, were often verging on suicidal, had a profound effect on the Germans' preparations for invading Britain in 1940. Churchill summed up the situation in September 1940 with one of his many famous speeches in which he said,

'The Navy can lose us the war, but only the Air Force can win it. The fighters are our salvation but the bombers alone provide the means of victory. We must therefore develop the power to carry an ever-increasing volume of explosives to Germany, so as to pulverize their entire industry and scientific structure on which the war effort and economic life of the enemy depends, whilst holding him at arm's length from our island.'

In 1588, only the Navy Royal had the ability to provide an effective offensive and defensive force, and Drake was determined to take the coming battle to the enemy in their own waters rather than sit back and wait.

In March 1587, eleven armed merchantmen, funded by their owners and sanctioned by the Queen, gathered in the Thames with the aim of intercepting Spanish ships bound from Lisbon for the East Indies. Due to delays in sailing, they were then joined by seven of the Queen's ships, led by Sir Francis Drake on the *Elizabeth Bonaventure* which had orders to intercept Spanish ships and possibly enter Spanish harbors. According to Ronald, Drake had a total of forty-two ships with him, whereas Moorhouse and others say there were as few as twenty-one. The Queen, her Privy Council, and the government knew that they could not destroy the Armada but hoped that this action would at least delay its sailing, possibly by a year, giving them valuable time in which to continue building up England's defenses. The fleet set sail for Plymouth on 2 April. On 9 April, after Drake had left Plymouth, the Queen then sent new orders, forbidding him from entering any Spanish ports but still allowing him to attack ships at sea. It might well be true that Drake, who was anxious to leave, had anticipated this and was determined to leave before the orders arrived. The Queen had recently received information that as many as three hundred ships were gathering in various Spanish and Portuguese harbors ready to join the Armada that was to sail from Lisbon. She might equally have sent the message later enough to miss Drakes sailing, allowing her to claim that she tried to prevent any subsequent actions that might take place.

Three days after leaving Plymouth, Drakes ships were sailing off Cape Finisterre—a peninsular off the Atlantic coast of Spain. During the following eleven days, whilst sailing towards the Portuguese coast, they were scattered by a large storm, and lost one of their pinnaces. When they finally arrived at Lisbon, Drake decided not to attack the harbor, as the risk of damage from the harbor's defenses was too great given the small number of ships moored there. They therefore sailed south around Cape St. Vincent and headed for Cadiz. In fact, they were sailing so fast that, when they arrived off the coast of Cadiz at 4 p.m. on Wednesday, 29 April, some of the slower ships were still struggling to catch up. Drake, in his Flagship, the *Elizabeth Bonaventure*, was accompanied by the *Golden Lion, Dreadnaught*, and *Rainbow* together with three large armed merchantmen of the Levant Company, these comprised the principal fighting ships under his command. On arrival, and with the element of surprise still upper-most in his mind, Drake held a Council of War aboard his flagship to outline his plans which centered on entering the mouth of the harbor as quickly as possible. When they sailed in at 8 p.m., their sudden and unexpected arrival caused panic throughout the town and harbor, where the majority of the sixty ships berthed were crewless and in some cases even without sails. Mattingly gives a vivid description of the scene when he says that men in the galleys, which were moored close to the seawall scrambled ashore. Ships with shallow draughts were able to beat out across the shoals while many of the larger ships were 'simply paralysed by surprise into inaction or blocked by the inaction of their neighbours. These swung helplessly at their anchors, huddled together like sheep who scent the wolf.'

The speed of his arrival and move in to the harbor caught most of the ships off guard, but the English ships were still met by a line of eight galleys led by Don Pedro de Acuna, a maneuver designed to block their way to the lower harbor. Drake dispatched the armed merchantmen to deal with the ships moored in the outer harbor whilst he led the Queen's ships to strike at the galleys and other defenses. Drake and some of the other navy ships opened fire on the galleys with their broadsides before the Spanish were able to move into position. The galleys were no match for the longer ranged cannons of the English ships, but they stood their ground to allow time for the ships in the harbor to escape to safer areas. English fire smashed their way through the galleys, nearly sinking two of them.

One ship in the harbor, the huge galleon owned by Santa Cruz, which he may well have been intending to use as his flagship for the Armada decided to fight. Drake's ships smashed her to pieces before she finally sank. This must have come as a shock to the other ships in the harbor who apparently offered no further resistance.

Drake's ships then lowered their anchors and set about removing anything useful or valuable from the ships they found. He then either manned them with prize crews to sail them back to England or burnt or sank the ones he did not want to keep. Occasionally, the Spanish, ineffectively fired off their long-range cannons from the old Matagorda Fort, which guarded the harbor, but, apart from one lucky strike on the *Golden Lion*, they did no damage. The Levant ships were positioned to prevent any interference from the galleys and to stop any ships leaving the harbor. One Portuguese ship dispatched by Drake with a prize crew was, however, intercepted by the galleys, which at close range pounded it with deadly fire before boarding and recapturing it. They found only five of the prize crew alive.

The following day, Drake, using the *Merchant Royal* as his Flagship as it had a shallower draught than the *Elizabeth Bonaventure*, led most of the Levant ships in to the upper harbor. Six of the galleys set out, in two lines, to surround the *Golden Lion* to which Drake responded by sending the *Rainbow* and six merchantmen to her assistance. The wind then picked up and the *Golden Lion* itself went on the offensive.

Having achieved what he wanted and not wishing to risk being around to face Medina Sidonia's land forces, the first of which had started to arrive, Drake prepared to leave, but the wind that had been so helpful suddenly dropped, leaving the English ships helpless in the harbor. The situation remained the same for nearly twelve hours, and although the galleys came out every so often to take shots at the English ships, and the fort continued to fire off ineffective rounds, no damage was done. The Spanish even launched fireships towards the English fleet, but their crews did not stay with them long enough to guide them into the English ships, so Drake's ships were either able to fend them off or towed them out of harm's way. Then, just after midnight, the wind picked up once again. At dawn, with many of Medina Sidonia's 3,000 troops continued to arrive, the galleys came out for a final time as Drake was preparing to leave, so his ships responded by dropping their anchors once again and prepared to fight. While the Spanish hoped to pick off an isolated English ship without engaging most of the fleet, their commander sent Drake a complimentary message, wine and some food. This was followed by an exchange of prisoners before Drakes ships sailed away.

Drake's ships had sunk, captured, or set fire to twenty-four ships, many of which had been destined either to take part in, or carry supplies to the Armada. News of Drake's actions spread rapidly throughout the continent, and as he cruised off the coast of Portugal, the presence of his fleet paralyzed Spanish shipping, with no ships willing to sail beyond the entrance to Lisbon harbor. This fear of facing Drake by a significant number of ships that were destined to take part in the Armada led to delays in Philip being able to launch his fleet that would have major consequences.

Bicheno also makes the point that one of the 'novel' aspects of the Cadiz raid was that its first priority was a military-strategic objective rather than profit.

During the next six weeks, Drake's ships blockaded a number of Spanish and Portuguese harbors and captured or destroyed a further one hundred smaller ships, including those carrying metal hoops and wooden staves destined to be made into storage barrels for the Armada.

Generally, most books report that the loss of seasoned barrel staves was to have a disastrous effect on the storage and preservation of water and food for the Armada, but interestingly Herman states that Spanish reports at the time do not support this and that Drakes raid did not significantly delay preparations in its build up.

Drake then set out for the Azores, but a storm dispersed his ships, many of which then headed for home. Eventually, he arrived back in Plymouth towards the end of June, his actions effectively resulting in an invaluable year's delay in the sailing of the Armada.

Chapter 5
Opening Rounds

It is worth noting, before we go any further, a problem with calendars. Two sets of dates are given for the progress of the Armada in different books and websites, which may lead to some confusion. These differences are due to use of two different calendars. The Julian calendar, introduced by Julius Caesar in 46 B.C., replaced the Roman calendar. In 1582, Pope Gregory XIII introduced the Gregorian calendar, which was adopted that year by France, Portugal, Spain, and Italy. Britain did not adopt the new calendar until 1752, when 2 September was followed by 14 September. This means that during the events of 1588, both sides were using different calendars, hence two sets of dates for the same events. I have used the corrected Gregorian calendar dates so that they correspond to the dates for the Battle of Britain.

Chapter 3 ended with the Armada about to set sail from Lisbon on 10 May 1588. Medina Sidonia held a Council of War at which it was decided that the Armada should sail as soon as possible. It left harbor the following day, but due to adverse wind conditions, it was unable to make it to the open sea, so the ships dropped anchor in the River Tagus. The weather continued to plague their progress so much so that after nearly three weeks at sea they had only reached the estuary at Belem, to the west of Lisbon. On 28 May, the weather started to calm down, and the wind switched to the south allowing them to finally leave the Tagus and they were sent on their way by gunfire from Castle St. Julian. Once at sea, the Armada sailed into a north-northwest breeze, which, although quite light, was sufficient to delay completion of its formation until the morning of 30 May. The large number of slower, less sea-worthy ships slowed the progress of the entire Armada to a crawl, so much so that by 1 June it had still not reached the Rock of Lisbon which was only 24 miles (40km) northwest of the harbor. It took a further eleven days to sail the 160 miles (257.5km) to Cape Finisterre, one of the western-most points on the North Spanish coastline.

By this time, the condition of the Armada's food and in particular its water supply, was becoming a major cause for concern. The number of soldiers and seamen falling ill with dysentery, scurvy, and other ship-borne diseases was having a severe impact on most of the ships' abilities to sail. Medina Sidonia had been sending messages to Philip, requesting the urgent deliveries of much needed supplies, and it was decided that the entire fleet should wait off Cape Finisterre for them to arrive. The Armada waited there for four days, but no supplied arrived. Medina Sidonia then decided that they could wait no longer, and they should therefore continue their journey in spite of the ever-worsening conditions of both men and supplies on board. By 16 June, when they had covered only 30 miles (42.8km) in twenty days, he called another Council of War, at which all but one of his advisors agreed to put in to Corunna on the northwest tip of Spain, to let the sick receive attention and to take on the supplies they desperately needed.

Most of the Armada reached the entrance to Corunna during 19 June, but the galleasses and most of the slower hulks, together with Recalde's squadron, who were guarding them, arrived after sunset and were advised to wait out to sea overnight so that they would be able to sail in to the harbor in daylight. Unfortunately, during the night, a strong, southwest gale blew up and those ships still at sea decided for safety sake that they would have to pull up their anchors and run with the wind rather than try to ride out the storm outside the harbor. The winds continued to blow until the afternoon of 21 June, by which time most of these ships had been scattered over a wide area. Once the storm had passed, Medina Sidonia sent out a number of his fast sailing pinnaces to find and retrieve them. However, by 24 June, thirty ships were still missing. Instructions had previously been given to all ships captains that, if any ships lost contact with the body of the Armada, they should either meet it off the Isles of Scilly or, failing that, join it in Mounts Bay, off Mousehole, on the south Cornish coast. It is interesting to observe that the last of the missing ships did not rejoin the Armada until 15 July.

On 27 June, Medina Sidonia called yet another Council of War at which it was decided that the Armada should stay in Corunna until all the ships had been repaired and taken on the provisions they so desperately required. Not only were the ships that had been caught at sea in need of urgent repairs, many of those moored in Corunna had also been damaged. Although King Philip was desperate for the Armada to get on with its mission, he agreed to Medina Sidonia's request and agreed to the delay. One of the most pressing problems the Armada faced was the urgent need to replace all the men that had fallen ill or died, which, it is thought, accounted for as many as one third of those on board when the ships left Lisbon.

Finally, at a Council of War on 20 July, it was decided that the Armada was at last ready to sail, but yet again wind conditions kept it in port. With as many replacement soldiers and sailors as they could find and as much food and water as the countryside around Corunna could provide, the Armada was at last ready to sail on 22 July, over a month after leaving Lisbon. On the same day, Howard and English fleet arrived back in Plymouth from their expedition to look for them. The Spanish were not the only ones affected by the weather, the English ships set sail on three different occasions to try to catch the Armada in port, but each time, they were beaten back by the weather.

On their return, the English fleet had only ten days provisions on board and less than two days' worth of gunpowder. As we have seen, one of the trade-offs, the English ships had to contend with for their sleeker design was the reduced storage capacity of their ships. This affected not only the amount of food and water they could carry but also the amount of shot and powder they had available for any action; a situation which would continuously dog Howard and his ships throughout the coming battle.

With all the problems of illness, supplies, and the lack of seaworthiness of many of his ships Medina Sidonia realized that once the Armada had reached Dunkirk, he could not afford to wait for Parma's army, barges, and ships to be ready to sail. He therefore sent a fast sailing pinnace on 25 July, to inform Parma that the Armada had finally set out on its journey. On 26 July, after four days at sea, the Armada was still making slow progress, and as the wind dropped, the entire fleet drifted until midnight. The wind eventually swung around to the north, increased in strength, and was accompanied by short, sharp showers. It then changed direction again, blowing from the west-northwest, and it continued to increase in strength to gale force conditions. This storm continued until midnight on 28 July, and although most of the Armada, which was by now southwest of the Isles of Scilly, managed to stay together, some ships had been scattered by the storm. The *Diana*, the flagship of the galleys, was so battered by the storm that it separated from the fleet and headed for shore, eventually running aground at Bayonne. Fortunately, everyone and most of its equipment and stores were safely rescued before she broke up. The other three galleys, which had also taken such a battering by the storm and were taking on so much water that they were liable to sink, were also allowed to leave and seek shelter along the French coast. Much to Medina Sidonia's relief, they never rejoined the Armada. The *Santa Ana*, the flagship of the Biscayan squadron, which had been damaged by the last storm, ran ahead of this one all the way up the Channel before it reached the port of The Hague, it too never rejoined the Armada. Many of the other ships were once again damaged, including Diego Flores' flagship, the *San Cristobal*, which lost her stern castle, and the *San Lorenzo*, flagship of the galleasses which lost its rudder. The Armada had now lost twenty ships before it had even reached the English Channel. Hanson informs us that Hawkins sailed through the same storm without any trouble.

The storm had blown itself out by the morning of 29 July, and Medina Sidonia was able to review the situation. He had lost all four of his galleys and one of his major warships, and forty other ships were also missing. The Armada undertook running repairs and continued on its journey towards the Isles of Scilly. Later that day, he at last received some good news: the missing ships were ahead of the rest of the Armada, having been collected together by Don Pedro de Valdes off the Lizard. By 4 p.m., when all of the sailors and solders got their first sight of the English coastline around the Lizard, the missing ships had rejoined the rest of the fleet; the Armada was at last almost back to full strength.

On the same day, a small ship that had sailed from Mousehole on the south Cornish coast, bound for France to collect a cargo of salt, came across a French warship. Its captain warned the Cornish sailors that the Armada had been spotted to the west, and not to head in that direction. The Cornishmen thought the news was so important that they abandoned their mission and raced westwards to find out where the Spanish were. Three hours later, they spotted a large number of ships in the distance, and, having confirmed that they were indeed the Spanish, they headed for home as quickly as they could sail. On returning to Mousehole, the captain set off for Plymouth to report his news. Later that day, two other ships arrived home with news that Spanish had previously been spotted north and south of the Isles of Scilly.

In the early hours of 30 July, Medina Sidonia found out from the captured crew of a Falmouth fishing boat that Howard, Drake, and the ships based in Plymouth were at sea. He then ordered all of his ships to drop anchor and called another Council of War. During this meeting, it was decided, against Philip's specific instructions, that the Armada would sail as far as the Isle of Wight and wait for news from Parma.

They realized that if they sailed further than the Isle of Wight and Parma was not ready to meet them when they arrived at Dunkirk, they would be vulnerable not only to the English fleet but also the shallow waters, sandbanks, and mudflats of the English and continental coasts. If they were able to moor in the eastern side of the Solent and land their troops on the Isle of Wight, they could probably then wait there until they received news that Parma's forces were ready to meet them; they could then sail to Dunkirk. Philip wanted them to capture a landing site on the Cape of Margate, the eastern-most part of the Kent coast, and then support Parma's invasion fleet as it crossed the Channel; a plan, which Parma had already said he did not have the ships in numbers, strength, or seaworthiness to fulfil. They also discussed the possibility of a surprise attack on the English fleet whilst it was moored in Plymouth. They however decided against this because the entrance was too narrow to be able to send in a sufficient number of ships together to be able to defend themselves against, or land enough soldiers to capture the coastal defenses which they considered to be too strong to be left intact. They also thought that the confined waters off Plymouth Hoe would limit their maneuverability and thus prevent them from being able to board and capture the English ships. This was a fundamental mistake, as Hanson points out, that if the Spanish ships had made a dash for Plymouth and risked the guns of the shore batteries, they would have caught Howard's ships trapped in the harbor by the prevailing winds. And given the number of soldiers they had on board, they may well have been able to over-run the harbor's defenses and take the city as well as the closely packed English fleet.

The English ships had arrived seven days earlier from their expedition to Corunna and were still in the process of loading their long awaited provisions, shot and gunpowder. So many of their ships companies had also been hit by dysentery and ship fever that press gangs were hard pushed to find replacements in the local area. They were therefore in no position to be able to defend themselves against a prolonged and determined attack.

Plymouth

While the Armada was approaching the Lizard on Friday, 29 July, news of their arrival reached Plymouth from one of Drake's screen of barques that he had set across the Southwest Approaches. As soon as this ship, the *Golden Hind,* and its captain, Thomas Fleming, arrived in Plymouth, he set out to find Howard and Drake. Interestingly, Fleming had a royal warrant out for his arrest for piracy. The famous story, which has been handed down as one of the great moments in English history then follows. Fleming found the two commanders playing bowls on the Hoe, and on receiving the news, Drake is supposed to have said, 'We have time to finish the game and beat the Spaniards too.' This story may or may not be true, but it was only written down thirty-six years after the event and the famous quote was not recorded until the 18th century. They may not have been playing bowls on Plymouth Hoe as we think of it; in Cornwall, bar skittles was also known as bowls at the time, so may have been playing skittles in a pub. Finally, although Fleming commanded one of Drake's ships, it would be odd that he should report the news to him rather than Howard, who after all, was the Admiral of the Fleet. (Incidentally, the word Hoe is an Anglo-Saxon word, meaning a sloping ridge that looks like an inverted foot or heel.)

When Fleming arrived, the tide had just turned and was flowing in to Plymouth Sound and the wind, which was blowing from the southwest, which would have blown the Spanish ships in to the harbor had they decided on this plan of action, would also have prevented the English fleet from leaving. There was effectively no alternative but to wait.

The tide would not turn until 9 p.m. that night, and the strength or direction of the wind was not expected to change substantially either. This meant that the English ships could not sail out of the Sound. Therefore, each ship was either towed out to sea by their rowing boats, hauled along cables attached to the shore, or pulled out in a series of moves whereby each anchor was rowed ahead of the ship, dropped into the water and the ship then pulled itself forward by winding in the anchor rope. The process of leaving the harbor was so slow that many of the ships were still leaving Plymouth over twelve hours after Fleming had arrived with the news they had all been waiting for. In fact, by dawn on Saturday, 30 July, only fifty-four ships had made it out in to the open seas and some were still leaving when Howard was preparing to engage the Armada for the first time.

The wind was still blowing from the southwest, and with the Armada almost off Fowey, some 20 miles (32.2km) west of Plymouth and although he could not see the Spanish ships, Howard called his ships to order because he knew that if he did not maneuver his ships to be behind the Armada, the Spanish would have the advantage of the wind. He, therefore, intended to lead his ships around the front of the Armada during the night so that he could take up a position behind it the following morning. By 3 p.m., the Armada, which was still making very slow progress up the Channel, was heading south of Eddystone Rock—an isolated outcrop which is almost 13 miles (20.9km) due south of Plymouth—when they got their first sight of the English ships through the rain showers that had been soaking them. When they saw the first of the English ships, they got a bit of a surprise, as they thought that most of the English fleet would be further up the Channel, guarding the Narrow Sea. Interestingly, the Spanish record seeing seventy-six ships, which is obviously an over-estimate. Their first impression on spotting the English fleet was that it was disorganized, and that being downwind they would be at a disadvantage. By sunset, they could clearly see the English ships and felt that they would be able to keep the weather gauge and engage the enemy in the morning, on their terms, so they dropped anchor between Eddystone and Dodman's Point—a promontory between Falmouth and

Fowey close to Mevagissey. This was also the first time that most of the English ships had seen the Armada, which must have been an impressive sight, as it was almost four miles (6.4km) across, and with each ship sailing approximately 15 paces (less than 40 feet [12m]) apart; it must really have looked like a wooden wall, or a single wooden fort, which in effect was its true function. Coincidently, it was thirty-four years to the day, since Philip had landed at Southampton to marry Mary Tudor at Winchester.

Tor Bay

During the night, the wind changed direction, and Howard made his move to get behind and, therefore, gain the wind advantage he needed for his faster, more maneuverable ships to be able to engage the Spanish on his terms, not theirs. Then, using their intimate knowledge of the local tides, wind, and sea conditions, he left a few ships down wind and in sight of the Armada to make them think that all of his ships were off Plymouth, while he led the rest of the fleet south and then northwest to position himself to the west and, therefore, upwind and behind the Spanish.

This local knowledge and experience would play a crucial part in the engagements that continued all the way up the coast in the days to follow. At around 5 a.m. on Sunday, 31 July, Medina Sidonia and the other commanders on the Armada, looked eastwards to where they had seen the English ships the night before, expecting them still to be there, instead, they could only see six ships—the rest were nowhere in sight. To their surprise, they realized that Howard and a large proportion of the English fleet had sailed past them during the night and were now behind them; they had therefore lost the tactical advantage that they briefly held the previous day.

The English now had a total of one hundred and ninety-seven ships, including thirty-four Navy ships, ranged against the one hundred and thirty ships of the Armada, and, as Rupert Matthews writes in *The Spanish Armada: A Campaign in Context*, that although most of the English captains had a relatively free hand, tactically they followed a set pattern. On each occasion that the Spanish were approaching somewhere where they would be able to land, the English ships positioned themselves to block their access and crowd the Spanish ships together until the possibility of a landing had passed.

When the Spanish saw that the English were behind them, they realized the problems they were now facing. The English ships were obviously faster, more maneuverable, and could take greater advantage of wind and sea conditions than they could. With the English ships positioned upwind of the

Spanish, the wind would tend to heel (tilt) them over towards the Spanish ships, thus, lowering the angle of their cannons towards the Spanish hulls. Conversely, the Spanish ships would heel away from the English, raising their line of fire above the English hulls and while exposing more of their own hulls to English fire.

If you add to this the problems of reloading the larger guns on the Spanish ships highlighted in Chapter one, as long as the English continued to stay upwind and avoid coming to within grappling range, the Spanish would be fighting a losing battle.

With the bulk of the English ships behind him, Medina Sidonia fired a signal gun, and the entire Armada turned and formed up in to its fighting formation with the Levant squadron and galleasses in front, the hulks in the middle, and the Guipizcoans and Andalusian squadrons forming the two wings which pointed towards the English ships; this was an act of remarkable seamanship. With most, but not all of the English ships at sea, the two fleets faced each other, but no one had ever seen this before, and no one quite knew what damage the weapons in each fleet could inflict on the other; this was a new type of battle. As Mattingly puts it:

'This was the beginning of a new era in naval warfare, of the long day in which the ship-of-the-line, wooden walled, sail-driven and armed with smooth-bore cannon, was to be queen of battles… In the beginning there was no name for the ship-of-the-line, and no idea how to use it. That morning off the Eddystone nobody in either fleet knew how to fight a "modern" battle. Nobody in the world knew how.'

Medina Sidonia was the first to offer battle, by raising his banner. In response, Howard sent out a pinnace, the *Disdain*, commanded by James Bradbury, to fire a warning shot across the front of the Armada, before raising his flags and standards, opening his gunports, and dividing his fleet in to two units. Such an act of chivalry was still regarded as being important. Howard then led his ships in line ahead and sailed off towards the left, landward, wing of the Spanish fleet. He had instructed Drake, Frobisher, and Hawkins to take the rest of the ships to attack the right seaward wing.

Matthews points out that the winged fighting formation to be adopted by the Armada had been 'agreed weeks earlier.' In response to Howard's move, Medina Sidonia fired a signal gun, 'and as the English warships bore down,' the Armada adopted this formation. Matthews comments that 'what had until then been a gaggle of ships without any apparent formation slowly shook itself out as the ships slipped into position.' He notes that 'the English were astonished to see the fleet adopt a tightly knit shape akin to that of a crescent moon, with the tracking tips of the crescent pointing backwards toward the English.'

Although Philip's instructions had been to avoid fighting to keep the Armada intact to meet with Parma, he thought that his warships could easily deal with the English fleet. However, Medina Sidonia's orders had always been to use the Armada as a defensive, rather than an offensive, force, so he wanted to draw the English ships towards the center of his formation so that the wings could close in and allow his ships to fight at close quarters. Howard was well aware of this and made sure to avoid it at all costs

Howard in the *Ark Royal* led the attack, firing his bow-chasers and then, as he drew up alongside the first of the Spanish ships, fired his broadside, the rest of the ships following him in a loose line astern formation. In response, Don Alonso de Leiva in the *Rata Coronada*, followed by the rest of the Levant squadron, turned to sail parallel with Howard to trade broadsides with his ships. Howard then turned his ships away to reload before sailing around the back of the Armada and repeated the exercise on the other wing. As Matthews and others report, 'the Spanish were not used to sustained enemy fire' and 'perhaps most unnerving of all was the sight of ship after English ship coming into range, running out its guns and then firing. As if in slow motion, the Spanish saw the death-dealing culverins coming towards them, and there was little they could do about it.' In an instinctive effort to get out of the way of some of the incoming fire, the wing began to move inwards towards the center of the Armada.

At the same time, Drake and his ships, started to perform the same pattern of attack on the other wing before deciding to concentrate on attacking one ship, the *San Juan du Portugal* with Juan Martinez de Recalde on board, who was Admiral of the Biscayan squadron and commander of the rearguard. Unfortunately, Drake's ships did not elicit the same response as Howard had, because Recalde turned to meet the English ships but none of the rest of his squadron followed. Isolated and facing Drake in the *Revenge*, Hawkins in the *Victory*, and Frobisher in the *Triumph*, together with four other ships, Recalde's ship sustained two hours of fire from some of our biggest cannons as they fired their broadsides at him, then turning around and firing again. Eventually, the rest of the Biscayan ships—including the *Gran Grin* and Medina Sidonia in the *San Martin*—came to his rescue. English fire had smashed the *San Juan du Portugal's* main mast and rippled through a large proportion of its rigging as they fired at will. As other Spanish ships came to its aid, the English ships retired. At the end of this engagement, Howard and the rest of the English commanders were disconcerted to see that given the amount of shots they had fired at the Spanish ships, they could see only superficial damage.

Although fighting was effectively over by 2 p.m., Medina Sidonia formed the Armada's fighting ships in to line-ahead squadrons to await further engagement with the English fleet. He hoped that Howard would be drawn in to another fight, closer in, so that the Armada's ship could board the English ships. In response, the English ships just sailed towards the Spanish, let off a few shots, and sailed away again. This was probably in attempt to keep the Armada busy, as both fleets sailed eastwards for another three hours until they had passed Plymouth. With no further action required, the English ships pulled away, and seeing no prospects of further action, Medina Sidonia regained his position at the front of the Armada, and Recalde bought the *San Juan* and the *Gran Grin*, which had also sustained some damage, into the protection of the Armada to make repairs.

With many of his ships now out position following the day's action, Medina Sidonia was keen to re-establish the Armada's formation before darkness fell; but in doing so, two incidents occurred within the Armada, which had a profound effect on both sides. The first was an increase in the strength of the wind and a deterioration in sea conditions. The second involved the *Nuestra Senora del Rosario* the flagship of the Andalusian squadron, which collided with the *San Catalina* as they tried to get in to position. The *Rosario* lost its bowsprit and most of its masts and sails, and although she was taken in tow to bring her towards the safety of the body of the Armada and make repairs, the tow rope kept breaking. As the wind began to blow harder, a section of her foremast broke away damaging the mainmast. She was now unmanageable, so her captain fired off a distress signal.

It seems that internal disputes between various commanders led to a decision by Don Pedro de Valdes, commander of the *Rosario,* not to repair his ship and not to fight with her even though she was one of the largest and most heavily armed and, therefore, most important ships in the Armada. Instead, he let his ship drift behind the rest of the Armada. Once again, Medina Sidonia came to his rescue in the *San Martin*, but after a while, he had to leave it to continue leading the rest of the Armada back into formation before darkness fell. This meant that the *Rosario* continued to fall further and further behind. The loss of this and the *San Catalina*, which were two of the most important fighting ships, was a severe blow to Medina Sidonia, as they carried more than 10% of the Armada's heavy cannons. As we will see, their later capture by the English helped our supply problems. About two hours after darkness, as the English fleet sailed past her, the Spanish fleet heard

94

gunfire, and then silence. Howard had decided that she was no further threat and so led his ships past her to continue tracking the rest of the Armada.

The Armada suffered another blow when an explosion in the rear gunpowder magazine on the *San Salvador*, the Vice-Admiral of the Guipuscoan squadron's ship ripped through the back of the ship and the top two decks. The explosion killed two hundred soldiers and sailors on board—in fact only ninety-two men were unhurt by the explosion. Medina Sidonia sent a couple of galleasses to tow it back in to the protection of the Armada and take off the dead and injured together with as many of the provisions, armaments, and gold as possible—the Armada's paymaster was on board the ship. She was then towed backwards away from the Armada to prevent the fire engulfing more of the ships structure and was only turned around once the fire was out. By noon, she was starting to sink and was left to drift behind the rest of the ships, without removing her cannonballs or gunpowder. Later that evening, Howard sent his cousins, Lord Thomas Howards and Sir John Hawkins to board her—they found fifty badly injured men still on board. She was the towed by the *Golden Hind* in to Weymouth, where the gunpowder and shot were removed and sent out to the English ships.

That afternoon, Howard called a Council of War. The English commander had been disconcerted to see that firing their cannons at a range beyond which there was no threat of boarding by the Spanish had resulted in no real damage; it was estimated that they had fired over three hundred cannonballs at the *Rosario* alone. The effective range of the heaviest English guns were 2,000–3,000 paces (1.6–2.4km), but it was not until later on in the running battles, when the English came in to around 300 paces (240m), a distance that was also within small arms fire, that they managed to do significant damage to any of the Spanish ships. In answer to the apparent lack of damage, the English increased their rate of fire. Space restrictions reduced the stock of cannonballs to approximately thirty per cannon, which with the higher rate of fire achieved by the English ships meant they would be constantly in danger of running out if resupplies were not forthcoming.

It was also decided that Drake would shadow the Armada during the night with his large stern lantern burning so that the rest of the English ships could follow at a safe distance. This was an eminently sensible decision on Howard's behalf given Drakes navigational and sailing skills, but as Hutchison comments, Howard did not reckon 'with his Vice Admiral's greed in the face of the enemy.'

Drake followed orders until around 1 a.m., and with no moonlight to help, it appears that he reverted to his usual behavior. He then put out his stern light and sailed off, possibly with the *Roebuck* alongside him, to take the *Rosario* as a prize, which as it drifted, collided with another Spanish ship, causing even more damage. Howard had given specific orders to leave it alone so that the English fleet could be maintained at full strength. When he reached the *Rosario*, having gone off 'to find some German ships that he thought he had passed,' Drake managed to persuade Don Pedro de Valdes to surrender. Not only was the *Rosario* carrying forty-six unused cannons and 2,000 cannonballs, which would prove invaluable to the English, but it had a large quantity of valuables and money onboard, which Don Pedro had prevented Medina Sidonia from removing. This money, a third of that carrying by the Armada, was destined to pay the wages of the soldier and sailors on board and the soldiers with Parma in the Low Countries. Drake had her taken in tow by the *Roebuck* into Torbay to be stripped of anything that could be useful, while Don Pedro stayed on board with Drake for the rest of the voyage as his guest. Most of the Spanish crew, however, died in English prisons. Interestingly, the amount of treasure recorded by Drake and del Valdez as being on board was significantly less than the amount claimed in Spanish records as being on the ship.

This ship, together with the *San Salvador*, that had been under tow by *Santa Maria de la Rosa*, until she had also been abandoned because she was sinking, were huge losses to the Spanish and huge gains for the English. However, when the rest of the English commanders heard what Drake had done, they did not believe his story; in fact, Frobisher called him 'a cowardly knave.'

During the night, Howard, who with the *White Bear* and *Mary Rose*, had been sailing ahead of the rest of the fleet behind Drake stern lantern until it went out. They later saw another lantern which they thought was on Drakes ship, and followed that. At first light, Howard found himself and the other two ships almost in the midst of the Armada with the rest of the English fleet nowhere in sight; he had been following the lantern on the Spanish flagship. He pulled away, but, due to lack of wind, it took nearly twelve hours for the English ships to reform by which time both fleets had passed Tor Bay, the next possible landing site for the Spanish. The English had therefore effectively lost an entire day's fighting due to Drake's actions, as both fleets now sailed on across Lyme Bay towards the Isle of Portland. Medina Sidonia noted that more and more ships were joining the English fleet, but these were actually supply ships, bringing out desperately needed provisions, shot, and gunpowder, which had been taken from all possible sources.

As Herman points out, the night before 'Drake saw the opportunity for some easy thieving and took it.' His actions had led not only putting his admiral in a dangerous position but also to the scattering of the entire English fleet. Howard then lost a full day of possible action whilst he had to reassemble his fleet.

Drake's rather weak explanation for his actions did not convince anyone, but as Hutchinson explains that 'Howard deemed it impolite to court marshal one of England's naval heroes at a time of national emergency—even though, through his actions, the English fleet had lost both time and distance in chasing the Armada.' He goes on to say that 'had the Spanish successfully landed in Torbay, the fault would have been entirely down to Drake and his lust for ducats.'

The Drake incident reminded me of the situation between Admiral Beattie and Admiral Jellico during the major First World War sea battle on the last day of May 1916, which is known as the Battle of Jutland. Beattie, who was in command of the 2nd Battle Cruisers Squadron, charged off to engage the Germany High Seas Fleet. Jellico, as the Admiral of the Fleet, was leading the slower more heavily armed dreadnaughts of the Grand Fleet, the most powerful navy in the world. Jellico could hear gunfire over the horizon but could get no information from Beattie as to where the Germans were. Beattie's battle cruisers were not considered to be 'Ships of the Line' and, therefore, were designed to engage other cruisers not the battleships of the High Seas Fleet. Due to his headstrong action, Beattie, who was another 'blue-eyed boy' of the navy rather like Drake, caused Jellico to miss the opportunity to bring his heavy guns to bear on the enemy and probably took away the chance of a decisive naval victory.

During a Council of War on board the *Ark Royal*, it was decided that Frobisher and four of the other slower ships would take up a more coastal position to keep the Armada away from potential landing places and to keep them moving. The others would take their faster ships and attack the seaward wing of the Armada, and Howard would use his ships to concentrate on the center of the Spanish formation. While Howard gave his commanders a great deal of freedom to use their own initiative, experience, and tactics, Medina Sidonia, however, allowed virtually no flexibility for his own captains.

That afternoon, Medina Sidonia called his Council of War and then reordered his ships once again with forty-three of his most powerful ships, forming a defensive line across the rear of the Armada commanded by Don Alonso de Leiva, because Recalde, his most experienced admiral, was still repairing his ship. Medina Sidonia himself, with Don Diego Enriquez in charge, led a smaller force of twenty of the main fighting ships—including the *San Mateo*, *San Luis*, *Florencia*, and *Santiago* plus three of the four galleasses—as a defensive formation in the front of the Armada. He was expecting to find more of the English ships ahead of him sailing down from

Dover, with, as he thought, Hawkins in command. One of the problems, which Medina Sidonia faced was that when the Armada was sailing in its crescent formation, it was some seven miles (11.3km) from tip to tip. This meant that the English could attack either wing, and he would have great difficulty in getting reinforcements to help those ships under attack. Medina Sidonia also noted that some of the ships that had come under attack fled to the center of the Armada for protection, which left the other ships in the wing more vulnerable. Howard thought that this change in formation indicated that the powerful rearguard was going to be used to protect the troop and supply ships during a landing along the coast.

Portland

At dawn on Tuesday, 2 August, as both fleets were approaching the Isle of Portland, the wind turned from the northwest to the east and increased in strength. This gave the Spanish the weather gauge and, therefore, the advantage for the first time since first sighting the English ships. Howard led the majority of the English fleet, which included the *Ark Royal*, *Victory*, *Elizabeth Jonas*, *Golden Lion*, *White Bear*, *Nonpareil*, *Mary Rose*, *Margaret and John*, *Merchant Royal*, *Centurion*, *Dreadnought*, and the *Swallow*, north-northeast to try to get past the Armada on its landward side. Taking advantage of the strengthening winds, this move took the Spanish by surprise. In response, Medina Sidonia with his vanguard, that had been shadowing the English Admiral, moved to intercept and block Howard's path. Howard responded by tacking across the back of the Armada to the south-southwest, to sail around it on its seaward side. As the English ships sailed past the rear of the Spanish fleet, which had the wind in their favor, the seaward element of their rearguard swung around to engage Howard. Their more landward section also turned to engage the rear of the English line. The ensuing battle between Howard and at least half of the Armadas fighting ships lasted all morning. All the time the English were trying to gain the weather gauge on the seaward side of the Armada and the Spanish were trying to get close enough to board them, the easterly wind gradually blew both fleets back westwards into Lyme Bay.

It should be remembered again that most of the battle was fought at walking pace, as Hanson so vividly points out, even if the cannon fire was intense, the speed at which the ships sailed meant that it usually took quite a long time before anyone could gauge what was going on, where your opponent was and what you should be doing, hence battles went on all day, often with only sporadic periods of real action. He reports that sometimes ships even dropped their anchors or loosened their sails to wait for the wind to change. On occasions, both fleets were even left drifting helplessly because of a change in the wind or tides.

Some books record that whilst Howard was attacking the center of the Armada, Drake and Hawkins's squadrons sailed seaward out of sight of the Armada to attack its offshore wing, but it is quite possible that Drake actually took no part in the battle, he may not have even been there at the time.

While Howard's running battle was developing with Medina Sidonia, and nine of the Armada's most powerful warships, Frobisher on board the *Triumph*, with five London merchantmen, the *Merchant Royal, Centurion, Margaret and John, Mary Rose* and *Golden Lion*, sailed in to the lee (west side) of Portland close to Portland Bill, the southern-most point of the island, and dropped anchor. It might be that Howard's and Hawkin's move was a tactical diversion, designed to pull Medina Sidonia and his ships away from Portland, to enable Frobisher and his older, larger ships to try to pass the Armada on its landward side.

The southern tip of Portland is an unusual place, with deep water right up to the base of the cliffs. There is a bank of sand and shells, two miles (3.2km) out to sea to the east of the island, known as the Shambles, which may be part of the original location of Chesil Beach. To the seaward side of this, there is a very strong tidal race, one of the strongest in Southern England, which projects seaward from the southern tip of the island. This tide race can generate tides, which could be lethal to any ships that tried to cross it. The landward section of the race flows eastwards at around 2 knots (3.7kph), the center flows eastwards at up to 7 knots (13kph), and the offshore race flows westwards at 1 knot (1.8kph). The different flow directions produce eddy currents, in which the water 'boils' as it wells up from the center of eddies and spirals outwards.

Frobisher positioned his ships in the quiet water behind (landward) the tide race and the Shambles, inviting the Spanish to come and fight him. Crowds of locals had gathered on the cliffs to cheer on the English ships, and it may well be that the ships were close enough to the cliffs for them to be able to throw food to those on board. Medina Sidonia, seeing Frobisher's 'plight' sent the four galleasses to attack him. In response, Frobisher used his ships boats to turn the *Triumph* and the other ships with him in to a firing position and awaited the galleasses. The galleasses were unable to cross the tidal race and never got closer than about 300 yards (274m) to the English ships. Every time they moved in to tidal race, it threw them about and swept them away. Their situation was made worse by the fact that Frobisher's ships were continuously firing at them with their longer-range cannons, whilst the galleasses shorter-range guns were unable to fire back with any effect. The still waters in which Frobisher had positioned his ships allowed them to use their lower gun decks for the first time, and they loaded their cannons with chain rather than round shot to maximize injuries to the crews and rowers rather than to the structures of the galleasses themselves.

The galleasses tried for nearly two hours to reach Frobisher's ships without success, after which Frobisher weighed anchor and led his ships swiftly out to join Howard and the rest of English fleet.

At around 10 a.m., as the heat from the sun increased, the offshore wind dropped, eventually to be replaced a southwesterly onshore wind. This gave Howard the weather gauge again and, on seeing the *San Martin* and other ships of the Spanish vanguard heading towards Frobisher, Howard together with the *Elizabeth Jonas*, *Galleon Leicester*, *Golden Lion*, *Victory*, *Mary Rose*, *Dreadnought*, and *Swallow* set out to help. Medina Sidonia saw Howard's move and led his ships to intercept him. Unfortunately, they did not manage to keep up with the English ships. Medina Sidonia also saw that Recalde, in the repaired *San Juan* was under attack by about twelve English ships, and dispatched some of his own ships to help him. In the meantime, Medina Sidonia's *San Martin* had fired at Howard on the *Ark Royal* and the *Ark* replied at close range, followed by the rest of the fifteen ships behind him. Once past, they turned around, reloaded, and sailed back past the *San Martin* firing their broadsides as they went. They then turned around again and made a third pass. The *San Martin* fought Howard's ships for an hour before any other Spanish ships came to its rescue, at which point the English pulled away. During the battle, which may have lasted until well into the afternoon, it is estimated that the English fired as many as five hundred cannonballs at the *San Martin*, which only managed to fire eighty shots in return. During the various running battles, the Spanish estimated that nearly 5,000 shots had been fired by the two fleets. The only other action of any note that evening was a small encounter between a few English merchantmen and a small force of Spanish ships on the outer, seaward side of the Armada.

The wind swinging around to the southwest also enabled Hawkins and Drake (if he was actually present) together with around forty ships, to mount their attack on the seaward wing of the Armada. This side of the Armada was more poorly defended because so many of the Spanish fighting ships were either engaged fighting Howard or Frobisher. Matthews records that the English ships 'cruised up the seaward flank of the store ships and opened fire…damage was done on a large scale, but Recalde in the only real fighting ship still on that flank defended well—putting his ship between Drake and the storeships.' Seeing this move, Medina Sidonia sent some of his ships to support Recalde and help defend the storeships, but, as we have just seen, he stayed to fight Howard—commander versus commander. When the support ships eventually arrived, they placed themselves with Recalde, between the English ships and the rest of the Armada.

At 2 p.m., Howard disengaged and Hawkins (and Drake) followed suit. The wind and morning battle, which had lasted around five hours, meant that the Armada had missed the high tide, which would have allowed it to sail in to Weymouth to the east of the Isle of Portland. The Spanish were now downwind of Weymouth, with no possibility of being able to gain access to the harbor and were heading out along the eastern half of the Dorset coastline towards the Isle of Wight and the Solent. Once again, the English had been able to make full use of their local knowledge of the coastline, winds, and tides to delay the Armada and keep them away from another deep-water harbor at high tide. Their seamanship enabled the English commanders to dictate the form and timing of the engagements. As Hanson points out, around the south coast, summer wind patterns are 'repetitive and predictable.' Usually, the wind blows northeast off the land early in the morning as the land surface warms up. Then at lunchtime, it drops, before blowing from the southwest on to the land in the evening as the land cools down. Calm conditions usually return during the night.

But as Matthews says, although 'the English congratulated themselves on having driven the Armada away from a landing place where Medina Sidonia had never intended to land,' the English were not to know that this was not part of his plan. As we have seen, Philip's instructions had been to head for Cape Margate and then cooperate with Parma to invade England; however, Medina Sidonia had in fact received secret instructions that he could land (as most of his admirals and soldiers had wanted) and take the Isle of Wight to force the Queen to negotiate. This was also where the English thought the Spanish were more likely to try to land. The battle was now moving towards one of its most crucial phases, as both fleets drifted along the Dorset coast.

That evening, both commanders called a Council of War. Hanson highlights the problems both commanders faced; the Spanish were dismayed to see that, even with the wind in their favor, they could not control the battle because the maneuverability of the English ships meant that they could gain the weather gauge and pull away whenever they wanted. The English were equally dismayed that, even though they were firing two or three times as fast as the Spanish and from a greater distance, their fire appeared to be doing no harm to any of the Spanish ships no matter how many shots they fired at them.

The English were almost out of shot and gunpowder again and would not be able to fight another battle without urgent supplies of both; they were also running low of food and water, therefore, one of Howard's main concerns was a desperate need for extra supplied. The Privy Council in London had ordered that almost all of the gunpowder and shot held in the Tower of London should be sent to the fleet, and between 23 and 26 July, it was on its way to Portsmouth and harbors in Kent. However, due to the running nature of the action, little of these supplies actually reached the fleet in time. In fact, some of it was still being transported to the fleet when they were following the Spanish in to the North Sea six days later. Until supplies arrived, Howard was happy to track the Armada and only engaging it when necessary. He had been able to use some of the shot and gunpowder taken from the Spanish ships which had been captured by the English, but these did not make up for the amount they had used.

Bicheno makes a moot point when he says that 'there has never been a war in which the expenditure of ammunition did not vastly exceed pre-war estimates.' The English ships were fighting 'a running battle for the Channel which was longer, more intense and would involve a far greater number of guns than any previous battle in history.' It was, therefore, hardly surprising that the navy started to run out of gunpowder and cannonballs.

Isle of Wight

At dawn, on Wednesday, 3 August, as the two fleets drifted along the Dorset coast and across Poole Bay one of the hulks, the *Gran Grifon* captained by Juan Gomez de Medina, carrying supplies for Parma and the Armada, began to fall behind the rest of the Spanish ships. English ships, which had been following the Spanish fleet at an extended distance, saw their chance and several ships, including Drake in the *Revenge* set out to attack it. *Revenge* fired three broadsides at her from closer range than previous engagements, and the rest of the ships with him followed his lead. For the first time, English firepower managed to inflict real damage on the hull of a Spanish ship. On seeing one of his ships in trouble, Recalde in the *San Juan* and three of the galleasses turned back to rescue her. In the ensuing fight, Spanish fire may have damaged or brought down Drake's main mast. The galleasses managed to tow the *Graf Grifon* back into the middle of the Armada, and in response to Spanish fire, the English ships fell back to join the rest of the fleet, bringing nearly two hours of action to a close. Both fleets then continued their eastwards drift, at walking speed, with no more engagements for the rest of the day. By the afternoon, the wind had died, and both fleets were approximately one mile (1.6km) apart and drifting southwest of the Needles, the sea stacks that project out from the western-most headland on the Isle of Wight.

Howard called a Council of War to review the action so far and see what changes were needed to make the shot and gunpowder he had available count. Until now, the fleet had generally sailed as a single unit with individual captains deciding which commander they wanted to follow. One problem Howard faced was the continuous flow of smaller ships wanting to join in the action. Most were too small, or too lightly armed to be of any use, and, therefore, they could not be regarded as frontline fighting ships. Many had younger members of important families on board, wanting to make their mark and increase their family's standing at court. They would often sail along with whichever commander they thought might give them the best opportunity to get their hands on any Spanish valuables that might come their way. In reality, generally all they did was to get in the way.

Howard (probably on the advice of Drake), Hawkins, and Frobisher— having seen how the Spanish ships fought as discrete units—now divided his own fleet into four separate squadrons, each with their own commander. This was the first time that such a structured division had been used by an English commander and set a precedent that would be used by all naval commanders in the future. It was also decided that each ship would follow their commander in 'line ahead' so that once a ship had fired its broadside at the enemy, it could peel away to allow the next ship in line to fire its broadside, and so on down the line. This set yet another precedent, which would be adopted and used to good effect by future generations of naval commanders for the next three hundred years.

Frobisher in the *Triumph* was joined by the *White Bear* and *Elizabeth Jonas*, two of the other great ships, and was tasked with attacking the landward wing of the Armada. Drake kept the ships that had originally joined him at Plymouth to concentrate on the seaward wing. The other Queen's ships were divided between Howard and Hawkins and were tasked with attacking the center of the Armada. Howard also planned to bring more of the armed merchantmen in to action by using twenty-four of them to attack the Armada during the night. It appears that this had not been attempted before and, if successful, would keep the Spanish awake all night. As Hanson says, this novel idea, even though it carried some risk to their ships, would mean that the English could have continuously hassled the Spanish, day and night, giving them little rest.

Unfortunately, the calm condition of the sea that night meant that Howard was unable to see whether this type of action would be successful or not.

At dawn, on Thursday, 4 August, when both fleets were south of St. Catherine's Point—the southern-most point on the Isle of Wight—three of the English squadrons were still becalmed to the west of the Spanish. We have already seen that Medina Sidonia and his commanders had decided that they should try to head for the eastern entrance to the Solent and land on that side of the Isle of Wight, to await news of Parma and his intensions. Medina Sidonia knew that he would have to try to reach the entrance to the Solent between 7 a.m. and 12 a.m., when the tides would be with him, if he wanted to be able to sail in to it. After midday, the tide—which was too strong for the Spanish ships to sail through—would be against him. He and the English also knew that for the following three days, the tides would prevent him from entering the Solent, so he only had one chance. Howard and his commanders could therefore make the most of their knowledge of the tides, winds, and coastline to prevent the Spanish from being able to sail into either the Solent or the relatively sheltered shores on the east of the island around Bembridge.

At first light, Medina Sidonia had let three ships—the *Doncella*, *San Luis de Portugal*, and the *Duquesa Santa Ana*—fall behind the rest of his ships to entice the English to attack them so that he could send ships from his rearguard to engage them. In spite of the calm conditions, Howard went for the bait. Hawkins sent out his rowing boat to tow the *Victory* towards the *Duquesa Santa Ana*, the furthest seaward of the three ships. When he was in range, he opened fire. Howard in the *Ark Royal* used his boats to tow him towards the *San Luis*, the ship in the middle, and Drake's ships, headed for the *Doncella*, the most landward of the three Spanish ships. It appears that Drake may not have actually been with them and might well have been out of action for most of the day whilst his ship was being repaired, equally, he may have transferred his flag to another ship in his squadron rather than miss any of the action. The Spanish responded by sending three of the galleasses—the *Zuniga*, *San Lorenzo*, and *Girona*—into action. They were also towing the *La Rate Coronada* with them, to give them additional firepower. Following a short but fierce fight, the wind picked up slightly, and the three English squadrons turned their attention to the ships of the Spanish rearguard.

Whilst the action described above was developing, Frobisher once again led a number of his squadron toward Dunnrose between Ventnor and Shanklin on the southeast coast of the island to take advantage of the local tides and wind condition. Just south of this section of the coast, there is another strong tidal race that flows at speeds up to 7 knots (13kph), which forms off St. Catherine's Point, to the east of Dunnrose. Frobisher might also have been using this fast flowing water to try to sail past the northern wing of the Armada to block its way in to the eastern entrance to the Solent. At this time of the day, inshore of the tide race, an eastward current was flowing along the coast at about 1 knot (1.8kph), and Frobisher, who was in the lead and sailing about 2 miles (3.2km) offshore, was being pushed along even faster than the rest of his ships and found himself on his own. Medina Sidonia saw his 'plight'—he appeared to be having trouble controlling his ship, the Spanish thought he may have broken his rudder—and turned the *San Martin* together with the Galleass *Patrona* to engage him. Frobisher responded with his broadside. The encounter probably lasted about thirty minutes, before a gentle southwest wind also allowed several of the other Spanish ships to move in to support of their commander. Meanwhile, Frobisher's other ships were still struggling to catch up with him. Recalde turned to intercept them and separate the *Triumph* from the other English ships. In response, most of Frobisher's ships turned and headed back towards the rest of the fleet. Two of the ships—the *White Bear* and *Elizabeth Jonas*—however, continued to try to join Frobisher. The *Sam Martin* and possibly three or four other Spanish ships tried to get closer to the *Triumph*. By this time, she was being towed by eleven of her boats in and out of the tide race to ensure that she stayed just out of range of the Spanish while being able to use her own guns. Eventually, the wind changed direction and began to blow from the south-southwest, and with high tide approaching, and the tide race also slackening, this gave Frobisher and his other two ships the opportunity they had anticipated to sail up the coast to position themselves off the Foreland (the eastern-most headland on the island) to guard the eastern entrance to the Solent. In fact, the breeze and tide was strong enough to enable his ships to move so fast that the closest Spanish ships could not keep up with him.

The same breeze also helped the rest of the English fleet. The *Mary Rose* and the *Nonpareil* from Drake's squadron, who had been waiting out to sea, moved toward Recalde to try to draw him towards them. On seeing Recalde's move, Howard led his squadron, which had been sailing behind the Armada about four miles (6.4km) offshore, in to the gap left by Recalde's ships—a maneuver which as McDermott says, 'entirely reversed the tide of the battle.' Instead of being able to strike the English ships, the Armada's formations were beginning to break down. As it tried to reform, Recalde's ships were attacked by Drake's squadron; and when Howard and Hawkins headed towards the actions, the entire Armada had to drop back to help protect Recalde's ships.

Drake's ships surrounded the *San Mateo* and continued to fire at it as the *San Francisco* and several other ships came to its rescue. During the ensuing running battle, the *San Mateo* received so much punishment that she started to drift towards the storeships, who responded by trying to get out of the way. This caused the seaward wing of the Armada to be pushed towards the shallow waters and the Bembridge Ledges, which may have been Drake's primary aim.

A short time later, having passed high water, the tide began to flow out of the Solent. With the English ships surrounding them, the Armada drifting slowly past Bembridge and across the eastern entrance to the Solent. It was gradually being 'pushed' towards the coastline near Selsy Bill; a stretch of coast, known as Owers Bank, which comprises shallow water, rocks, and sandbanks that project out into the Channel. As Hanson relates, the English tried to do the same thing to the French in 1545, but the wind changed direction and saved them. This time, it was the quick reaction of Medina Sidonia's pilots that saved the Spanish.

At 3 p.m., on seeing the imminent danger, Medina Sidonia fired a signal gun to tell the Spanish ships to cease fire, reform, and follow him out to sea.

That night, there was a thunderstorm in the Channel, which helped push both fleets further up the Channel.

The English were now down to their last reserves of cannonballs and gunpowder, but this action meant that the Armada had missed the last safe landing place available to it until it reached the Kent coast, by which time Howard knew that he would have Seymour's ships to support him. In fact, two days earlier, the Privy Council had ordered Seymour to join Howard, but on hearing the news that the Armada had passed the Isle of Wight, they recalled him so that he could maintain his watch for and movement by Parma on the other side of the Channel. Medina Sidonia took the opportunity to transfer some of the food, shot, and gunpowder from the hulks—that was destined for Parma—to his fighting ships in anticipation that the English would continue the fight the following day. He also decided that he would sail across to France/Holland to find out where Parma was and how close he was to being ready for the invasion rather than head for the Kent coast and wait for him there. Medina Sidonia did not know that the English ships were now in a desperate situation as well with regard to shot and gunpowder, which meant that they would be unable to challenge him until they had been resupplied.

As the threat to Portsmouth, Southampton, and Isle of Wight passed, army commanders were able to send out provisions, cannonballs, and gunpowder from their stores to the English ships. Gunpowder was also sent by the local Trained Bands. The English even tried to buy gunpowder from the Low Countries and Germany, but none would arrive in time. With both fleets closing in on the Straits of Dover, Seymour with his squadron was at last able to join Howard's ships; and for the first time, the English fleet would be up to full strength. He was also able to bring supplies with him and obviously, supply lines to Howard's ships from London and the Tower were significantly shorter. Having passed the Sussex coast, supplies were bought out from its harbors too.

The rest of the light winds of 4 August were replaced on 5 August by virtually no wind at all, consequently, the two fleets, which were often barely a mile (1.6km) apart, slowly drifted eastwards past Hastings towards Kent and the French coast. Howard had decided that he would not attack the Armada again until they were closer to Kent, where they would be trapped between his ships and those of Seymour and Wynter.

During the night, the winds increased, but died again the following morning. On Saturday, 6 August, with the ships moving at no more than 2mph (3.2kph), the Armada made its way slowly away from England and towards the French coast, which it sighted at 10 a.m. Medina Sidonia's pilots had informed him that the entrance to Dunkirk, where he was supposed to meet up with Parma, was too narrow and too dangerous for the Armada to enter. They also told him that once in there they would be extremely vulnerable to both the English fleet and the Dutch 'Sea Beggars'; therefore, even though Calais was in French hands rather than Spanish, it was the best and probably only option he had. Finally, during the afternoon, when it was 4 miles (6.4km) off the French coast in an area known as the Calais Roads, Medina Sidonia fired a signal gun, and the entire Armada dropped anchor. He might well have hoped that the English would miss this move and sail past, but Howard reacted immediately and signaled the English ships to do the same, dropping their anchors in Whitesand Bay, which was only a 'long culverin shot away from the enemy'—the English therefore retaining their tactical advantage. The Armada was now anchored off an enemy coast with over a hundred English ships close behind it. The Dutch had also responded to English requests for support and had twenty-four ships ready to blockade the coast to prevent Parma's sailing. They also had thirty-two ships patrolling off Sluys and another one hundred and thirty-five covering the seas off Antwerp.

At 7 p.m. that evening, Wynter arrived with his ships, and Seymour's ships arrived an hour later. As Matthews says:

'…the English were gathering in strength. They now had about as many ships present as were in the Armada. The daunting sight was too much for some—several men from the Armada deserted that night.'

Chapter 6
Crunch Point

Early in the morning on Sunday, 7 August, with the English fleet anchored off chalk cliffs of Calais in Whitesand Bay within firing distance of the Spanish fleet, both admirals viewed each other's fleets with foreboding. For the English, the news was slightly better. Seymour with the Narrow Sea Squadron had arrived the previous afternoon from the northwest, which bought the total English fleet up to one hundred and forty ships. He had finally been able to leave his station, patrolling off the Kent coast in case Parma made any attempt to sail. He probably could have joined in the action much sooner if communication between England and the Low Countries had been better. Seymour and his valuable squadron had been kept back to patrol the narrowest section of the Channel because neither the Queen nor the Privy Council trusted that Justin of Nassau and his 'Sea Beggars' would be ready and able to face Parma and his invasion fleet if it left Dunkirk. What they did not know was that he was well prepared and had kept his ships, which were armed with long-barreled guns, out of sight in the hope that Parma would think that he had none and come out in to the open where Nassau's ships could destroy them.

Nassau was equally annoyed with the English because with Seymour on patrol he knew that Parma would not make a move. He even tried to persuade the English to withdraw Wynter and Seymour from patrols off the coast so that Parma would attempt to come out, but the English were less convinced of their abilities than the Dutch. The 'Sea Beggars' had twenty-four ships at sea, with possibly as many two hundred and fifty other stationed elsewhere. What Nassau, Medina Sidonia, Howard, the Queen, and Privy Council did not know was that Parma was nowhere near ready, did not have the fly ships required to defend his barges which themselves were totally un-seaworthy (see below). In fact, Parma had already decided that the entire endeavor was a lame duck and he was not even in Dunkirk, something Medina Sidonia was about to find out. Just as the Spanish and English arrived at Calais, Nassau bought his ships out to lay off the coast at Dunkirk.

Before we continue to look at the crucial naval action of that day, it is important to find out what both the Dutch and Parma had been doing. There are significant differences reported about the preparedness of both of these parties with regard to the anticipated invasion. While some authors indicate that Parma was ready, most indicate that he had virtually given up on the idea of being able to mount an invasion. Equally, some accounts suggest that the 'Sea Beggars' were a potent force, while others think that this is rather overstated.

Medina Sidonia sent a number of messengers to find Parma while he was making his way up the Channel. One arrived back on 7 August with a note from Parma, saying that everything would be ready. He claimed that he had barges disposed along the coast, even though the messengers could only see a handful. He also claimed that he had 5,000 troops in Nieuport ready to embark within six days. However, the messenger reported what he had actually seen at Dunkirk. The barges were not sturdy enough to make the crossing, they were effectively unarmed, there were no flyboats to protect the barges, and the troops were still in their camps inland. Medina Sidonia then sent his private secretary to find Parma to find out what was really going on, and to demand that he set a date that he would be ready to meet up with the Armada. He was to tell Parma that the Armada could only stay off the coast of Calais for perhaps two weeks. His secretary reported back that, in his view, Parma would need at least two weeks to be ready for any invasion. Medina Sidonia then sent the Inspector General of the Armada to talk to Parma. Matthews describes how, on the evening of 7 August, Parma left Bruges 'to personally supervise the embarkation—knowing that it was all a charade.' As we have seen, it appears that Parma had already given up on the idea of being able to put together an invasion fleet, let alone get it across the Channel. Medina Sidonia was at last becoming aware that Parma was not coming, and that the proposed invasion, and therefore the entire purpose of bringing the Armada was lost; but without more information, he could not be sure of Parma's intentions.

On the morning of 7 August, with his entire fleet now in position, Howard called a Council of War on his flagship. He had no idea where Parma and his army were, or what their strength was. He saw numerous small ships and boats passing between the Armada and Calais and was sure that they were either bringing news of Parma or were providing help. After all, France was now to all intent and purposes under the Control of the Guise's and the Holy League. He would probably have been greatly relieved to know that in spite of Medina Sidonia's requests, the Governor of Calais, Gourdan, was maintaining the ports strict neutrality by only allowing the Spanish to take on food and water, and none of the gunpowder or cannonballs that they desperately needed. He would also have been relieved to know that Medina Sidonia was desperately trying to find out the same information about Parma.

Both admirals knew that the current spring tides would enable the Armada to come out of Calais and sail for Dunkirk where Medina Sidonia was expected to rendezvous with Parma's flyboats and barges. The strong tides had caused problems the night before, leading to four of the Spanish ships becoming entangled with each other. It had also meant that most of the Spanish ships put down two and sometimes three anchors to be able to hold themselves in position. French and Spanish pilots had told Medina Sidonia that the dangerous shoals, sandbanks, and shallow water made their position extremely precarious so to improve their defenses he had arranged his warships so that they formed a defensive shield between the English fleet and his hulks and armed merchantmen, which were anchored closer into shore.

As we have seen, having sent a number of messages off to Parma, Medina Sidonia finally got a reply, Parma could not be ready to meet him for at least six days, and he could not get his troops, barges, and fly boats down to Calais. The Armada would, therefore, have to sail up to Dunkirk. Medina Sidonia realized that he could not afford to hang around in Calais that long with the English sitting in a controlling position out to sea, and, therefore, he was going to have to decide what he was going to do next.

The English were also still in need of re-supplies of food, water, and ammunition which was being sent out from England. As they watched and worried about the small ships passing between the Armada and Calais, the Spanish were equally concerned about all of the small ships they saw coming to the English, because they knew they were sitting in a vulnerable position which would be idea for an attack using fireships. Even worse, they knew that the Italian engineer, Frederico Giambelli, who devised an extreme version of fireships which they referred to 'Hell Burners' was in England. These had been used in 1585 to blow up a bridge that Parma's army had built to gain access to a castle they had under siege at Scheldt. Hanson provides a very vivid description of the 'Hell Burners' at Scheldt and how they worked, which helps to explain the Spanish nervousness. Giambelli had the *Hope* and *Fortune*, two 70-ton (71 tonnes) ships whose hulls he lined with stone and brick. He then packed them with 7,000lbs (3,175kg) of gunpowder, shot, chains, shards of broken iron, and rocks, and sealed them in with fire-proofed timbers covered with lead sheeting on which he put more rocks and wood. He used clock-operated flintlocks built by a Dutch watchmaker as triggers.

As the two ships approached Parma's bridge, they were set alight and crashed in to it. Soldiers defending the bridge jumped aboard the ships to try to put the flames out and cut the fuses they had found leading into the hulls of the ships. With curious onlookers observing what was going on, all of a sudden both ships blew up—it was said that the explosion could be herd 50 miles (80km) away. It killed eight hundred soldiers.

Stafford, who was in Paris as one of Walsingham's double agents, had also been spreading misinformation. According to Mattingly, he had told them that the English were preparing 'many strange fireworks and diabolical inventions' and added that Giambelli was helping to construct defenses in London; no wonder that the men on the Armada were nervous. In fact, Giambelli was constructing a barrier across the Thames, which consisted of a chain supported by small boats tied to one hundred and twenty ships masts that had been driven in to the riverbed. However, following its completion on 31 July, it was broken by the next flood tide.

Howard's Council of War decided, at Drake and Wynter's suggestion, that they should use fireships and in response, Howard sent Sir Henry Palmer in the *Antelope* back to Dover to organize them. He had already pre-empted this request a few days earlier, and nineteen small fishing boats had been prepared, and were waiting ready to be used. But it was decided that it would take too long to sail them over. Also, the Spanish would see them coming and would prepared for any attack. They therefore concluded that they would have to use boats that were already with them that night rather than wait any longer. Drake offered one of his own ships as did Thomas and Hawkins, a number of the other captains then did the same until they had eight ships. These were the *Thomas Drake, Barque Bond, Barque Talbot, Hope Hawkins, Bear Yonge, Elizabeth of Lowerstoft,* and one other, un-name ship. These were stripped of their stores and packed with anything that was combustible. They also had tar barrels tied to their bows, and had their cannons double loaded so that they would blow themselves apart once they got too hot. The English then waited with the eight ships tied in line abreast across the front of the fleet. With the expected strong tide that would be flowing straight towards the Spanish ships that night, Howard gave orders that once the fireships had done their work, the English fleet would engage the heaviest armed Spanish ships in the hope that with them destroyed or put out of action the others would surrender or risk being destroyed. It was also decided that once the Spanish had been flushed out, Howards would take most of the Royal galleons and attack the ships closest to shore, Wynter and Seymour would concentrate on those in the center, and Drake, Hawkins, and Frobisher would attack the ones furthest offshore.

Just after 4 p.m., Howard sent out a pinnace to check the tides. It circled the *San Martin* and twenty-six other ships moored close by, before firing four shots and turning back to rejoin the rest of the ships. This came as a surprise to most of the Spanish, and only the Galleass *San Lorenzo* managed to fire two shots in reply. The pinnace may have been sent out to annoy the Spanish, or it might have been on a reconnaissance mission and decided to have a pot shot anyway whilst it was there.

Medina Sidonia knew what was coming and sent orders to set up a screen of eighteen pinnaces and rowboats, which could be used to grapple the fireships and tow them out of harm's way. He also sent instructions to all of his ships that if any of the expected fireships got through the defensive screen, they were to cast off the anchors and tie them to buoys so that they could immediately sail and regain the moorings. Everything was now set, all both sides had to do was wait and watch.

Just after midnight, Howard fired a signal gun to release the fireships. The skeleton crews—commanded by Captain John Young on the *Bear Yonge*—climbed aboard, cast off the ropes, and set the sails. The wind was blowing from the south-southwest straight towards the Armada, and the spring tide was also flowing towards the moored Spanish fleet at 3 knots (5.5kph). The English had chosen ships that were larger than normal for use as fireships in order to make the Spanish task of trying to stop them harder. Their size also heightened the Spanish fears that they really were 'Hell Burners.'

As the fireships, sailing under full sail, headed towards the Spanish screen, the fires were set, so too were their rudders so that they would stay on course, the crews then scrambled into the waiting row boats which would take them back to the safety of their own ships. By the time the fireships reached the Spanish screen, they were completely alight. The waiting pinnances managed to get hold of and tow the first two fireships out of harm's way, but the English had sent them down so close together that the Spanish did not have time to get to the other ones. As the next two approached the Spanish ships, their guns exploded, throwing burning hot metal and other debris in every direction (none had been loaded with barrels of gunpowder because it was in short supply). The Spanish crews panicked, and the remaining fireships broke through the screen. Medina Sidonia fired off a signal gun, warning the rest of the ships of the approaching fireships, but presumably, all of the ships' captains had been watching all night in anticipation of their arrival. It took them ten minutes to pass through the screen and reach the Armada, most of the Spanish captains panicked, cut their anchor ropes, tried to set their sails, and get out of the way. Do not forget, the wind was blowing straight towards them, so they had to turn before they could catch sufficient wind to be able to control where they were going and be able to sail out to sea. The scene was complete panic and mayhem with ships getting in each other's way; it was too late when the Spanish realized that the fireships weren't the dreaded 'Hell Burners.' In the strengthening wind, most sailed out of harm's way and just kept going. In the morning, the Spanish ships would be spread out along the coast towards Flanders and Dunkirk. In the confusion, the Flagship of the Galleasses, the *San Lorenzo* got tangled up with the *San Juan de Sicilia* and lost control of its rudder. The tide and wind then pushed it towards the shore.

McDermott makes an interesting point when he says that it appears that neither Howard nor any of his commanders had anticipated the scale of their success and how to take advantage of it. Therefore, they kept to the decision made at the Council of War that Howard would lead the attack in the morning. This meant that they lost the opportunity to attack individual, vulnerable ships and would have to face a steadily reforming Spanish defensive formation. As McDermott puts it, 'That precious breathing space preserved the greater part of the armada from early destruction.'

Maybe, the primary aim of the fireships was to disrupt the Spanish formation, with the English expecting them to regain the anchorage and keep them awake, as they had planned to do several nights before. Equally, as we saw above, Howard had ordered the English heavy ships to engage their Spanish equivalents, which goes some way to explaining why many of the 'more vulnerable stragglers' were saved.

Only Medina Sidonia's *San Martin* and four other ships—the *San Juan*, *San Marcos*, *San Felipe,* and *San Mateo*—followed their admirals orders and came back, anchoring a mile (1.6km) from their original position, and at first light, those were the only Spanish ships he could see. The fireships had passed through the Armada without causing a single fire on board any ship, but by their action, the Spanish captains had, for the first time, broken their regimented formation, which had prevented the English from being able to inflict any real damage on them. Medina Sidonia intended to use his five warships to block and engage the English fleet in order to protect the rest of the Armada, as the pinnaces he sent gathered it back together.

At first light, the entire English fleet set off in pursuit of the Spanish. Howard had handed over command to Drake so that he could go and capture or plunder the stricken *San Lorenzo*, which was grounded and was listing badly towards the shore, leaving her guns pointing uselessly in to the air. Howard took the whole of his squadron which him, which, remember, comprised all the Queen's galleons. Consequently, they would be missing

113

from the battle to come for the next three hours. The shallow seas prevented Howard and the *Ark Royal* from reaching the galleass, so he sent more than eleven smaller ships, including the *Margaret and John*, which also beached to attack it. People, including the Gourdan, the Governor of Calais, and his wife had gathered to watch the action, as they had done the previous day. Defensive small arms fire from the galleass was intense, killing a number of the Englishmen before the captain of the galleass was killed; the defenders then fled, leaving the ship to the English. The English losses during this action were the worst the fleet would suffer during the entire campaign. The governor allowed the remaining Englishmen to take all the plunder on board but insisted that the ship itself and its guns were his to rightfully salvage. When the English tried to take more than they should, he fired cannon shots at them from Calais Castle. It is said that the English even robed some of the onlookers of their jewelry before they left.

When his men had returned to their ships, Howard took his squadron out to catch up with the rest of the fleet, which, by the sounds of gun fire over the horizon, was activity engaged with the rest of the Spanish fleet.

One of the big questions is why did Howard decide to leave leading the English fleet for between two and three hours, in what would be their decisive moment to go off in pursuit of a prize, just as Drake had done a few days earlier?

Various reasons have been given, including greed, but it was probably more than that. McDermott explains that Howard had received a number of critical messages from the Privy Council, asking why he had not been able to capture any prizes as Drake 'the blue-eyed boy,' had done, to pay for the extra cost of gunpowder, cannonballs, and provisions. Feeling the pressure and seeing the *San Lorenzo* as an easy target, maybe Howard decided that if he captured it along with the money on board, it might go some way to countering such unfounded criticism. As John Barratt says in his book, *Armada 1588: The Spanish Assault on England:*

'The English had carried off about 20,000 ducats and fourteen chests containing other valuable. But they had suffered more casualties in the attack on San Lorenzo—including twenty drowned in their hasty departure—than in the whole of the rest of the campaign.'

Before we follow both fleets towards Gavelines and the coming battle, we ought to go back and see what Parma was up to. He was short of money, struggling to build up anything like an invasion fleet, and was skeptical of the entire idea. Whiting gives us an insight into his preparations and problems:

114

'Although the boat builders had been imported from the Baltic and Italy for the task [of building flyboats and barges], he had to rely on captured Dutch labour for the manual work. Could there have been sabotage? Certainly, good timbers had been intermixed with rotten ones. At an embarkation exercise several had left their troops standing neck-high in the water when they promptly sank!'

Mattingly adds that the carpenters and shipwrights worked as slowly as they could and even stopped working altogether when they had not been paid. They often used rotten and green wood as well as good timbers so that many of the barges had to be taken apart and rebuilt. He also says that they could not find enough cannons for the flyboats and not enough seamen to sail them.

Parma did not have the pilots to guide them, and the barges could only put to sea in near perfect, calm condition as they were not seaworthy, and any waves would have sunk them. They had no masts or sails, no armament to defend themselves—they were flat-bottomed tubs. He had insufficient flyboats to protect them and was expected to join up with the Armada, which would provide defensive cover for all of his troops and equipment, at sea, either off the coast of Dunkirk far enough out that the deep draught ships of the Armada could meet him. This would leave him open to attack from the Dutch flyboats who could intercept his force before they could reach deeper water; or, according to Philips plans, off the Kent coast, where his entire journey would be open to attack from the English fleet unless, somehow, the Armada had been able to neutralize it. Is it any wonder that he had effectively given the entire idea up as a bad job?

At first light, Drake was leading his squadron and the entire English fleet, apart from the ships that were with Howard, in to battle. As he gained on Medina Sidonia in the *San Martin*, who was sailing at the back of the four ships that had anchored with him after the fireship attack, the *San Martin* turned to meet him. It was now approximately 9 a.m., and the most decisive and intense battle was about to begin, which would last almost nine hours.

Chapter 7
The Big Day

We could begin with a quote from Thomas, which sums up this most important of days:

> 'Monday 8 August, starting on midnight on Sunday with the attack by fireships at Calais, was a red-letter day in the annals of England's long maritime story. It was a long-drawn-out, seemingly endless day of battling, lasting from long before daybreak right through till after sunset, although at the time, in the blur of battle, sea, wind, rain, explosions and gunsmoke, it was not seen in terms of victory.'

The weather was deteriorating with rising seas, strengthening winds, and decreasing visibility—all of which would complicate the forthcoming battle. As usual, the English had the wind and, therefore, the tactical advantage, and many of the Spanish ships were either very short of, or already out of, gunpowder and cannonballs before the battle started. The day began badly, when Francisco de Bobadilla, the Senior Army General, during a court martial, sentenced two captains to be hung because they had disobeyed Medina Sidonia's orders to heave to and wait for the English. The captain of the *Santa Barbara* was actually hung, and his body was sailed through the fleet as a warning, the other, the captain of the *San Pedro*, was let off. As many as nineteen or twenty other captains were also sentenced to serve as oarsmen on galleys.

Following the relatively unsuccessful display by the English cannons during the previous gun battles, Howard and the rest of the English commanders had resolved to move in much closer to the Spanish this time in order that they could inflict real damage. Consequently, during the first engagement of the day, Drake sailed to within 50–100 yards (45.7–91.4m) of the *San Martin*, the Spanish flagship, which had been trying to sail away from the shore to allow the rest of the Armada room to reassemble. It turned so that its broadside would be facing the *Revenge* and opened fire. Drake, still approaching, waited until he was close enough. He then replied, firstly with his bow-chasers, and then turning side-on to the *San Martin*, with his broadside, before sailing away to allow each of the ships in his squadron, who were following him in line astern, to follow suit. In this brief encounter, the *Revenge* had been hit by as many as forty cannonballs from the *San Martin* whilst the *San Martin* would eventually receive one hundred and seven hits, one of which went clean through both sides of the ship. Once they had all fired at Medina Sidonia, Drake led them to the northeast, firing at each of the other Spanish ships that had stayed with their commander before going off in pursuit of the other Spanish ships. The results of this battle would depend on the best leadership, the best tactics, and the best resources.

Drake's squadron was followed by that of Frobisher, Hawkins, and finally Seymour. Frobisher sailed almost to within grappling distance of the *San Martin* before opening fire. When Hawkins ships arrived, Frobisher's ships made room for them to join in. Hawkins then set off to find some other ships, while Frobisher stayed to fight. On seeing their admiral's predicament, the other four ships that had been with Medina Sidonia overnight turned to come to his defense, and Frobisher set about them as well. Several of these ships were badly damaged in this firefight, so much so that they lost the ability to fight back. This element of the battle ended at around 3 p.m. when the Spanish ships were approximately seven miles (11.2km) off the coast of Gravelines.

The decrease in range and difference in the rate of fire between the two fleets now began to play a significant role in the battle. The Spanish were firing at an average of one shot per hour whilst the English were firing between three and four shots in the same period. Hutchinson records that excavation of Armada shipwrecks indicates that the Spanish rate of fire may have been as low as three shots per day. Hanson provides a vivid description of the damage and mayhem inflicted on the *San Martin*

'The lighter weapons on the deck and upper gundeck pulverised the upperworks of the *San Martin*, chain—and bar-shot shredded rigging, sails, spars and yards, while dice—and hail-shot wreaked terrible havoc among the close-packed soldiers lining the rails to discharge their small arms. Meanwhile the heavier cannons on the *Revenge's* lower gundeck, close to the waterline, battered the *San Martin's* hull. Even its four-inch oak planking and close-packed timbers could not withstand such an onslaught from 30 and 60 pound [13–26kg] shot, fired at a range so close that smouldering powder residue and spent wadding drifted over the enemy decks like snow. Already weakened by the previous battles, the hull was pierced by shot still glowing and smoking from the furnace of the cannons. Smashing through the planking, each cannonball unleashing a blizzard of arrow-sharp splinters and shards of oak, filling the air like swarm of murderous hornets, ripping stabbing, blinding, maiming and shredding flesh from bone, and driven with such force that some jagged shards embedded themselves in the planking of the opposite hull, quivering like thrown knives.'

Drake and Hawkins had set off in pursuit of some of the other ships, and by mid-morning, they were in amongst a group of Spanish ships that had gathered around five galleons—*Rate Encoronada*, *La Reganzona*, *San Juan de Sicilia*, *San Christobal*, and the *San Juan of Castile*. At 11 a.m., the two English squadrons, possibly with the addition of Seymour's ships, began their attack.

Wynter had sailed past this firefight in search of other ships and found another group of storeships gathering around two more galleons. He attacked at close quarters; and, in an effort to get out of the way of his ships, two of the Spanish ships collided. At one point, the *San Felipe* was surrounded by as many as seventeen English ships, and was hit by more than a hundred cannonballs before it was able to join the others.

By late morning, when Howard had rejoined the rest of the English fleet, some semblance of order was returning to the Armada. As we have seen, Medina Sidonia had already sent out a number of pinnances to catch up with and bring back his dispersed fleet, which started to assemble in a rather ragged formation downwind of him. Returning to Calais would have proved difficult for most of these ships, as they would have had to sail against the wind. He and the other four galleons with him were engaged in a rear-guard delaying game designed to allow the rest of the Armada to form their defense formation with the remaining fighting ships, including the three surviving galleasses, forming the familiar wings either side of the more lightly armed merchantmen and hulks. There were now approximately sixteen fighting ships, including the three galleasses in each wing.

Howard and Seymour's squadrons attacked the *San Felipe* and *San Mateo*, both of which had been heading back towards the *San Martin* to draw some of the deadly fire that it was now suffering. On seeing their predicament, Recalde in the *San Juan* also came back to support them so that both ships and the *San Martin* could be sailed back towards the rest of the Armada. Barratt reports that at one point, Wynter's ship was so close to the *San Mateo* that one of his sailors jumped on to the *San Mateo* and was 'cut to pieces.' As the *San Mateo* was being rescued, the *Begona* and *San Juan de Sicilia* came under fire. By this stage in the battle, most of the Spanish fighting ships were out of either shot and gunpowder or were running critically low, even though some of the hulks were carrying supplies of both for Parma's army. Unfortunately, little if any of these stores had been transferred to the Armada's galleons while they lay at anchor off Calais. Consequently, as Barratt so graphically illustrates, 'as a result, some of Medina Sidonia's finest ships could only endure the enemy fire in silence.'

By mid-afternoon, the English began to pull back as they were also getting critically short of cannonballs and gunpowder. Even Seymour's ships were getting low, in spite of the fact that until this days' fighting they had not had to use any of their shot or gunpowder.

The *San Martin* received around two hundred shots in its rigging, sails, and hull; and the *San Felipe* and *San Juan* were both severely damaged during this engagement. The *Vanguard* and *Rainbow* in particular inflicted significant damage to the *San Martin*, including disabling the rudder, and causing a large number of casualties. The *San Mateo*, which had also been joined by the *San Luis*, went to rescue the *San Martin* but was crippled by gunfire. The *Doncella* (a hulk) and the *Zuniga* (a galleass) came to the *San Felipe's* rescue and managed to take off three hundred crew whilst she was slowly sinking, but they had to leave the most badly wounded on board. The *Doncella* itself was also slowly sinking.

The *San Filipe* ran aground between Nieuport and Ostend. Some of the crew were rescued by pinnaces sent out by Parma, before she was captured by the Dutch who managed to refloat her. She later sank whilst they were towing her back to Flushing. The *San Mateo* also ran aground somewhere between Ostend and Sluys but kept fighting for nearly two hours before the crew surrendered to the Dutch. At sunset, the *Maria Juan* sank with the loss of ninety-two sailors and one hundred and eighty-three soldiers on board—only eighty members of the crew were rescued. In fact, this was the only ship sunk by English gunfire throughout the entire campaign. Hanson provides a vivid description of the state of the ship, explaining that some of her masts and her rudder were shattered, water was pouring in through holes in her hull punched through by cannonballs. She was so low in the water that the sea was flooding her decks, and the soldiers and crew on board were climbing the rigging to get to safety. When she sank, she took two hundred and seventy-five people with her.

At about 4 p.m., the wind swung around to the northwest and increased in strength, and the tide was also running towards the coast. By now, the Armada was in real trouble, its defensive formation, which had held to a greater or lesser extent for most of the day had started to break up; its main fighting ships, which, remember, Howard's Council of War on 7 August had determined should be the main targets for attack, were beset from every side. They were running or had run out of shot and were effectively only being defended by small arms fire. Worse still, the English and the weather were slowing driving them towards the shallow waters off the coast; a coast where 'at low tide shrimp fishermen worked the offshore sandbanks from horseback,' and a coast that the English sea captains knew well. The Spanish could see the predicament they were in and could see that if the English guns did not finish them off, then the sandbanks or the 'Sea Beggars' would.

By 5 p.m., the Armada had reformed into its familiar crescent shape, and the English ships began to pull back. Sea conditions were choppy and getting worse, and the wind was strengthening. Four of the Spanish ships, which were struggling to hold their close formation within the main body of the Armada, collided and became entangled with each other. At the same time, Seymour had led his squadron in to an attack on the Armada's landward wing. The *Santa Ana*, *Santa Maria de la Rosa*, *San Pedro*, *Gran Grifon*, *San Juan de Sicilia*, *Valencera*, *Begona*, and the *La Trinidad Valencera* were also severely damaged, and the *Regazona* was sitting low in the water. Given the description of the fighting on board the *San Martin* above and considering that she was one of the main targets for the English, most reports say that it sustained only light causalities compared to many of the other Spanish ships,. The *San Martin*, together with Recalde's *San Juan* probably made the most effective use of their guns out of all of the Spanish ships.

Again Hanson provides a powerful impression of what it must have been like in the midst of the battle, noting that such a barrage had never been seen or heard before, leaving ships crews 'battle-shocked.' So much smoke filled the air that ships would appear and disappear from sight with only the flashes of cannons giving away their locations.

In fact, visibility due to the weather and gun smoke was so bad that Medina Sidonia climbed to the top of a mast on the *San Martin* to be able to see what was going on and where the rest of his ships were. Hanson explains that often, because of the smoke, both sides could only distinguish friend from foe by the sound of fire. Spanish ships were identified by their irregular fire, whereas the English sounded like a drum roll.

With more than two hundred and sixty ships taking part in the battle, this was the first great sea battle in modern history. Although in reality, probably no more than twenty-five to fifty English ships were actively engaged in the majority of the fighting, and these would probably have been the largest Queen's ships. Barratt adds that although the *Mary Rose*, *Hope*, *Elizabeth*

Bonaventure, *Dreadnaught*, *Swallow*, and *Elizabeth Jonas* had all been in the thick of the action, 'notable perhaps, by his absence was Sir Francis Drake.'

Seymour and Wynter's ships, with their relatively fresh crews and stocks of ammunition inflicted the heaviest damage to the Spanish ships. Many of the rest kept their distance, probably because their owners decided that there was no need to risk their own ships unless really necessary. This may have meant that there were not enough English ships actively engaged in the battle to turn it into a decisive victory. Equally, it was generally only the larger first-rate fighting ships on the Spanish side that were involved in the fiercest fighting. As the battle continued, the Spanish formation began to break up with individual ships or small groups of the ships, becoming isolated from the rest, leaving them open to being picked off by the English.

Many of the English ships were as far north as Lowestoft by this time, and with most of them almost out of ammunition, food, and water, all they could do was shadow the Spanish. While the majority were watching for the Armada's next move, hoping that it would be driven on to the sand banks, Howard called a Council of War. It was decided that Seymour, much to his annoyance, should be sent back to guard the Narrow Seas again to prevent Parma coming out. His ships were to leave at twilight to prevent the Armada from seeing them go; they set sail at about 7 p.m. Even now, Howard did not know the state of the Dutch ships and their preparations for action. English losses were low, with only three hundred killed or seriously wounded. On the Spanish side, some 3,000 men were either wounded or dead.

What, you may ask was Parma doing during this crucial day? He had started to embark his troops in his barges, even though this may have been just a face-saving exercise, but with the fire offshore, and news of the battering the Armada had taken, he disembarked them and returned to camp.

All through the night and into the following morning, the Spanish ships were gradually pushed closer and closer to shore. At dawn, one of their ships set off a distress signal. The *Hope* was the closest ship to it, but just as she arrived, the Spanish ship's hull cracked and it sank with all its crew on board.

During the morning, the wind continued to push the Spanish ships slowly towards the sandbanks. With no cannonballs left for their long-range guns, they prepared to fight rather than be shipwrecked. Then suddenly at 11 a.m., the wind increased in strength, swung around to the south-southeast (some versions say it blew from the west-southwest). This change in wind direction and a cloak of heavy rain, which reduced visibility significantly, allowed the Armada, out of sight of the English, to pull away from the coastline, which was now only a short distance away. By the time the rain—which had only lasted for half an hour—had cleared, the Spanish were out of range of the

English cannons and heading northwards. The fighting was over, but the danger for both sides still remained.

Thomas includes a rather telling quote from one of Medina Sidonia's staff on board the *San Martin:*

'We saw ourselves lost or taken by the enemy, or the whole Armada drowned upon the banks. It was the most fearful day in the world, for the whole company had lost all hope of success and looked only for death.'

You can only imagine the relief they felt when the wind changed direction, and they were able to sail out in to open water.

The English took up their familiar trailing position and waited for the arrival of much needed supplies, content once again to track the Armada, which tried to reform in to its usual crescent formation. As Mattingly says, neither fleet was now in a position to continue the fight. Barratt explains that:

'The Battle of Gravelines would prove to have been the decisive engagement of the Armada Campaign... Certainly, however, it was not as great a victory for the English as has often been claimed... Yet in many ways the seven or eight hours of intense fighting that day had been a traumatic experience for the Spaniards, and would prove to have destroyed any will among the majority to renew the fight. This was not so much because of the losses suffered as a result of close-range English gunnery, but the final realisation that the English could never be brought to fight on Spanish terms.'

The Spanish resolved, at a Council of War, to fight and return to meet Parma if possible, or sail for Norway, Scotland, or Denmark to make repairs so that they could then sail south again to fulfil their mission. However, if the wind direction remained the same, they were to sail around Scotland and Ireland to take as many ships as possible back to Spain. 'It was their duty to save as many as they could of the Kings ships.'

The Spanish lost eight ships, including one sunk purely by gunfire, although many more had been severely damaged. In comparison, the English had got off lightly. It is interesting to note that the first English ship to be sunk by Spanish gunfire did not occur until 1592. Not a single shot had managed to pierce any of the English ships hulls; in fact, it was later proved that, because of their poor quality, most of the Spanish cannonballs shattered either as they left the guns or when they impacted on the English ships. Equally worrying was the fact that most of the Spanish ships had left their anchors in Calais when they desperately tried to get out of the way of the English fireships. Their lack of anchors would prove to be even more critical from now on, and even if many of their crews had not been killed or wounded, the battered condition of their ships and the fact that they were entering unknown waters would prove to be the real danger.

We have seen that the English were now desperate for shot, gunpowder, food, and drink. Some was available, but it was difficult to get it to a fleet on the move where knowledge of its whereabouts and future position would depend on the subsequent intentions and movements of the Armada. Newcastle had been asked to provide supplies and sent four ships—the *Daniel*, *Galleon Hutchins*, *Bark Lamb*, and *Fancy*—out with them. Berwick supplied whatever it had and stationed it on Holy Island so that the English fleet could pick it up if it passed by. Some supplies, presumably some of those that had been chasing it up the Channel, did reach the fleet from the south of England, but it was nowhere near enough.

As they followed the Spanish up the North Sea, the leading English ships managed to overtake the trailing Spanish ones on a couple occasions; in response Medina Sidonia slowed the Armada down ready to engage the English, who in returned pulled back, happy to track the Spanish out of harm's way.

It was midday on Friday, 12 August, (some books give this as 13 August and some say it was 14 August) when they were 90 miles (144km) off Newcastle that the English lost sight of the Spanish. Howard sent two pinnaces to find and follow them whilst he led the rest of the English ships towards the Firth of Forth to get much needed supplies. The next day, when they were still 40 miles (64km) off the coast, the wind changed to the northwest and drove them back down the North Sea. As they were expecting the Spanish to do the same, with the aim to finally try to meet up with Parma, the danger was still not over. However, the Spanish continued their journey northwards, up the Scottish coast and safety, as they thought. The English finally lost sight of them on Sunday, 14 August, but Howard and the whole of England were still worried that they may turn and head back to Channel; they had no idea the battle was over. On 16 August, the wind, which had continued to increase in strength, dispersed the English fleet, leading to individual and groups of ships to sailing in to harbors from Lowestoft to Margate. A number of them gathered at Harwich on Thursday 18 the same day that the Queen arrived to review her troops at Tilbury (see below). Due to their lack of food and fresh water, most of the English ships were in a sorry state when they made shore, and as Herman notes:

'…as if on cue, typhus broke out on board the English ships just as they ran out of food. They could not have followed the Armada even if they had wanted to. The *Elizabeth Jonas* lost two hundred of her five hundred crewmen. Some ships did not even have enough fit men to weigh anchor. Soon sick and starving English sailors and soldiers lay helpless in the streets of Dover and Rochester. And then there was still the threat of Parma, waiting in his lair at Dunkirk to strike.'

Chapter 8

The Window Closed

Before we look at the progress of the Spanish ships as they try get home in chapter 9, let us have a look at what Parma was up to and the situation of the land forces in England.

Parma was in Dunkirk on 9 August to oversee his men and the invasion barges; but when the barges started to sink under the weight of the soldiers, it confirmed to him that he could not mount an invasion. We have seen that he also heard the rumble of gunfire out to sea and must have had at least some idea of what was going on off the coastline. He must also have seen, or been alerted to the fact that the Dutch were now roving up and down the coastline in their fast, shallow draught fly-boats, waiting to pick off Spanish ships that were in trouble or prevent him from leaving harbor. He must have also realized by this stage that Medina Sidonia and the Armada, unless they won the battle that was raging out to sea, would be in no position to escort his vulnerable barges across the Channel. Although Seymour was incandescent at being sent back to protect our coastline, Howard had been right to do so, given that Parma was at last making some attempt, even if it may have been only half-hearted, to put to sea. The threat was not yet over and, as we have seen, would not be for many days to come.

The Earl of Leicester was nominally in charge of the land forces with Sir John Norris, the Lord Marshal being in charge of the training and disposition of Trained Bands in the coastal counties between Dorset and Norfolk. Although, as McDermott says, Leicester thought of himself as 'supreme commander' of the army the soldiers under him 'regarded him as a troublesome irrelevance.'

When the Armada was first sighted on 29 July, just over 2,000 members of the Trained Bands in Cornwall were mobilized. They were joined by bands from Devon and Somerset as they followed the progress of the Armada along the coast. Once the threat had moved further eastwards, the majority of them returned to their harvesting.

Although this mobilization on paper sounded encouraging, most of the troops as we have seen were only poorly armed, and their commanders were not speaking to each other.

It might well have been that the Trained Bands of Cornwall and Devon were particularly enthusiastic as the majority of the sailors in the English fleet came from those counties. They therefore may have had first-hand knowledge of what the Spanish had been doing and consequently had a greater connection to the threat they and the country were facing.

It was indeed fortunate that the Queen and Privy Council had realized that they would have to depend on the navy to defend the country, as they had no standing army and no prospect of forming one.

Tilbury, on the north side of the Thames estuary, was part of the original outer defensive line around London, and it was here that Leicester had started to form his defenses as early as 3 August. The first of the Essex Trained Bands arrived on 8 August. One of the problems that the assembly of the forces required to defend not only the capital but the coast faced was the continuous lack of money available to the Queen and Privy Council to pay them or provide food. The situation so severe that on 5 August, an order had to be given to stop any more soldiers from going to Tilbury unless they had their own food with them. Hanson reports that the next day 4,000 men stationed near Dover, who had not been paid and had no provisions started to desert.

As we saw in Chapter 6, a defensive boom, which stretched from Tilbury on the Essex side of the River Thames to Gravesend on the Kentish side had been constructed by the Italian inventor of the 'Hell Burners.' This comprised a series of masts and boats chained together with explosives on them, which were supposed to explode if the boom was rammed by any ships. In fact, as we have seen, it had broken under its own weight the day it was completed. It was also supposed to carry a roadway, which would enable the troops stationed at Tilbury to cross quickly in to Kent to meet Parma if he landed in that county. Interestingly, by 9 August, the Privy Council already had news from captured Spanish soldiers from the *San Lorenzo* that Parma was intending to land at Dover, even though Leicester thought he would make for the Thames. It is therefore also interesting to consider why the Queen and the Privy Council allowed him to set up camp at Tilbury, which as McDermott explains, may have been a way of keeping him busy without him being able to do any harm to either the situation or his men. In other words, give him something to do that will keep him out of the way and prevent him from doing something stupid, or annoying, or endangering anyone else.

In Kent, there were nearly 5,000 members of their Trained Bands who were based at Sandwich and Shornecliff, which is close to Folkestone, with a reserve at Canterbury. Their strength and tactics would only allow them to hold the line while slowly retreating towards London, destroying anything the Spanish could use on their way.

It was then hoped that this would give Leicester time to bring him troops back towards London to make a final stand together with the 10,000 armed men already preparing to defend the capital. Requests were sent out across the country between 16 and 20 August for Trained Bands to gather in London. Those from the surrounding counties made it, but ones from further afield were still on the road when it was realized that the threat was over, at least for that year. As McDermott notes:

'The organization of this force, and the manner of its deployment around St James's Palace, presaged the apocalyptic atmosphere of 1940, when Churchill and the more ambulatory members of his cabinet would vow to fight every inch of the panzers' advance through Whitehall.'

Thomas also notes another similarity to 1940 in that other orders were issued saying that anyone 'not in actual service were to "stay put" and not clog roads with refugees.'

On paper, there were nearly 30,000 troops to the south of London, 4,500 in East Anglia and 34,000 to the west of the capital. This would indeed be a significant force, but remember, they would have been up against well-trained, extremely experienced Spanish and other foreign troops, and to make thing worse, much of the armaments available to the Trained Bands in the Home Counties had been stripped out to supply those based in London.

On 18 August, Queen Elizabeth left St. James's Place to take a processional barge down the Thames to review her troops at Tilbury. Much has been written about her visit, which need not be repeated here. She even stayed overnight in a nearby manor house, Arderne Hall, so that she could come back the following day. News, most of it wrong, had been filtering through to London. It included stories that Drake had been killed or captured, that the English had lost up to fifteen ships, a rumor probably based partly on the dispersed nature of the English fleet and their haphazard arrival in so many different ports. There was even a rumor that a storm had dispersed the Dutch 'Sea Beggars' blockade, enabling Parma to prepare to launch his invasion fleet on the next available Spring Tide. Even with all this uncertainty, the Queen and Privy Council had ordered the disbandment of all but 6,000 of the troops now at Tilbury without really knowing where the

Armada was and what its next moves might be. Most authors put this down as a cost cutting measure given that the Queen would have to pay for everyone once they were there, but Hutchinson points out that after several years of famine, the men were needed to bring in the harvest. Five days later, the camp closed completely.

During her visit, she received news from the Earl of Cumberland about the progress of the battle off Gravelines and chasing the Armada up the North Sea. Everyone, including Howard and Drake, expected the Spanish to try to either sail back down the North Sea to Denmark or put in to a port somewhere on the Scottish east coast, to make repair, re-provision, and be ready to meet up with Parma. Howard urged the Queen and Privy Council to keep as much of the fleet in being, with the crews, rested, replaced and the ships repaired, replenished, and ready to meet any possible threats. At the time of her visit, there were over fifty ships moored in Margate Roads, seventeen on patrol with Seymour, and thirty-eight at Harwich. Howard wanted those ships that were in a fit state to be available should the Armada be sighted or Parma try to make a move. To this end, he requested that the fleet be divided in two with those ships which were in need of repair and replenished to be kept in Margate Roads until replacement crews could be impressed whilst the others that were considered to be in an operational state should be stationed off the Downs.

During her visit to Tilbury, to rouse the troops the Queen made probably her most famous speech:

'My loving people, we have been persuaded by some that we are careful of our safety, to take heed how we commit ourselves to armed multitudes for fear of treachery; but, I do assure you, I do not desire to live to distrust my faithful and loving people. Let tyrants fear, I have always so behaved myself, that under God I have placed my chiefs' strength and safeguard in the loyal hearts and goodwill of my subjects; and, therefore, I am come amongst you as you see at this time, not for my recreation and disport, but being resolved, in the midst and heat of battle, to live or die amongst you all—to lay down for my God, and for my kingdoms, and for my people, my honour and my blood even in the dust. I know I have the body of a weak and feeble woman; but I have the heart and stomach of a king—and of a king of England too, and think foul scorn that Parma or Spain, or any prince of Europe, should dare to invade the borders of my realm; to which, rather than any dishonour should grow by me, I myself will take up arms—I myself will be your general, judge, and rewarded of every one of your virtues in the field. I know already, for your forwardness, you have deserved rewards and crowns, and, we do assure you, on the word of a prince, they shall be duly paid you. For the meantime, my Lieutenant General [Leicester] shall be in my stead, than whom never prince commanded a more noble or worthy subject; not doubting but by your obedience to my General, by your concord in the camp, and your valour in the field, we shall shortly have a famous victory over these enemies of my God, of my kingdom and of my people.'

A rousing speech designed to inspire her troops and send a clear message across the country and continent. As we have seen, she and the Privy Council had already ordered the partial demobilization of the army on 16 August, it was further reduced on 22 August. Hanson describes the Queen's actions at Tilbury as pure theatre when the Armada was already sailing northwards. I think this is quite harsh, given that Howard, Drake, and her other seamen were still sufficiently worried about the Armada's whereabouts, and the possibility that it might still try to meet up with Parma's forces in the Low Countries. As we have seen, the Queen and Privy Council knew that the navy was really their only hope for defending the country. Equally, I am sure that they were well aware that having called the Trained Bands out, they could do it again if necessary.

Interestingly, although the speech above is famous, it might not be the speech that the Queen delivered, as Hanson records, the only person to provide an eyewitness account of the speech was James Aske, who recorded that much of the well-known version of the speech bears hardly any relation to what he heard.

Whatever she said, the speech marked an important point in the self-awareness of England and the Elizabethan era that together with the roving actions of its privateers and merchantmen helped lay the foundations for the British Empire and the principal of freedom on the seas.

Having paraded at Tilbury, the Queen moved across the Thames to Kent to continue her tour; she was at Erith on the 21, returning to London on or about 23 August. On 28, Justin of Nassau sailed in to the Downs with forty of his flyboats to report that Parma only had less than eighty barges in which to bring his troops across the Channel and that, the immediate threat of invasion was effectively over not just for now but probably for the rest of the year.

With invasion a receding possibility, Elizabeth and the Privy Council felt confident enough on 30 August to plan a victory celebration. In fact, a full celebration did not take place until 18 September when a number of captured Spanish flags were hung in St. Paul's Cathedral. Another celebration was held in Norwich on 2 October, but the grand official celebrations of the countries God-given victory was held on 24 November (one source quotes 29 November), following a thanksgiving service in St. Paul's Cathedral on 4 October. A final service was again held in St. Paul's on 4 December.

Chapter 9
They Think It's All Over

As we saw at the end of chapter 7, Howard, and the majority of the English fleet stopped following the Armada when it was some distance out to sea, off the Firth of Forth on Friday, 12 August because the wind changed direction to the northwest, which meant that it could no longer make landfall in Scotland. We also saw that the English ships were very short of gunpowder and shot and equally short of food, water, and beer. Of these three, it was beer that usually caused the most concern, for it was felt by the seamen that they could put up with most shortages but they could not do without their beer.

Medina Sidonia called a Council of War on 13 August after they had lost sight of the English. Their ships were in a poor state to make it back to the Low Countries, so they discussed either heading for Scotland, Ireland, or trying to make it back to Spain; it was unanimously decided that they should try to make it back to Corunna. As they headed northwards, the heavy seas, rain, fog, and cold winds made it very difficult to keep the fleet together, but in the main they succeeded.

Most of the ships in the Armada had incurred severe damage from the English cannons, so much so, that some were barely seaworthy, including the *Sam Martin* that, according to Thomas 'leaked like a colander.' Damage to her hull included a large hole just above the waterline, which the ships divers had struggled to repair. The *San Juan's* mainmast was sufficiently weak that she could not raise any sails, and the *San Marcos* had three thick cables wrapped vertically around its hull to hold it together. Disease was widespread with up to 3,000 men suffering from Typhus and a further 1,000 suffering from serious wounds inflicted during the fighting. The shortage of food, water, and wine meant that, for the first time rationing was uniform across the entire Armada regardless of rank or status. To save water and food as they sailed up the North Sea, they threw all of the horses and mules overboard, action that led to accounts of the sea being covered in died and dying animals.

The Armada continued its slow progress up the North Sea and planned to sail between the Orkney Isles and Fair Isle, an isolated island midway between the Orkneys and the Shetlands. To a large extent, Medina Sidonia and his mariners had managed to keep most of the ships together so far; but on 14 August, there occurred 'a great storm' which lasted for forty hours. Before they turned westwards, three ships, which were struggling to keep up with the rest of the Armada in the prevailing conditions, turned eastward, probably with the intention of trying to make it to Norway or back down to Denmark, but they were never seen again. The combination of the weather and the state of the ships meant that survival was now largely in the hands of the individual commanders.

Following the capture of three Scottish fishing boats on 15 August, the Spanish used their captains as local pilots to guide them around and through the islands off the north of the Scottish mainland.

As they continued northwards on 17 August through two days of freezing rain, the *Gran Grifon*, and a number of other ships, including *Castilla Negro*, *Barca de Amburg,* and the *Trinidad Valencera* started to fall behind. On 1 September, the *Barca de Amburg* fired a distress gun to signal that she was sinking. The *Gran Grifon* and *Trinidad Valencera* managed to rescue three hundred men from her before she went down. On 3 September, the remaining three ships lost contact with each other. The *Castillo Negro* sank, taking her entire crew with her, and the *Trinidad Valencera* made it as far as Loch Foyle on the County Donegal coast with four hundred and fifty men. These included survivors from the *Barca de Amburg* who managed to make it to shore before being massacred on 16 September. Two days after dropping their anchor, she broke up, taking all the sick and wounded on board with her. The *Gran Grifon* was in a sorry state. Following her involvement in many of the running battles in the English Channel and off the coast at Gravelines, she could only sail with the wind to her stern a situation that meant she could only go where the continuously changing winds took her, she therefore made little progress on the her journey home. For three days, she sailed northeast, then the wind changed direction and pushed her towards the Irish coast, where the crew managed to make emergency repairs. She then set sail again but was pushed back towards Scotland on 23 September. On 27 September, she made landfall on Fair Isle, where two hundred and eighty members of her crew made it to shore before she was wrecked on the rocks; they had originally passed the same island six weeks earlier. Eventually, they made their way back to the Scottish mainland where they joined up with other survivors before sailing to France and finally making all the way home to Spain.

On Thursday, 18 August, the wind shifted to the northeast. Medina Sidonia and his pilots thought that they should be far enough north to be clear of the Orkney Isles and Fair Isle, so they turned west-southwest towards the Atlantic and home. On 19 August, they were able to buy dried fish from some local fishermen which went some way to alleviating their hunger. Medina Sidonia called another Council of War where it was decided that they should avoid the Irish coast, which was considered to be extremely dangerous. It also had the additional hazard of being patrolled by English soldiers. By now, there over 3,000 sick on board his ships, which only added to his problems of looking after the wounded. They had very few medical supplies, and everyone was living in increasingly insanitary conditions. During Saturday, 20 August, the wind turned to the south, which began to force them northwards. The following day, the pilots thought that they were sufficiently clear of the Irish coast that they could at last begin their journey southwards.

The majority of the Armada had still managed to stay together; and by Monday, 22 August, they were about 70 miles (122.6km) northwest of Rockall, when they were hit by the first of a number of severe gales, which lasted for eighteen hours. Because many of the ships were in such a poor condition, they were unable to keep station and ended up having to sail with the wind—a move that scattered the Armada over a wide area. One ship even ended up close to Iceland. This storm was followed by a similar one ten days later, which scattered them even further. Weather conditions were so bad that after fourteen days of sailing, they were virtually back where they started. During those two weeks, they had lost seventeen ships, including the two remaining galleasses. Hanson and others observe that when English ships sailed through the same storms they reported no damage.

By 27 August, once the gale-force winds and driving rain had abated a number of the ships managed to find each other and Medina Sidonia held another Council of War on board the *San Martin*. His main concern was to get as many of the surviving ships as he could safely back to Spain. In the end, Ricalde headed for North-West Ireland with around fifty ships with the intention of making repairs and re-provisioning his ships. Medina Sidonia with the other ships turned southwards to sail clear of Ireland and its notorious coastline with the intension of sailing straight for home. It must be remembered that most of the captains had never sailed in these waters before, and their maps unfortunately did not include the 40-mile-wide (64km) western protrusion of County Mayo. It was known that Ricalde had at least been to the shores of Southern Ireland before, so many of the other commanders with him, whose ships and men were in such a bad condition, reluctantly followed him. His fateful actions resulted in more than twenty-six ships becoming wrecked on the Irish coast in an episode that Thomas describes as a 'drama, horror, tragedy, and indescribable inhumanity.' He explains that the loss of these ships and the situation their crews faced were a direct result of three different problems. Firstly, weather conditions had meant that they had not been able to accurately locate their position for some time. Secondly, their ships were effectively unseaworthy, and finally, as they had cut their anchor cables in their rush to escape the fireships at Calais, they had insufficient anchors with them to keep them from being smashed on the rocky coastline or being grounded on the sandy beaches.

The first messages recording the Armada off the Irish coast were sent to London via Dublin on 20 September, which said that twenty ships had been sighted off the coast.

Whilst heading for the Irish coast, Recalde's *San Juan de Portugal* lost contact with the *Rata Encoronada*, the *Duquesa Santa Ana,* and the *San Pedro el Mayor* that was being used as a hospital ship, plus three hulks. The *Rata Encoronada* landed on the Irish coast in Tullaghan Bay, County Mayo on 21 September, where, unfortunately, her only remaining anchor could not hold her, and she ran aground. Luckily, everyone on board made it to shore before setting fire to the ship. Two days later, six hundred survivors marched northwards to where the *Duquesa Santa Ana* had anchored, intending to repair her so that they could sail back to Spain. On route, other survivors swelled their ranks, bringing their total to around 1,000 men. Following repairs, which were only partially successful, they decided that the ship would not make it to Spain, so they headed northwards back towards Scotland. Unfortunately, bad weather drove them on shore once more at Loughros Mor; this time the ship was wrecked. Once again, they set off on foot, marching up the coast to meet up with around three hundred crew from the galleass *Girona* that had moored in Donegal Bay. These 1,300 men then set sail in the *Girona* on 26 October again heading for Scotland. However, yet again they encountered bad weather on 28 October that drove them on to the rocks of the Giants Causeway on the County Antrim coast. This time, their luck ran out and all but nine of the men on board drowned.

On 20 September, the *Lavia, Santa Maria de Vison,* and the *La Juliana* made it to shore in Streelagh Sound, County Sligo. Four days later, gale-force winds caused all three ships to run aground and break up in fewer than three hours, killing over 1,000 men; three hundred men survived. Once ashore, the survivors were attacked by English soldiers, local Irish inhabitants, and Irish and Scottish mercenaries, who robbed them of all of the valuables before killing them. The *Santiago* ran aground in Broadhaven, County Mayo with no survivors, and the *El Gran Grin* was wrecked on Clare Island, in Clew Bay, County Mayo, where the survivors were robbed and killed by locals. There are also reports that two ships anchored outside Ard Bay, in Galway were deliberately lured onto rocks by signal lights before locals stripped the bodies and plundered both ships. The *San Juan de Sicilia* ran aground in Tobermory Bay on the Island of Mull where most of the crew were met by English soldiers before they blew the ship apart.

During a storm on 21 September, the *San Juan de Bautista* and Recalde's *San Juan de Portugal* ran in to each other in Dingle Bay, County Kerry. Shortly afterwards, the *Santa Maria de la Rosa* sailed into the bay and put down her anchor. Unfortunately, the winds and seas were too strong for the anchor to hold her, and she was blown on to rocks and began to break up; all but one of her crew were killed, the survivor was later captured and hung. When the storm abated the crew of the *San Juan de Bautista*, which had already taken the surviving crew of one of the hulks that had been in trouble, were transported across to Recalde's ship before setting it alight to prevent her falling into enemy hands.

Recalde eventually made it back to Corunna on 7 October, but he died two days later. The *San Juan Bautista* also made it back to Spain, landing at Santander a week after Recalde. *The San Pedro el Mayor* eventually managed to set sail but strong winds drove her up the English Channel and on 7 November, she ran aground on the rocks of Bolt Tail adjacent to Bigbury Bay, 14 miles (22.5km) east of Plymouth. The galleass *Zunieja* made it as far as Liscannor Castle on the Irish coast where she moored so that the crew could try to repair her rudder. She set sail again on 23 September but was hit by yet another gale and eventually sailed in to Le Harve, where convicts on board made a run for it. Almost a year later, the Spanish tried to set sail in her again but she was caught in a further storm and ended up back in Le Harve; she never sailed again.

The *San Marcos*, which was in an extremely distressed condition, sailed in to the Shannon estuary where she sank after her crew set fire to her. The *San Esteban* was wrecked off Doonbeg, County Clare, drowning most of those on board; the survivors were rounded up and executed. The *La Anunciada* was wrecked close by in Scattery Roads, on the River Shannon.

In most cases, the survivors were killed by English soldiers who were worried that if too many Spaniards made it ashore they could overwhelm the English forces stationed in the country, leaving it open for Spain to try to use it as a base for a future invasion of England. The local Irish people, which the

Spanish described as 'heathens,' had a different point of view, as Hanson relates, although they hated the English, superstition had it that if you saved someone from drowning, the sea would claim one of your own family instead. Therefore, even when the Spanish managed to survive ship wrecking, the locals often just stood by and watched as they drowned on the beaches. If they made it to shore, they were usually robbed before the English arrived and killed them.

Whiting adds to this by telling us that this belief was based on the legend of the Sea God Lir, whose 'ancient right [it was] to claim whom he wished.' He also points out that the same superstition existed on the islands of Orkney and Shetland.

Although most books include stories of massacres by the English and Irish, often the local Irish people would shelter, look after, and help survivors get back to the continent. Hutchinson records that 6,751 of the people who sailed with the Armada died, of which 3,750 drowned or died from hunger or disease in Scotland and Ireland. Of those that made it ashore, 1,500 were killed by the English or Irish, and only seven hundred and fifty men survived.

The majority of the main fighting ships—including the ten galleons of the Indian Guard, seven of the ten galleons of Portugal, eight of the Andalusians, seven of Oqueudo's squadron, six of Recalde's ships, and two of the ten Levantine galleons—made it home, because they had followed Medina Sidonia's lead and advice. This is impressive given his lack of maritime experience—something to remember when reading the next chapter. Hutchinson also records that the Spanish lost as many as sixty-four ships out of the one hundred and thirty that arrived off the English coast on 29 July, whereas the English only lost the eight fireships which they used at Calais during the night of 7 August. The returning ships bought back less than 4,000 of the 7,707 sailors that set sail with it and only 9,000 of the 18,703 soldiers (a casualty rate of over 49%). Set against the huge Spanish losses, the English only lost one hundred and fifty men killed in action.

Chapter 10

Scapegoats in the Aftermath

Medina Sidonia was severely ill with a fever and dysentery during the journey back to Spain and rarely came out of his cabin. Following his arrival at Santander, he valiantly tried to sort out the many problems caused by the returning ships, but was too ill to do so. The ports and their townsfolk were simply overwhelmed by the large numbers of ill and dying who came ashore. To compound the problem, the fact that they had not been paid meant that those capable of looking after themselves were unable to do so because they had no money.

Following Philip's approval, Medina Sidonia was relieved of his duties; and in October, he was able to begin his journey home. He was conscious that many Spaniards blamed him for the enterprise's failure and the death of so many of their seamen and soldiers, so he tried to avoid as many towns as possible, particularly the ones in which important and wealthy families, who had sent their son's and father's on the great expedition, lived. By the spring of 1589, he was well enough to be able to walk around his estate. In spite of the personal courage and leadership he had shown, he knew that the Spanish people would never forgive him for his failure even though he continued to serve both Philip and his son for another twelve years.

It is said that when the Philip finally found out the extent of the Armada's loss and the failure of the enterprise, he put it down to God's displeasure with him and his country's sins. He understood the main reasons for the defeat, including a lack of securing a deep-water port on the French, Dutch, or English coasts, the lack of long-range cannons, and the significantly different sailing qualities of the ships that made up the Armada.

The war with England would continue, and he quickly gained support from many cities who pledged money and resources to be able to build a stronger, better-equipped fleet to send another Armada; in fact, as we saw in the introduction, he sent three more. However, it appears that the defeat took its toll on him, as it is said that he aged more quickly after the event. He also thought that Parma had let him down and sought to replace him as quickly as possible.

Across Europe, the defeat had wide implications and 'brought a feeling of great relief.' Henry III in France felt he was able to resist the pressures and maneuverings of the powerful Guise's and The Holy League, which enabled Protestants to take up political and other influential positions again. The Dutch were eventually able to break Spain's hold, and other countries, particularly Italy, were relieved to see that Spain was not the all-powerful, all-conquering nation it had once been. Many others were relieved to see that it would not necessarily be in a position to dominate Europe as it had done in the past.

But what of the English ships and crew? When the English ships made it to harbor, it was clear that they had suffered only light damage but had largely run out of food, water, gunpowder, and shot. Ship-borne diseases however had hit their crews hard. Complaints started almost at once about how a great victory had been lost by a lack of provisions, shot, and gunpowder reaching the fleet, all of which had been promised but not delivered.

The Queen appears to have been annoyed that so few Spanish ships had been captured, leaving her with less prize money than she would have liked, particularly given the precarious nature of her finances. It was also clear that she and her Privy Council did not understand or appreciate the tactics Howard and his commanders had employed. Their tactics were continuously being adapted during the running battles from the time the Spanish were first sighted, to the chase up the North Sea. The Queen complained about the lack of attempts to board and capture Spanish ships. To some extent, this complaint is hardly surprising, given that the English ships were being used in a way that had not been tried before, particularly on such a large scale, but her ships had not been designed for that purpose, they had been designed and had been deliberately used to fight at arm's length rather than the traditional method of coming in close and boarding. Although these tactics may not have provided the prizes the Queen and her Privy Council desperately needed, given that they were nearly bankrupt by the time the Spanish turned for home, the English fleet would have been at a distinct disadvantage, given the number of soldiers on board the Spanish ships if they tried to board any Spanish ships.

One myth that continues to this day surrounding the defeat of the Armada is that the English ships were much smaller than their Spanish counterparts. In fact, size for size there was very little difference except that the English being 'race-built' did not have the towering castles fore and aft on their ships.

The English did not, as I remember being taught, "sail in under the Spanish guns." As we have seen, the fighting ships of both fleets had been designed for two completely different tactical fights. Hanson points out that 'the design of the warships, heavy weapons, munitions and gun carriages of the English Grand Fleet in 1588 was not just years but two full generations ahead of those used by the Spanish.'

In response to the Queen's and the Privy Councils criticisms, Sir Walter Raleigh published a strong defense of Howard's conduct and tactics during the fight. Interestingly, publication of the report was delayed until after the Queen's death. Although Raleigh's views were not universally accepted, it has always been the case, even up to the present day, that ships are rarely sunk by gunfire alone. Another point that Hanson makes is that most of the ships in the English fleet and their captains were privateers who may not have wanted to sink Spanish ships which would have prevented capturing any valuables or cargo on board which could be turned in to a profit. They may also have not wished to risk losing their own ships in any ensuing firefight.

Although it was a lack of provisions, shot, and gunpowder that led to Howard's stalking tactics in the North Sea, illness and fatigue amongst his men must have also played a part in his and his Council of War's decisions. There was no need to risk damage to the English ships when they might still be needed to stop Parma. Equally, although the Queen and her Privy Council had already started to demobilize her forces at Tilbury before she went to inspect them, they and their mariners did not know for certain, as some authors indicate, that the threat from the Armada and Parma had really passed.

Put simply, the Queen's finances could not support a standing army for any length of time; and by demobilizing the majority of the soldiers, it saved her money, however, some of those soldiers had to sell their arms to raise the money just to enable them to return home. It was probably thought, that if required, the Trained Bands could be called to service once again if needed. Other activities of the Queen show just how tight finances were, but some of her actions deserve reproach, for instance, Hanson informs us that she required Hawkins to account for 'every item of expenditure on powder, shot and supplies.' He explains that:

'The earl of Sussex, who was in charge of provisions was, "subject to scathing criticism and ostracized at Court for answering Howard's pleas for munitions without the Queen's authorization" and "victualler Marmaduke Darrel was imprisoned in the Tower after exceeding his orders and purchasing more victuals for the fleet than had been authorized by the Queen."'

Another money saving exercise included the discharge of the entire fleet apart from the Narrow Sea's Squadron, on 30 August. Why? Because once the seamen and soldiers on board had been dismissed, the Queen would not have to pay for their upkeep. It appears that most, both fit, sick and injured, were also dismissed without receiving the pay they were already due. By 14 September, the fleet had been reduced from one hundred and ninety-seven ships to just thirty-four, which presumably included most of the navy's own ships, thus, relieving the Queen of the cost of hiring ships that had not been supplied by individuals, town, or ports (at their own expense). The ships that had come from west country harbors were sent home with only one day's provisions, for a journey that could take them up to five or six days.

In theory, when they left Plymouth, the ships had been provisioned until 7 September so why did they run out of food so quickly? Was it a case, as so often happened, that the amount of food and drink that was supposed to have made its way to the fleet was significantly greater than actually arrived? We know that they were still loading the ships when they were ready to leave Plymouth and that some of the provisions were left behind. But we also know that ships were bringing out supplies to the English throughout their passage eastwards. In fact, fifteen ships carrying provisions were sent out to the fleet on 17 August, but only three of them made it. One of the basic problems for those in charge of supplying the fleet was trying to rendezvous with ships that were continuously moving.

Although Howard, Drake, and the other commanders did what they could to argue and press for more food, including paying for it out of their own pockets, the lack of provisions exacerbated the desperate conditions on most of the ships, which led in many cases to more than half of the ships companies going down with, scurvy, typhus, and dysentery. Howard had also tried to fumigate the ships to prevent the continuous spread of disease but the clothes the men wore, the only clothes they had, were often riddled with the lice and fleas, leading to illness.

Many of the sailors were sent home without pay. Howard and the other commanders had to fight the Admiralty for years afterwards to be paid the prize and ransom money they and their crews were owed. In fact, Howard, Drake, and the others were, never fully reimbursed for the money they had paid out.

As we have seen, at a Council of War on 1 September, it was decided to divide the fleet in to two with the ships that were fit enough to take to sea being based in the Downs whilst the ones with too many sick on board were to be sent to Margate. Even with new pressed men taken from Essex, Suffolk, Norfolk, Sussex, and Hampshire, it was thought that many of the ships did not have enough men in them to be able to set sail even if the Spanish were to return.

Howard not only used his own money to pay for food, he tried hard to find them accommodation in and around Margate. Even so, as many as half the crews died within a couple of weeks of the battle.

One of the outcomes of the appalling state of provision for the sick and injured seamen was Howard's, Drake's, and Hawkins establishment in 1590 of the Chatham Chest, a fund which every serving seaman paid in to, which was then used to support the sick and injured. It was also used to provide pensions and pay for burials. This was world's first health and pension scheme.

Following the defeat of the Armada, most of the popular credit went to Drake rather than Howard or any of the other commanders who had played such a vital role the action. It is open to debate as to whether there was any bitterness between Howard and Drake in particular. We know that Frobisher was particularly angry at Drake's behavior, but there seems, as is often the case, that there was a split between Howard's and Drake's supporters. Unfortunately, it was Drake, one of the Queen's and the Privy Councils 'blue-eyed boys,' who became the national hero that everyone remembers. It is interesting to note that Howard was not asked to lead the fleet next time it sailed, and Drake would never achieve the success that he had prior to the Armada.

As we have seen, Frobisher was very anti-Drake and had been for a long time. Sir Walter Raleigh, Lord Sheffield, Lord Thomas Howard, and the Earl of Cumberland were also Howard supporters, whereas the Earl of Essex, who had taken over as the Queen's favorite after Leicester's death and was a great rival to Raleigh's for the Queen's affections, was anti-Howard. As a result of this, Howard's reputation was caught up in the continuous power play that surrounded Elizabeth's court, a situation which may have helped Drakes reputation. After all, it is Drake that was and still is, generally regarded as the person who won the battle, but it was he who had been one of the chief advocates of the 'stand-off' tactics, which the English fleet had been designed to make best use of its ships. In fact, as Mattingly points out, recent reassessments of the battle have shown that Howard tactics were the only ones he could have used in order to make sure that the English fleet remained an effective force. We will see that similar comments have been made with regard to the way in which Sir Keith Park and Sir Hugh Dowding fought the Battle of Britain.

There is one final quote I would like to add from Mattingly's book:

'Historians agree that the defeat of the Spanish Armada was a decisive battle, in fact one of the decisive battles of the world, but there is much less agreement as to what it decided. It certainly did not decide the issue of war between England and Spain...as the episode of the Armada receded into the past it influenced history in another way. Its story, magnified and distorted by a golden mist, became a heroic apologue of the defence of freedom against tyranny, an eternal myth of the victory of the weak over the strong, of the triumph of David over Goliath.'

Part 2. 1940:

The Battle of Britain

Chapter 1
Fundamental Changes

In their book *The Battle of Britain*, Richard Hough and Denis Richards ask the question 'when did the Battle of Britain really begin?' Not an unreasonable question! They then answer this question with:

"'A not unreasonable answer is that the Battle of Britain began when the Wright brothers flew." So wrote the American historian Alfred Gollin, who went on to show that of all the governments to express an interest in the Wright brothers' achievements, Britain's was the first.'

Hough and Richards go on to explain that with the creation of the Royal Flying Corpse (RFC) in 1912 and its naval and army wings, there was a clear division of objectives. The navy would be responsible for preventing an enemy approaching the UK, and the army units would be responsible for pushing them back into the sea, if they made it to shore. The army units would also be responsible for dealing with any enemy aircraft that crossed the British coast with the navy providing air cover for ports and naval bases. The army concentrated on purely reconnaissance tasks for aircraft, and the navy, under the guidance of the energetic and adventurous Winston Churchill at the Admiralty, developed scout, and bomber aircraft. This meant that the two sides of the RFC rapidly grew apart and finally separated, as the army and navy took aviation in two different directions.

In 1914, the Admiralty was given responsibility for defense of the British Isles whilst the army focused on activities abroad, and on 1 July 1914 formed the Royal Naval Air Service (RNAS). However, as the army's air arm grew, some of its aircraft were redesignated to provide defensive cover for London. This development continued until February 1916 when it was given responsibility for air defense of the entire UK.

Following German air raids on London, a new defense system was introduced, known as the London Air Defence Area (LADA). This comprised naval aircraft that provided cover along the coast, together with a zone of anti-aircraft guns situated 25 miles (40km) out from the center of London. The Army provided air cover inside this zone with additional guns situated in London itself. Hough and Richards report that, Brigadier General Ashmore, who was in charge of LADA, thought that although airplanes were the first means of defense, they would be ineffective unless supported by a ground control system. Such foresight proved to be of fundamental importance some thirty years later. With no radios, aircraft were directed from the ground by large white arrows pointed in the direction of the enemy, they could not communicate with the ground, and they could not communicate with each other except by hand signals and waggling their wings.

In 1917, the Germans mounted a series of night-time raids on London, which resulted in some deaths, but more importantly, a significant degree of shock. This led to recommendations that the government establish an Air Ministry that would be independent of both the army and the navy, but would be their equal. It would be charged with responsibility for all airplanes previously under the control of the other two forces. The new Air Ministry was established in January 1918, and the Royal Air Force (RAF) came in to being on 1 April 1918 with Hugh Trenchard as its first leader.

At the end of the First World War, the Royal Air Force comprised one hundred and eighty-eight front-line squadrons, which made it the largest air force in the world. Of these, sixteen were designated for defense of the UK. Within two years, this total had been reduced to only twenty-five squadrons, with seven of them allocated to home defense.

Following the war, the newly established RAF was continuously under threat from the other two senior services. Hough and Richards report that even though the RAF had been significantly downsized, it appeared that the War Office and Admiralty both wanted to break-up the service and claw-back their 'lost' air-arms.

At the time, and for much of the 1920s, it was envisaged that if another conflict were to start, it would be with France, not Germany, as France was the only European country with military forces capable of challenging Britain. This, together with tight finances, influenced much of the UK military planning for most of the next two decades, as Chaz Bowyer writes in his book *Fighter Command:*

'...the defence of the United kingdom was considered to be completely safe in the hands of the Army and, especially, Britain's traditional first-line defence, the Royal Navy.'

In 1922, Hugh Trenchard, Chief of Air Staff and the person who is considered to be the 'father of the Royal Air Force,' was informed by the government that he could have fourteen bomber and nine fighter squadrons for defense of the UK. Following a change in government in 1923, they said that this would increase to a total of fifty-two squadrons within five years, comprising thirty-five bomber and seventeen fighter squadrons. The fighter squadrons were to include thirteen non-regular units, including six Auxiliary Air Force squadrons, while another seven would comprise a special reserve. At the same time, the new government established the Observer Corpse, which would play such an important part in the defense of the country during World War Two. There would also be a new command that would be responsible for control of all bomber, fighter, ant-aircraft guns, and searchlights used in the defense of the country. This new command, which was formed in 1925, was given the name Air Defence of Great Britain, or ADGB for short. It was designed to provide protection southwards from the Thames estuary to Bristol. Although Trenchard had been promised fifty-two squadrons within five years, by 1928, this total had only reached thirty-one, and by 1932, there were still only forty-two.

In 1930, Trenchard stood down as the Chief of Air Staff, and his position was taken over by John Salmond who had previously been in charge of ADGB. Trenchard never got the fifty-two squadrons he thought he had been promised; and by the 1930s, British fighters were falling behind those of the continent both in numbers and quality.

In 1934, following the failure of disarmament talks in Geneva, the government and those in charge of the military reassessed the threat from Europe and decide that the emergence of Nazi Germany would now be considered the greatest threat rather than France. They also thought that Germany might be in a position to start a major conflict as early as 1938 or 1939. In response to this new and escalating threat, the government decided to enact a rapid expansion of the RAF to seventy bomber and thirty-five home-based squadrons by 1942. To cope with this massive expansion, the RAF was reorganized in to separate commands, namely, Bomber, Fighter, Coastal, and Training commands. Added to these were the Balloon, and Reserve and Maintenance commands. This expansion could only work because of the foundations of organization and logistics that had been so carefully laid down since the First World War by Trenchard and his staff, in particular by Hugh Dowding. The ADGB area was also extended up to the River Tees. In 1938, with the ever increasing possibility of war, this was further extended northwards to beyond Newcastle. The introduction of radar (RDF) cover along the entire southern and eastern coastlines also meant that fighter control could be extended well out to sea, removing the need for an outer ring of anti-aircraft guns, but this was only achieved after a long period of experimental and development work.

As mentioned above, during and certainly shortly after the First World War, the RFC and then the RAF recognized that one of the most important elements needed for an effective command and control system was a method of communicating between aircraft in the air and controllers on the ground. Another essential element was an early warning system that included the ability to detect approaching enemy aircraft as far away as possible. These requirements led, during the 1920s and 1930s, to the establishment of a number of experimental programs many of which came within the remit of the Air Defence Experimental Establishment (ADEE) at RAF Biggin Hill. These included experiments with acoustic wells, mirrors, walls, and horns. The Signals Experimental Establishment moved to Biggin Hill in 1916, and the Wireless Experimental Establishment arrived in 1918. The Anti-aircraft School, which among other things investigated how to link acoustic detection and then RDF to search lights and anti-aircraft guns was also moved to Biggin Hill. Experiments were also conducted from the airfield with radio detection finding (RDF), which involved aircraft from the resident 32 squadron from 1936. As Peter Osborne relates in his book *RAF Biggin Hill: The Other Side of the Bump:*

'It is impossible to estimate how influential good radio communications were when faced with a determined enemy; air to ground/ground to air and air-to-air telephony would become vital for effective command and control, an aspect of aerial warfare which [as we shall see later] was not widely appreciated in the Luftwaffe' who '...in time honoured tradition they tended [to] rely on past experience and could not see that radio telephony would be vital in any future, fast evolving combat zone.'

Dowding was tasked by Trenchard to oversee this important experimental and development work, and so had a very good understanding of its potential before he took charge of the newly established Fighter Command, based at Bentley Prior in Middlesex, on 1 May 1936. Huge Caswell Tremenheere Dowding, who had also been in charge of Supply and Research for the RAF since 1930, is described by Bowyer as 'totally honest, utterly professional, and wholly dedicated to his responsibilities.' He adds that 'despite an austere outward appearance [Dowding] could almost have been chosen for his role by destiny.' During his time in charge of Supply and Research, 'his far-sighted and down-to-earth policies were to have a huge bearing upon the state of Britain's air defences by the outbreak of the war in 1939.'

Hough and Richards comment that he understood the changes that he regarded as essential to transform Fighter Command in to the command that would be required to fight in the future, and that he had the grit, determination, and character to see that this transformation would be achieved.

During his time in charge of supply and research, the specification for a new fighter was also developed, which led to Hawker and Supermarine submitting designs that would eventually become the Hurricane and Spitfire. Dowding also 'put the full weight of his office and personal enthusiasm behind the development of a new device—radio direction finding (RDF), which years later became more widely known as Radar [a term introduced by the Americans].'

When Dowding took control of Fighter Command in 1936, it comprised only eighteen squadrons of Bristol Bulldogs, five of Hawker Demons, six equipped with Gloster Gauntlets, and three with Hawker Furies, all of which were biplanes. These were gradually to be replaced by the first of the six hundred Hurricanes and three hundred and ten Spitfires which were ordered on 3 June 1936 and which were expected to be in service by 1939. However, by March 1939, although Fighter Command now comprised forty-five operational squadrons with four hundred aircraft and a further one hundred and sixty in reserve, only five squadrons were equipped with Hurricanes, the rest still used biplanes armed with only one, two, or four guns. Previously, in 1935, Squadron Leader Ralph Sorley had identified that the next generation of faster aircraft would require more guns to be able to shoot down enemy aircraft and suggested that they should initially be armed with four, then six and finally with eight 0.303 inch (7.6mm) caliber machine guns; the provision of eight machine guns was included in the specification for the new generation of monoplane fighters. To give some indication of how rapidly the introduction of the new eight gunned fighters occurred, by September 1939, when war broke out, Fighter Command's Hurricane squadrons increased from five to twenty-one, and there would also be twelve squadrons of Spitfires. It also had five squadrons of Bristol Blenheims light bombers, which had been hastily converted to act as fighters by the addition of gun packs under their fuselages.

When Dowding took command, he wanted all of his airfields to be equipped with concrete runways, which would allow his fighters to be used in any weather, but this idea was met with some resistance from the Air Ministry. Bowey relates that he also met significant opposition from members of the Air Staff and others when he requested thing such as a system of camouflaging aerodromes and bulletproof windscreens for his fighters.

Traditional thinking within the upper echelons of the air force together with every air force around the world held the view that bombers were the key to the defense of the country, but following the Munich Crisis in 1938, attention turned towards building up the number of fighter aircraft in the RAF. Dowding tried on numerous occasions to get the government and the Air Ministry to state how many fighter squadrons they thought he would need to mount a defense of the country, but he was never really given an answer. This would prove crucial when it came to war and the Battle of France, when Dowding had to fight to save his fighters from being lost in that conflict. Bowyer makes the following observations on Dowding's contribution to the build up to war:

'Dowding was a realist, and his immense foresight, coupled with meticulous planning, was to provide a ground organisation for Fighter Command by 1940 that withstood the cruellest testing under war conditions and continued to function. Added to this perspicacity was Dowding's immediate and deep grasp of virtually all the new technical facets of that embryo organisation—RDF, armament, air rocketry, even cannons for aircraft; all came within his aegis of research and development at some stage. Never one to shrink from unpleasant facts, he also foresaw that under wartime conditions of any air assault on England, his precious fighter squadrons would inevitably be depleted in strength in any battle of attrition; and therefore laid down plans for rapid interchanges of war-weary units and fresh squadrons between the far north of England and Scotland and the units in the "forward zones" of southern England.'

Before we look at the operational tactics which Fighter Command would use in defending Britain, it is worth looking at the basis on which the Air Staff made their predictions of the quantity and effects of bombing and the Blitzkrieg on Britain. In *Invasion: 1940*, Derek Robinson points out that they overestimated the effectiveness of the Luftwaffe bombing and the expected loss of life in London. They predicted that the Luftwaffe would drop 100,000 tons (101,600 tonnes) of bombs in fourteen days which was more than the total they eventually dropped on the capital during the entire war. They also estimated that bombing would kill 600,000 and injure a further 1,200,000 in the first six months of aerial bombing.

The professionals and politicians were therefore predicting heavy bombing and enormous causalities, because 'the bomber would always get through.' Although, as Robinson highlights, their figures were way off the mark, it had an added, unforeseen, advantage in that our defenses and air force were being expanded to meet this perceived threat, probably to a larger size than the politicians would have allowed if the figures had been more accurate.

In the build up to war, Fighter Command's tactics were based on the premise, held all the way through the 1930s, that any attack would be conducted by massed bombers, flown in close formation without the need for fighter protection. This was partially based on the idea that if Germany were to attack, it would only be able to do so from airfields in Belgium and Holland, from which the limited range of German fighters, would have restricted their usefulness. Few, if any, considered that airfields in France would become available to the Germans. Equally, there appears to have been little consideration of the idea that the Germans would provide their fighters with long-range drop-tanks, which fortunately was an idea that the Germans themselves also saw as a low priority.

Alongside the idea that bombers would be the preferred method of attack, was the concept that dog-fighting—fighter-versus-fighter combats—were a thing of the past. To enable fighters to bring as many guns to bear on enemy bombers as possible, a set of six well-defined and rather complicated fighting area attack tactics were introduced, in which fighters flew in multiples of three, in 'vic' (V) formations. These involved the lead aircraft, leading the formation so that all three aircraft acted almost as a single airplane. This meant that the two wingmen spent most of their time concentrating on keeping position with the fighter leader rather than looking at where they were going or looking at what was going on around them. As Johnny Johnson, one our most famous fighter pilots wrote in his book, *The Story of Air Fighting*, 'a wingman found it impossible to keep a good lookout and watch both his leader and his target.' Many squadrons were still trying to adhere to these tactics at the beginning of the battle when it was clear that they would not work. As Chaz Bowey puts it, strict compliance with Fighting Area Attack Tactics by squadron leaders and the more experienced pilots who had no war experience meant that:

'...tragically, many such squadron commanders who failed to release their minds from the bonds of blind obedience were among the earliest casualties of 1939–40; often in circumstances of their own making in which younger pilots, faithfully following their leader, were also dragged into an unnecessary oblivion.'

Robinson concurs with this, adding that Luftwaffe tactics were usually good whilst the RAF's tactics often verged on suicidal.

Those that abandoned the fighting area attack tactics often adopted the Germans fighting formation, a formation, which is still largely used today. An explanation of this formation, its origins, and development is provided later on in this chapter when we look at the origins of the Luftwaffe, its expansion and training.

The Air Ministry was sufficiently alarmed at the public arrival of the Luftwaffe in 1937 that they tried to instigate a rapid increase in the size of the Royal Air Force and aircraft production, on a scale equal to their estimates of the expansion of the Luftwaffe, but the Chamberlain government rejected the plan. Winston Churchill, who was on the opposition benches at the time, had been concerned about German military developments for some time and had been pushing the government for several years to re-arm, but with little success. Following the rejection of its plans, the RAF suggested a compromise, which enabled it to get the increase in fighters it had requested but with a slower increase bomber production.

In 1938, the Air Ministry reported, in answer to the government, that neither it nor any of its allies would be able to stand up to the Germans for more than a couple of weeks should they invade Czechoslovakia. In response to this news, the government continued with diplomatic negotiations but also instigated a large increase in aircraft production, which was designed to provide the air force with 12,000 aircraft within two years.

One of the key components designed to enable RAF airplanes to compete with the new Luftwaffe aircraft was the development and introduction by Esso and Shell of 100-octane fuel. This gave our aircraft a significant boost in performance compared to the German aircraft which were still using 87-octane aviation fuel.

As early as 1936, the government introduced a system of shadow factories. They also urged other organizations to switch to aircraft manufacture in an effort to increase production and further disperse it to prevent its potential destruction from air raids. As Arthur Ward recounts in *A Nation Alone: The Battle of Britain—1940:*

'…the dispersal system encouraged a much broader manufacturing base than had previously been available. Soon furniture-makers, coach-builders, and panel-beating firms were engaged in the manufacture of aircraft parts. Dispersal also ensured that no single factory—and, consequently, target—produced all the components for a particular machine. The wisdom of this policy was demonstrated when the birthplace of the Spitfire, Supermarine's Woolston factory at Southampton, as badly damaged during the Battle of Britain. Production of the immortal fighter, though impaired, continued apace at other locations.

'One of the most important factories to take on this work was Morris's car works at Castle Bromwich. William Morris, better known as Lord Nuffield, not only offered his factory to the Air Ministry to build new aircraft but also offered his invaluable organisational skills.'

Ward includes the following:

'...soon the mighty Nuffield organisation had rolled up its sleeves and was heavily involved in the accelerated rearmament programme...under his [Nuffield's] control the CRO (Civilian Repair Organisation) charged Morris Motors with the recovery, repair and redistribution of damaged or unserviceable military aircraft. Battle-damaged or simply worn-out aircraft did not long lay idle on airfields and even during the heat of battle were withdrawn to CRO factories for repair to ensure they were back in action in as short a time as possible.'

The repair system worked so efficiently that a damaged Hurricane could be back in action within four to five days and sometimes within twenty-four hours. By the middle of July, the system was operating so well that they were repairing an average of one hundred and sixty fighters a week with unrepairable aircraft being stripped of any useable components.

As mentioned briefly above, one of the key players in the success of Fighter Command was Squadron Leader Ralph Sorely, who became the commanding officer of 8 Squadron in 1931. In 1933, he moved to the Operational Requirements section at the Air Ministry where he was in charge of the section that drew up Operational Requirement F.36/34. This laid out the requirements for an eight-gunned, single-seat, monocoque fighter, with an enclosed cockpit and retractable undercarriage: a requirement that led to the design and production of the Hurricane and Spitfire.

Hawker Hurricane 1—a single-seat fighter powered by a Roll Royce Merlin III engine, which gave it a maximum speed of 328mph (529kph).

It was armed with eight Browning 0.303 inch (7.7mm) machine guns, four in each wing located in a single group.

Supermarine Spitfire 1—a single-seat fighter powered by a Rolls Royce Merlin II engine, which gave it a maximum speed of 362mph (549kph). It was armed with eight Browning 0.303 inch (7.7mm) machine guns located in three, dispersed positions in each wing.

In addition to these two famous fighters, Fighter Command also used the follow aircraft types during the coming battle:

Boulton-Paul Defiant—a two-seat, single-engined fighter, It had no forward-firing guns but did possess four Browning 0.303 inch (7.7mm) caliber guns in a powered turret located behind the pilot. The Rolls Royce Merlin III engine gave the aircraft a maximum speed of 304mph (489kph).

Gloster Gladiator—a single-seat biplane powered by a Bristol Mercury engine that gave it a maximum speed of 257mph (414kph) It was armed with four Browning 0.303 inch (7.7mm) machine guns, two of which were fitted in the nose and the other two located under the lower wings.

Bristol Blenheim I—a two-seat, medium bomber, powered by two Bristol Mercury engines. It had a maximum speed of 285mph (460kph) and was armed with four Browning 0.303 inch (7.7mm) machine guns in a semi-retractable turret. Some Blenheims were also fitted with a four-gun pack under the center of their fuselage so that they could be used as fighter aircraft.

Bristol Beaufighter I and IF—a two seat fighter, powered by two Bristol Hercules engines that gave it a maximum speed of 321mph (518kph) It was armed with four 20mm Hispano cannons in its nose and six Browning 0.303 inch (7.7mm) machine guns in its wings. The IF version was fitted with an Mk IV Air Interceptor radar.

Another of the key components of the new defense strategy was the introduction of radar. In the spring of 1939, General Wolfgang Martini, the Head of Signals in the Luftwaffe, became increasingly concerned and intrigued by the tall masts that were being constructed along the English coastline. He thought that these masts, 350 feet (106m) high and built in groups of three, must be, in some way, designed to be used for either radio or radar (or RDF—Radio Direction Finding as it was known at the time).

The Germans, independently from Britain, had been designing and were building their own radar system, which used a parabolic 'dish.' This operated on a short wavelength of between 0.5m and 1.5m. As the British system looked significantly different to theirs, the Germans thought that if these masts were part of a radar system, the British were significantly behind them in its technology and development. Although the Germans had operational, gun-laying radar in 1939, they had originally used radar as an early warning system around their naval bases and to direct anti-aircraft fire.

In order to determine the function of these masts Martini reactivated the airship LZ 130 *Graf Zeppelin*. In May 1940, the LZ 130—packed with radio receivers, cathode-ray tubes, and aerials—was sent on a mission to fly up the East coast of England, out of sight of land, to try to detect any radio signals that might be being transmitted from the masts. Martini and the operators on board scanned all of the wavelengths they expected the British radio signals to be using if the masts were being used as part of a radar system, and found nothing but background noise. Fortunately, what they did not realize was that the British system used significantly longer wavelengths of between 10m and 13.5m. During its flight, British radar operators had been following LZ 130 on their radar sets and, according to Brian Johnson in his book *The Secret War*, when the Germans signaled back that they had found nothing, and were turning for home, they reported their position incorrectly, and the English were sorely tempted to tell them their true location. The radar system, known as Chain Home, continued to develop into an overlapping system that gave radar cover along the entire east and south coasts from the River Tay in Scotland to Southampton. In August 1939, Martini set out on a further test flight, but once again, he and his crew were searching for the wrong wavelengths; and in the end, the Germans concluded that the British did not have a functional radar system. As Robinson points out, 'when they [German's leaders] failed to take seriously Britain's chain of radar stations…that was a major blunder.' As he explains, 'because it did not fully understand British radar, the Luftwaffe underestimated its importance. Since it was not important, it could be easily destroyed.' As we will see later, when the Luftwaffe failed to destroy the radar towers, rather that keep trying, they gave up.

The British system allowed the RAF to look out over the North Sea and English Channel. Depending on the height at which they were flying, it could detect aircraft at varying distances, for instance, an aircraft flying at 5,000 feet (1,524m) could be tracked from 40 miles (64km) away. If it were flying at a height of 30,000 feet (9,144m) it could be spotted at a distance of between a 120 miles and 140 miles (193–225km). The one weakness in the Chain Home system was its inability to detect low flying aircraft. To counter this problem, scientists developed a version of a gun-laying radar, which became known as Chain Home Low. This used 1.5m long radio waves similar to that used by the Germans, but from 185 feet (56m) high masts, which allowed the operators to detect and track low flying aircraft at a distance of 50 miles (80km) from the British coast.

What advantage did the system of radar cover and information sorting and distribution (see below) give the RAF? Much of the work involved in developing filter rooms, sector controls, and the operations maps used to track and control friend and foe was undertaken at RAF Biggin Hill. This, together with radar cover for most of the south and east coasts, enabled operators to track enemy aircraft up to 100 miles (160km) from our coast. As Johnson points out, this was all achieved in secret over four years and at a cost of only £10 million. It was soon to prove very cheap at the price.

Radar provided one of the most effective and important elements of the British early-warning system. As Johnny Johnson wrote, 'Radar and radio provided the means of close control from the ground, and fighter pilots, fighting within the radar shield,' so that 'fighter squadrons could be used economically so that the cathode tube had the effect of multiplying the fighter strength several times…Fighter Command provided an invaluable guard which gave Britain, for the first time in the history of air warfare, the means of defending our island home.' Robinson adds that 'radar gave Fighter Command the invaluable benefit of time—time to plot the raids and plan the interceptions, time to get the defenders airborne and climbing.'

In February 1940, there were twenty-one operational radar stations and by July, this had increased to fifty-one with the inclusion of thirty Chain Home Low units.

It is worth remembering, however, that the world's first interception of bombers by aircraft, assisted by radar occurred on 18 December 1939 when Luftwaffe fighters intercepted a number of Wellington bombers during a raid on Wilhelmshaven. The first air-to-air radar directed interception occurred on 2 July 1940, when a Blenheim shot down a Dornier 17 bomber. It is also important to note that even with the benefit of information from radar, frequently fighters scrambled in 11 Group (see below), particularly from airfields close to the coast, were often still climbing when they had to intercept German formations which, as we shall see later, put them at a distinct disadvantage.

To make full use of radar and other developments, Dowding introduced a new system of command and control. This was based around giving commanders on the ground, that had a clearer picture of events as they unfolded, control of the fighters rather than Station Commanders or even Squadron Leaders, who could only react to the local situation as they saw it.

One of the biggest advantages of the new system was that it removed the need for the old system of mounting standing patrols, in which aircraft flew around in a particular area until the enemy were detected. Such patrols involved aircraft staying in the air, often for lengthy periods of time before encountered the enemy. With the new system, aircraft could be held in readiness on the ground and only sent up when needed, saving fuel and flying time for their pilots. It also enabled controllers to determine how many aircraft would be needed to counter a particular attack. This avoided sending too few or too many aircraft, and helped to prevent them from being caught on the ground when being rearmed or refueled. The tactics, which were used under the new system, were also developed at RAF Biggin Hill from 1936 onwards and resulted in the world's first complete air defense system based on radar.

Another key component of Dowdings warning system was the Observer Corpse, who took over observing and tracking enemy aircraft once they had reached the British coastline when the numbers of aircraft and their flight paths could more accurately observed. As Sinclair McKay records in *The Secret Listeners: The Men and Women Posted Across the World to Intercept the German Codes for Bletchley Park*, these volunteers manned observations post that were 'structures of the purest simplicity' that were often 'basic wooden huts' that could 'barely shelter the volunteers from the weather.' Nonetheless, the vital information they provided was fed straight to representatives of the Observer Corpse standing next to Dowding in his control center at Bentley Priory.

When Fighter Command was formed in 1936, Dowding realized that to be able to defend the country, he needed a system that would integrate the early warning information that radar and the Observer Corpse would provide, together with other intelligence. This system of aircraft control would allow him to position and make maximum use of the limited forces under his command. Being able to fulfil this ambitious project involved a complete redesign of the existing communications system, which was still based, to a large extent, on experience gained during the First World War. Over a period of four years, his new system came together and, as Derek Wood and Derek Dempster put it in their wonderful book, *The Narrow Margin:*

'...piece by piece the giant jigsaw puzzle was assembled, each section interlocking exactly with the next. Warning of attack came first from radar. From the coast it was the responsibility of the Observer Corpse and the information was passed to Fighter Command and the fighter groups. From there the orders were relayed to the fighting sectors, where with

H.F. [high frequency] radio, "Pip Squeak" [see below] and high frequency direction finding the controllers could direct the Spitfires and Hurricanes to the attack at the right place and time and guide them safely back to base.'

For operational requirements, the country had been divided in to four areas, with a fighter group in each one. 10 Group covered the South West and South Wales; 11 Group covered the South and East from Bournemouth to just west of Oxford and eastwards across to the coast to just north of Ipswich; 12 Group covered the area north of 10 and 11 Groups to a line from just south of Southport on the North West coast to south of Bridlington on the North East coast; finally, 13 Group covered the area north of 12 Group, including Scotland.

Every group had its own headquarter linked to the Fighter Command's Headquarters at Bentley Priory in Middlesex. Each group was sub-divided into a series of sectors systematically labeled from A to Y from Dorset around the east of the country as far as Edinburgh and Glasgow. Each sector contained a principal airfield, known as the Sector Station, which looked after a number of satellite airfields to which it could position its aircraft.

Fighter Command HQ at Bentley Priory contained a map, which covered the entire country, while each of the Group HQ's had a map covering their own group plus adjacent areas. Finally, each Sector Station had its own map which covered its own sector and adjacent areas. Thus, the entire country was covered by a series of linker-locking maps on which markers, indicating the movement of both British and German aircraft, or formations were plotted. The wall of each Operations Room contained a 'Totaliser,' or Tote, which comprised either a slotted blackboard, or light system which showed the 'state' of each squadron. The Totes in Sector Control rooms showed only the squadrons based at, or temporarily called in to their sector, whereas each Group operations room showed the state of all squadrons in their group. In Fighter Command HQ's Operations Room, the Tote showed the state of every squadron in Fighter Command. The Tote board used colored lights to indicate the state or readiness or action of every flight in every squadron. There were fourteen different states of readiness from top to bottom on the board, which gave the controllers a detailed picture of the resources available to them. The fourteen stages were:

Relaxed
Available 30 minutes
Available
Ordered to readiness
At Readiness
Ordered to standby
At Standby
Ordered on Patrol
Left ground
In Position
Detailed to Raid
Enemy Sighted
Ordered to Land
Landed and Refueling

The Tote board also showed the controller how many pilots and aircraft were available for each squadron.

In each of the control rooms at station, group, or HQ level, people then plotted the paths of enemy and Fighter Command aircraft that were being provided by radar stations, the Observer Corpse, and Fighter Command airfields, and any other sources that were available, on a giant map table of their respective area. Before this information could be plotted, it was 'filtered' in the Filter Room. This pulled all of the incoming information together and, as the name implies, filtered it out so that spurious or conflicting information did not impact operational effectiveness.

To make sure that controllers knew how up-to-date the information was that they were looking at, the entire system worked on a very clever structure based on a clock, the face of which was divided into five-minute colored sections. As the clock's minute hand passed from one colored section to another, the plotters changed the colors on the aircraft markers.

To allow controllers to be able to identify and direct individual aircraft a system called 'Pip Squeak,' instigated by a Squadron Leader Chandler, was installed in each aircraft. This automatically cut in to the aircraft's high frequency radio system for fourteen seconds every minute to send out a radio signal, which could be triangulated, by three or more receivers. This then told the controllers the exact location of the aircraft without the pilot having to determine where he was. Before a fighter took off, the ground controllers would advise each pilot to set his 'Pip Squeak' to a particular time setting, thus, he could 'see' the position of four individual aircraft over a 15-second period every minute. It also meant that he could 'watch' up to four squadrons of aircraft at a time. The code word for 'Pip Squeak' was *Cockerel*, and if a pilot had forgotten to set his 'Pip Squeak' or had accidentally forgotten to turn it on when he was in the air, the controller could identify which aircraft it was and inform the pilot that his Cockerel was not crowing.

The other key component, which turned this fighter control system in to a complete defense system, was the inclusion of other forces in the Operations Room. At Fighter Command HQ for instance, the Commander-in-Chief of the anti-aircraft defenses and the Commandant of the Observer Corpse, together with liaison officers from Bomber and Coastal Command, the Admiralty and a representative from the Ministry of Home Security, accompanied Dowding. This enabled each of the other services to evaluate the action as it developed and coordinate their responses.

Wood and Dempster explain that the entire system worked because everyone, from Dowding down to all the Sector Controllers, could see all the up-to-the-minute information through the use of the same synchronized colored clocks. This allowed Dowding and his group commanders to assemble their aircraft where and when they were needed to maximize their effectiveness.

Wood and Dempster add that it was not until the Luftwaffe radio monitoring service and German Post Office set up a number of listening stations along the French coast that they realized the importance of the radar stations and the level of control Fighter Command controllers had while directing their aircraft to intercept Luftwaffe raids.

Before we move on, it is also worth saying something about how the communications, radar, and operation control system fitted together, and here, according to Paul Brown and Edwin Herbert in their book *The Secrets of Q Central*, the town of Leighton Buzzard comes to the fore.

'*Q Central*' was the code name for RAF Leighton Buzzard, the RAF's central communications station. This was the home to No. 26 (Signals) Group who operated 'the largest telephone exchange in the world.' It was realized that using land telephone lines was far more secure than radios, and therefore, RAF Leighton Buzzard was the hub for all communications that would eventually be linked to every theatre of the war and would also house all communications for the army and navy, as well as those for MI5, MI6, and MI8.

It was only a few miles from Bentley Priory and housed an emergency filter and operations room that could be used if Bentley Priory was destroyed. Bletchley Park '*Station X*,' the home of the *Enigma* code breakers, was also fairly close by and No. 60 (Signals) Group, who ran and coordinated all of the radar stations, was housed in Oxendon House which was also in Leighton Buzzard. This unit moved from Bawdsey on the Suffolk coast two days before the outbreak of war when it was thought that the Germans knew the existence of the radar experimental and development work being undertaken there.

Although the work at Bletchley Park has been rightly acknowledged for shortening the war, Brown and Herbert point out that 'without No. 60 Group, and the men and women who invented, improved and then ran the radar stations from Leighton Buzzard, the war might well have been lost already.' Equally, the operations of the '*Y Service*,' the wireless interception operation that listened and copied down all enemy radio transmissions, was critical to the work of Bletchley Park. As McKay relates, 'It was Y Service operatives who listened in on the entire German war apparatus, every hour, every minute of every day; it was these young people who were the first to hear of any tactical shift, any manoeuvre, any soaring victory, any crushing defeat,' and that 'accuracy in relaying these coded enemy messages could mean the difference between life and death.' So that they too were truly on the frontline, copying and transcribing every message and relaying it to Bletchley and the various commanders. However, unlike the code-breaking work carried out at Bletchley Park, 'the efforts of those men and women are sadly and curiously uncelebrated today.'

As a lead in to the next part of our story, the homes of the 'black propaganda studios' at Milton Bryon, the Country Headquarters of the Political Warfare Executive at Woburn Abbey, and RAF Tempsford, which was one of the most secret airfield in the world that was used to fly special agents in and out of the occupied Europe, were also nearby. The Signal Intelligence Unit at RAF Chicksands and later in the war RAF Little Horwood, that would house two special communications units, were also close to Leighton Buzzard.

Following on from this, and before we look at the development of the Luftwaffe, I would like to include another aspect of the Battle of Britain which is not usually included in the narrative, but which played an important part in protecting our airfields and war industry, namely deception. In his book, *The Hidden War*, Seymour Reit provides an interesting insight in to the activities of those charged with coming up with imaginative ways of deceiving the enemy (on both sides) or diverting their attention away from their intended target. But why should this be important? As Reit relates, in the Battle of Britain, the Royal Engineers and Home Guard worked tirelessly to provide deceptions that would convince the Luftwaffe and German High

Command that British defenses were stronger than they really were. This work included '*Q*' lights, fake airfields, dockyards and shipyards, factories, as well as imitation fuel and supply depots, each of which diverted bombing from real targets.

Along the coastline, fake gun emplacements were established to fool the Germans into thinking that the coastline was better defended that it really was. Inland numerous camouflaged strong points, minefields, and other hidden explosive devices were installed to delay any invading forces. I can remember many years ago, talking to an artist and cartoonist, named Sid Gallard, who lived on the Isle of Wight. He had been one of three people charged with patrolling and protecting three miles (4.8km) of the Dorset coastline during the early part of the war. He said that they only had one rifle between them and so they built a number of gun emplacements along their section of the cliffs which comprised broomsticks and sand bags together with other painted weapons.

Even before the evacuation at Dunkirk, Sir John Turner, who was a staff officer in the army, started developing deception work with regard to our airfields which employed two rows of parallel flares, designed to look like flare paths on emergency runways. The flares were set off by men on the ground and were usually positioned several miles down the flight path of German raiders from the real airfields so that they would think that they had reached the airfield and drop their bombs early. To help the deception, a complete blackout was maintained on the real airfield. As Reit says, even given this apparent success, there were objections from some in the RAF:

'Turner and his assistant, Group Captain A. G. Bond, weathered the criticism and won approval to go ahead… The British at this stage of the war, were short of fighter pilots and aircraft but not of lighting equipment, the original crude flares were soon replaced by strands of electric lights, shaded to simulate the dim outlines of operational [air] fields. The patterns, called "Q lights," became fairly elaborate: in additions to runway markers, many of the decoys had red obstruction lamps, landing "V"s, taxi aprons; and recognition beacons: and on some, floodlights mounted on wheels were pulled along the runway to resemble the "landing lights" of incoming planes.'

Reit also includes the comments of a pilot who said that:

'…on the ground in the daytime, the decoys looked pathetic. Just a collection of old wooden poles with a tangle of wires and electric bulbs strung here and there. But when we flew over the same spot at night, the effect was amazing. It was quite impossible to tell a fake from the real thing.'

Initially, there were problems with some RAF aircraft trying to land at some of these '*Q*' sites, so Turner and his men added a line of nine red lights across the ends of the 'runways' which looked similar to the light on the real airfields but which the RAF pilots knew indicated that they were fake airfields. Following their success, other aspects of a real airfields were added to some of them. Coastal Command asked whether it would be possible to add fires so that it would convince German pilots that when they dropped their bombs they started fires. In response, fire baskets, known as '*Starfish*' were added, which were triggered electrically to simulated strings of bombs exploding.

To try to convince the German bombers and reconnaissance aircraft that the real airfields had sustained the damage they had actually inflicted on the '*Q*' sites, Turner's department, together with scenery makers from the British film industry, created a series of canvas bomb craters which could be pinned out along runways and across airfields that would not restrict aircraft operations. They even went as far as making two different types, some which could be used in sunny conditions and others with a more subdued effect for use in cloudy weather.

The system of '*Q*' sites, of which there were hundreds, were so successful that they were extended to include factories and even railway yards. Again, they were placed within a short distance of the real thing so that suspicions would not be raised by targets being in the wrong place, but they would be far enough away to make sure that the real targets were missed.

To try to counter daylight raids, they developed '*K*' sites, which comprised full-scale airfields with all the attributes of the real thing but made out of canvas and wood. To maintain the realism, fake aircraft and vehicles were continuously moved around and repositioned on them, they even took delivery of supplies which were stored in the open and then moved. Each '*Q*' site could be operated by two men, but it took over two hundred people to look after a '*K*' site, consequently there were far fewer of them.

Were these really useful, or were they as some at the Air Ministry thought a diversion of resources? Reit records that Colonel Charles W. Hinkle of the U. S. Department of Defense reported that the '*Q*' and '*K*' airfields attracted four hundred and forty Luftwaffe raids compared to four hundred and thirty aimed at real airfields.

The diversion of a significant amount of German bombing not only from our airfields but also from our aircraft factories, armament factories, and transport networks played an important part in our being able to defend ourselves and eventually go on the offensive.

To finish this section, I could not resist adding another cautionary story, which Reit includes, about a German decoy airfield:

'…built in occupied Holland, [it] led to a tale that has been told and retold ever since by veteran Allied pilots. The German "airfield," constructed with meticulous care, was made almost entirely of wood. There were wooden hangars, oil tanks, gun emplacements, trucks, and aircraft. The Germans took so long in building their wooden decoy that Allied photo experts had more than enough time to observe and report it. The day finally came when the decoy was finished, down to the last wooden plank. And early the following morning a lone RAF plane crossed the Channel, came in low, circled the field once, and dropped a large wooden bomb.'

Having looked at the formation of the RAF and Fighter Command in particular, and the preparations for war, let us turn our attention to the Luftwaffe.

Following the end of World War One along with many other restrictions, the Germans were prohibited from forming an air force. However, from the 1920s, General Hans von Seekt, the Chief of Army Command, had been instrumental in establishing the development of a secret air force, brokered in a deal between Germany and Russia. This would allow Germany to set up a military flying school on Russian soil at which it would also be able to test its new and developmental aircraft. Between 1924 and 1932, almost two hundred and fifty 'elite' German fighter pilots and observers were also trained there.

In Germany itself, there were no restrictions on the establishment of glider clubs, which sprang up all over the country. In fact, so many were formed that within a short period of time they had over 50,000 members. Germany was also allowed to develop its own airline, Lufthansa, which was allowed to train and employ additional pilots. The airline was instrumental in developing and bringing in to service aircraft, such as the Junkers Ju 52, which would provide almost all of the future Luftwaffe's transport aircraft for much of the war. As Hough and Richards explain, the national airline also had ground facilities and pilot training sessions that were beyond those required to run and maintain an airline at the time. Many of their airliners were also designed to be easily converted into bombers when required.

This meant that when Hitler became Chancellor in 1933, much of the fledgling Luftwaffe already existed. He eventually bought his 'new' air force out of the shadows, allowing a rapid expansion under the command of Herman Goering, a World War One pilot. Erhard Milch, another well-known World War One pilot was put in charge of its planning and development. Originally, much of the work was conducted under the guise of a Civil Air Ministry; but within this organization, all the necessary infrastructure for the air force was established, usually under the premise of developing civil air traffic control. Hitler accelerated Milch's plans to such an extent that it resulted in an air force that could be used quickly; however, it did not have the long-term planning behind it that would be required to fight an extended war.

There were other more basic problems for the Luftwaffe from the beginning, as Williamson Murray identifies in his book *Luftwaffe: Strategy for defeat 1933–45:*

> 'German's strategic position, as well as the rather confined nature of the strategic arena in Western and Central Europe, also tended to make her military leaders pay scant attention to logistics. Put very simply, in the two World Wars British, and particularly American, generals had to think of logistics and supply before they considered operational matters. Their first problem was how to get there. The Germans, on the other hand, were, in a sense, already there and had to solve the operational and tactical problems of war immediately. In the confined space of Central Europe their tendency to pay less attention to logistic matters was not necessarily disastrous.'

Germany also lacked the natural resources it needed for mobilization. This was particularly true with regard to oil, aviation fuel, and iron ore. To make things worse, most of their imports had to come past Britain and the ever-watchful eye of the Royal Navy. This meant that their industry could rarely work to its full capacity. Consequently, part of Hitler's rush that led to war in 1939 was the need to secure the resources his military ambitions required. There were additional problems. As the German economy was in a very fragile state, it found it difficult to obtain the external financial help it needed. Consequently, the limited resources it could purchase were targeted towards building up the armed forces, and because Goring considered himself to be Hitler's right-hand man, this meant that the needs of the Luftwaffe took priority over the other services.

Murray provides an interesting insight into why Germany found itself in a war years before it had anticipated and before it was militarily ready to conduct one. The military high command thought that the army had serious deficiencies in equipment and training. Even though Britain and its European allies had not been deterred from opposing Germany following its invasion of Poland, Hitler thought that with his Nazi-Soviet Non-Aggression Pact and the supply of raw materials from the Balkans, Germany could withstand any blockade. However, imports did not live up to expectations with a fall in value of 57% between January 1939 and January 1940. They also faced significant reductions in their petrol reserves from 2,400,000 tons (2,438,512 tonnes) at the start of the war to 1,600,000 tons (1,625,675 tonnes) by May 1940. Petrol supplies also fell from 300,000 tons (304,814 tonnes) in September 1939 to 110,000 tons (111,765 tonnes) in the following April. This goes a long way to explain why Hitler wanted and needed a short conflict. He knew that Germany did not have the capacity or the capability to fight a potentially long war. It also helps to explain, together with the economic constraints, the lack of reserves and long-term planning in the armed forces.

Throughout the 1930s, one of the tactical reasons for giving the expansion of the Luftwaffe preferential treatment was the thought that it would be required to prevent France and Poland from making a pre-emptive strike on Germany's military build-up. Early in the Luftwaffe's development, it was realized that they would need a large, four-engine, heavy bomber, and indeed, two different types were under development. However, the need to concentrate on the production of fighters and the particular focus on dive-bombers, together with technical problems regarding the engines required to power large bombers, led to their development being stopped.

Some indication of the rapid speed of expansion is revealed in the following figures: in 1938, they had five hundred and eighty-four combat aircraft with a production rate of one hundred and eighty aircraft a month; but by 1939, this had increased to 3,609 combat aircraft, five hundred and fifty-two transports, and a production rate of seven hundred aircraft a month.

Although the fledgling Luftwaffe were producing a large number of new pilots, what they needed was a way to give them the opportunity to hone their skills and try out their new equipment. They found this in the Spanish Civil War where, through the Condor Legion, they were able to cycle through many of their pilots, giving them invaluable combat experience.

It was also during this conflict that the Luftwaffe developed their fighter tactics, and in particular, the 'Route,' a pair of aircraft, a leader and wingman, and the *'Schwarm'* finger-four formation. As we have seen this formation, flying as a basic fighting unit, has become standard practice throughout the world, but it was born from a shortage of fighter aircraft. When the Luftwaffe sent their fighters with their Condor Legion, they had insufficient aircraft to fly in their usual three-aircraft 'V' formations. They, therefore, had to revert to flying in pairs, initially flying in line abreast. When more Bf 109s arrived, the pairs were doubled up in to the finger-four formation in which the widely spaced aircraft could cover each other's tails and fly with more freedom than that imposed by the tight formation practices developed during the inter-war period.

The Condor Legion and Blitzkrieg gained a formidable reputation during the Spanish Civil War which sent shockwaves around Europe and America. It seemed that this fearsome new form of 'lightning war' was unstoppable. In fact, much of this reputation was based on partially correct information. The Germans were supposed to have flattened the town of Guernica, causing massive civilian deaths; but in reality, they destroyed only half of the town (which was bad enough). Most of the civilian population had stayed out of the town because the Germans had already done the same thing to the town of Durango, which they bombed for four days previously. As Guernica was on a major crossroad and rail center through which Republican forces had to travel, and there was an important arms factory on its outskirts, most people avoided the town on that fateful market day when twenty-seven bombers and ten fighters attacked. Although the Germans failed to hit either the factory or any of the major bridges in the town, the attack was as much a demonstration to show that bombers were unstoppable, a premise, which we have seen the RAF and other air forces used in the inter-war period when designing their strategic and development plans.

The Germans used this attack to show the people at home and those in the rest of Europe the frightening efficiency and terror of their 'lightning war' machine to try to dissuade their neighbors from trying to put up any resistance. It was also used as an implied threat to their towns, cities, and civilian populations.

During the build-up of the air force, the Luftwaffe had developed six key aircraft that would prove their worth in Spain and be used against the rest of Europe, these were the:

Messerschmitt Bf 109E – A single-seat fighter powered by a Daimler Benz DB601 engine that gave it a maximum speed of 357mph (575kph).

It was armed with two 7.9mm machine guns on its engine crankcase and two 20mm cannons in its wings.

Messerschmitt Bf 110 – A two-seat, long-range fighter, powered by a two Daimler Benz DB601 engines that gave it a maximum speed of 349mph (563kph). It carried four 7.9mm machine guns and two 20mm cannons in its nose, and one 7.9mm hand-operated machine gun in the rear of the cockpit.

Junker Ju 78 'Stuka' – A two-seat dive-bomber, that was powered by a single Junker Jumo 211A engine that gave it a maximum speed of 232mph (374kph). It carried two 7.9mm guns in its wings and one reward-facing, hand-operated gun in the rear of the cockpit. It could carry a single 1,100lb (499kg) bomb under the center of its fuselage and two 110lb (50kg) bombs, one under each wing.

Junker Ju 88 – A medium bomber powered by two Junker Jumo 211B engines that gave it a maximum speed of 286mph (461kph). The crew of four comprised a single pilot and three gunners/navigators/bomb-aimers. It carried three 7.9mm machine guns mounted in the front and rear of the cockpit and one in the under-fuselage gondola. Its normal bomb load comprised 3,968lb (1,801kg) carried under its wings.

Heinkel He III – A medium bomber powered by two Daimler-Benz DB601A engines that gave it a maximum speed of 247mph (398kph). It was armed with three 7.9mm machine guns located in the nose, dorsal and ventral positions. It carried a crew of three, comprising a single pilot and two gunners/navigators/bomb-aimers. It was able to carry a bomb load of 4,410lb (2,002kg).

Dornier Do 17 – A sleek, medium bomber powered by two Bramo 323P engines, giving it a maximum speed of 265mph (427kph). It carried between four and eight 7.9mm machine guns in the front, rear, and middle of the aircraft. Its normal bomb load was 2,200lb (1,000kg) and it carried a crew of one pilot and four gunners/navigators/bomb-aimers.

Chapter 2

European Matters

Following the reoccupation of the Rhineland in March 1936 and the Anschluss (annexation) of Austria in March 1938, Hitler's ambitions in Europe were clear, but the rest of Europe, including Britain, were neither prepared nor had the desire to enter into another conflict so soon after the end of the First World War, which after all, had been the war to end all wars.

Everyone watched nervously as Germany continued to flex its muscles, but as we saw in chapter one, Britain did not sit back. The government ordered a rapid expansion of the Royal Air Force and Royal Navy, but this would take time.

Things came to a head during the Munich Crisis in September 1938, when Hitler made clear his intensions to annex the Sudetenland from Czechoslovakia to protect its German speaking communities in the north, southwestern, and southern parts of the country. British Prime Minister, Neville Chamberlain flew to Munich together with leaders from France and Italy to negotiate a compromise with Hitler. In the process, the borders of Czechoslovakia were redrawn in accordance with Hitler's wishes, and Chamberlain arrived home with his famous piece of paper—'peace for our time'—which signified the 'symbolic desire of our two people never to go to war with one another again' and 'a pledge to assure the peace of Europe.' This is usually portrayed as the actions of a Prime Minister prepared to give up everything for peace, but, as Robinson so rightly says, 'Chamberlain was an optimist but he was no fool. Peace was not the best policy, it was the *only* [his italics] policy' at that point in time.

In response, as we have seen, the Government decided to increase the rate of rearmament still further, but the peace did not last, as six months later and on 15 March 1939, the Germans invaded Czechoslovakia.

One of Germany's primary reasons for invading Czechoslovakia was the need to gain control of its natural resources. Although the Czechoslovakian armed forces had been mobilized, Hitler's threat to destroy Prague, using the same tactics—Blitzkrieg—that it had so vividly employed in Spain, led to Czechoslovakian capitulating.

Having faced no intervention from the British or French in the process of invading Czechoslovakia, the Germans turned their attention to Poland, where their armed forces crossed the border on 1 September. When German bombers were sent into Polish airspace, they caught the Poles still in the process of mobilizing. Even though bad weather prevented an all-out air attack on military and industrial targets, the Germans still managed to strike a significant blow. By 6 September, they were halfway to Warsaw, and when the weather cleared, large-scale attacks were not required. For, although the Polish Air Force fought fiercely against overwhelming odds with their largely outdated fighters, they could only do so for a couple of days. To make things worse, the Polish Army disintegrated in the face of the fast moving German forces. By the time that Poland had been defeated, their losses and casualties were a staggering, with 70,000 dead, a 133,000 wounded, and 700,000 taken prisoners of war.

Although the fight was short and ferocious, the Germans, and the Luftwaffe in particular, did not have everything their own way. As Robinson notes, even though the Polish airmen were flying old aircraft, they managed to shoot-down a total of five hundred and fourteen German aircraft, which included seventy-eight bombers, thirty-one Stukas, sixty-seven reconnaissance machines, twelve Bf 110s, and sixty-seven B f109s.

Having conquered Czechoslovakia and Poland, the Germans turned their attention to Western Europe.

On 7 April 1940, the Germans attacked Norway and Denmark without a declaration of war. Almost two months earlier, the *Altmark*, a German supply ship, carrying British prisoners of war captured by the pocket battleship *Admiral Graf Spee*, had been intercepted by ships of the Norwegian Navy in Norwegian waters. Having searched the ship three times, the Norwegians sent her on her way, only for her to be stopped whilst still in Norwegian waters by HMS *Cossack*. During this encounter, fighting broke out and was only stopped when the German crew were overwhelmed. On searching the ship, the British sailors found and released the prisoners. The ship was then allowed to continue its voyage.

The Norwegians were furious that Britain had boarded a ship in its territorial waters when they were trying to maintain their neutrality. The Germans were even more concerned because Swedish iron ore, which they desperately needed, and which was being shipped out of the Norwegian port of Narvik might also come under British control. In fact, they were importing something like 10,000,000 tons (10,160,469 tonnes) of iron ore from Sweden at the time.

The British Home Fleet, as part of *Operation Wilfred*, under the leadership of Admiral Sir Charles Forbes, set sail from Scapa Flow on 7 April, the same day that the first elements of the German invasion fleet put to sea, to lay mines between the Norwegian coast and its outer islands in an effort to prevent the Germans shipping out Swedish iron ore through Narvik. They also put in to place *Plan R 4* which involved occupying Narvik and other important locations, but this was overtaken a day later by *Operation Weserubung*—the German invasion of Norway, which was designed to secure their iron ore supplies. It would also give them access to Norwegian harbors and Fjords from which they could mount counter attacks on Britain shipping as part of their planned siege of the UK. Unfortunately, due to bad weather and misjudgment from those in London, the bulk of the British fleet failed to find the German ships. Although HMS *Glowworm* (a destroyer) attacked the German Heavy Cruiser *Admiral Hipper* before she received significant damage, at the which her captain then rammed the German ship, inflicting a 40m-rip in her side; *Glowworm* sank with the loss of 111 men. While going to *Glowworm's* rescue, HMS *Renown* (a British battlecruiser) encountered two German Battlecruisers, the *Scharnhorst* and *Gneisenau*.

Although the British rushed ships and aircraft to the country, the Germans quickly captured key Norwegian towns, cities, and ports, using paratroopers, fighters, bombers, and transport aircraft, but not everything went their way. During the attack on Oslo, the forts defending the harbor managed to sink the *Blucher*, one of the Germans Heavy Cruisers. Other losses included the *Karlsruhe* and *Konigsberg*, both Light Cruisers as well as eleven destroyers and eight submarines. A significant number of the Germans larger warships sustained damage that was sufficient to require an extended period in harbor for repairs. These included the three ships mentioned above as well as the Pocket Battleships *Lutzow* and *Admiral Sheer* which were also damaged, as were the Light Cruisers *Leipzig* and *Emden*. In fact, according to Murray, by the time operations were over, 'the German Navy had ceased to exist as an effective surface force.' They had one heavy cruiser, two light cruisers, and only four destroyers left in home waters, 'the remainder of the fleet was either at the bottom of the ocean or in dry dock undergoing repair.' He continues, 'The naval staff compounded the inevitable naval losses that went with such a campaign by what can only be categorized as strategic incompetence.' They were afraid that the war could be over before they had had the opportunity to show what their two Battlecruisers (*Gneisenau* and *Scharnhorst*) could do and so they made the fatal decision—following repairs—to send both ships out into the North Atlantic where they suffered sufficient damage to put them out of action until the following winter. Consequently, their absence during any invasion of Britain would have been significant.

Having secured their targets in Scandinavia, the Germans turned their attentions to Belgium and Holland, which they attacked on 10 May. As with Poland, both national air and ground forces were quickly overwhelmed; in fact, they effectively ceased to exist after the first day's fighting. The Germans also inflicted a significant amount of damage on RAF and French units in the area as well. By 13 May, the Germans had control of three vital bridges over the River Meuse. Bomber Command threw aircraft at the Germans and the remaining bridges in suicidal attempts to stop their advance. It was only when the Luftwaffe bombed Rotterdam with He 111 bombers that the Dutch Government surrendered.

Bruce Lewis's book, *Aircrew: The Story of the Men Who Flew the Bombers*, includes many stories of the heroism from the bomber crews, the following is typical. This relates to this early period of the conflict, when Bomber Command was fighting a desperate battle to stop or at least slow down the Germans advance. This incident follows the Germans first use of radar to intercept British bombers (see chapter 4) during which, half of the bombers were shot down:

'As a result of these disastrous set-backs, and in view of further tragic losses sustained during the short but hopeless Norwegian campaign the following April, a change of policy was forced on Bomber Command. It was vital to conserve the small number of bombers and the limited supply of crews then on squadron strength.

'On 12 May, 1940, the CO of 12 Squadron told his men that it was vital to destroy two large bridges that spanned the Albert Canal near Maastricht in Holland. This was the only chance of stemming the Wehrmacht's headlong advance. Making no bones of the fact that the mission was suicidal, he called for volunteers. Every pilot, observer and wireless operator/air gunner in the squadron stepped forward.

'Six crews were picked for the job. The [Fairey] Battles took off. In spite of intense opposition, one of the bridges was hit and partly destroyed. None of the aircraft returned from that mission.'

At the outbreak of the war, Fighter Command had only thirty-seven of the promised fifty-two squadrons to defend the UK. The government then sent four of them—numbers 1, 73, 85, and 87, all equipped with

Hurricanes—to France to help fight the Germans. Dowding was also instructed to bring a further six squadrons up to a mobile state in preparation for service in France. When the Germans invaded Norway, two more squadrons, numbers 46 with Hurricanes and 263 with Gloster Gladiators, were sent to help with its defense. Following the rapid defeat of Norway during which most of the Gladiators were lost, 46 Squadron was flown on to the aircraft carrier HMS *Glorious*, which was then sunk, losing all of the aircraft on board.

At a Cabinet meeting on 9 May, the government decided that Britain would be Germany's next target and therefore gave approval for an increase in both fighter and bomber production; they also decided to increase production of anti-aircraft guns. The following day, the Germans started their offensive against France, and the British government formed the Local Defense Volunteers (dad's army). Within six days, 250,000 men under the age of sixty-five had joined; and by mid-summer, this had grown to over 1,000,000. Eventually, they were given the far more familiar name, Home Guard, and swapped their armbands for uniforms. Most were still largely unarmed, except for tools and weapons they might have to hand. In his book, *A Nation Alone: The Battle of Britain 1940*, Arthur Ward explains that part of the Home Guard comprised a group of people known as 'auxiliaries.' These were men, such as gamekeepers, miners, woodsmen, fishermen, and poachers, all skilled in shooting and explosives, who were to hide and attack the Germans when they invaded. However, in *Churchill's Ministry of Ungentlemanly Warfare: The Mavericks Who Plotted Hitler's Defeat*, Giles Milton explains that these men actually formed into Auxiliary Units and were in fact highly trained specialists who had nothing to do with the Home Guard. They were established under a very secret organization originally known as MI(R), but later became MDI, and were directly answerable to Churchill, who had appointed himself Minister of Defense (even though there was no Ministry of Defense).

MI(R)/MDI specialized in inventing, developing, and building novel armaments for use in guerrilla warfare and then set up twelve guerrilla units to defend the British coast (which had been divided into twelve sectors). Each sector had its own geographical requirements, which meant that each unit comprised men with intimate knowledge of their own area and the skills required to operate within it. Each sector had its own field commander, with Peter Fleming (brother of Ian Fleming) in charge of the most important Kentish sector. Each unit was trained in the arts of sabotage, survival, and Guerrilla warfare with the aim that they would scatter and hide across the countryside and wait to ambush the enemy and their headquarters, following an invasion.

Ward writes that 'Many hideouts were constructed in the grounds of some of Britain's grandest homes, as experience in France had shown that German generals selected lavish accommodation for their command centres.' The men were then expected to lay in, wait, and attack from their hideouts. Milton describes how they were to inflict as much death and destruction on the invading Germans as possible before they were either killed or captured. Incidentally, after their offices in London were bombed, MDI moved in to 'The Firs,' a large manor house only 12 miles (19km) from Bletchley Park (another Leighton Buzzard connection). Churchill then established what he referred to as his Ministry of Ungentlemanly Warfare which combined MI(R) and the Whitehall department Section D (D for destruction); it's official name was the Special Operations Executive (SOE).

On 10 May, Churchill became Prime Minister, taking over from Neville Chamberlain. Although he was a member of the Conservative party, a significant proportion of the party disliked and did not trust him due to his rhetoric and past failures. They thought that he was a reactionary and many of them would have preferred Lord Halifax as Prime Minister. As we will see later, Churchill's position, at least in his first month in office was not entirely secure.

On 12 May, another four squadrons—numbers 3, 79, 501, 504 again equipped with invaluable Hurricanes—were sent to France to help in the desperate fighting. As Bowyer, together with virtually every other author points out, Dowding had already lost almost a third of his aircraft and 40% of his fighter pilots, trying to stop, or at least slow down the German advance.

By 13 May, Fighter Command had lost over two hundred Hurricanes in France. It was at this point that Dowding took one of his most important and dramatic decisions with regard to the outcome of the Battle of Britain that everyone was now expecting following battles on the continent. Bowyer relates that Dowding requested the opportunity to talk directly to the Cabinet to be able to state his case for the prevention of any more of his fighters being directed to, and lost on the continent in defense of the French. He knew that if and when France was to fall, he would need as many defensive fighters as possible to defend this country.

The meeting took place on 15 May in the Cabinet Room in Downing Street. Sitting next to Churchill, and following the Prime Minister's assessment of the situation in France, Dowding presented his case for not sending any more of his precious fighters to help in the defense of that country. As the meeting progressed, Dowding felt that neither the Prime

Minister nor the other people present had grasped the seriousness of the situation, so he presented a graph that he had made earlier that day at his Head Quarters at Bentley Priory. This showed the number of fighters that had already been lost and what the situation it would be if losses continued at the same rate. As he placed the graph in front of Churchill, Bowyer records that he said, 'If the present wastage continues for another fortnight we shall not have a single Hurricane left in France *or in this country*' [Bowyer's italics]. He then sat down 'while Churchill sat glaring at the graph. It brooked no argument. Dowding had been forced to fight his case alone; the Chief of Air Staff, Newell, and other Air Ministry representatives present took no part in the discussion.'

To emphasize what he had said and to try to make sure that Churchill and the Cabinet did not change their minds, he sent the following letter on 16 May:

'Sir

I have the honour to refer to the very serious calls which have recently been made upon the Home Defence Fighter Units in an attempt to stem the German invasion on the Continent.

I hope and believe that our Armies may yet be victorious in France and Belgium, but we have to face the possibility that they may be defeated.

In this case, I presume that there is no-one who will deny that England should fight on, even though the remainder of the Continent of Europe is dominated by the Germans.

For this purpose, it is necessary to retain some minimum fighter strength in this country and I must request that the Air Council will inform me what they consider this minimum strength to be, in order that I may make my dispositions accordingly.

I would remind the Air Council that the last estimate which they made as to the force necessary to defend this country was 52 Squadrons, and my strength has now been reduced to the equivalent of 36 Squadrons.

Once a decision has been reached as to the limit on which the Air Council and the Cabinet are prepared to stake the existence of the country, it should be made clear to the Allied commanders on the Continent that not a single aeroplane from Fighter Command beyond the limit will be sent across the Channel, no matter how desperate the situation may become.

It will, of course, be remembered that the estimate of 52 Squadrons was based on the assumption that the attack would come from the eastwards except in so far as the defences might be outflanked in flight. We have now to face the possibility that attacks may come from Spain or even from the north coast of France. The result is that our line is very much extended at the same time as our resources are reduced.

I must point out that within the last few days the equivalent of 10 Squadrons have been sent to France, that the Hurricane Squadrons remaining in this country are seriously depleted, and that the more Squadrons which are sent to France the higher will be the wastage and the more insistent the demand for reinforcements.

I must therefore request that as a matter of paramount urgency the Air Ministry will consider and decide what level of strength is to be left to the Fighter Command for the defences of this country, and will assure me that when this level has been reached, not one fighter will be sent across the Channel however urgent and insistent the appeals for help may be.

I believe that, if an adequate fighter force is kept in this country, if the fleet remains in being, and if Home Forces are suitably organised to resist invasion, we should be able to carry on the war single-handed for some time, if not indefinitely. But if the Home Defence Force is drained away in desperate attempts to remedy the situation in France, defeat in France will involve the final, complete and irremediable defeat of this country.

I have the honour to be,

Sir,

Your obedient Servant,

H.C.T. Dowding,

Air Chef Marshal,

Air Officer Commanding-in-Chief Fighter command, Royal Air Force.'

Having said and done all of this to try to ensure that Fighter Command was not bled dry in France, Dowding found out that his fears were well founded, because even as he was driving back to Bentley Priory, the Cabinet reverse their decision and requested that four more squadrons be sent to France. In response, Deputy Chief of Air Staff Shotto Douglas sent eight flights (twenty-four aircraft) instead.

The following day, during a visit to France, Churchill requested that a further six should be sent to the continent even though there were neither the airfields nor the facilities there to support them. Finally, even though he had not backed Dowding at the previous day's meeting, Air Staff Cyril Newell, the Chief of Air Staff, decided to move only six flights of fighters to forward airfields along the south coast so that could operate over France and return to their airfields each day.

Following his return from the meeting in Paris, and having read Dowdings letter, Churchill decided that no more fighters would be sent to help defend France.

Although Dowding may have felt that Newell had not backed him in the crucial meeting with Churchill and his cabinet, it was Newell's overall responsibility to look after the needs of both the air force and the army in France, and it was his ultimate backing for Dowding's request which helped win the debate, together with the speed at which the Germans overran France, Belgium, and Holland.

Up to the end of the evacuation of Dunkirk (see below), the equivalent of twenty squadrons of fighters, a total of four hundred and thirty-two aircraft, had been lost in France, leaving Dowding only four hundred and forty-six operational aircraft to mount a defense of the country; and if the Germans attacked immediately, only three hundred and thirty of these were Hurricanes or Spitfires.

Before we look briefly at the historic evacuation of the British Expeditionary Force (BEF) from Dunkirk and its implications for the defense of the UK, it is worth returning to the position of Churchill and Lord Halifax just before and during the first part of the evacuation. In his book *Five Days in London May 1940*, John Lukacs provides a really interesting insight into the operation of the War Cabinet and the options open to it, as well as the 'power struggle' between Halifax and Churchill. Does this matter? As Lukacs says, 'the five days are from Friday through Tuesday, 24 to 28 May. Then and there Adolf Hitler came closest to winning the Second World War.'

When Churchill took over from Chamberlain, he did so because the Conservative Party did not want Chamberlain to do anything else that would make the situation worse. As we have seen above, Churchill was pro-French and Chamberlain was, to some extent, pro-German, as were many of the aristocracy and upper classes. The government was well aware of the situation on the continent, as were governments further afield. On 24 May, President Roosevelt wrote to the Prime Minister of Canada suggesting that Canada and the Dominions should press Churchill to send the British Fleet across the Atlantic before Hitler's peace terms could include it. Churchill had written to Roosevelt on 21 May about the possible situation if Britain were defeated.

The following day, during a meeting of the highest council in Paris, General Weygand said that the French should not have joined in a war that they were not prepared to fight in. Remember, Britain and France had an agreement to stand together. There had already been contact between the French and Italians about the possibility of Italy acting as an intermediary with Hitler. Italy had not joined the war at this point. During a War Cabinet, Halifax was given permission to talk to the Italian Ambassador about Britain-Italian relationships within a general European settlement that included Germany.

At just before 7 a.m. on Sunday, 26 May, the order to begin the evacuation of Dunkirk—*Operation Dynamo*—was given. Two hours later, Churchill held a War Cabinet; this was much earlier than usual. The day had been designated as a National Day of Prayer. A delegation from the French Government arrived in London and Halifax met the Italian Ambassador. The War Cabinet was made fully aware of the bad news from France and to add even more gloom to the situation they were also told that the Belgian King was about to surrender the country to Germany. The Belgian Government moved to Paris intending to continue the fight. It was clear that an evacuation of the BEF would have to be mounted, but that there was no guarantee of success, in fact, the prospects of evacuating only a few of the solders seemed a reality.

A few days earlier Churchill had asked the Chiefs of Staff to consider what would happen if France dropped out of the war. Their response, titled 'British Strategy in a Certain Eventuality' concluded that Britain could continue the fight if the RAF and Royal Navy could remain in control over Britain, and if the USA would support us.

During the third War Cabinet of the day, the position of France was again discussed, and Lord Halifax outlined the likely outcomes of talks with Italy. It was thought that Hitler would impose unlimited term on Britain if we gave up without a fight. Halifax also thought that it would be foolish not to accept terms if they guaranteed Britain's independence, but Churchill thought that whatever the outcome, if we gave up without a fight we would surely lose our independence. As Lukacs says, 'in the last days of May 1940 the fate of Britain—indeed the outcome of the Second World War—depended on two things. One was the division between Churchill and Halifax. The other was the destiny of the British Army crowding back into Dunkirk.'

At 4:30 p.m. on Monday, 27 May, the second War Cabinet of the day was one of the crucial meetings during the four days. Halifax decided that he had to confront Churchill. He said that the British should make contact with Mussolini to discuss his 'Suggested Approach.' Churchill disagreed, saying that Britain should stand by France rather than negotiate around her, and so rejected Halifax's ideas completely.

With the publics shock at the surrender of Belgium and the dawning realization of the situation of the British Expeditionary Force (BEF) in France, during the War Cabinet on the morning of 28 May, Churchill agreed

178

to make a statement in Parliament about Dunkirk. Having spoken in Parliament about the grave situation in the town and harbor, and the evacuation of the troops, he then called another War Cabinet at 4 p.m. During this meeting, Churchill said that he was afraid that the French would try to draw Britain into negotiations with Hitler before they would have to surrender so that they could end the war and remain independent. Churchill considered this to be a 'slippery slope' from which Britain could not get away. Before ending the meeting at 5 p.m., Churchill said that the War Cabinet would meet again at 7 p.m. He then called a meeting of the wider 'Outer Cabinet,' during which he said that Britain would not negotiate with Hitler and that it would be better to fight on rather than lose control of the Royal Navy plus 'much else,' and end up being a slave state with a puppet government. During the reconvened War Cabinet, Churchill outlined what he had just said at the lager meeting, and got the War Cabinets full backing. Halifax tried one last vein attempt to try to persuade them that they should make an appeal to the USA, but Churchill said that it would be better to stand against Germany and command America's admiration. They should fight on no matter what the outcome of the evacuation at Dunkirk would be. Churchill was now in control and the backing for Halifax diminished.

The Germans continued to push the Allied forces back until they reached the outskirts of Dunkirk on the north French coast, when, to everyone's surprise, Hitler ordered them to stop. A number of reasons have been put forward for this dramatic move, it might have been to allow Britain to pull its troops out in the hope that they would accept Hitler's peace terms; that the German Army needed to consolidate its forces having pushed so hard and so fast across the country; it might also be that Hitler called it so that the army could conserve and reorganize its forces ready to capture the rest of France. One thing is certain; Goering had assured him that Luftwaffe could finish off the British and French on its own, without the army. In reality the Luftwaffe actually faced its first serious air battles since Spain and, for the first time, it was fighting against at least some modern fighters.

Dunkirk then was one of the most critical times in British Army history, if the troops were not evacuated from France and had been taken prisoner of war, we would have been left in an impossible situation. In his book, *Dunkirk: The Necessary Myth*, Nicholas Harman separates fact from fiction, and makes the following observations:

'It became clear that, as with all good working myths, parts of the traditional Dunkirk story are true. The truth of the other parts is poetic rather than literal. In particular I struggled for a while to substantiate the familiar belief that an armada of civilian "little" ships' played a significant part in the rescue of the army. The little ships operated only on the last two days of the British evacuation, and then to very little effect. Civilian volunteers could not come forward earlier, since the whole affair was kept from the public until three-quarters of the army was safe at home.'

Operation Dynamo, the code name for the withdrawal of troops from Dunkirk began on 26 May 1940 and lasted until first light on 4 June. The person responsible for organizing the evacuation was Admiral Bertram Ramsay; he expected to be able rescue as many as 45,000 troops, but by 29 May 72,000 British troops had already been evacuated using British and French channel ferries guarded by warships from both nations. This meant that within three days, one third of the British Army had already been rescued from France, primarily from the harbor at Dunkirk and not from the beaches which were too shallow for even small craft to come in close enough for the troops to reach. In fact, 30 May was the only day on which more troops were evacuated from the beaches than from the harbor. The following day they managed to rescue a fifth of the total number of soldiers evacuated and it was at that point that they proposed giving up on the idea of rescuing people off the beaches.

It is interesting to note that it was not until the BBC 6 o'clock news that evening (31 May) that the British people were first told about the evacuation; it had been a complete secret until then. Following the public announcement civilian volunteers began to come forward and a further 26,000 were rescued from the beaches.

In total 186,587 British and 124,999 French troops were rescued, of which only 18,575 troops were rescued by civilian volunteers from the beaches. More than 200,000 French and 50,000 British soldiers were left to hold the perimeter of the town against the Germans whilst the evacuation took place, and these were later captured by the Germans. The French saw the 'abandonment' of so many of their troops whilst they held 'the line' as a disgrace, but again as Harman shows:

'In the end, despite what the French saw as the great British betrayal of their allies, the vast majority of both armies got away to England. Well before the end the Germans had given up their attempts to take the town by their main force, or to frustrate the evacuation. Their best soldiers, and their entire modern Air Force, were transferred to the more important operation of advancing on Paris and bringing all France to its knees.

Dunkirk became a sideshow. The rescue of the last tens of thousands of French soldiers proved pointless, since none of them got back into the fighting before the order by their government to surrender.'

Following the arrival back in Britain the army was in a desperate state. They had left almost all of their equipment in France including 2,472 guns, 63,879 vehicles, including four hundred and forty-five tanks (only twenty-two made it home), 20,558 motorcycles and half a ton of stores; many soldiers arrived home without even their uniforms. Only the two divisions that had arrived back from Brittany came home with their equipment largely intact. With so much basic equipment missing, the army was in no fit state to provide an adequate defensive force if the Germans were to continue their advance across the Channel. Of the nearly 125,000 French troops rescued from Dunkirk, most disembarked in either Southampton or Weymouth. When General de Gaulle offered those who had arrived in the UK a choice of either remaining here to fight with the Free French Army or return home, all but two hundred of them sailed for home.

In addition to the soldiers rescued from Dunkirk, a further 4,000 were recovered from Boulogne and 1,000 from Calais.

It was often thought, by the troops trapped on the ground that the RAF had abandoned them, but this was again a false observation. Bomber Command put a great deal of effort and sacrificed numerous aircraft and, more importantly, aircrew, in bombing German forces well behind the British and French lines. Equally, with all of his remaining fighters now back in Britain, Keith Park, and 11 Group, endeavored to maintain, when weather permitted, almost continuous air cover above and behind the beaches. He tried his best, at first, to send individual squadrons in to theatre, with replacements taking over as fuel ran low, but he soon discovered that single squadrons were relatively ineffective and vulnerable to the large numbers of German aircraft attacking the beaches, town, and harbor. He then decided that it would prove more effective to lengthen the gaps between standing patrols so that he could increase the numbers of squadrons in the air at the same time. He started with two squadrons and eventually increased this to units of four squadrons operating together.

Hough and Richards report that during the evacuation, the RAF flew one hundred and seventy-one reconnaissance, six hundred and fifty-one bomber, and 2,739 fighter sorties over Dunkirk and the surrounding area; and during the operation, they lost ninety-eight Hurricanes and Spitfires. Park was only allowed to use up to eighteen squadrons each day. And by the end of the evacuation, all but three of Fighter Command's squadrons had taken part in the operation, giving their pilots invaluable flying and fighting experience. (The term Sortie is derived from the French word for exit and is used for the deployment of a military unit, in this case a single aircraft flight, from a defensive strongpoint to mount an attack.)

The Luftwaffe also lost a significant number of aircraft and, more importantly, experienced aircrew during the fight. By the time that France surrendered, the Luftwaffe had lost around 1,389 aircraft of all types since the start of their invasion of Poland and the RAF had lost nine hundred and fifty aircraft, or almost half of its front-line strength. Of these, Fighter Command lost four hundred and fifty-five Hurricanes in France, of which three hundred and seventy-eight were either destroyed on the ground or had to be abandoned as non-airworthy. At the same time, the Luftwaffe lost three hundred and sixty-seven fighters, most of which were Bf 109s, their main front-line fighters.

The rotation of fighter squadrons through 11 Group not only gave many more pilots invaluable experience, it proved to be a key strategy that would be used throughout the coming Battle of Britain, which differed significantly from Goering's approach. Dowding would continuously rotate his squadrons so that pilots who had been in combat were moved to airfields away from most of the action to be able to rest, re-equip, and if necessary rebuild ready to enter the fray again. German pilots had to remain in frontline operations until they were either captured, wounded, died or were promoted and moved away.

The disparity comes back once again to the fact that the two sides had a completely different view of the war. Hitler wanted; or rather needed, a quick victory so that he could turn his attention to Russia, and Goering put virtually all of his best aircraft and aircrew in to front-line operations, keeping very few in reserve. In other words, the Germans were betting on, and had planned for, a short, sharp fight, similar to their previous successes. Britain had been planning for a lengthy conflict, which meant that Fighter Command had to make sure that it had the reserves of aircraft and, if possible pilots, to spread the load, without exhausting either.

On 14 May, the British Government formed the Ministry of Aircraft Production under the leadership of Lord Beaverbrook. It focused on the production of Spitfires and Hurricanes, together with three different bomber types. This had an immediate effect, as by June, planned production of the two fighters had been two hundred and sixty-one airframes whereas the aircraft industry actually turned out three hundred and twenty-five airplanes. In July and August, planned production had been six hundred and eleven while they produced nine hundred and seventy-two airplanes. British fighter production was usually double the rate of the Germans. Total fighter production for the two sides gives some indication of how prepared they both were for the forth-coming battle; in 1940, German aircraft industry produced 3,382 Bf 109s and Bf 110s, while the British built 4,283 single-seat fighters.

The principle fighters on both sides were short-range aircraft, which meant that Goering had to largely restrict his bombers to attacking the southeast of England where he could provide some fighter protection, or allow them to range further afield to attack RAF bases, aircraft factories and the like unprotected. Dowding could afford to keep many of his fighters out of reach of the Luftwaffe and, even if things became too hot in 11 Group, he could pull those squadrons back north of London and still be able to fight. He also had a sizable reserve, which was continuously being bolstered by increased aircraft production and the repair organizations. His only restriction would be the number of pilots he had available.

But this is still in the future; let us turn our attention back to Dunkirk. What was the outcome of the Luftwaffe's attempt to bomb the troops on the beaches and harbor? Goering had urged Hitler to let the Luftwaffe take care of Dunkirk, but fog kept many of his aircraft confined to their bases for three days and even when his bombers were able to attack the troops concentrated in the harbor, town and on the beaches, they suffered significant losses at the hands of Fighter Command. Even his beloved Stukas had problems, as many of their bombs just buried themselves in the sand so that it either reduced the effectiveness the explosions or prevented them from exploding completely.

They also faced additional problems. In spite of the higher accuracy of dive bombing attacks which Goering and his staff had made a priority when planning the development of the Luftwaffe, hitting the small boats, or even the larger ships proved more difficult than had been anticipated. The RAF, who had not followed the same philosophy, would have found it even more difficult to bomb the German invasion barges, tugs and steamers, had they set sail during any invasion attempt.

On 27 May, at the height of the evacuation, with an eye on the Germans next move, the British Chiefs of Staff decided that their main priority was to prevent the Luftwaffe gaining air superiority over the Channel and Southern England; a pre-requisite for an invasion.

Even though Inspector General of the Luftwaffe Milch thought that the British were now in such a weak position and had convinced Goering that an invasion should take place at once, Hitler thought Britain would settle for peace. He wanted the Luftwaffe to 'teach the British a lesson' and is recorded as telling his valet: "It is always good to let a broken army return home to show the civilian populations what a beating they have had." Hitler said to someone else that "the blood of every single Englishman is too valuable to shed. Our two people belong together, racially and traditionally—this is and always has been my aim even if our generals can't grasp it."

It appears that Hitler could not make up his mind as to what he wanted to do with Britain, and, as was his nature, he was telling different people different stories. As we have seen, it appears that he thought Britain would accept his peace terms, and, as we shall see, following the surrender of France, he went on holiday. Perhaps this was one way in which he could stall his Army and Air Force leaders from their push to keep going?

With the overrun of France, one of the biggest questions left unanswered, was what would become of the French Navy, which comprised the second largest fleet in Europe after the Royal Navy?

On 3 July, *Force H* of the Royal Navy under the command of Vice Admiral Somerville, comprising the Battlecruiser HMS *Hood*, two Battleships HMS *Valiant* and HMS *Resolution* together with the Aircraft Carrier HMS *Ark Royal*; two Cruisers, HMS *Arethusa* and HMS *Enterprise*; and 11 Destroyers, arrived at the Algerian port of Mers-el-Kebir. Their mission, code-named *Operation Catapult* was to persuade the commander of the French ships anchored there to either surrender their ships to the British, scuttle them or, as a last resort for the British ships would sink them.

Previously, Admiral Darlan, the Minister of Marine had sent messages to the French Navy across the globe that in the event of a French surrender, their commanders were to either sail for America or prepare to scuttle their ships to prevent them falling in to German hands. He added that, following the issue of these orders, they were to accept no other orders, including his, from any other admiralty. So when Somerville arrived with orders for the commanders of the French ships to either join the British, disable their ships, or sail for the West Indies, they ignored him.

The French remained in harbor all day, until, at 5:54 p.m., when the British opened fire. They hit the Battlecruiser *Dunkerque*, causing the crew to beach her but not before she managed to fire off a couple of shots at HMS *Hood*. The *Strasbourg*, the other Battlecruiser in harbor, was also hit but managed to escape. Later, she was struck by two torpedoes launched from HMS *Ark Royal's* Swordfish and limped in to Toulon, where she was scuttled two years later. These were significant loses, as both battlecruisers were more powerful that the *Scharnhorst* and *Gneisenau* and the only ship in the Royal Navy that could match their speed was HMS *Hood*.

The action at Mers-el-Kebir lasted less than an hour, as Herman vividly describes, 'before the smoke clearer, the bulk of the French naval power at Mers-el-Kebir was either aflame or at the bottom of the sea.' Of the two battleships, *Bretagne* was hit, blew up, and capsized, and the *Provence* was so badly damaged that she was left as a wreck. The airplane carrier *Commandant Teste* tried to make a break for safety with the *Strasbourg*. At the end of this brief but decisive action, 1,297 French sailors were dead. Whilst the attack was taking place, French ships including the battleships *Courbuet* and *Paris*, which were moored in British ports were also seized. Those in the West Indies were disabled. The Battleship *Richelieu*, berthed in Dakar, was attacked and put out of action. Those in the port of Alexandria, which included three battleships and a light cruiser, agreed to disarm.

According to Robinson, this action, known as 'the deadly stroke' at Oran 'amazed and impressed the whole world.' It may have been one of the reasons why, in spite of Hitler' pressure, both Spain and Turkey stayed out of the war. It certainly made an impression on the Americans who 'discovered a fearlessness and a ferocity in Britain that dissolved all those stories of a nation on its knees, helpless before a looming invader... The deadly stroke had been the most powerful form of propaganda. If Britain was prepared to do this to her ally, what might she do to her enemy?' And what was Hitler's reaction, he 'went ballistic' and then went to the Eagles Nest in the Austrian Alps for sixteen 'days of inaction.' For more information about this dramatic episode in Royal Navy history, it is worth reading Warren Tate's excellent book *The Deadly Stroke*.

Following Dunkirk, and having taken the French Navy out of the equation, Churchill felt that as long as the country and Fighter Command could withstand the expected bombing, whilst Bomber and Coastal Commands, together with the Royal Navy could delay the expected invasion for three months, the country could keep going indefinitely.

One of the big questions that has been asked ever since the completion of the evacuation at Dunkirk has been: why, having pushed so far and so fast across the continent did the Germans effectively stop and let the British get away? To try to find the answer, we need to look at how and why the Germans were preparing and planning an invasion of Britain.

Chapter 3

Preparing for Invasion

I think an appropriate way to begin our look at the German and British preparations for invasion could be based around a quote from Robinson when he says that there are 'Two powerful myths. The first is that Fighter Command alone prevented an invasion. The second is that an invasion force would inevitably have conquered Britain. Both untrue.' The reason for including this here is to put the rest of this chapter in to context. No matter what Robinson infers, Fighter Command was not and had never been designed to, nor asked to prevent an invasion. Their task was to prevent the Luftwaffe from gaining air superiority over Southern England, a job they achieved.

Robinson claims that the Luftwaffe gained air superiority over the Channel for brief period, which is not strictly true. As we shall see, the Royal Navy withdrew some of its ships and diverted convoys away from the area due to heavy bombing. We will also see that Fighter Command were not driven from the skies above the Channel, but avoided flying over it and to conserve their strength they avoided unnecessary combat over the sea.

It was not Fighter Command's job to stop an invasion, that would have been the responsibility of Bomber Command, Coastal Command, and the Royal Navy, but it would have been their job to provide fighter cover, no matter what the cost. With regard to the 'other myth,' as we shall see, the Germans would have struggled to achieve an invasion; but, as with the Spanish Armada and the Spanish invasion plans, from the British point of view, we could not afford to take that for granted, even if we had known it at the time.

When the Germans began their invasion of Western Europe, the Fuhrer's '*Directive Number 6*,' titled 'for the Conduct of War,' stated that the purpose of the conflict was to defeat the Allied armies, and secure as much land in Northern Europe to be able to mount an air and sea campaign, and a blockade, against Britain. As we have seen, at the time Hitler was not considering an invasion as he was convinced that Britain had neither the forces, equipment, nor the appetite for war. The capture of Norway, which gave him access to harbors and airfields in Norway, further tipped the balance in Germany's favor. As Robinson puts it, following Dunkirk, as far as Hitler was concerned, he thought that 'the British won't come back from this.' We were on our own, and Hitler was convinced that the Americans would not help, and that the Commonwealth countries were too far away to offer any assistance. But the destruction of the French Navy sent out a clear message, to which the Americans and Canadians responded.

Having steamrollered their way through Belgium, Holland, and Northern France, the Germans stopped! Why did they not continue their push and strike England straight away? It appears that the speed of the German victory caught them as much by surprise as it did the British and her European allies. Although the Blitzkrieg is famous for the Panzer divisions, most of the German Army were infantry soldiers who usually traveled on foot, as they had only a limited number of motorized transports. Equally, the majority of their artillery guns and supplies were still pulled by horses. To be able to consolidate their gains in Northern Europe and be able to take control of the rest of France, they needed to stop to establish their supply lines and new bases, and to give their troops some rest. The Luftwaffe had similar problems; they too had to establish, reorganize, and equip airfields in Northern France, and reorganize their air fleets in France and Norway ready to fight the RAF. The English Channel and the North Sea posed a new element to the way they could operate which they had not had to face so far.

At the same time, it appears that Hitler had gone on holiday and Goering was enjoying himself in France. Hitler left for his headquarters in the Black Forest on 22 June and stayed there until 11 July. He still appears to have wanted a peace deal with Britain, but to help push us in the right direction, he decided that the Luftwaffe should destroy the RAF. He also wanted the Luftwaffe to mount a bombing campaign designed to destroy our food stores, bring terror to our streets, and maintain a siege on the country. If these measures failed, his last option would be a full-scale invasion.

At a meeting between Grand Admiral Raeder and Hitler on 20 June, before Hitler went on holiday, the admiral put forward his plans not—as Robinson says—because he thought the German Navy was capable to mounting an invasion, but 'to be ready to pre-empt any stupid proposals from elsewhere.' The Admiral told Hitler that the navy had no ships available with which to mount an invasion, and no landing craft. He did, however think that within a couple of weeks he might be able to scrape together up to forty-five river barges, which would be nowhere near enough to mount an invasion, but they were at least a start. When they met again on 11 July, at Hitler's Eagles Nest, in the Austrian Alps, Raeder told him again that the navy did not have the resources to mount an invasion. He said that to do so would risk the effectiveness of the few operational ships he still had available to mount an effective blockade on Britain. However, two days later, Hitler met with the von Brauchitsch, Commander-in-Chief of the Army, who was keen to build on its successes. He wanted to mount an invasion as soon as possible. He presented Hitler with a plan that would see three separate attack groups cross the Channel to land along a 225-mile (360km) front along the English Channel, stretching from Ramsgate in the southeast to Lyme Bay in Dorset in the southwest. One attack group would set out from Calais, another from Le Havre, and a third from Cherbourg. This would involve more than 500,000 soldiers, 1,000s of horses, and hundreds of tanks. The Army viewed the task as equivalent to 'a mighty river crossing'; Hitler approved the plan immediately.

The Navy were stunned by both the decision and the plan. They had neither the ships, barges, nor the manpower to mount and protect such a large crossing, and Raeder said that he could only support such a plan if the front were reduced to less than 50 miles (80km), for example from Folkestone to Beachy Head. There was, therefore, a fundamental mismatch in the basic requirements of the two services; the army needed a wide front to be able to succeed whilst the navy needed a narrow one that they could defend. In the end, a compromise was reached whereby the front would be 80 miles (120km) wide.

The final invasion plan involved four fleets sailing from six different ports:

Fleet B would sail from Rotterdam, Ostend, and Dunkirk, with hundred tugs or trawlers towing two hundred barges towards the English coast between Folkestone and Dungeness.

Fleet C would comprise another hundred trawlers or tugs with two hundred barges, together with fifty-seven steamers towing an additional one hundred and fourteen barges, which would set sail from Calais and would land between Rye and Hastings.

Fleet D would set out from Boulogne and head for Hastings and Eastbourne with one hundred and sixty-five tugs or trawlers towing three hundred and fifty barges.

Finally, Fleet E would set out from Le Havre with two hundred motor boats and one hundred motorized sailboats, heading for Brighton. An additional twenty-five tugs or trawlers with fifty more barges would meet up with Fleet D in the Channel.

To protect these, the German Navy had only six destroyers based in Cherbourg and another two at Flushing.

One of the basic problems with each of these plans was that Hitler, rather like Philip of Spain in 1588, was in total control and kept his ideas to himself. He would not allow anyone else to try to co-ordinate such a vast operation. Because of this, each service, army, navy and air force, went their own way, and rarely, if ever, talked to each other, and, when they did speak, it was with 'forked tongues.'

Hitler was back in Berlin by 19 June, when he addressed a meeting of the Reichstag in which he said that, 'a great empire will be destroyed, an empire which was never my intention to destroy or harm.' This has a similar ring to the prophesy of Dr. John Dee in 1588, that one empire would rise whilst another would fall.

On 30 June, Goering signed an operational directive for war against England. The Luftwaffe's targets were to be Fighter and Bomber commands airfields together with armament and aircraft production factors. However, most of these targets were north and west of London and therefore, they would be relatively immune to large-scale bombing, particularly if the bombers needed fighter protection.

On 16 July, Hitler approved a directive (*number 16*) to his High Command to start preparations for a possible landing operation against England, code-named *Sealion*. He still hoped that Britain would accept his terms for a peace, but with no response to his settlement proposals, he confirmed his intention to invade England. Hitler thought that even though Britain was in a hopeless position it was not going to opt for his peace plans, he therefore decided to proceed with his invasion plans. Milton explains that 'The plans were meticulous—far more so than the Norwegian invasion.' It included the use of death squads to round up around 3,000 'notable people.' Britain's 300,000 Jews were to be interned 'with a darker fate awaiting them,' and 'all able-bodied men between the ages of 17 to 45 were' also 'to be interned and then transported to the continent.'

Operation Sealion was extremely ambitious given that the Germans had not tried to launch such an operation before and appeared to lack many of the resources necessary to mount an invasion on any realistic scale. The projected date for the completion of all preparations for invasion was set for mid-August, only a month away, but one of the preconditions for any invasion to take place was for the Luftwaffe to gain air superiority over Southern England.

During the fighting in May, the Luftwaffe lost a total of 1,044 aircraft, including one hundred forty-seven Bf 109s and eight-two twin-engined Bf 110s. In June they lost a further hundred Bf 109s and twenty-six Bf 110s; these losses, over a two month period were equivalent to 15% of their total number of fighters. They also lost six hundred forty-three bombers over the same timescale.

By mid-August, the Luftwaffe reported a total strength of 1,610 bombers, and 1,155 fighters, which were divided in to five Luftflotten. Luftflottes I and IV were kept back for defense of Germany, Luftflotte II was based in Northeastern France and the Low Countries, Luftflotte III was based in Northwest France, and Luftflotte V was based in Norway. The latter three air groups, II, III, and V, comprised a total of 2,800 aircraft of which 1,800 were bombers. Although these totals look impressive, and were similar to the figures the British had for the German strength, all was not as it seemed. The Luftwaffe had significant serviceability problems, and could only count on the availability of some nine hundred and forty-four bombers of all types, and eight hundred and twenty-four fighters, including both Bf 109s and Bf 110s. Against this, Fighter Command had around six hundred fighters, but this included Boulton Paul Defiants, Gloster Gladiators, and Bristol Blenheims fitted with gun packs. These were divided amongst the four Fighter Command Groups with seven squadrons in 10 Group, nineteen squadrons in 11 Group, fourteen squadrons in 12 Group, and twelve squadrons in 13 Group.

Unfortunately, although the Luftwaffe thought that they could take on Fighter Command and defeat it, the German Army were only playing a bit part now that the continent was secure, and the German Navy had suffered significant losses during their Norwegian campaign that they could not realistically support an invasion. It would therefore fall on the Luftwaffe to take the brunt of the action for the time being. Of course, Goering would have had it no other way; his over confidence, even arrogance, ensured that the Luftwaffe would take up the mantle. Unfortunately, he was not the same kind of leader as Dowding; he had not been intimately involved in its development and was not concerned with the day-to-day running of 'his' air force. As John Ray adds in *The Battle of Britain: Dowding and the First Victory, 1940*, he did not have a grasp of the 'logistics, strategy, aircraft capabilities, technology, and engineering—in other words, just about everything to do with air power.'

Hitler was equally to blame, for as Ray explains, he 'never demonstrated wide awareness of the value of either air fleets or navies; subsequently the waters of the Channel proved too great an obstacle for his land-based, military thinking.' He adds that 'in a sense, the defeat of Britain was a side show...at this stage his mind was divided between the two objectives, and settling with Britain never held the monopoly of attention required for the success of such a venture.' The other objective was the invasion and conquest of Russia.

On 30 July, Hitler told Goering to speed-up his preparations for the defeat of the RAF in preparation for an invasion. The following day he said that *Operation Sealion* must be ready to sail by 15 September, a month later than originally planned; it was later put back to 21 September. By then, the army was prepared, and the Navy had miraculously put together the invasion fleet even if it did not have the capital ships to defend it. He also wanted *Eagle Attack*, the start of the destruction of the RAF, to begin by 5 August— an operation he expected to take between eight and fourteen days to complete. Goering had said that he could wipe out the RAF in two weeks. This later changed to a prediction that the Luftwaffe would be able to defeat Fighter Command in four days and it would then take another four weeks to finish off the rest of the RAF and the British aircraft industry.

Goering had planned five days of fighting and bombing within an area of between 100–150km south and east of London, followed by three days of operations 50–100km outside London, and finally, a further five days of action within a 50km circle around the capital itself. German Intelligence estimated that the RAF had between four hundred and five hundred fighters in Southern England which the Luftwaffe were expected to destroy within the timescale set. Their aim was to gain control of the skies over the southeast, which meant destroying all of Fighter Command's aircraft in that area. One of the problems the Germans faced was that if Fighter Command losses became too great, they could always pull their aircraft back to the North and West of London, a move that would have taken them out of range of the Luftwaffe's fighters. It would also have caused Fighter Command significant delays in their reaction times and reduced their effective range, and increased their flying time. Dowding would have been most reluctant to do this. All that the Luftwaffe could realistically do was fight a war of attrition with Fighter Command, a game Dowding was astute enough to avoid.

The final plans for the start of air operations, *Eagle Day*, were completed by 6 August but bad weather initially delayed the expected start date until 8 then 10, it finally began on 13 August. Even then, as we shall see in chapter 6, fog and cloud prevented the launch of the planned large-scale air raids. The Luftwaffe were short of fuel and spare parts, they also had only two hundred and sixty-five Ju 52s, their main transport aircraft. They were short of pilots due to losses sustained during the fighting so far and had to draft inexperienced pilots from training units to replace them. They were also short of steel and bombs, so Hitler decided that they should build concrete bombs and fill them with shrapnel. Robinson records that 'When war came, 20% of the bomber units, 30% of the Stuka units, and at least 50% of the fighter units were seriously below strength.'

As we have seen, the German Navy eventually managed to collect sufficient landing craft, but what other ships did they have available to support an invasion?

One of the elements of German forces that has only occasionally been mentioned so far but would be an important part of any invasion of Britain is the German Navy led by Grand Admiral Raeder. Following the Munich Crisis, Hitler ordered a massive expansion of the German Navy under his *Plan Z*. This called for the size of the navy, the Kriegsmarine, to increase to eight hundred ships and 1,000 U-Boats during the period 1939 to 1947. This included ten new battleships and battlecruisers, four aircraft carriers, fifteen armored ships, five heavy cruisers, forty-four light cruisers, and one hundred and fifty-eight destroyers and torpedo ships. Restrictions on the supply of raw materials meant that when Karl Donitz, who was in charge of the U-Boats force, clashed with Goering over the provision resources, the priority given to aircraft production, meant that the navy would never have the vessels it required and had been promised.

In January 1939, Hitler had agreed to a plan that would provide Raeder with a navy large enough to challenge the Royal Navy. He also assured him that there would not be a war with Britain before 1944, but, as we have seen, following the invasion of Poland only eight months later, Britain and Germans were indeed at war. As Robinson says, 'all of his [Raeder's] grandiose plans were dissolving about him,' and to make things worse, the Norwegian campaign cost him half of his destroyers and put two of his biggest ships in harbor for repairs. So Germany went in to the war with a largely modern but significantly weaker navy than the British, and as we have seen, their only opportunity to acquire a significant increase in their naval resources, through the capture of French Navy ships, was taken away by the bold action of the British Government and the Royal Navy.

At the start of the war, the German Navy comprised two old battleships, which were kept in home waters for coastal defense, two battlecruisers, three pocket battleships (equivalent to our heavy cruisers), three heavy cruisers, six light cruisers, twenty-one destroyers, and fifty-nine submarines.

With the German surface fleet significantly under strength, even allowing for the imminent completion of the *Bismarck* in August and *Tirpitz* later in the year, Hitler planned to use U-boats as the main means of enforcing a blockade on British naval and merchant shipping, in order to deter Britain from interfering with his European ambitions. To do so, as we have seen, he needed to capture Norway to allow his ships and submarines access to harbors away from British home waters. Until then, they had to pass under the eyes guns and torpedoes of the Royal Navy and RAF as they sailed through the Straits of Dover or around the top of Scotland.

Even while the evacuation at Dunkirk was under way and the Germans were beginning to consolidate their gains across Northern Europe, Hitler issued a directive to the Luftwaffe to initiate air attacks against British aircraft production and our main seaports in retaliation for RAF Bomber Commands attacks on the German industrial heartland, the Ruhr (see below).

Intervention by ships of the Royal Navy was regarded as being one of the crucial factors in preventing a successful invasion, as Robinson puts it, 'the RAF could not have stopped the invasion fleet, and the Luftwaffe could not have guaranteed its safety.' He quotes Herr Von Plehwe, who was Assistant to the Head of the German Army's liaison staff at the German Navy's headquarters, "I would like to lay great emphasis on the fact that the decisive deterrent to the operation was the expected large-scale intervention by the British fleet."

In his book, Robinson describes what might have happened had the Germans launched their invasion fleet. The German Navy had only eight destroyers available to protect it, whilst the Royal Navy had forty-two based in eastern and southern coast harbors; these comprised six destroyers at Plymouth, sixteen at Portsmouth, and twenty at Sheerness and Harwich, together with two light cruisers.

Robinson explains that these would have caused havoc amongst the invasion barges, tugs, and ships with little real sea-borne opposition. He tends to underplay the usefulness of the RAF, and although Fighter Command may not have been able to do much about the naval operation, Bomber Command, Coastal Command, and the Fleet Air Arm would have thrown everything they had at the slow moving and extremely exposed flotillas. Equally, if troops and armor made it ashore, they would have faced heavy and sustained attacks from the air. Finally, if an invasion looked likely to succeed, I am sure that the heavy units of the Home Fleet would have sailed down from their main base at Scapa Flow, no matter what the risk, to intervene to protect the mainland.

What ships did the Royal Navy have available to bombard the invasion fleet as it built up in French, Dutch and Belgium harbors and to disrupt and destroy them once they were at sea?

In 1939, they had fifteen battleships and battelcruisers with another five battleships on order, a single aircraft carrier in operation with six more under construction. It also had sixty-six cruisers with an additional twenty-three under construction, one hundred and eighty-four destroyers with fifty-two on their way, and sixty submarines with nine being built, and almost three hundred armed patrol boats in home waters. This was a formidable force. In comparison, the French which, as we have seen, was the second largest navy in Europe, comprised two battleships, one aircraft carrier, three cruisers, and twenty-two destroyers stationed in the Channel and Atlantic waters. Whereas, as we have seen, the Germans had two battleships, two battlecruisers, three pocket battleships, three heavy cruisers, six light cruisers, twenty-one destroyers, and fifty-nine submarines.

In the next chapter, we will review the disposition and operations of both the Royal Navy and Bomber and Coastal commands during the build-up to a potential invasion.

I have so far concentrated, quite rightly, on Fighter Command and its central role in the build-up and involvement in the Battle of Britain. But let us turn our attention to the other fighting elements of the RAF. At the start of the war, Bomber Command, under the command of Air Marshal Portal, comprised thirty-three squadrons divided between five different groups:

No. 1 Group which was largely equipped with Fairey Battles formed the Advanced Air Striking Force which flew to France in support of the British Expeditionary Force.

No. 2 Group, equipped with Bristol Blenhiems based in East Anglia.

No. 3 Group, which flew Vickers Wellingtons from East Anglian airfields.

No.4 Group, which was equipped with Armstrong Whitworth Whitley bombers based in Yorkshire.

No. 5 Group, equipped with Handley Page Hampdens flew from airfields in Lincolnshire.

Later an additional group, No. 6, was formed with airfields to the west and north of London, and others in Scotland.

As Graham Warner records in his wonderful book *The Forgotten Bomber: The Story of the Restoration of the World's Only Airworthy Bristol Blenheim:*

'...at the start of the war the RAF had more Bristol Blenheims in service than any other type of aircraft, a total of 1,089 as opposed to less than 200 each of the other main bomber types.'

Bomber Command were in immediate action as soon as war was declared and on 10 May, they attacked industrial targets in the Ruhr. In those early days, accuracy in bombing was poor, with only 30% of bombs falling within five miles (8km) of the target. They were soon to realize that the established philosophy on which most air forces had been built would not work, as Warner says:

'Once the "shooting war" really started in May 1940, the fallacy of the theory [that the bomber would always get through] was demonstrated at great cost by the very heavy losses incurred by RAF bombers of all types during daylight operations, as well as by Luftwaffe bombers to the RAF fighters in the Battle of Britain. Both Air Forces were soon forced to resort to far less accurate night bombing, for which both were equally unprepared.'

In this early stage of the war, Bomber Command was equipped with only medium and light bombers, in numbers that were insufficient to provide an effective force; but they flew every mission, even though many were suicidal. The Fairey Battles, which were supporting the Allied troops were slow, poorly armed, and carried a small bomb load, but the crews pressed home attacks even though they knew that the chances of survival were slim. In an effort to avoid civilian casualties, most of the early raids involved dropping nothing more dangerous than leaflets until Germany launched their attacks on Belgium, Holland, and France.

In the first six months of the war, Bomber Command flew a hundred and sixty-two night raids over Germany. Following German air raids on Rotterdam, Bomber Command switched to bombing raids and reconnaissance photography of enemy airfields; and communication systems, such as railway lines, as well as stations and goods yards. They also attacked oil facilities and power stations in the Ruhr in an effort to slow down and disrupt the build-up of German forces. They were tasked with attacking German naval ships in an attempt to drive them out to sea so that the Royal Navy Home Fleet, based in Scapa Flow could deal with them.

Following the evacuation from France, and as the threat of invasion of Britain increased, they flew almost continuous raids against the harbors and rivers where the invasion barges were being assembled. They were also involved with laying minefields across the Channel and around the invasion ports.

In his book, which details the activities of Bomber Commands 2 Group, Michael Bowyer includes many interesting instructions given to the group squadrons during this period of the war. I have included several of them in an effort to show how intense and desperate Bomber Command was in its efforts to stop, or at least slow-down or disrupt the Germans invasion plans.

For Bomber Command, the Battle of Britain began on 19 June, when they started to conduct air raids on enemy airfields in France. They were told that in the event of an invasion force taking to the sea, any of its aircraft that were not under the control of the army at the time were to concentrate on bombing enemy vessels. If the enemy managed to land on British beaches, they were to concentrate on attacking troop-carrying ships and barges even if German warships were in the area and also instructed to bomb the invasion beaches.

Operations Instruction 38 sent out on 3 July, stated:

'The enemy are using airfields and landing grounds in France, Belgium and Holland… The intention is to destroy as many aircraft as possible on the ground thus forcing the enemy to withdraw. Airfields are to be attacked by sections escorted by fighters, or sections or individual aircraft using cloud cover when definite information is received from fighter reconnaissance.'

A further instruction issued on 9 July said that:

'Barges and other shipping are reported concentrating in waterways in Holland and north Belgium. Attacks on these are to be given high priority. Reconnaissance is being undertaken by Blenheims of Coastal Command and 2 Group aircraft on missions to Germany. Most profitable areas for attack are likely to be: two canals running east from Zwolle, canal and river running south from Zwolle to the Rhine, the area in the vicinity of Rotterdam and around Antwerp, Ostend and Dunkirk.'

The following was a special signal sent from the Air Officer Commanding:

'You must bear in mind that your forces may have to play a most important part in repelling an invasion of this country, and you should be prepared at short notice to divert your squadrons to the attack of the invading enemy forces at points of departure and subsequently at sea, and points of landing in this country. To meet the threat of invasion twelve aircraft are to stand by (at each station) every morning at 20 minutes notice from twilight to sunrise.'

Those based in Scotland were tasked with attacking any German warships which put to sea, day or night. Bomber Command also increased its raids on targets, such as aluminum plants, aircraft factories and assembly plants, oil supplies and storage depots, and shipping in German ports, which included the *Bismarck* docked in Hamburg, and the *Deutschland* which was at Kiel. Warner highlights the importance of these operations with regard to delaying or preventing an invasion. He explains that even during the battle, wartime propagandists focused on the deeds of Fighter Command's Spitfires and Hurricanes without acknowledging the role of aircraft, such as the Blenheim which undertook dangerous day and night attacks on the barges and ships building up for the invasion, and points out the heavy price paid by the Blenheim and Fairey Battle aircrews during often suicidal missions.

By August, the threat of invasion grew even greater as the Battle of Britain intensified, and Bomber Command aircrews were told that:

'Attacks will be pressed home, regardless of cost. Each crew should aim to hit one vessel with one bomb and machine-gun the enemy whenever possible. Squadrons equipped with gas sprays are to be ready to operate with the shortest possible notice, but it will only be used as a retaliatory measure.'

The other flying Command, which played a significant role in the Battle of Britain was Coastal Command. This was formed after the break-up of the ADGB, on 14 July 1936 under the control of Commander Air Marshal, Sir Frederick Bowhill. Its headquarters were established at Northwood, Middlesex, which is the current Headquarters of the British Armed Forces.

Coastal Command comprised three groups, No. 18 based in Scotland, No. 16, in Southeast England, and No. 15 which covered Western England, the Southwest Approaches, and the Irish Sea. It had a total of nineteen squadrons which included six equipped with flying boats. Their main duties included covering convoys in the North Atlantic, the North Sea, and the Channel; watching for enemy ship movements; hunting German submarines; and air-sea rescue duties. A lack of adequate of aircraft and pilots during the early months of the war led to aircraft and crews from the navies Fleet Air Arm being loaned to the command.

Before we take a look at the operations of these two commands, let us turn our attention back to the army.

We have seen that the army had left an enormous quantity of equipment at Dunkirk; and when they arrived home, they had no more than five hundred heavy guns, fifty infantry tanks, and one hundred cruiser tanks. Robinson reports that when General Alan Brooke took over from General Ironside as Commander-in-Chief of Home Forces on 20 July, there were no existing plans for home defense. Following General Alan Brookes visit to the 50th Division, which was spread across Hampshire, Dorset, and Somerset, he wrote in his diary, that he was appalled to see it without the equipment it needed. In fact, the only troops that could be considered well equipped were those that had returned from Brittany. In his book *Hitler's Armada: The Royal Navy & the Defence of Great Britain April—October 1940*, Geoff Hewitt itemizes the army's resources, following Dunkirk as 2,300 machine guns, thirty-seven armored cars, three hundred and ninety-five light tanks, thirty-three cruiser tanks, seventy-two other tanks, four hundred and twenty field guns, and one hundred and sixty-three medium and heavy guns.

As we have seen, Hitler believed that Britain would remain isolated, the Americans would not join them, and the nations of the Empire were too far away to provide help in time.

On 1 June, having watched the plight of the British, and, given the messages of utter despair coming from the likes of Joseph Kennedy, the American Ambassador to Britain, President Roosevelt asked for a report from the American navy and army about what equipment they could spare that could be sent over to Britain. By 11 June, this equipment was being loaded on to ships bound for England. It arrived on 9 July, and, as Robinson, says, 'over night, 200,000 British troops were armed...the Canadians sent 75,000 rifles as well.' The British Government had also bought up the entire production capacity of the Thompson Machine Gun Company in Chicago, the producers of the famous Tommy gun, who were producing 5,000 guns a month. It is interesting to note that although we were desperate when the Americans gave us this equipment, it may not have been as good as it seemed; the rifles were 1917 American 'Springfield' rifles which used 0.3 inch (7.62mm) caliber bullets which made them incompatible with the standard British 0.303 inch (7.69mm) caliber Lee Enfield Mk4 rifles used by the army.

They also supplied us with fifty destroyers as part of the 'Destroyers for bases' agreement. In return for these ships, the USA was granted 99-year leases on British possessions in the Bahamas, Jamaica, St. Lucia, Trinidad, Antigua, British Guiana, Bermuda, and Newfoundland to build military bases. I can remember my uncle Jack telling me that he was part of the crew of one of the American ships when they sailed them back from America. He said that they were so old and rusty that they were really only good for the scrapyard! It is hardly surprising that Britain was prepared to give up so much, as Parker reports in *The Battle of Britain July–October 1940: An Oral History of Britain's 'Finest Hour,'* following the Munich Crisis, our gold and dollar reserves, together with saleable assets in the USA were down to £775 million and dwindling fast. It was estimated that they would be completely gone by the end of 1940. With Britain facing Germany alone, and with no certainty of success, it was hardly surprising that some important voices in Washington were cautious of supporting us at the time. So when the British also asked for twenty torpedo boats, the request was blocked in congress by invoking an old law that prohibited America from selling armed vessels to a belligerent nation. Some in the corridors of Whitehall suspected that the Americans were waiting to see if they could 'pick up the pieces of the British Empire' if Britain was successfully invaded.

However, Britain was preparing to stand-alone. Hence, Parker informs us that on 9 August 1938, London had a practice blackout and that by September, over 1,000,000 feet of trenches (304,800m) had been dug in the city and that 99% of the city's population had been issued with gas marks. Within a year, 1,500,000 Anderson air-raid shelters had also been built.

The British knew that if the Germans wanted to invade, they would probably need to secure one of our harbors on the south or east coast, hence their defenses were increased. All of the main harbors were covered by extensive, heavy gun emplacements, their entrances were also protected by minefields and submarine nets. If an invasion looked imminent, instructions had been given that harbor entrances could be blocked by sunken ships, and that docks and harbor facilities could be destroyed to prevent the Germans from being able to use them. Along the coasts where landings were likely, beaches were mined, tank traps installed, and areas, such as Romney Marsh, were to be flooded using a system of dykes which had been first installed during the Napoleonic War. In land, one of the biggest perceived threats was from German paratroops and gliders, neither of which were as effective as the British or Germans' imagined. Fields were dug up, and overhead cables were installed. Explosives were positioned in pipes under roads close to the coast. Holes were being dug in flat-lying areas, and wooden stakes were being planted in open fields together with old farm machinery to obstruct parachutists and aircraft. In addition to all of this, a 400-mile-long (643km) defensive system was introduced from Maidstone to Bristol that was designed to protect London and the industrial areas in the midlands.

By July 1939, 8,000 pillboxes had been built at strategic locations and a further 17,000 were under construction. All road signs and station names were removed, place names were covered up, and famous landmarks boarded-up to prevent them from being identified.

The Home Guard had even made 1,000,000 Molotov Cocktails for use against tanks and other motorized vehicles. Finally, a complete blackout was strictly enforced and a number of petrol stations in the southeast were also set with explosives because, according to Ward, 'in France, the petrol-fuelled Panzers had simply queued up at garages and helped themselves to what was available.'

Churchill also threatened to incinerate any invaders by pumping burning oil in to the sea; in fact, for this to work, the sea's surface would have to be flat calm—the idea was eventually dropped. We saw from the instructions given to Bomber Command that as a last resort the government were even prepared to use its stock of poisonous gas if it was first used by the Germans.

The coming battle would have to be fought over the fields, coastline, towns, and cities of Southern England and therefore, unlike most the other battles it would be fought in full view of a significant proportion of the British people. Again, Parker adds a vivid description of the situation, when he explains that, unlike most battles fought far from home, the Battle of Britain played out in full view of the British public and international press. It became a 'spectator sport on a vast scale,' which rather than lowering public morale, raised it—it became personal. As news reports spread out across the world, and particularly across the Atlantic, they captured 'the attention and admiration of many people in America who in other circumstances might have been indifferent or hostile to what was happening on the other side of the Atlantic.'

Each day, during the period known as the Phoney War, which lasted from the end of the invasion of Poland in September 1939 to start of the Battle of France in May 1940, the Luftwaffe sent over bombers and reconnaissance aircraft to test British defenses and harass shipping in the Channel and along the south and east coasts. From a British point of view, it was considered too dangerous for naval ships to operate in the area, so convoys had either be re-routed around the west coast or they had to depend on air cover from Fighter Command for protection, a system which usually required up to six aircraft at a time. This was therefore not a period of inactivity as the name might suggest, as it allowed both air forces to replenish their battered squadrons, replace, and train replacement pilots, and it gave them the opportunity to gain at least some flying and combat experience before the real battle, which everyone knew was coming, began in earnest.

In his book *The Battle of Britain: Dowding and the First Victory, 1940*, John Ray makes the following observation, that although the RAF had put up a great fight over the French beaches, towns and countryside, there was a feeling of dread about the forth-coming battle given the speed that the Luftwaffe had crushed all before it. However, he points out that those successes were more down to the weakness of their opponents rather than the strength of the Luftwaffe. This meant that when the time came to face Fighter Command across Britain's natural defensive wall, the seas surrounding us— in particular the North Sea, English Channel and Western Approaches—and a fighter force that had been specifically built for the defense of the country, the Luftwaffe was faced with 'unattainable goals.'

He adds that, one of the main problems faced by the Luftwaffe was that Hitler thought, or hoped, that Germany would not have to fight in a war 'beyond the continent.' As have seen, he had decided that Britain had neither the capability, ability, nor the heart to challenge his authority or power in Europe. This was one of the reasons mentioned earlier why Germany virtually abandoned the development and production of, for example, a long-range, four-engined, heavy bomber. It meant that the Luftwaffe would be going in to a long-range bombing campaign with only medium-range bombers carrying a medium bomb-load. They had also put a great deal of their efforts in to designing and producing bombers capable of being used as dive-bombers that, although they proved extremely effective when used in combination with the army, were far less effective one their own.

With the expansion of the Luftwaffe following the Munich Crisis, Hitler included thirteen of the planned fifty-eight bomber squadrons for use against the Royal Navy and British shipping—these were known as the 'Pirate Formations.' Thirty of the remaining squadrons were designed to attack Britain whilst only fifteen were designated for attacks on France.

As we have seen during the build-up and defeat of the Spanish Armada, knowing what your enemy is thinking and doing, is one of the most important aspects of warfare. It allows you to make better use of limited resources and hopefully gives you at tactical advantage. One of the most important developments in both Germany and Britain was the use, by the Germans, of a code system known as *Enigma*.

Like so many aspects of the story of the Battle of Britain, and the Second World War in general, the story behind *Enigma* is immense, and therefore I can only include the briefest of outlines here.

This is a good time to introduce Frederick William Winterbotham, an RAF man who had been in charge of distributing *Ultra* intelligence as it was known, deciphered from *Enigma* messages at Bletchley Park in North

London. This was the home of a giant early computer, designed to 'crack' messages that the Germans sent using special machines, which they thought, all the way through the war were unbreakable.

The Germans depended heavily on radio communications to direct the Blitzkrieg across Europe, but one of the problems with using radio was that it is open to be received by both sides in a conflict unless you can, somehow 'scramble' the message. As Brian Johnson puts it, '*The Secret War,*'

'Without a quick, easy-to-operate and secure encoding system, there could be no radio; without radio there could be no Blitzkrieg... Enigma was the solution.'

The Germans developed a system, which used machines, comprising a series of cogs that they could send and receive messages securely. Each cog had 26 letters on it, and most machines had between four and eight cogs. By continuously changing the setup of the cogs, the Germans thought that it would be impossible to decipher their messages and for a while, it was. Again, Johnson gives a vivid description of how *Enigma* worked:

'The military Enigma, as used by the Army and Luftwaffe, had 10^{21} possible initial setting of the machine; for the Navy Enigma, which would use four operational rotors out of the eight, the figure would be 10^{23}... The Germans must have considered the possibility of one or more being captured: to try all the possible settings of the machine, even with the aid of a modern computer, could take fifty years. [Remember this was written in 1978 and computer power has moved on incredibly since then.] No wonder the Germans had confidence in the security of the codes.'

In fact, the Germans, who may have had as many as 200,000 machines in operation, used the system throughout the war and were never aware that its coding system had been broken. They used it for almost all routine and operational communications, which allowed the British to keep a very close eye on what they were up to.

The Poles were the first to detect and start to try to break the codes in December 1932; they then involved the French and eventually the British. In this country, the work to break the codes was carried out by Room 47 at the Foreign Office, the cover name for the code and decipher school at Bletchley Park, a country house in Buckinghamshire. It was here that some of the best mathematicians in Britain were involved in code breaking. In the grounds of Bletchley Park, there were a number of huts dedicated to either breaking, deciphering, or deciding on the tactical importance of the *Enigma* messages. The information they were handling was so important that it was known as the '*Ultra Secret.*' Huts 3 and 6 were used for deciphering army and air force messages, and huts 4 and 8 concentrated on navy ones. A card index was held in C block. Once the messages had been decoded, they were sent to the Watch Hut which housed German speaking intelligence officers who then interpreted them in to English and passed them on to people in other huts, depending on the importance of the information they contained. Each 'hut' was not, as we might assume, a single hut, but might be, as the system expanded, a group of huts which kept the same designation. The machines used to break the codes were known as 'bronze goddesses.' Later on in the war, these were developed, by the post office and the BBC, in to the world's first computer which was known as the 'Colossus Mk1.'

With regard to the build-up to Battle of Britain, the first decoded massages that were successfully broken occurred during the Norwegian Campaign in April 1940. From then on, 'the quality and number of intercepts rose steeply until, by the Battle of France in early May, the codebreakers in hut 6 were reading a significant proportion of the Enigma traffic.' Decoded intelligence helped provide information that led Churchill and the War Cabinet to decide to evacuate the British Expeditionary Force from France.

Johnson also describes how the system worked and what type of information the code breakers used:

'The intelligence aspect of Enigma was the province of other huts at Bletchley—principally Hut 3, where skilled interpreters pieced the information together. Nothing was too small; everything, however trivial, was collated and filed in a huge card index containing hundreds of thousands of names, units, postings, supply requisitions, details of promotions, courts martial and leave of absence. A transfer of a single Air Force Lieutenant could reveal an impending attack. The card index grew until it was virtually the archive of the entire German Command structure.'

Eventually, the system worked so well that often the British knew information and could read it in real time, sometimes before the German commanders it was being sent to had received it. With regard to the Battle of Britain specifically, Johnson includes a quote from Winterbotham, who was not only the Head of the Air Intelligence Branch and the 'guardian of Ultra intelligence' but was also Churchill's personal representative, he reports that Dowding told Winterbotham that being able to read Goering's messages enabled him to devise his own tactics. This included observing Goering's increasingly desperate use of larger and larger numbers of fighters in the hope that Dowding would send more of his own aircraft into the skies. As we will see, Dowding would do the opposite. He also saw when Goering changed from bombing his airfields to turning his attention to London:

'...then came the amazing signal for the Luftwaffe bombers to change from attacking the fighter airfields to London. That was a change of policy by Goering which saved us.'

Churchill considered the '*Ultra*' information to be so important and of such value that his military leaders could not act on any of it unless they could find another way in which the information could have been gained so that the Germans would not become suspicious and begin to wonder whether their *Enigma* system had been compromised.

In his book *The Ultra Secret*, the first publication to talk about *Enigma* and the work at Bletchley Park, Winterbotham explains that although the Germans used it for fairly mundane communications, dealing with logistics etc. the Army and Luftwaffe also used it to keep a close eye on all aspects of the their forces including resources, distribution, strength and disposition. It appeared that the German armed forces were told to use '*Ultra*' as a system of communication rather than 'blocking up' telephone landlines with 'non-operational traffic.' Consequently, the British were able to keep as accurate a record of the German's military activity and planning as the German commanders had.

Having said that, not all signals were 'broken,' and not all 'broken' signals told all the story. For instance, on 23 May 1940, at the height of the retreat back to Dunkirk, Bletchley Park decoded a signal which informed the two German Army groups to push ahead and encircle British and French troops. With this information to hand, as we have seen above, Churchill and the Chiefs of Staff decided to instigate '*Operation Dynamo*,' the evacuation from Dunkirk. What the signal did not say, and Churchill did not know, was that Hitler was actually on the battlefield when the instruction was given and that he canceled subsequent orders, leading to the halt of the German advance. This delay, with the British and French in full retreat and the Germans making swift and decisive advances, possibly prevented them from cutting off, decimating, or capturing both allied armies.

Winterbotham includes some very interesting information which others have either agreed with or disputed:

'...ever since I had met Hitler for the first time in 1934 I had felt that his desperate desire for peace with Britain was no bluff. I knew that above all he genuinely feared the British as an enemy, and now that France was virtually finished, he obviously wanted peace in the west before he set out on the great mission that possessed his soul—if he had one—the destruction of Communist Russia. I believed he was deliberately letting the BEF go home... I believe that if Hitler had let his victory-drunk armies and air force loose there would have been little for the small boats to pick up. Did Hitler let the BEF go home, having stripped them of all their armour? We now know that soon after Hitler ordered his tanks to stop closing in, he addressed his military staff in France. According to one German general who was present, Hitler told them exactly what he told me in 1934: it was necessary that the great civilisation Britain had brought to the world should continue to exist and that all he wanted from Britain was that she should acknowledge German's position on the continent. He went on to say that his aim was to make peace with Britain on a basis which she would regard as compatible with her honour to accept. All his efforts, as we know, were rejected. This time he had totally misjudged the mood of the British people.'

The rest, as they say, is history.

There is significant disagreement over the usefulness of decoded *Enigma* information during the early part of the war and its use during the Battle of Britain. Hough and Richards report that by the start of the Dunkirk evacuation, Bletchley Park were reading around 1,000 messages a day. Robinson disputes the usefulness of *Enigma* with regard to Dowding strategies and includes a comment from Edward Thomas, who worked on *Enigma* during the war. Thomas explained that there were three main reasons why *Enigma* decrypts were of little value to Dowding. Firstly, the Luftwaffe were still sending most of their communications by telephone or dispatch rider. Secondly, it took too much time for most of the '*Ultra*' messages to be deciphered so operational intelligence often arrived after the event. Finally, the Luftwaffe used code words to identify its targets so, even if an '*Ultra*' message was decoded in time, the people at Bletchley and Fighter Command Head Quarters could not necessarily decode the target.

Robinson therefore thinks that *Enigma* was 'never more than a bonus' for Dowding during the battle. However, with the huge card index system that Bletchley had been developing, the mere movement of particular airmen or units, for which Bletchley knew their function, could indicate when a raid was likely to take place, what type of raid it might be, and what the likely target was. In his book about the Luftwaffe, Williamson Murray comments:

'...what is clear is that "Ultra," in combination with "Y" Service (the British radio listening service) intercepts of German radio traffic, gave the British an increasingly accurate picture of the German order of battle as air operations continued into September.'

Before we leave the story of *Enigma*, it is worth adding one other anecdote. During the crippling attacks by German U-boats in 1941, the German Navy had introduced a new code known as *Hydra*, which had still not been broken at Bletchley. On 8 May 1941, the Royal Navy corvette *Aubretia* and the destroyers HMS *Bulldog* and HMS *Broadway* captured *U-110* (not the Americans and *U-571* as portrayed in the film) with, not only its *Enigma* machine, but its rotors and cipher code books intact before the captain had had a chance to destroy them. This enabled the code breakers to 'break' the new *Hydra* System, which helped turn the tide against the U-boats by re-routing convoys around the U-boat 'wolf packs.' It also helped locate and sink their 'milk cows,' the fuel supply ships, and submarines. It should also be said that German Naval Intelligence were able to intercept and read the Royal Navy's signals until August 1940 when they changed their codes, and as Hewitt notes, even then they were able to read signals sent out by the Merchant Navy. As an interesting aside, it is worth reading a book that I bought during a visit to Bletchley Park in 2018 called *Code Breakers: The true story of the Secret Intelligence Unit that changed the course of the First World War*, written by James Wyllie and Michael McKinley. This covers the development of listening, code breaking and other intelligence operations during that war which 'founded Britain's modern intelligence services.'

Ray records that in 1939, 'Beppo' Schmid, the leader of the Intelligence Branch of the Germans Operational Staff, who was infamous for his incorrect predictions, claimed that the British defenses were weak and our air force and that of France was out of date. This may have been true prior to 1939, but rapid changes had taken place since then. His information did not take account of the huge strides that British industry and our armed forces had made in a very short period of time when, as we have seen, Britain trebled production while the Germans only doubled theirs.

Another aspect of intelligence that is worth adding at this stage was the use of spies. A fear of spies gripped the nation, and to some extent, the Government, and the military encouraged this paranoia, because it meant that the general public would remain on their guard. But was this paranoia justified, were the Germans sending over hundreds of spies, and were there spies on every corner? The Germans did send spies, twenty-four in fact, but as with most of the spies which crossed the Channel to Britain, they were usually picked up by the British within hours or days of their arrival (see below for the stories of the six sent over in 1940). Peter Fleming says in his book *Operation Sea Lion* that in September 1940, 'a shower of spies descended on the United Kingdom; all were taken into custody by the British Authorities. They were for the most part low-grade agents who had not completed their training.' Can you really count six spies as a shower? Fleming also records that the British sent over large numbers of caged carrier pigeons designed to be used by people on the continent to send back any information they could about the German military build-up, disposition, and operations. However, he observes that 'the birds who returned in the summer of 1940 carried, at best, only simple, pathetic messages expressing faith in victory or hatred of the Boches.' For both sides then there were problems in knowing the disposition and likely movements of the opposition's armed forces. Fleming summarizes the situation from the British point of view like this:

'...it is not quite true to say that in the field of intelligence the British, once more, lost every battle but the last; but certainly it was late in the day before they arrived at a correct forecast of German strategy. There were several reasons for this. They overestimated the operational strength of the German Navy; they assumed, prudently but as it happened wrongly, that German plans for invasion were more advanced and more workmanlike than in fact they were; and above all they found it impossible to believe that Hitler, who for all their derision still remained a formidable and hypnotic figure, would come at them, as Julius Caesar and the Duke of Normandy had, by the shortest and most obvious way.'

He adds that:

'...as long as counter-invasion intelligence remained largely a matter of guesswork, the British tended to guess wrong; but from the moment, in the last days of August, when a body of relevant evidence began to come their way, they interpreted it sensibly and got the answer more or less right.'

Even before they had broken and could make use of the *Enigma* codes, in March 1940, MI5, Bletchley Park, and the British Radio Security Service

(BRSS) had been able to intercept radio traffic between the Hamburg German Intelligence Service and a spy ship in the North Sea. This enabled them to break the cipher used to communicate with German agents by radio and meant that MI5 could locate newly arrived spies. By then, MI5 already had its Double Agent system operational.

In his book *Operation Fortitude: The Story of the Spy Operation that saved D Day*, Joshua Levine relays the stories of the six German spies sent over by General Alfred Jodl, the Chief of Operations Staff at Wehrmacht High Command, who wanted a network of spies in place to relay information about British defenses, suitable landing beaches etc. The operation, code-named *Lena* was also going to use the spies as guides for the soldiers once the invasion army had landed.

Of the first four spies recruited for the operation, only one could speak some English and one could speak no English at all. Two of them were given the choice of either becoming spies or being sent to a concentration camp. All four came across on fishing boats on 3 September. Two landed near Dymchurch on the Kent coast, the first of which was arrested within an hour of landing and the other some thirty minutes later. The other two landed near Lydd, which is approximately 9 km south of Dymchurch. At around 9 a.m., the following morning one went into a local pub and asked for a bottle of champagne cider. When he was told by the landlady that he would have to come back in an hour, he left. She was already suspicious, and when he returned, he ordered half a pint of milk. When he left, she asked two men to follow him, and when they asked him to get into a car to go to the police station, he surrendered. The forth spy actually managed to transmit a message back to Hamburg to say that he had landed. During the evening of 5 September, he was spotted by the police, and when they found that he could not speak any English, they arrested him.

Another spy, who was Swedish, was dispatched on 5 September. His arrival near the village of Denton in Northamptonshire was already anticipated by MI5, who were waiting for him. As he parachuted down from the aircraft he had been traveling in, he was knocked unconscious. He was found dazed and confused and, after he had been arrested and was being questioned, he said that a second spy was also coming across. Under the control of MI5, he sent a message back to his controllers saying that he had arrived safely and would start work. The second spy, a Dane, arrived by parachute near the village of Willingham, Cambridgeshire on 19 September. He was arrested the following day by members of the Local Defence Volunteers. Under MI5 control, he too sent a message back announcing his safe arrival. MI5 had just been able to add two more spies to their Double

Cross network; in fact, the Dane became the longest serving double agent MI5 had during the war. German spies were therefore of no use to the German Intelligence Service, even though many of them continued to pass 'valuable' information back to them throughout the war.

British Intelligence was convinced that an invasion would occur along the east coast where the flatter beaches would make any landings easier and, even when German invasion barges started to assemble in French, Belgium and Dutch ports, which indicated south coast targets, they were still convinced that this was a diversionary tactic. One of the problems that such an interpretation could cause was the transfer of troops by road and rail across London and the surrounding area once an invasion was underway. If they had chosen the wrong area, this would have been a similar problem to that faced by the army in 1588 based a Tilbury.

Equally, the Germans needed to know what forces the British had and where they were positioned to give an invasion the best possible chance of success, and, although Jodl thought that the British Army was poorly equipped and ill prepared, Hitler thought that they faced a 'defensively prepared and utterly determined enemy.' German Intelligence had only basic information on the disposition of the British Army and, as Fleming points out, although their estimates were close to the mark, most of the units were located in totally different places, a fact that would have had a significant impact on any invasion.

Not only was it important to know what your enemy was doing but it was equally important to convince the populace of your message. We have seen that during the Phoney War, Bomber Command was restricted to dropping leaflets across Germany and the occupied countries, while the Germans established a number of radio stations, the first, which was called La Voix de la Paix, broadcast in France during the German advance. This radio station was supposed to be a French station, run by Frenchmen and broadcast from French soil. It was designed, as Fleming puts it, to be 'an agent of alarm and defeatism.' The Germans viewed it to be a success and consequently decided to use the same tactics on Britain. Fleming recalls that they set up a radio station called the New British Broadcast Station (NBBS) that began to broadcast in late February 1940. It used The Bonnie, Bonnie Banks of Loch Lomond as its signature tune and closed its broadcasts with the National Anthem. Presumably, the Germans, equally pleased with its results, then established three more stations, the Workers' Challenge, Caledonia, and the Christian Peace Movement. Fleming explains that each one was designed to 'spread disinformation, fear and unrest or division, including the presence of a well-organized Fifth Column.' In his book, he includes several examples of the way in which these were used, all of which were fairly misleading, but were designed to unsettle the British public with continuous reports of an imminent invasion.

Rather like the perceived and, possibly real, threat of a Catholic uprising or at the very least Catholic support for Spanish troops once they had landed in 1588, the perceived threat of German sympathizers living in Britain was equally real. As we have seen in the above quotes, the Germans played on these fears, particularly the existence of a Fifth Column. But, what was the infamous and much dreaded Fifth Column?

The expression Fifth Column originates from the Spanish Civil War, when General Franco's nationalist forces comprised four separate columns that were closing in on Madrid from four different directions. A separate Fifth Column was already based in, and ready to operate in Madrid. It was known that there were a small number of Fascists in Britain, but as Fleming explains, the idea of a Fifth Column was designed to spread suspicion and fear that their numbers were far greater than they really were. It also played on the idea of the Trojan Horse, where spies and saboteurs were coming across from the continent in amongst all the refugees from France, Belgium, and Holland.

In response, the Government introduced new laws, which were used to intern people suspected of collaboration or even expressing negative views. But as we have seen, Germans spies were usually caught as soon as, or soon after they landed and frequently 'turned,' so that establishing a real Fifth Column would have been extremely difficult. Nonetheless, perception is a powerful weapon, and you can hardly blame the British public or even the Government for being paranoid when, as in 1588, an all-conquering military force was facing them across the narrow divide of the English Channel poised ready to strike. Even if they had known that in both conflicts, the Germans and Spanish were neither ready nor capable of invading, the threat could not have been greater.

In 1940, the British were convinced that the Germans would send over paratroopers, who could land anywhere, at any time. The perceived threat was real and was based, as Fleming points out, on the psychological affects German airborne forces had when they parachuted in to locations all over the Low Countries on 10 May. This resulted in an almost hypnotic paranoia whereby people thought that groups of possibly disguised, heavily armed paratroopers could be landing anywhere and everywhere, at any time.

Little did they know that, in reality, paratroopers, at least in the early part of the war, were far from the perceived menace? Their parachutes were difficult to control, and paratroopers were extremely vulnerable when descending and landing. But the Government and military were sufficiently 'spooked' by the treat that they issued orders that people should try to shoot then down as or before they landed. Fleming quotes orders that were given to shoot at paratroopers, particularly when there were more than five together, as they had to be German because the maximum number of crew in any British aircraft was five.

Chapter 4
Attack Is the Best Form of Defense

Most of Europe had fallen to the German's in a relatively short period of time. The army had left much of its equipment in France, the RAF had taken a beating, and Hitler was intent, if possible, to try to convince Britain to give up in the face of what appeared to be an overwhelming opposition. On 4 June, Churchill replied during a long speech in the Home of Commons with:

> 'I have, myself, full confidence that if all do their duty, if nothing is neglected, and if the best arrangements are made, as they are being made, we shall prove ourselves once again able to defend our Island home, to ride out the storm of war, and to outlive the menace of tyranny, if necessary for years, if necessary alone.
>
> 'At any rate, that is what we are going to try to do. That is the resolve of His Majesty's Government—every man of them. That is the will of Parliament and the nation.
>
> 'The British Empire and the French Republic, linked together in their cause and in their need, will defend to the death their native soil, aiding each other like good comrades to the utmost of their strength.
>
> 'Even though large tracts of Europe and many old and famous States have fallen or may fall into the grip of the Gestapo and all the odious apparatus of Nazi rule, we shall not flag or fail.
>
> 'We shall go on to the end, we shall fight in France, we shall fight on the seas and oceans, we shall fight with growing confidence and growing strength in the air, we shall defend our Island, whatever the cost may be, we shall fight on the beaches, we shall fight on the landing grounds, we shall fight in the fields and in the streets, we shall fight in the hills; we shall never surrender, and even if, which I do not for a moment believe, this Island or a large part of it were subjugated and starving, then our Empire beyond the seas, armed and guarded by the British Fleet, would carry on the struggle, until, in

God's good time, the New World, with all its power and might, steps forth to the rescue and the liberation of the old.'

We have seen that Francis Drake led a famous and very important attack on Cadiz as a pre-emptive strike on the build-up of the Armada, but was there an equivalent action in 1940? The simple answer is no, but why? In 1940, the situation was different; in the previous chapters, we have seen that Europe had been swiftly overrun by rapidly moving German forces on land and in the air. Our armed forces now faced the possibility of defending the country against an enemy which could attack from as far south and west as the French-Spanish border and northwards as far as Northern Norway. The Germans had spent their time since the fall of France re-organizing their air fleets, re-equipping and re-enforcing their newly acquired airfields and building up their coastal defenses.

Hitler and his high command had decided that in response to Britain's rejection of their peace offers that we would have to be dealt with through the threat of, and possibly the launch of, a sea-borne invasion. Fighter Command was busy preparing itself for the inevitable onslaught that everyone knew was coming, but what were the Royal Navy, Coastal Command, and Bomber Command doing? The answer is, a great deal. Even though they did not undertake a headline winning, pre-emptive killer strike similar to that of Drake, their actions were of fundamental importance in not only disrupting the build-up of the German invasion fleet and hassling the Luftwaffe, but, as we shall see, in leading to a fundamental change in the course of the coming battle.

First, we will turn our attention to the Royal Navy, the senior service. We have seen that the Germans were engaged in a very hasty plan to build an invasion force that, with the best will in the world, would need exceptional weather conditions and a great deal of luck to be able to cross the Channel. We have also seen that the German Navy took a hammering during its Norwegian campaign that left it desperately short of the large warships that would be needed to escort and protect an invasion fleet.

In his excellent book *Hitler's Armada: The Royal Navy & the Defence of Great Britain April-October 1940*, Geoff Hewitt details the activities of our navy during the Battle of Britain as a counter balance to its usual omission from books on the subject. Much of the following is therefore based on, or quoted from his book. The basic premise of his argument can be summed up in the following quote 'in simple terms, for an opposed invasion, whilst control of the air was desirable, control of the sea was essential, and this remained firmly in the hands of the Royal Navy throughout.' Hewitt comments that neither Fighter, Bomber nor Coastal Command could do sufficient damage to the invasion fleet and supporting ships should they sail, and concludes that, in 1940, 'the Luftwaffe was simply not able to sink or disable Royal Navy warships in sufficient numbers by day to protect an invasion force from destruction, and at night would have been unable to sink any warships at all.'

Although Hewitt tends to imply that Fighter Command in particular would have been incapable of stopping an invasion, and therefore he links the Battle of Britain directly to an invasion; in doing so, he is missing the point. The job of Fighter Command was to prevent the Luftwaffe gaining air superiority over Southern England. Attacking and defeating an invasion fleet was not in their remit and their primary aircraft—the Spitfire and Hurricane—were designed as short-range fighters not fighter-bombers, bombers, or even ground attack aircraft. Equally, the Royal Navy played no effective part in the Battle of Britain because it was an air battle. However, a fleet-in-being, as we saw with the Navy Royal in 1588, is a most powerful force to other navies; and, as we saw in the previous chapter, the Home Fleet was indeed a powerful force.

It appears that those in charge of home defense were convinced that if the Germans were to invade they would most probably head for the east coast of England. On 16 September, they had the following ships (as recorded in Hewitt's book) dispersed in eastern and southern ports within striking distance of an invasion fleet (the times given in brackets refer to sailing times from the named port to the Straits Dover):

Dover (one hour) – two motor torpedo boats (MTBs);
Harwich (three and a half hours) – six destroyers and eleven MTBs.
Portsmouth (three and a half hours) – one light cruiser, fourteen destroyers (including a French ship), six MTBs, and five Dutch torpedo boats.
Southampton (three and a half hours) – two destroyers.
Sheerness/Chatham (four hours) – two light cruisers and eighteen destroyers.
London (four and a half hours) – one MTB.
Portland (five hours) – two MTBs.
Plymouth (eight hours) – one battleship, two cruisers, and eleven destroyers (including two French and three Polish ships).
The Humber (ten hours) – three cruisers, five destroyers, and eleven MTBs.

In addition to these ships, the Home Fleet had been divided between Scapa Flow and Rosyth in Scotland. There was a battleship, an aircraft carrier, four cruisers and seven destroyers remaining at Scapa Flow that were twenty-six hours sailing time from the Straits of Dover. Two battleships, a battlecruiser, three cruisers, seventeen destroyers and an MTB, had been stationed at Rosyth, which was only eighteen hours away.

Although it has been said that the Royal Navy was kept out of the way for fear of air attack, it had a powerful force assembled ready to sail if required given that an invasion would take anything up to eleven days to complete. The evacuation at Dunkirk had shown that it was difficult to bomb ships even when they were moored close together at sea or in harbor. If, and when the Home Fleet sailed, given the limited bomb aiming technology available in 1940, the Luftwaffe would have found it extremely difficult to destroy or even disable our ships. Equally, although as we shall see, Bomber Command had had some success in bombing barges assembling in French, Belgium, and Dutch harbors, they would have found it as difficult as the Luftwaffe to bomb them once they had put to sea. Therefore, their job, and that of the Royal Navy in the first instance, was to prevent the invasion fleet from sailing.

On 20 July, the Admiralty had decided that the Home Fleet would not risk entering the southern part of the North Sea unless the German's larger warships set sail. Following their rather disorganized operations off Norway, when the Royal Navy ships fired off a third of their anti-aircraft ammunition and only shot down four aircraft, the Commander-in-Chief of the Home Fleet decided that his ships should not 'operate within range of shore-based aircraft.'

Between the beginning of April and the end June, the Royal Navy had suffered the loss of an aircraft carrier, two cruisers, and seventeen destroyers—these were significant losses, but the fleet was large enough to withstand them. The Admiralty knew of the damage done to the German Navy during their Norwegian campaign but were unsure of its future capabilities. Raeder planned, as a precursor to invasion, to use some of his larger ships, together with a number of liners in a diversionary invasion named *Operation Herbstreise*. The intension was to direct this towards the north east coast between Newcastle and Aberdeen in order to draw as many of the Home Fleets ships away from the south coast as possible.

It was clear that all the while the Home Fleet remained 'in being,' it was a direct threat to any German plans. Although the Norwegian campaign and the evacuation of Dunkirk had shown the vulnerability of warships to air attack, it was thought that the Home Fleet could inflict serious damage to any invasion force without paying too high a price to its own ships.

As I have said, the Royal Navy did not play a direct part in the Battle of Britain, but they were equally as active as Bomber and Coastal commands in attacking Germans invasion forces. Most nights, destroyers, motor-torpedo boats, and occasionally cruisers would sail up the French, Belgium, and Dutch coast to check on the build-up of invasion shipping, lay mines, and bombard harbors with almost no damage to themselves. At the same time, Royal Navy and allied minesweepers were busy keeping sea-lanes and the entrances to British harbors free of German mines.

This was particularly important as the laying of four mine fields to prevent Royal Navy access to the invasion fleet whilst it was at sea was one of, if not the main form of defense the German Navy could provide given its desperate shortage of ships. Two mines fields code-named *Anton* and *Bruno* were to be laid between Brighton and Le Harve. A third, *Caesar* would be placed across the Straits of Dover, and the last *Dora* was designed to keep the Royal Navy ships based in Plymouth out of the area. Unfortunately, the Germans had neither the mines available to achieve this plan nor the capability to maintain the minefields once they had been laid.

Before we leave the attempts to disrupt and destroy the Germans ability to attack the UK by air and sea, and concentrate on the Battle of Britain as it unfolded, it is worth adding one other action proposed by the Royal Navy which harks back to 1588, namely *Operation Lucid*. As Hewitt explains, 'Operation Lucid, which envisaged attacking German barges and shipping assemblies with a weapon Drake or Howard of Effingham would have understood—the fireship.'

It was planned to use three old tankers filled with 50% heavy oil, 25% diesel fuel and 25% petrol, which would be ignited and sailed in to different harbors to cause havoc and destruction amongst the tightly packed ships and barges. These attacks on Calais, Ostend, and Boulogne were first planned for the night of 25–26 September, but unfortunately, the chosen tankers were in such a poor state that the mission was postponed until 2–3 October. Bad weather that night and the following night led to further cancelations and a final attempt was planned for the night of 7–8 October. However, adverse weather and the poor state of the tankers led to yet another cancelation. With the subsequent dispersal of the German invasion fleet, no further attempts were made after that and the idea was dropped.

Having looked briefly at the operations of the Royal Navy during the Battle of Britain we should now turn our attention of the activities of Bomber and Coastal commands. It must be remembered that, although Churchill had been the First Lord of the Admiralty, a position that so pleased the Royal Navy that on his return in May 1940 they sent out the message 'Winston is back' to its ships worldwide, he was also a strong supporter of aerial bombing. He realized the importance of forcing the Germans to defend their own country, and declared in September that:

'The Navy can lose us the war, but only the Air Force can win it. The fighters are our salvation but the bombers alone provide the means of victory. We must therefore develop the power to carry an ever-increasing volume of explosives to Germany, so as to pulverize their entire industry and scientific structure on which the war effort and economic life of the enemy depends, whilst holding him at arm's length from our island.'

Following the mauling of their squadrons during the Battle of France, both commands prepared to do their part in trying to prevent an invasion. Although the official start date for the Battle of Britain is 10 July, for Bomber and Coastal Command, the battle started as soon as the Battle of France ended and continued until the night of 12–13 October when the last raid on the invasion barges was conducted—they had been gradually dispersing since 24 September.

Even before the Battle of France had begun, Fighter Command had been engaged with a little publicized battle of their own that is sometimes known as the Battle of Scotland, which lasted from October 1939 to April 1940. The commands aircraft were engaged in a series of skirmishes against mainly He 111 bombers and reconnaissance aircraft probing defenses around the Firth of Forth and Scapa Flow. In fact, the Luftwaffe's first attempt to bomb Britain occurred on 16 October 1939 when a number of bombers tried to attack warships moored in the Firth of Forth. This attack led to Fighter Command's first engagement with the Luftwaffe in home waters when 602 (City of Glasgow) and 603 (City of Edinburgh) squadrons Spitfires attacked the approaching bombers. It was one of the latter's fighters which claimed the first of Fighter Command's 'kills' of the war. The first bombs to fall on British soil fell, but did not explode in the Shetland Isles on 22 November.

If the actions of Bomber and Coastal Command were so important to the outcome of the battle, why do most books on the Battle of Britain overlook or often provide only cursory reference to their activities? As Larry Donnelly observes in his excellent book *The Other Few: The Contribution Made by Bomber and Coastal Command Aircrew to the Winning of the Battle of Britain:*

'The gallant exploits of the Fighter Command aircrew during the Battle were made evident to the public by the reports in the press and on the wireless; also by the sight of the vapour trails high above them during the air battles. But unseen beyond our shores were the continuous day and night operations being carried out by our Bomber and Coastal Command aircrews. Perhaps it was because they were based near sleepy villages and hamlets far from the Metropolis, and operated out of sight, that they received so little recognition, except for the laconic daily reports on the wireless.'

In the previous chapter, we saw that Bomber Command had been divided in to a number of groups each equipped, primarily with a specific type of aircraft. This meant that each group could take on a specific range of targets, thus, 2 Group, which was principally equipped with Bristol Blenheims were to bear the brunt of flying daylight raids against enemy airfields, shipping and the build-up of invasion barges. The Battle of France had shown how vulnerable the Blenheims and the Fairey Battles were to enemy fighters and ground fire during daylight raids but they continued their policy of mounting these raids with equally disastrous results for their aircraft and aircrews.

The fact that these operations continued shows the seriousness and desperation of the situation we were in. Steps were taken to try to reduce casualties in these near suicidal raids; future daylight attacks could only take place when weather conditions were suitable. To give the aircrew and their aircraft the best chance of surviving during a sortie, they required cloud cover in which they could hide. Cloud however produced its own problems, not only for the Blenheim crews but for all of Bomber Command's airmen. Bomb aiming was still primarily a visual skill in the early years of the war; this meant that if a bomber crew could not see it they were unlikely to be able to deliver their bombs on target. When fighter aircraft were available they were sent with the Blenheims for protection; these operations gradually increased during the battle as the invasion fleet built up and attacks on German airfields increased.

3 Group equipped with Vickers Wellingtons, 4 Group with its Armstrong Whitworth Whitleys, and 5 Group's Handley Page Hampdens were tasked with attacking a wide range of targets, including enemy airfields; aircraft manufacturing and storage; shipping ports and harbors; oil production and storage facilities; marshaling yards and communication networks. To reduce potential losses, all of their raids were only to be conducted at night. The Whitley squadrons in particular were given responsibility of conducting most

of the long-range raids, including those against the aircraft industry in Northern Italy.

Coastal Command's primary tasks were to provide reconnaissance patrols across the North Sea, English Channel, Irish Sea and out in to the North Atlantic in search of German submarines, E-Boats, shipping, surface raiders and warships. They undertook these missions at least twice each day and operated a wide range of aircraft including Avro Ansons, Lockheed Hudsons, Bristol Blenheims, Shorts Sunderland flying boats, and Westland Lysanders. The limited speed and range of the Anson meant that it was restricted to near-shore convoy duties. For long-range patrols, Coastal Command used the awesome Sunderland, nicknamed the 'flying porcupine.' These could operate over Norwegian waters, the North Sea and out in to the Atlantic. Slow moving Lysanders were used at night to intercept German spy missions. Other important tasks involved photo-reconnaissance flights using Blenheims and Spitfires. We have already seen that Fleet Air Arm (FAA) units had been seconded to bolster hard-pressed Coastal Command squadrons. These were equipped with aircraft, such as the Fairey Albacore and Fairey Swordfish that were used to attack shipping and drop mines along the enemy coastline. The Swordfish was an aircraft that was effectively out-of-date when it entered service in 1934 but which undertook many of the most famous FAA attacks including the destruction of the Italian fleet at Taranto.

On 18 June, Churchill made one of the historic speeches of the war in which he made the point that:

'What General Weygand called the Battle of France is over. I expect that the Battle of Britain is about to begin. Upon this battle depends the survival of Christian civilization. Upon it depends our own British life, and the long continuity of our institutions and our Empire. The whole fury and might of the enemy must very soon be turned on us. Hitler knows that he will have to break us in this Island or lose the war. If we can stand up to him, all Europe may be free and the life of the world may move forward into broad, sunlit uplands. But if we fail, then the whole world, including the United States, including all that we have known and cared for, will sink into the abyss of a new Dark Age made more sinister, and perhaps more protracted, by the lights of perverted science. Let us therefore brace ourselves to our duties, and so bear ourselves that, if the British Empire and its Commonwealth last for a thousand years, men will still say, "This was their finest hour."'

Simon Read in his book *The Killing Skies: RAF Bomber Command at War*, records that on 20 June, the Air Ministry sent Bomber Command a directive instructing them to focus their air raids against targets that would have an immediate effect on reducing the scale of air attacks on Britain. This directive set one of the primary agendas for taking the war to the enemy—the destruction, or at least disruption of Germans aircraft industry and oil production.

The following summaries of Bomber and Coastal commands operations during the crucial period which includes the Battle of Britain and the so-called Battle of the Barges are based on details recounted in Donnell's book.

From 1 July, German shipping and U-Boats were the primary targets for Coastal Commands aircraft as they provided sweeps across the North Sea as far as the Norwegian coast, the English Channel, and the Southwest approaches. Their Swordfish were engaged in night-time raids on barges and shipping moored in harbors and river estuaries such as the River Maas in Holland. Their Blenhiems also attacked barges as well as German ships attempting to clear British-laid minefields; they also bombed the harbor facilities at Brest.

Bomber Command's objectives included the Dortmund-Ems Canal, which continued to be an important target throughout the build-up of shipping and barges for the invasion. Daylight raids focused on attacking airfields in France and Belgium together with the German aircraft industry and marshaling yards where German personnel, equipment, and supplies were being assembled.

On 3 July, following Churchill's concerns that an invasion could be attempted at any time, Air Marshal Portal decided to switch the focus of his operations from German industry to the build-up of invasion forces, airfields and the German aircraft production. As his Operational Instruction 38 (as recorded in Michael Bowyer's book) explained:

'The enemy are using airfields and landing grounds in France, Belgium and Holland... The intention is to destroy as many aircraft as possible on the ground thus forcing the enemy to withdraw. Airfields are to be attacked by sections escorted by fighters, or sections or individual aircraft using cloud cover when definite information is received from fighter reconnaissance.'

The following day, another directive arrived which said that targeting German shipping was a new priority 'with emphasis on German warships and the invasion ports along the occupied coast.' We saw in the last chapter that other directives were produced in rapid succession, as the situation deteriorated and additional targets were added.

A revised list of targets was issued that included the aluminium plants at Cologne, Lunne, Ludsigshafen, and Grevenbroich; the airframe assembly plants at Wismar, Lutzkendorf, Bremen, Dieschausen, Gotha, and Kassel; oil targets at Bremen, Hamburg, Hanover, Ostermoor, Gelsenkirchen, Monheim, Reisholtz, Schulau, Castrop, Rauxel, and Bottrop; shipping in Hamburg docks, Kiel, Bremen docks, Wlihelmshaven, and Brunsbuttel.

On 9 July, aircraft attacked Stavanger in Norway. Night-time raids targeted naval facilities along the German coast including Kiel, where the *Scharnhorst* was berthed and the *Tirpitz* at Wilhelmshaven. They also targeted the harbor facilities and ship-building at Cologne, Dortmund, and Hamburg. Hampdens, the only Bomber Command aircraft capable of carrying 'M' (magnetic) mines, were engaged in laying mines outside the entrances to important harbors and river estuaries. The previous night, fifty-two aircraft had been used in the largest bombing operation to date targeted at oil and industrial facilities together with marshaling yards.

On 10 and 11 July, Blenheims of Bomber Command were sent out on daylight raids to bomb airfields and industrial facilities. Many failed to find their targets and strong ground defenses or enemy fighters shot a number of them down.

Bad weather from 12 to 17 July restricted daylight operations for both commands with only a small numbers of aircraft attacking barges, shipping and airfields; the weather was so bad on 14 July that all operations were canceled. In spite of the weather, Bomber Commands night operations continued. On 12 July, most of their aircraft were grounded but Whitleys still set out to bomb the dockyards at Kiel and an oil depot at Emden, but their effectiveness was limited by poor visibility over the targets. During the following three nights, raids were conducted against targets across Northern Germany, including oil facilities and the German aircraft industry together with the usual mine laying operations. The weather so bad on the night of 16 July that all operations were canceled apart from leaflet drops over France.

Read records that another directive was issued on 13 July that instructed Bomber Command to focus on fifteen selected targets, ten of which were important aircraft industrial sites and the other five were oil production and storage related.

With a gradual improvement in the weather on 18 July, Coastal Command was boosted by the transfer of two squadrons of Blenheim fighters, which joined in convoy escort operations and reconnaissance flights along the French and Belgium coasts. The following night, the commands

Blenheims and Hudsons attacked shipping at Emden. Bomber Command launched forty-two Blenheims to attack airfields across Northern France as well as barges and shipping in Boulogne during the day on 18 July. That night, Wellingtons of 3 Group attacked aircraft storage facilities at Rotenberg and Diepholz, as well as oil refineries and airfields. 5 Group's Hampdens attempted to bomb a wide range of targets including an aircraft factory at Gotha, the cruiser *Admiral Scheer* berthed at Kiel, and the *Tirpitz* at Wilhelmshaven. Whitleys of 4 Group attacked oil storage units and industrial sites throughout the Ruhr.

With a general improvement in the night-time weather, Coastal Command increased its attacks on the coastline of France, Belgium, and Holland. On the night of 20 July, they bombed the oil storage tanks at Vlaadingen and the docks at Ghent. Over the following two nights, some of the commands Blenheims and Hudsons bombed barge concentrations at Amsterdam whilst its Swordfish were laying mines off the coast. The Hudsons returned to Amsterdam on the night of 23 July, and the Blenheims attacked oil storage tanks at Flushing.

Meanwhile, bad weather during the day once again affected Bomber Commands daylight raids. On 20 July, Blenheims set out to bomb Luftwaffe airfields, naval and industrial sites, but only two aircraft reached their targets. Over the following two days, all daytime operations were canceled; and on 23 and 24 July, Blenheims once again set out on missions, which failed to find their targets due to adverse weather conditions over the continent. Night operations were also affected. On 20 July, their targets were oil facilities and industrial factories across Northern Germany together with the Dornier factory at Wismar. Following their mauling during the Battle of France, Fairey Battle squadrons were back in operation on the night of 21 July. Their raids again focused on airfields, oil production and storage, barges and shipping but also included strikes by the heavier bombers on German aircraft production, including attacks on the Fieseler factory at Kassel, Dornier's at Wismar, and the Focke Wulf works at Bremen.

Poor weather on 25 July again restricted both commands daylight operations to reconnaissance flights. These included Photographic Reconnaissance Unit (PRU) Spitfires, which were now operating with Coastal Command. When the weather improved, apart from a blip on 30 July, both commands resumed their attacks on the build-up of barge concentrations, but these operations were restricted by a lack of essential cloud cover so vital for the Blenheims to have a chance of reaching their targets and avoiding detection. At night, Bomber Command again concentrated—particularly with their heavier bombers—on attacking the build-up of forces designed to defeat Fighter Command and take part in the expected invasion.

Both sides knew that the ideal tides, necessary for mounting an invasion, i.e., high tide just before mid-day, would occur during two periods, 20–26 August and 19–26 September. These tides would provide the invasion fleet with the best opportunity to undertake a significant proportion of the Channel crossing under the relative protection of darkness. As the earlier period would be too close for the Germans to gather the required ships and barges, the British and Germans knew that mid to late September would be the critical time for any invasion.

August opened with Coastal Command steadily increasing the number of reconnaissance flights designed to monitor the build-up of invasion barges and tugs, the disposition of the German Navy's surface fleet, submarines, E-boats, and activity at Luftwaffe airfields and marshaling centers. On 8 August, both commands attacked airfields on the Channel Isles. In the first third of the month, Bomber Commands 2 Group's Blenheims concentrated their daylight raids on enemy airfields, but once again, they could only fly when cloud conditions offered some protection. At night, the heavier bombers continued to target oil production and storage facilities, marshaling yards, and naval units, including the battleships *Gneisenau* in Kiel and the *Bismarck* at Hamburg. Hampdens were still employed, laying minefields outside the invasion harbors.

During the middle third on the month, Coastal Command stepped up reconnaissance flights that covered the coast from the French-Spanish border to Norway as invasions forces continued to increase. They were also busy as usual providing air cover for convoys and hunting for submarine and surface raiders. On 17, 18, and 19 August, Fairey Battles, escorted by Blenheim fighters, attacked ships in the Port of Boulogne, while Swordfish were busy laying mines at night. 2 Group's Blenheims conducted daylight and night-time raids on airfields and oil targets when conditions allowed. Hampdens and Wellingtons continued their attacks on German military infrastructure as well as railways, power stations, aluminum plants, the Krupps factories at Essen, and oil refineries. They also caused significant damage to the Dortmund-Ems Canal on the night of 12 August. The Whitleys of 4 Group used their longer range to significant advantage by attacking aircraft production in Northern Italy. On the nights of 13, 14, 15, and 18 August, formations of up to thirty-two aircraft flew over the Alps to bomb the Fiat works at Turin and the Caprioni works at Milan.

Until now, both the British and Germans had tried to avoid all-out bombing of civilians, but, as Parker reports:

'In August 1939 Goering had used a Swedish go-between to obtain assurances from the British that they would not be the first ones to bomb heavily populated areas. When Rotterdam had been bombed, the British had taken it to be the end of this mutual agreement and had launched attacks on the Ruhr, against, in theory, industrial targets.'

Bad weather on 20 August led to Bomber Command restricting its daytime operations to keeping up the pressure on enemy airfields while all night sorties were canceled. Although the weather improved slightly the following day, all operations involving Wellingtons and Whitleys were still canceled, although Hampdens were able to attack German oil facilities. The same day, Coastal Commands Swordfish were involved in mine-laying duties and Blenheims continued their airfield attacks, whilst Battles were used against German E-Boats. On 24 August, the night that Luftwaffe bombers accidentally dropped bombs on London (see chapter 6)—Whitley bombers returned to Milan and targets in Southern Germany, including the Messerschmitt works at Augsburg. The following day, Coastal Command launched a hundred and twenty-nine aircraft for their daily anti-invasion and anti-submarine sweeps; these included the first of seven days of attacks on oil storage tanks at Cherbourg. That night, one hundred and two aircraft from Bomber Command set off for air raids on a number of sites in and around Berlin. These included Wellingtons and Whitleys targeting the Siemens factory, and Hampdens attacking the Henschel works.

During the remainder of the month, weather conditions severely affected Blenheim daylight operations against Luftwaffe airfields, but Coastal Command still launched night-time raids on airfields and barge concentration. Their Fairey Albacores attacked shipping in Boulogne and their Swordfish were also busy laying mines. At night, Bomber Command's Blenheims kept up their harassing attacks on airfields and continued to bomb industrial targets and marshaling areas. Its Hampdens headed for oil and gas installations and, on 31 August bombed the BMW factory and airfield in Berlin. The commands Wellingtons and Whitleys also attacked the city. Wellingtons struck the Junkers factory at Dessau, while Whitleys were sent once again to bomb the Fiat works in Milan and the Caprioni factory in Turin. They also attacked the Fiat works in Torino and a magneto factory in Sesto San Giovani. Bomber Commands bombers were now increasing pressure on Germany's military industry by targeting sites across much of the country.

As Bowyer comments:

'As September dawned the fate of freedom hung in the balance. Fighter Command was certainly doing well, and 2 Group's attacks on airfields seemed worthwhile. Invasion fear reached fever pitch, German long-range guns were hurling shells on to the south coast, and the Luftwaffe was relentlessly hammering Britain. It seemed to make sense to continue cloud-cover operations, and the need to sink the barges was becoming paramount.'

Operations in September continued with Coastal Commands daily sweeps, reconnaissance, and patrols. Most days they also provided cover for convoys. Their nocturnal activities included bombing shipping, barge concentrations, and harbor facilities with their Blenheims and Swordfish; these were joined from 2 September by Bristol Beauforts. It was thought that to-date the RAF had destroyed or damaged up to 20% of the invasion barges in the 'Battle of the Barges.' Swordfish and Beauforts were also used to lay minefields across river and harbor entrances. Bomber Command operations continued with Blenheims, Battles, and Hampdens attacking barge concentrations, shipping and harbor facilities. Blenhiems also continued their harassment of enemy airfields. Wellingtons targeted aircraft production and storage facilities, marshaling yards and oil and electricity installations. They were also sent to bomb military stores in the Black Forest, Grunewald Forest, and the Hartz Mountains. Whitley bombers ranged across Germany, hitting Berlin, the BMW works in Munich and Spandau and the Bosch factory in Stuttgart. They also continued to cross the Alps to bomb aircraft production in Milan and Turin and a power station in Genoa.

Read records that on 7 September the Government 'issued its invasion warning…the Royal Navy and RAF were placed on their highest alert and the army was ordered to battle stations along England's southern coast.' Donnelly adds that at 8 p.m. that evening, 'Cromwell' the code word indicating that an invasion had been launched, was mistakenly issued triggering the ringing of church bells, a traditional way of warning the public of an invasion. Roadblocks were established and the Home Guard set off on armed patrols. Wood and Dempster report that even part of Operation Banquet, Flying Training Commands part of the anti-invasion plans was initiated.

Bad weather on 12 September led to the cancellation of both day and night operations. Even so, a few Wellingtons still managed to bomb marshaling yards in Emden and Flushing. Although the following day, the weather improved, a lack of cloud cover led to Blenheim attacks on barges and airfields being canceled.

With the second optimum invasion period approaching (19–26 September) from 13 September Bomber Command focused most of its operations on barge concentrations and shipping. This meant that not only were its Blenheims targeting any harbors or estuaries, which contained barges, its Hampdens, Wellingtons, and Whitleys were now targeting them as well. Wellingtons also kept up their pressure on marshaling yards in Germany, Holland, and Belgium whilst Whitleys bombed railways. They also made a return trip to the *Bismarck* in Hamburg. Hampdens joined in, barge bashing together with their mine laying operations.

By 15 September, there were one hundred and two barges at Boulogne and this had increased to one hundred and fifty two days later. By 18 September, the Germans has amassed 1,004 invasion craft in the Channel ports with another six hundred at Antwerp.

Coastal Command managed to maintain their anti-invasion and anti-submarine sweeps together with intense reconnaissance missions over all of the invasion harbors. On 14 September, aircraft from Coastal Command undertook their first night-time torpedo attack and three days later, when weather conditions improved, Bomber Command flew their largest force to-date, causing considerable damage to Dunkirk, Calais, Boulogne, Cherbourg, and Den Helder.

Large-scale, anti-invasion attacks continued for the rest of the month and were only interrupted on 19 September by bad weather. By the end of the month, 60% of Bomber and Coastal commands bombs, totally some 1,400 tons (1,422 tonnes), had been targeted at the invasion ports. The rest of their missions were focused on military supplies and transport system. Following this period of intensified activity against all aspects of a potential invasion, the Air Ministry (as quoted by Read) is said have issued the following proclamation, 'the crews of Bomber Command are following the precedent set by Sir Francis Drake even though they are singeing the moustache of a bloodthirsty guttersnipe, not the beard of a Spanish King.'

The arrival of October and a general deterioration in the weather signaled the approach of winter that meant that the possibilities of an invasion receded. The last invasion-focused attack occurred on the night of 12–13 October. Following that, Bomber Command changed tactics and went on the offensive to show that the RAF was capable of striking back, resulting in the start of its Strategic offensive which developed throughout the rest of the war.

On 12 October, having missed the ideal period for the weather and the tides, Hitler had to make a decision, would he continue to postpone launching an invasion in the hope that the Luftwaffe could somehow gain the all-important air superiority over the English Channel and Northern England or should he abandon the idea altogether. The RAF had sunk two hundred and fourteen barges and twenty-one transport ships that were destined to take part in the crossing. Although the Germans had seven hundred barges in reserve, these raids, together with the actions of the Royal Navy and deteriorating weather conditions, led to the Germans dispersing some of their invasion fleet in order to give it some protection. Wood and Dempster include the following from Field Marshal Keitel, Supreme Command of the German Armed Forces:

'The Fuhrer [he wrote] has decided that from now until the spring, preparations for Sealion shall be continued solely for the purpose of maintaining political and military pressure on England.
'Should the Invasion be reconsidered in the spring or early summer 1941, orders for a renewal of operational readiness will be issued later. In the meantime, military conditions for a later invasion are to be improved.'

In his book, *The Most Dangerous Enemy: A History of the Battle of Britain*, Stephen Bungay summarizes the possibility of Sea Lion succeeding thus:

'The best that can be said for Sealion is that it was a terrible gamble. Everything had to go right: the three services had to co-operate very closely; the RAF had to be neutralised, the Royal Navy had to be deterred by mine, U-boats and air attack (bearing in mind that the Luftwaffe had only a handful of obsolete He 115 torpedo-bombers and did not have a bomb heavy enough to penetrate the deck armour of the British battleships); and the weather had to benign. The river barges taking the troops across were to be towed in pairs by tugs and could only make about three knots [similar to the speed of the Armada in 1588]. They would be swamped by anything more than a light swell... Only a decisive victory in the air could have given Sealion any prospect of success. All depended on the other part of the plan—the Luftwaffe's Eagle assault.'

Arguments still continue over whether the Fighter Command or the Royal Navy should be given the credit for preventing an invasion (few include Coastal and Bomber Command in these arguments even though it is clear from the above that they played equally important parts in the anti-invasion actions). Similarities can be made between the German's invasion fleet in 1940 and Parma's in 1588, neither of which, given the sea condition required and those common in the English Channel, could have stood much of a chance of succeeding with the barges available. However, this does not diminish the perceived threat the country faced on both occasions, or the importance of either the Navy Royal in 1588 or RAF's Fighter Command in 1940. Both were fighting for their lives and the lives of everyone in Britain.

Having looked at the operations of Bomber and Coastal Commands let us go back to Fighter Command and the air battle against the Luftwaffe.

Chapter 5
Opening Rounds

A number of different dates have been proposed for the start of the Battle of Britain, including 4 June, which marks the end of the evacuation from Dunkirk and 1 July when the Channel Islands were invaded. The official date for the beginning of the Battle has been set as 10 July, when the Luftwaffe began their heavy air raids on Channel and coastal shipping. Even though Hitler viewed these as only minor raids designed to keep up the pressure on the British government to accept peace terms, they formed an important escalation in German attacks. The end of the battle is almost invariably taken as the end of October.

The battle is often divided into different phases based on changes in the Luftwaffe's strategy. However, depending on the approach taken by different authors, the dates of the phases vary. Some authors include four phases, while others, including the RAF Museum divide the action in to five. In the following chapters, I have followed the four-fold phasing:

Phase 1: 10 July–7 August – reconnaissance flights, attacking Channel convoys, radar stations, and coastal towns.
Phase 2: 8 August–6 September – major attacks designed to destroy Fighter Command in the air and on the ground.
Phase 3: 7 September–5 October – the start of the Blitz – massed attacks on London and other major cities, aircraft factories, and a switch to night-time bombing.
Phase 4: 6 October–31 October – heavy night-time bombing and the use of daytime fighter-bombers.

Before we look at the course of the Battle, it is worth saying something about the weather, that great British obsession. Goering had stated that given four or five days of good weather, he could gain victory over Fighter Command. But, as we all know, the one thing that is guaranteed in Britain is that the weather is unpredictable, and so it proved to be during the summer of 1940. The weather that summer is often depicted, or thought of, as being a long, hot, dry period, with clear, blue skies onto which the vapor trails produced by the high-flying, twisting, and turning aircraft were etched. The reality is somewhat different. That summer, like many others here in the UK, was changeable, with no long-lasting, settled period of either good or bad weather. This changeability would have a profound effect on the course of the battle. The Luftwaffe needed an extended period of good, clear weather during which they could inflict the maximum damage on Fighter Command and its infrastructure so that it could gain air-superiority over Southern England and the English Channel. On the other hand, Fighter Command needed poor weather during which they could repair damaged airfields, support convoys, repair, and re-equip its squadrons and generally recover, or at least get some respite from the Luftwaffe's attacks—the weather corresponded to Fighter Command's wishes.

As part of his analysis of the Battle, Brown includes a summary of weather conditions. He divided the 114-day duration of the Battle into eight phases based on weather conditions. They can be summarized as:

Phase 1: 10 July–24 July – the weather was generally poor.

Phase 2: 25 July–10 August – a period of mixed weather with some fine days in between.

Phase 3: 11 August–18 August – a period of generally fine weather.

Phase 4: 19 August–23 August – five days of poor weather.

Phase 5: 24 August–9 September – a period of almost continuous fine weather with only one poor day.

Phase 6: 10 September–22 September – a combination of fine and poor weather in which the fine days were interspersed by period of poor or mixed weather.

Phase 7: 23 September–2 October – a period of fine weather.

Phase 8: 3 October–31 October – generally poor weather.

During the critical period of the battle from 11 August to 15 September when Fighter Command was under the most intense pressure, the weather was generally quite good, but there were crucial breaks, enough to provide the respite Fighter Command needed to be able to keep going.

I do not intend to give a blow-by-blow account of all of the action, when there are so many good, detailed, day-by-day, and overview accounts of the battle already available, but I intend to try to give a 'flavor' of the scale, intensity, and impact of the action. In doing so, I have combined information from many of the books included in the bibliography. However, it is noticeable that some conflict of information exists, so I have tried, as much as possible, to include the most consistent details. To keep the story of the battle in-line with that of the Armada, I have combined several of the 'phases' in to the same chapter, whilst separating out 15 September as the most important day. I am quite aware that authors such as Price point out that 18 August was 'the hardest day,' however, 15 September is celebrated as the day 'we won' the battle, as German tactics and the threat of invasion changed significantly from that date onwards.

On 1 July, Fighter Command had fifty-one operational squadrons and 1,103 pilots. As Ray puts it:

'…the crux of the forthcoming battle was a struggle between two sets of single-seat fighters and, of these, the Germans had about 760 serviceable Bf 109s, while the RAF possessed some 700 Hurricanes and Spitfires.'

A number of authors make similar statements about this being a battle between single-seat fighters, in order to bring the numbers on both sides in to a kind of balance, however, they ignore that fact, as far as Dowding and Park were concerned, the German bombers were always to be the main targets for their fighters. In other words, they were not just fighting Bf 109s, but everything the Germans threw at them.

By the first week of July, the Luftwaffe were beginning to time the arrival of their fighter sweeps over the south coast and Southern England to coincide with Fighter Command's aircraft returning to their airfields following their standing patrols.

To try to find out what the Germans were doing on the continent, Fighter Command had been carrying out reconnaissance patrols, but these flights were generally intercepted or disrupted by the Germans until they were replaced by dedicated photographic reconnaissance Spitfires.

On 8 July, there were seven different convoys at sea, each of which required fighter protection. One of the convoys was attacked by a formation of Do 17s—Biggin Hill's 610 Squadron was scrambled to go to its aid, but during the ensuing fight, they lost one of their Spitfires. 79 Squadron's Hurricanes were also scrambled but were bounced by a formation of Bf 109s, which managed to shoot down two of the of their aircraft, both of whose pilots were also killed.

Phase 1: 10 July–7 August

The first phase of the battle, known as *Kanalkampf*—the battle over the Channel—lasted for three weeks and has been defined by the Luftwaffe's attacks on convoys and shipping. They also attacked widely spread opportunistic targets designed to entice Fighter Command in to an air battle out over the sea, where their aircraft and pilots were more likely to be lost. Most of the action was centered on two areas, the first between the Isle of Wight and Weymouth, and the other along the Straits of Dover. Convoys in the Straits of Dover could also be shelled by the long-range guns stationed on the French coast. (These could shell the town and harbor of Dover as well.) There is also some suggestion that Hitler may have been using this initial phase of the battle to show to the British people what was in store for them if they continued to reject his peace terms.

As we will see, one of the aspects which the Germans could not foresee, nor control, was the unexpectedly poor weather for this time of the year. As well as Dowding's refusal to be drawn in to a battle of attrition, the weather hindered Goering's plans to weaken and hopefully destroy Fighter Command in preparation for invasion.

Wednesday, 10 July

10 July dawned dull and miserable; and at 7:30 a.m., three Spitfires from 66 Squadron based at Coltishall in Norfolk were scrambled, in pouring rain, to intercept a Do 17 on a reconnaissance mission, looking for coastal convoys. They located it off the coast of Great Yarmouth, and shot it down forty-five minutes later.

At 10:30, the radar stations at Dover and Foreness picked up another Do 17 and some twenty to thirty Bf 109s heading for the Kent coast and the Thames Estuary, where they found a convoy, code-named *Bread*. In response, six Spitfires from 74 Squadron, based at their forward airfield of Mantson were scramble. (Fighter Command had recently changed from moving individual flights to entire squadrons to forward operating airfields.) Two of their aircraft were damaged by the Bf 109s but the rest continued to head for and attack the Dornier, which managed to make it back to its base before crash landing. Four Spitfires engaged the Bf 109s and managed to inflict some damage before twelve more German fighters arrived on the scene together with nine Spitfires from 610 Squadron that had been scrambled from their forward base at Gravesend. During the resulting skirmish, one of 610 Squadron's Spitfires was hit and had to make a forced landing at Hawkinge airfield on the Kent coast above the cliffs at Folkstone.

Things quietened down until just before 2 p.m., when radar once again detected a build-up of German aircraft to the west of Calais. This turned out to be a large formation of around twenty Do 17s, plus thirty Bf 110s and more than twenty Bf 109s intent on attacking the *Bread* convoy, as it continuing its journey past Folkstone. Six Hurricanes from Biggin Hill's 32 Squadron, who were providing cover for the convoy, called for help. Fighter Command responded by scrambling an equally large force, comprising Spitfires of 56 Squadron based at their forward airfield at Manston, 74 Squadron from Hornchurch, six Spitfires from 64 Squadron at Kenley, and 111 Squadron's Hurricanes from Croydon. The Spitfires and 32 Squadron's Hurricanes headed for the German fighters while 111 Squadron's Hurricanes attacked the bombers. During the fight, a Hurricane from 111 Squadron clipped a Do 17, ripping off one of the fighters wings, which caused both aircraft to crash in to the sea. By the end of the fight, Fighter Command had a further three Hurricanes and four Spitfires damaged, while the Luftwaffe lost two bombers and ten fighters, they had however managed to sink one of the ships in the convoy.

At 15:30, between sixty and seventy Ju 88s bombers attacked Swansea and Falmouth, both of which were virtually undefended as, at this point in the battle, Fighter Command had not established 10 Group, designed to provide fighter cover for South Wales and the West Country. 92 Squadron, based at Pembrey, were scrambled too late to intercept, allowing the bombers to bomb an ammunitions factory in Swansea and targets in Martlesham. They also caused a large amount of damage in Falmouth, bombing a power station, the railway, shipping, and killing thirty people. During the day's activities, thirteen Luftwaffe aircraft were shot down for the loss of six British fighters.

Thursday, 11 July

Thick fog and low cloud with thunderstorms in the midlands and north made flying almost impossible in some areas. Even so, the Luftwaffe sent out reconnaissance flights in search of convoys along and around the east and southeast coast of England.

At 7:30 a.m., ten Ju 87s supported by around twenty Bf 109s attacked a convoy in Lyme Bay, Dorset. Aircraft from Middle Wallop and Warmwell were scrambled to intercept. However, before they could reach the dive-bombers, their fighter escort caught six Spitfires of 609 Squadron and shot two of them down. Fortunately, the Stukas did not manage to sink any of the ships.

As the morning progressed, the weather over the southwest began to clear, and the Germans launched an attack, using Ju 87s escorted by between twenty and forty Bf 110s. In response, 609 Squadrons Spitfires based at Middle Wallop that had only recently landed from the previous action, were scrambled to intercept the dive-bombers over Portland. Unfortunately, they were bounced by the Bf 110s and lost two aircraft. Whilst the Ju 87s were inflicting only slight damage on Portland, Hurricanes of 601 Squadron arrived from Tangmere to support 609 Squadron; they managed to shoot down two Ju 87s and two Bf 110s. At almost the same time, twelve He 111 bombers were detected heading towards the Isle of Wight and Portsmouth supported by an equal number of Bf 110s. Again, 601 Squadron were sent to intercept with the squadron dividing in half to attack each formation. Those targeting the Bf 110s managed to shoot two of the long-range fighters down, whilst during the attack on the bombers, two of the Heinkels collided and a third was shot down for the loss of a single Hurricane, which was actually shot down by Portsmouth's own anti-aircraft guns.

At around the same time, a He 59 seaplane (a twin-engined biplane), protected by twelve Bf 109s was spotted off Deal on the Kent coast. Six Spitfires from 54 Squadron based at the satellite airfield of Rochford (Southend) in Essex were scrambled to intercept. During this engagement, two aircraft were lost by both sides, and a Spitfire and Bf 109 collided in mid-air during a head-on attack.

A Do 17 was spotted off Walton-on-Naze, on the Suffolk coast, which 66 Squadron's Spitfires were tasked to intercept. Although the Spitfires managed to damage the Dornier, one of their aircraft was also damaged during the fight.

Along the south coast, Ju 87s and He 111s attacked the town and shipping at Portsmouth, killing nine people and injuring fifty others. They also attacked other targets around the Solent, Weymouth, and Portland. During this fight, Fighter Command lost two Spitfires and the Luftwaffe lost a He 111.

Friday, 12 July

Bad weather continued with heavy rain in the north, fog in the Channel, and occasional thunderstorms and low cloud in the southeast and southwest. However, the low cloud cleared during the late morning to leave a nice sunny afternoon over most of Southern England. To strengthen fighter cover in the south and southwest, 152 Squadron were transferred from Acklington in Northumberland to the Sector Station of Middle Wallop in Hampshire.

A convoy, code-named *Booty*, sailing along the east coast off Orfordness caught the attention of the Luftwaffe, who dispatched He 111 and Do 17 bombers to attack it. In response, Fighter Command scrambled the Hurricanes of 85 Squadron from Martlesham Heath. As an increasing number of German bombers headed towards the convoy, additional Hurricanes from 151 Squadron at North Weald and 17 Squadron at nearby Debden were scrambled together with 242 from Coltishall and 246 from Duxford. The British fighters managed to shoot down or damage at least five of the bombers—the damaged aircraft crash landing on their flight home.

A number of other widespread raids were also launched, including a lone He 111 that bombed Aberdeen, killing twenty-nine people and injuring a further hundred. The bomber was then shot down by Spitfires from 603 Squadron. Ju 88s, one of which was shot down, also attacked the airfields at Exeter and St. Eval. During the day, three Hurricanes and one Spitfire were lost in accidents—losses that Fighter Command could well do without. Fighter Command also lost a further four fighters while the Luftwaffe lost eight aircraft.

Wood and Dempster report that RAF Intelligence had discovered, before the war, that the Luftwaffe were trying to use British radio broadcasting stations as navigation beacons. As all of the BBC's transmitters were in or close to potential targets, it was decided to synchronize transmissions between groups of transmitters so that German bombers could not use them.

Saturday, 13 July

Although the weather was gradually improving, the day dawned with fog across Southern England, which cleared to be replaced by low cloud during the morning. A formation of He 111s swept over the Channel in search of a convoy code-named *Bread* and were met by the Hurricanes of 43 Squadron from Tangmere. During the afternoon, as the convoy sailed along the Dorset coast, further raiders, including Do 17s escorted by Bf 110s, were sent to attack it. These were intercepted by Hurricanes from 56 Squadron based at North Weald and 238 Squadron from Kenley, together with Kenley's 64 Squadron's Spitfires. During the ensuing battle, six Do 17s, one Spitfire, and four Hurricanes were shot down. An additional Spitfire was also lost in an accident.

Two other convoys, sailing off the coasts of Harwich and Dover were also attacked. An air battle developed over the latter involving 56 Squadron's Hurricanes against almost thirty-six German fighters.

Wood and Dempster report that some British pilots had reported being shot at by Hurricanes which had RAF marking but which might have been captured Belgium aircraft being used by the Luftwaffe.

Sunday, 14 July

The *Bread* convoy continued its passage eastwards under high cloud, only to be attacked by German fighters. Another convoy was also attacked in the Straits of Dover, together with the airfield at Hawkinge. In response, Fighter Command scrambled the Hurricanes of 111 Squadron from Croydon and 615 Squadron based at Kenley, together with the Spitfires of 74 Squadron from Hornchurch and the Spitfires of 610 Squadron from Biggin Hill. During the ensuing dogfight, four Hurricanes were lost for the downing of one German aircraft. This was the famous combat radio broadcast by the American reporter Charles Gardner, who was broadcasting live for the BBC from Dover at the time.

During the day, Fighter Command issued instructions to its squadrons to shoot down any He 59s, even if they bore Red Cross markings. He 59s had been spotted circling above convoys and were believed to be acting as observation aircraft as well as rescuing downed German aircrew. Hitler claimed that shooting down such aircraft was an act of "cold-blooded murder."

Monday, 15 July

The weather deteriorated again with much of the southern half of the country was covered by low cloud and the occasional thunderstorm. As the cloud cover began to break around mid-day, the Germans launched an attack, using fifteen Do 17s, on the *Pilot* convoy, which was sailing along the Thanes Estuary. They were intercepted by aircraft from 56 and 151 Squadrons. At almost the same time, He 111s based in Scandinavia attacked industrial areas and docks along the east coast of Scotland. These were intercepted by the Spitfires of 603 Squadron, based at Dyce, who managed to shoot down one of the bombers.

During the early afternoon, Heinkels were also used to attack the Westland aircraft factory at Yeovil in Somerset, the railway at Avonmouth, and the airfield at St. Athan in South Wales. At Yeovil, they managed to damage the runway and one of the hangars before they were driven away by the Hurricanes of 213 Squadron that had flown up from Exeter, and the Spitfires from 92 Squadron based at Pembrey.

Shortly after 2 p.m., Do 17s were again sent to attack the *Pilot* convoy—they were engaged by Hurricanes from 56 and 151 Squadrons, both based at North Weald.

Tuesday, 16 July

With improving weather conditions, the Luftwaffe again launched a couple of widespread raids. In the late afternoon, bombers based in Norway attacked Fraserburgh and Peterhead in Scotland, but were intercepted by the Spitfires of 603 Squadron, who managed to shoot down one of the bombers. Another raid, which occurred at teatime, was intercepted off the Isle of Wight by Spitfires from 601 Squadron who managed to shoot down a Ju 88.

Wednesday, 17 July

Hitler issues his directive, outlining the plans for invading Britain. Air activity followed a similar pattern to that of 16 July where the bad weather would restrict the number of reconnaissance flights looking for convoys and other potential targets.

Just before lunchtime, three He 111s attacked the fuel depot on the Isle of Portland but were intercepted by Spitfires from 601 Squadron who managed to shoot down one of the bombers.

In the early afternoon, as 64 Squadron's Spitfires were patrolling off the Sussex coast when they were 'bounced' by Luftwaffe fighters who managed to attack and disappear before the Spitfire pilots had seen them.

A formation of Heinkels, without a fighter escort, set out from their base at Stavanger on the Norwegian coast to attack a chemical works in Aberdeen. On their return journey, they were intercepted by three Spitfires from 609 Squadron based at Turnhouse who managed to shoot one of the bombers down.

Luftwaffe bombers also struck Bristol and attacked shipping off the coasts of Dartmouth and the Isle of Wight. Fighter Command responded to each raid shooting down a He 111 and Ju 88 without loss.

Thursday, 18 July

Weather conditions continued to improve slowly, and in response, the Luftwaffe launched a series of raids against different channel ports. With the realization that the British were using radar to provide early warnings of their raids, the Luftwaffe initiated the practice of sending over early-morning fighter sweeps. To begin with, the radar operates interpreted these as bomber formations and in response Fighter Command launched fighters against the raids. As the radar operators gained more experience in differentiating between fighter and bomber formations, they were able to give better advice on incoming aircraft. However, as the fighter-sweep sent on this morning was interpreted as a bombing raid, 11 Group scrambled the Spitfires of 610 Squadron based at Biggin Hill, who were subsequently 'bounced' by the German fighters who managed to shoot down one of the Spitfires.

The Germans also attacked the coastguard station at St Margaret's Bay, just north of Dover, and sunk the Goodwin lightship that was stationed on the edge of the treacherous Goodwin Sands off the Kent coast between Ramsgate and Dover.

In the afternoon, the Germans launched a large raid on the south coast, comprising Ju 88s and Do 17s escorted by Bf 109s. These were intercepted by the Spitfires of 152 Squadron from Warmwell in Dorset, and 609 from Middle Wallop in Hampshire—however, in the process, 609 Squadron lost two aircraft.

To further strengthen the air defenses in the southwest of England, Dowding moved a flight of Gloster Gladiators from their base in the Shetland Islands to Roborough, on the northern outskirts of Plymouth. In return, 232 Squadron, based at Wick in the north Scotland, sent a flight of their Hurricanes to the Shetlands to cover the loss of the Gladiators.

Friday, 19 July

Most of the country experienced rain showers with sunny intervals, with clearer conditions over the English Channel.

In the early morning, four Do 17s made a surprise attack on the Rolls Royce aero-engine factory in Glasgow, where they inflicted significant damaged.

This was to be a critical day for the Defiants of 141 Squadron based at Biggin Hill, who had recently moved south from Edinburgh. In the morning, they initially flew to West Mailing before moving to the forward base at Hawkinge, overlooking the cliffs above Folkstone. At 12:32, they took off to patrol over the Channel at 5,000 feet (1,524m). Three of the squadron's aircraft had to turn back due to engine problems, whilst the remaining nine continued their patrol. Unfortunately, shortly afterwards, they were 'bounced' by between fifteen and twenty Bf 109s of JG 51, who quickly shot six of the Defiants down. The remaining three only just made it back to Hawkinge due to the timely arrival of 111 Squadron Hurricanes, following their move from Croydon to Northolt.

During the late afternoon, radar detected a raid building up over Calais before it set out to attack Dover. 11 Group scrambled 64, 32, and 74 Squadrons in response, but being out-numbered by the Luftwaffe by almost two-to-one, they were unable to shoot any of the enemy aircraft down. By the end of the day's fighting, the Luftwaffe had fared better than Fighter Command, losing two aircraft compared to the loss of ten British fighters. Five Fighter Command pilots had also been killed and another five were wounded.

In Berlin, Hitler made his 'Last Appeal to Reason' speech as 'the victor' for the British to use reason and common sense to give up the fight. He also chose the occasion to promote a large number of Luftwaffe officers to the rank of General.

Saturday, 20 July

Weather conditions over the south coast and the Channel followed those of the previous day, while areas further north experienced the occasional thunderstorm.

The Germans continued to concentrate their efforts on attacking shipping along the east coast, through the Straits of Dover, and the English Channel, in an effort to draw Fighter Command out over the sea. At this stage, Fighter Command were still mounting standing patrols, which although they gave air cover to shipping, meant that they were vulnerable to attack, particularly by German fighters. With a number of ships at sea, Fighter Command's aircraft would again have a busy day.

During the afternoon, 238 Squadron's Hurricanes were in action over Swanage on the east Dorset coast, where they were providing cover for a convoy code-named *Bosom*. The squadron lost one aircraft while they were trying to prevent Bf 109s reaching the convoy. 501 Squadron's Hurricanes were also scrambled to intercept an incoming raid comprising Stuka dive-bombers escorted by Bf 109s. They met the enemy aircraft as the convoy was sailing south of Weymouth.

By 6 p.m., when the ships were approaching the Straits of Dover, another large formation of Stukas escorted by some fifty Bf 109s and Bf 110s headed eastwards towards the convoy. 32 Squadron, based at Biggin Hill, who were patrolling over the Channel, managed to 'bounce' the enemy aircraft and in the process, shot down two and damaged a further four Stukas. The Hurricanes of 615 Squadron and Spitfires of 610 Squadron who were also based at Biggin Hill then arrived on the scene. The Bf 110s assumed their usual fighting defensive circle and retreated across the Channel, whilst the Bf 109s joined in the dogfight, only to lose five aircraft.

65 Squadron's Hurricanes were also in action off the French coast, and 56 Squadron's Hurricanes attacked a number of Ju 88s off the Essex coast, shooting down one of the bombers. 603 Squadron were also in action off the coast at Aberdeen.

Apart from fighting over *Bosom* most other engagements were limited, even so, during the day's action, Fighter Command lost three aircraft and the Luftwaffe lost nine.

Sunday, 21 July

With the arrival of generally fine weather throughout the day, the Luftwaffe's tactics of sending over wide-spread raids continued, with Dornier bombers attacking targets along the Scottish coast, and single raiders or reconnaissance aircraft targeting the south and east coasts. A formation of twenty German aircraft attacked a convoy code-named *Peewit*. 238 Squadron, flying from Warmwell, shot down a Dornier bomber and a Bf 110 that had been shadowing another convoy off the Dorset coast. Having been alerted to the presence of the convoy, the Luftwaffe sent a formation of Dorniers escorted by Bf 109s and Bf 110s. They reached the ships as they passed south of the Isle of Wight but were intercepted by 238 Squadron who had been joined by 43 Squadron from Tangmere. The Hurricanes managed to break-up the bomber formation south of the Needles (the most western point on the Isle of Wight) just as the nine Bf 110s started to dive-bomb the ships. This was the first time that Bf 110s had been used as dive-bombers during the battle. After the dive-bombers turned for home, the British fighters chased them all the way back to the French coast.

Monday, 22 July

The weather continued to improve, and with it, small raids were launched against shipping in the Channel. These raids caused only slight damage because of the limited numbers of targets. Losses of aircraft on both sides were also limited.

Interestingly, Sea Gladiators of 804 Squadron Fleet Air Arm flew their first operation during the battle from their base at Wick, which is almost the furthest point north on mainland Scotland.

Tuesday, 23 July

Due to increasing losses, the Admiralty had begun to re-route shipping away from the Channel area. As a consequence, there were fewer opportunities for the Germans to entice Fighter Command in to battle, because Dowding was determined to meet any attack with only sufficient force to prevent that attack. He had made it clear to his pilots that they were not to engage the enemy unless it was necessary. Even so, the Luftwaffe still undertook attacks against shipping off the east coast, during which Fighter Command shot down three aircraft for no loss.

Wednesday, 24 July

With generally improving weather and fewer British ships at sea, the Luftwaffe turned their attention to launching a large number of raids on inland targets.

Just before 8 a.m., radar detected a formation of Dorniers with a large fighter escort heading for a convoy entering the Thanes Estuary. In response, the Spitfires of 54 and 64 Squadrons were scrambled. Although they did not manage to shoot down any of the bombers, 54 Squadron lost one of its aircraft whilst engaging with the German fighters.

Some three hours later, another formation comprising nearly twenty Do 17s escorted by more than forty Bf 109s were detected heading for the same convoy. This time, 54, 65, and 610 Squadrons, all equipped with Spitfires, were scrambled to intercept the raid, which they met over the town of Margate on the north Kent coast. The bombers turned for home having lost three of their number, and the Spitfires then engaged the Messerschmitts, resulting in a number of them being damaged, for the loss of a single Spitfire from 54 Squadron.

A number of lone bombers also ranged across the country, one of which, a Ju 88, joined the circuit at Brooklands before dropping twelve bombs on the airfield. Even if the raiders' actions were audacious, it caused little damage. Additional raids were mounted against shipping in the Bristol Channel. During the day's action, the Luftwaffe lost six aircraft; Fighter Command recorded no losses.

Dowding continued the re-shuffling of his squadrons with 43 Squadron moving from Tangmere to Northolt and 1 Squadron moving in the other direction. 264 Squadron equipped with Defiants moved from Duxford north to Kirton-in-Lindsay in Lincolnshire and 141 Squadron, also equipped with Defiants, were moved to Prestwick in Scotland.

Thursday, 25 July

Overnight, rain cleared to be replaced by fine weather for the rest of the day.

German radar that had been installed on the French coast opposite Folkstone to detect Allied shipping, initiated the first raid of the day when it located a convoy, code-numbered *CW8*. This comprised twenty-one ships that were sailing through the Straits of Dover and were heading for Portland on the Dorset coast. Initially, around mid-day, forty German fighters were dispatched, flying at low level, to attack the convoy. They were met by the Hurricanes of 32 and 615 Squadrons. This attack was followed by a formation of around sixty Stukas who attacked the convoy, sinking five ships and damaging five others. The dive-bombers were also joined by nine fast-moving E-boats, and were further supported by the heavy guns located along the French coast. To counter this attack, 54 Squadron joined the fight. The E-boats were intercepted by HMS *Boreas* and HMS *Brilliant*—two Royal Navy B class destroyers. Unfortunately, these were also dive-bombed and HMS *Boreas* suffered sufficient damage that it had to be towed into Dover harbor; twenty-two members of the crew were also killed. HMS *Brilliant* escaped the raid unscathed.

Within an hour, another raid, comprising thirty Ju 88s and fifty Bf 109s headed for the same convoy. Spitfires of 64 Squadron, who were mounting a standing patrol over the ships, were joined by the Hurricanes of 111 Squadron and together they went into attack. 111 Squadron mounted their now traditional head-on attack designed to frighten and break up the bomber formation. Just as many of the German aircraft turned for home and with 64 and 111 Squadrons also heading for their airfields to refuel and rearm, more Bf 109s arrived on the scene. With the additional new protection, the bombers turned back to renew their attack, sinking five ships and severely damaging four others. However, just as the bombers began their attack, 56 Squadron's Hurricanes arrived on the scene from North Weald, and they were also joined by the Spitfires of 64 and 54 Squadrons. During the ensuing fight, 64 and 54 Squadrons lost three aircraft each, while the Luftwaffe lost sixteen aircraft.

Later that day, Dowding continued his policy of rotating tired and depleted squadrons in 11 Group with 54 Squadron moving to Catterick in North Yorkshire, to be replaced by 41, who moved in the opposite direction to Hornchurch.

Friday, 26 July

Bad weather returned with low cloud and heavy rain, blanketing much of the south of the country. Even so, the Germans launched a raid on ships south of the Isle of Wight, to which 601 Squadron based at Tangmere responded. They managed to shoot down two of the bombers for the loss of one of their own aircraft.

A second raid was mounted around mid-day in the same general area, to which 238 Squadron at Middle Wallop were scrambled; they managed to shoot down one of the escorting fighters without loss.

Smaller raids, usually employing lone-raiders, were also dispatched across the country, hitting Hasting, Weymouth, Bristol, Aberdeen, and targets to the north of London. In the Channel, three steamers were sunk.

Saturday, 27 July

Again, weather conditions were poor with low cloud over the English Channel and occasional rain in the midlands and over the North Sea.

Shortly before 10 o'clock in the morning, a large raid comprising around thirty Stukas, with a large fighter escort, was mounted against a convoy code-named *Bacon* that was sailing off Swanage, on the Dorset coast. Fighter Command responded by scrambling Hurricanes from 238 Squadron based at Middle Wallop, who joined the Spitfires of 609 Squadron that had been mounting a standing patrol over the convoy, just as the dive-bombers were preparing to attack. Unfortunately, the Luftwaffe fighters managed to prevent most of the British fighters from reaching the dive-bombers, even so 609 Squadron shot down one dive-bomber and damage another one for the loss of one of their own aircraft.

During the afternoon, the Luftwaffe attacked two other convoys, one off Harwich and the other off Dover. During the Harwich-bound raid, Heinkel bombers managed to sink HMS *Wren*, a Royal Navy destroyer. The Dover raid involved Bf 109s that were being used as fighter-bombers for the first time. During a second raid on Dover itself, Ju 88s and Ju 87s bombed the harbor and military barracks. They also managed to sink HMS *Codrington* in the harbor, which broke its back. Bombers also sank and damaged two other naval ships sailing off the east coast.

In response to these and previous losses, the navy decided that they could no longer risk their ships in the harbor at Dover. Unfortunately, their decision meant that Fighter Command would have to increase the number of standing patrols to provide protection for convoys in that area and in the Thames

Estuary—a situation that Dowding was keen to avoid in order to prevent the unnecessary exposure and loss of his valuable aircraft.

Wood and Dempster report that the increasing number of attacks on Dover led the Air Ministry to issue special orders to Fighter Command to intercept incoming raids further out to sea. This meant that they would have less warning of any approaching raids and less idea of where the raids were bound. Fighter Command would therefore need to bring more squadrons in to 11 Group to be stationed at the forward airfields of Manston and Hawkinge. Intercepting raids further out-to-sea would also mean a greater potential loss of aircraft and pilots, as they would be further away from their airfields if they got in to trouble. Wood and Dempster also report that, in order to reduce the increasing number of aircraft lost or damaged through accidents, Dowding posted two flying discipline officers to each station, to make sure that pilots were taking eight hours rest a day, and a day off a week from flying.

Sunday, 28 July

Although the day dawned bright and clear, the expected early morning raids did not materialize. However, around mid-day, radar stations at Dover, Rye, and Pevensey detected the build-up of two large raids in the area around Calais that started out towards Dover, but then turned back. With the navy's decision to abandon Dover as a base, the Luftwaffe had achieved one of its goals.

At 2 p.m., radar detected the build-up of another raid, comprising more than sixty He 111s escorted by over forty Bf 109s that were heading towards Dover. In response, Hornchurch scrambled the Spitfires of 41 and 74 Squadrons, the latter stationed at their forward airfield at Manston. 111 Squadron's Hurricanes and those of 257 Squadron were also scrambled from Croydon and Northolt respectively.

Thirty minutes later, 74 Squadron led by 'Sailor' Malan, were the first to make contact with the enemy, the others followed soon after. With the Spitfires heading for the escorting Bf 109s, the Hurricanes attacked the bombers. During this encounter, the famous Luftwaffe pilot Werner Molders was wounded; and although his Messerschmitt was damaged, he managed to nurse it back to base. However, his injuries were sufficient to keep him out of the battle until September. Five Bf 109s and two He 111s were shot down, with a further eight aircraft lost in other attacks, whilst Fighter Command lost five fighters.

Monday, 29 July

With the weather remaining good across the country, at five in the morning, a Ju 88 bomber set out to bomb Crewe, but the aircrew got lost and eventually ran out of fuel and crashed near Bexhill in Surrey.

Twenty-five minutes later, a flight of Spitfires from 24 Squadron based at St. Eval in Cornwall, intercepted and shot down another Ju 88 close to Plymouth. A He 111 was also shot down on its way to bomb the aircraft factory in Bristol.

During the early morning, radar stations along the Kent and Sussex coast detected the build-up of a large formation of aircraft crossing the Channel; this comprised more than sixty Bf 109s escorting forty-eight Ju 87 dive-bombers. Spitfires from 41 Squadron at Manston, and Hurricanes from 501 Squadron at Hawkinge were the first to encounter the enemy. With the advantage of height, the escorting Bf 109s were able to counter 41 Squadron's attack, shooting down one of the Spitfires and damaging four others, for the loss of two of the dive-bombers. 56 Squadron from North Weald, 64 Squadron from Kenley, and 43 Squadron's Hurricanes from Northolt, who were already airborne, then joined the other British fighters. They intercepted the Germans over their target, Dover, just as the dive-bombers were about to attack. In the ensuing dogfight, which involved nearly two hundred aircraft, four of the dive-bombers were shot down, and one of 65 Squadron's Hurricanes was also lost. Anti-aircraft guns around the harbor managed to shoot down two other Stukas.

Shortly after this engagement, attacks were mounted on two convoys in the Channel. During the first attack, defensive balloons bought down one of the low-flying Ju 88s, whilst the convoy's anti-aircraft guns shot down another. Bf 110s attacking the second convoy off the coast at Orfordness were driven off by Hurricanes from North Weald's 151 Squadron, but not before two of the squadrons aircraft were damaged.

In the afternoon, a formation of twenty He 111 and Do 17 bombers were detected heading for the east coast near Harwich. The Spitfires of 66 Squadron based at Coltishall, together with Hurricanes from 17 Squadron at Debden, and 85 Squadron at Martlesham Heath were scrambled to intercept them. In the resulting fight, two of the Heinkels were shot down.

Tuesday, 30 July

Low cloud and occasional rain throughout the day meant that there was little action, apart from Ju 88s attacking a convoy off the east coast just before lunchtime. Bombers also flew limited raids against Orfordness,

Clacton, and Harwich whilst 603 Squadron based at Montrose in Scotland, shot down a He 111.

Wednesday, 31 July

The weather returned to balmy summer conditions with a cloudless sky and rising temperatures. Just before nine in the morning, a Sunderland flying boat from the Australian Air Force was covering a merchant cruiser that was heading for Plymouth to undergo a refit, when a Ju 88 arrived on the scene. The Sunderland managed to drive the bomber away before it could inflict any damage.

At around 11 o'clock, a formation of Ju 87s attacked a small convoy in the Channel.

During the afternoon, small, widely scattered raids occurred along east coast with bombers attacking shipping near Lowestoft and Great Yarmouth.

3:30 p.m. saw the last action of the day when a formation of Bf 109s were spotted heading for Dover. In response, four squadrons were scrambled, including the Spitfires of 74 Squadron from Hornchurch, which were the only aircraft to find and engage the enemy formation. During the developing dogfight, four Bf 109s were damaged, whilst 74 Squadron lost two Spitfires with another aircraft badly damaged. The German fighters had been sent over to shoot down the newly installed barrage balloons. These would feature as a regular target for fighter sweeps in the coming days, as their pilots, short of Fighter Command aircraft to shoot at, looked for alternative targets.

Other raids followed with more than fifty bombers flying towards the Isle of Wight before being turned back by defending fighters. This was followed by a smaller formation of over twenty bombers following the same course, which managed to get through to their targets without interception.

So far, the Luftwaffe had concentrated on attacking shipping, sinking eighteen steamers and four destroyers. They had also attacked elements of the aircraft industry in order to draw Fighter Command in to battle and to weaken its strength. However, on this day, Goering reported to Hitler that all of his aircraft were now ready at twelve hours' notice to begin their main air attack on England.

During July, the Luftwaffe had lost two hundred and seventy aircraft compared to Fighter Command's one hundred and forty-fine. As Patrick Bishop reports in *Battle of Britain: A Day-by-Day Chronicle*, more worrying for Dowding was the fact that Fighter Command had lost eighty flight commanders and squadron leaders during the month, and 'of those left, only about half hadn't any real experience of combat,' whilst 'those who had been involved in the fighting were approaching physical and mental exhaustion.'

Hitler issued *Directive 17*, the plans to launch an all-out attack on the RAF timed to begin on or around 10 August. Consequently, air activity over the next few days would be limited as the Luftwaffe relocated many of its squadrons closer to the coast and in particularly closer to the coast opposite Fighter Command's 11 Group airfield's.

Thursday, 1 August

With temperatures continuing to rise and early morning cloud clearing over the south of England, the day would provide ideal conditions for the Luftwaffe to try yet again to draw Fighter Command into battle, but this was proving difficult to achieve.

In a conference at The Hague, Goering told his Luftwaffe Commanders—Albert Kesserlring Commander of II Luftflotte, Hugo Von Sperle Commander of III Luftflotte, and Hans-Jurgen Stumpft Commander of V Luftflotte—that the raids on shipping had failed to draw Fighter Command in to battle. Luftwaffe Intelligence had realized that Dowding was only sending sufficient numbers of aircraft in to action to counter the raids, allowing other aircraft to replace them when they needed to land to rearm and refuel. Their intelligence also reported that, in their estimate, Fighter Command had been reduced to around five hundred aircraft; in fact, Fighter Command actually had almost 1,000 fighters either with operational squadrons or in storage ready for use.

At just before 1 p.m., two convoys code-named *Agent* and *Arena* were sailing off the Yorkshire coast, when a formation of bombers were detected heading for them. The Hurricanes of 607 Squadron based at Usworth (on the outskirts of Sunderland) and the Spitfires of 616 Squadron at Leconfield in Yorkshire were scrambled to intercept the raid, but due to very low cloud, they only found one Ju 88 and a Do 17.

At 2:30 p.m., the radar at Pevensey picked up what appeared to be a number of German aircraft over the Channel. These turned out to be a single Henschel Hs 126 short-range, reconnaissance aircraft, which was located and shot down by Hurricanes from 145 Squadron eight miles (12.8km) off the coast at Hastings. They also found another Hs 126 which they shot down, and damaged a Ju 88 for the loss of one of their own aircraft.

An hour later, a formation of He 111s attacked Norwich, hitting a railway station, the Boulton-Paul aircraft factory, and a wood yard. These attacks killed six people and injured forty others. No RAF fighters were scrambled to intercept this raid. Further south, smaller encounters were taking place along the Essex coast. These included the interception of two Dornier bombers near Harwich, one of which was shot down while the other aircraft escaped with some damage. Additional action occurred off the coast of Sussex.

During the night, the Germans dropped their 'Last appeal to reason' leaflets, most of which fell on open farmland. Tradition has it that, local people took great delight in using copies not eaten by cattle and sheep as toilet paper.

Friday, 2 August

The English Channel and the Straits of Dover were covered by low cloud, whereas the rest of the country was enjoying fine weather. Once again, air activity was limited to isolated attacks on Channel convoys and widespread, small-scale attacks that were difficult to detect and required only limited response.

This was the day that 303 Squadron, a third squadron crewed by Polish pilots was officially formed at Northolt. They would join their fellow Polish pilots—that had already formed 302 Squadron two weeks earlier—in training, and preparation for front-line service at Leconfield, and 301 Squadron that had formed on 22 July at Bramcote near Nuneaton.

Saturday, 3 August

The Luftwaffe General Staff issued the plans for *Alderangriff* (*Eagle Attack*). This was to comprise three separate phases:

Phase One: Five days in which attacks would be concentrated in a 60–90 mile (96–144km) radius around London.
Phase Two: Three days in which attacks would be concentrated in a 30–60 mile (48–96km) radius around London.
Phase Three: Raids would be concentrated within a 30 mile (48km) circle around London.

The day dawned with dense fog over Southern and Eastern England that was gradually replaced by low cloud. Again, the Luftwaffe limited themselves to widespread, small-scale attacks, as if they were testing the country's air defense. These included an early morning attack on a convoy off the east coast and the sinking of a trawler, which claimed to have shot the bomber down. Other attacks took place from Edinburgh to Falmouth,

Swansea to Liverpool, and Birmingham and Crewe. Off the Scottish coast, a steamer claimed to have shot down two Heinkels.

Sunday, 4 August

Even though the weather was a slight improvement on the previous day, the Luftwaffe was still fairly inactive with most flights being restricted to the southwest of the country. Fighter Command managed to shoot down four aircraft.

Monday, 5 August

This turned out to be a fine day, with only high cloud to spoil the view. The Luftwaffe sent out a number of raiders looking for convoys and other shipping. They also sent over a number of fighter sweeps during the day, including a large-scale sweep during the afternoon, in an attempt to draw Fighter Command in to combat. However, once again, Downing was not going to fall in to their trap. During the day's scattered attacks, including one on a convoy in the Straits of Dover, Fighter Command shot down six aircraft for the loss of only one of its own fighters.

Tuesday, 6 August

The weather deteriorated with strong winds and low cloud, which reduced still further any air activity. Only seven enemy aircraft came close to the coastline, and there was also limited activity against shipping in the English Channel.

Goering met with his commanders to lay out his plans for future attacks. Luftflotte II, based in northeast France, Holland, and Belgium were to concentrate on attacking the east coast of England, the Thames Estuary, and parts of Southern England. Luftflotte III, based in Northwestern France, were to focus their air offensive on the area west of Portsmouth, the Bristol Channel, and South Wales. Luftflotte V, based in Norway, were to attack Northern England, Scotland, and the Royal Naval Home Fleet base at Scapa Flow. The air fleets were also ordered to strike target further inland during their night attacks.

Goering's intention was to continue to try to draw Fighter Command in to combat by increasing the number and spread of raids. The actual bombing was of secondary importance to trying to shoot down British Fighters so that the Luftwaffe could gain the all-important air superiority over the invasion area. As part of Goering's plans, the number of fighters required to protect the bombers was doubled. The fighter pilots were also ordered to stagger their height above the bombers. To assist them in their additional duties and to give them more time to provide protection for the bombers, many fighter units were transferred to the area around Calais to enable them increased combat time over the Channel and Southern England.

Wednesday, 7 August

Once again, with the weather continuing to deteriorate, the day saw little action apart from the occasional reconnaissance flights looking for shipping. Even so, Fighter Command flew a large number of sorties and shot down four aircraft.

The lull in action caused partly by variable weather and Goering's change of tactics, meant that Fighter Command was able to continue to build up its forces. The limited numbers of British aircraft that the Luftwaffe had encountered so far led Goering and Luftwaffe Intelligence to underestimate Fighter Command's strength. As far as Goering was concerned, all he needed was four or five days of good weather to be able to defeat Fighter Command and establish air superiority over the English Channel and the southern and southeastern coast of England. However, through careful use of his aircraft and aircrew, Dowding had been able to significantly strengthen his forces. Between 30 July and 7 August, Fighter Command had increased its front-line fighter strength from five hundred and eighty-seven to seven hundred and twenty aircraft, and its aircrew from 1,200 to 1,465. This was partly achieved by the activation of two of the Polish squadrons (302 and 303) already mentioned and one of the Czechoslovakian (310) squadrons.

Chapter 6

Crunch Point

Phase 2: 8 August–6 September

Goering had set 10 August as *Adler Tag* (*Eagle Day*), the start of *Adlerangriff* (*Attack of the Eagles),* but as we will see, continuing poor weather delayed this until first thing on 13 August. Even then, things did not go according to plan, because poor weather delayed the start of the planned large-scale attacks until mid-day. This marked a significant change in tactics; convoys and shipping were no longer important targets, although aircraft production facilities remained a priority. The main focus of air attacks would now be Fighter Command's airfields and infrastructure.

Thursday, 8 August

The day began with showers in the southeast of England, which cleared during the afternoon; there were bright, sunny conditions in the west.

Hitler gave orders 'to all units of Luftflottes II, III and V, *Operation Adler Tag*, within a short period you will wipe the British Royal Air Force from the sky.' Within an hour of Hitler delivering this message, it had been intercepted by Bletchley Park, decoded, and was in the hands of both Churchill and Dowding. This confirmed the information gained from aerial reconnaissance flights, that the Luftwaffe had been moving their aircraft closer to the coast and explained the relative lack of activity in the last few of days.

Although the Luftwaffe's main targets were to be Fighter Command's airfield's, they could not let a large convoy of twenty-five ships plus their naval escort of nine ships—the first for nearly two weeks—pass them by. This convoy *CW9*, code-named *Pewitt* was sailing through the Straits of Dover and the English Channel, before heading for the Atlantic. The ships had assembled off Southend the evening before, with the intention of passing through the Straits of Dover during the hours of darkness. However, before dawn, they were detected by the German Freya radar, which alerted German E-boats to their presence. These attacked just after dawn, sinking three ships and damaging a number of others.

Early that morning, the Luftwaffe joined in the attack, launching three hundred Ju 87 dive-bombers escorted by around one hundred and fifty Bf 109s. After British radar detected the build-up of this force, Keith Park called five 11 Group squadrons based at Biggin Hill and Kenley to readiness, and called on 10 Group for support from one of their squadrons. Biggin Hill's aircraft were scrambled to intercept the raiders over the Channel before they could reach the convoy and in the ensuing fight, the RAF lost four Spitfires and their pilots, with another two aircraft damaged and an additional Spitfire having crash-landed on a beach. The Luftwaffe lost a single Bf 109, but a further five crashed in France trying to make it back to their bases. One ship had been slightly damaged.

Just before 2 p.m., as the convoy continued westwards, the weather improved and as it passed south of the Isle of Wight, a second large force of fifty-seven Ju 87s once again escorted by thirty Bf 109s and twenty Bf 110s, this time from Luftflotte III, attacked it. The Hurricanes of 43, 145, 238, and 257 squadrons, and a single squadron (609) of Spitfires were scrambled to intercept the raid. When they arrived, the Ju 87s were already inflicting a significant amount of damage on the ships. As the diver-bombers began to turn for home, a large dogfight developed between the fighters, during which two Hurricanes, three Ju 87s, a Bf 110, and three Bf 109s were shot down. During the course of the action, the dive-bombers managed to sink four ships and badly damage seven others.

Shortly after this raid had left the scene, a new force arrived comprising eighty-two Ju 87s, escorted by seventy Bf 109s and Bf 110s that had also headed out from the Cherbourg Peninsular. 145 Squadron, which had been scrambled to meet the original attackers, landed back at their base at Westhampnett, where they were quickly rearmed and refueled so that they too could meet this new threat. 43 Squadron also arrived and engaged the Bf 109s, shooting down three. They were followed by 145 Squadron who were now flying their third sortie of the day. Even though they shot down three dive-bombers and damaged five more, other Stukas inflicted even more damage on the convoy. In fact, out of the original twenty-five ships that set sail from Southend, only four made it to Poole or Portsmouth without any significant damage. This was the most heavily attacked convoy of the entire Battle of Britain period. During the air battle, Fighter Command lost thirteen Hurricanes, with another five damaged, and one Spitfire plus two damaged. They had also lost twelve pilots with another three wounded. The Luftwaffe lost eight Bf 109s, a Bf 110, and seven Ju 87s, with two Bf 109s, five Bf 110s, and 11 Ju 87s damaged.

Friday, 9 August

Rain and thunderstorms caused the postponement of Luftwaffe operations and once again gave Fighter Command time to replace their losses. Initially, Goering had set the following day for the start of *Adler Tag*, but as the day wore on, it was clear that the poor weather conditions would continue for at least another day. Even so, a single bomber attacked the shipyards in Sunderland, before being shot down by Hurricanes from 79 Squadron based at Acklington. A Heinkel bomber, one of six bombers searching for shipping targets, was shot down off the Yorkshire coast, and a Ju 88 was shot down off Plymouth. During the day, Fighter Command also lost three aircraft.

Saturday, 10 August

As we have seen, although this had originally been set as the date for the start of *Adlerangriff*, with thunderstorms and showers continued over much of the country, German air activity was again limited to reconnaissance flights and isolated raids. These included attacks on RAF West Mailing, in Kent, where a Do 17 dropped bombs close to the airfield, and a lone Do 17 supported by the Bf 110s of EG 210 that attacked Norwich.

During the early morning, a small raid made its way towards a convoy sailing close to Swanage in Dorset, but the bombers turned back for before they made contact with the ships. Another small convoy was attacked by bombers close to Lowestoft, and individual ships were attacked close to Beachy Head and the Pembroke coast. A lone bomber was spotted and chased away from the northeast coast close to Blyth in Northumberland.

It is also reported that this was the day that Vichy France offered to supply two hundred pilots to the Luftwaffe to fight in the battle.

Sunday, 11 August

The day began clear but clouded over in the afternoon. German reconnaissance flights had predicted that this would be the start of the break in the weather that Goering required to be able to mount *Operation Adlerangriff.*

In order to continue to rest and rebuild squadrons that had been in the thick of the action, Fighter Command moved a number of them from 11 Group. 501 Squadron moved from Kenley to Biggin Hill and was replaced by 1 RCAF Squadron, a newly commissioned Canadian squadron. 266 Squadron moved south from Wittering in Lincolnshire to Hornchurch in Essex, 85 Squadron moved slightly northwards from North Weald to Debden (which was in neighboring 12 Group), and 303, one of the Polish squadrons, moved to Northolt. Further afield, 141 Squadron swapped Prestwick for Turnhouse.

At 8:30 in the morning, the Luftwaffe mounted a fighter-sweep, comprising more than thirty Bf 109s and thirty Bf 110s, over the port and town of Dover. This fighter-sweep was designed to force Fighter Command to scramble aircraft towards the Kent coast and away from the Portland, where the main attack would be heading. In response, 11 Group scrambled Spitfires from 74 Squadron that had moved to their forward base at Manston together with 64 Squadron at Kenley, and 43 Squadron based at Tangmere. Just as 74 Squadron was about to engage the Bf 110s, they were set upon by some of the Bf 109s and lost one aircraft. 64 Squadron managed to shoot down two Bf 109s over the Sussex coast.

Just before 10 a.m., Ventnor radar station detected a large force building up over the French coast—this was to be the main raid. In response, Park called a number of squadrons to readiness, and as the potential target area was close to, or within 10 Group area, Brand bought a number of his squadrons to readiness as well. Once the direction of the raid—the largest to date—had been identified as the Portland-Weymouth area, 145 Squadron at Westhampnett, 152 Squadron at Warmwell, 213 and 87 Squadron's at Exeter, 238 and 609 Squadron's at Middle Wallop all within 10 Group, and 601 Squadron at Tangmere—in 11 Group—were scrambled. The attacking force comprised fifty-six Ju 88s and twenty He 111s escorted by sixty-seven Bf 110s and thirty Bf 109s. A huge dogfight developed during which the bombers managed to hit factories, a gasworks, and oil storage facilities in and around Portland and Weymouth. Losses in the air on both sides were significant, with the Luftwaffe losing two Ju 87s, six Ju 88s, two He 111s, fifteen Bf 109s, and ten Bf 110s, a further fifteen aircraft were damaged. Fighter Command lost six Spitfires and twenty-one Hurricanes, including five from 238 Squadron, whilst one Spitfire and five Hurricanes force-landed. Of even more significance, they also lost twenty-six pilots.

As soon as the British fighters landed, they were refueled and rearmed, ready to fight again. In fact, many of the pilots were in combat four times during the day. At almost the same time, a German fighter sweep appeared over Dover and tried to shoot down barrage balloons protecting the harbor.

Just before mid-day, the Germans attacked a convoy code-named *Booty* off the east coast of Essex near Clacton, with Do 17s bombers escorted by Bf 110s acting as fighter cover. Fighter Command launched two squadrons from Debden and one from Hornchurch in response, losing three aircraft in the ensuing flight. Two of the ships in the convoy were seriously damaged by bombs.

At 2 p.m., yet another attack took place off the Kent coast, this time close to Margate. This raid, which was aimed at a convoy and its escorts, in the Thames Estuary, comprised forty-five Do 17s bombers, together with ten Ju 87s and fifteen Bf 109s. 74 Squadron, who were already airborne, were redirected southwards to intercept the raid, and 54 and 111 Squadrons were scrambled to join them. During the fight, 74 Squadron lost two aircraft whilst 111 Squadron lost four of their Hurricanes. As we have already seen, 111 Squadron were rapidly becoming famous for adopting the dangerous technique of frontal attacks to break up bomber formations; but in adopting these tactics, they were particularly vulnerable to mid-air collisions. The squadron would fly, line abreast, towards the enemy bombers, and at the last minute, before colliding with them, they would dive underneath the enemy aircraft. Usually, the bomber pilots' nerves would crack first, and the bomber formations would scatter in an effort to avoid the rapidly approaching Hurricanes.

Although most of the ships in the convoy suffered only slight damage, a destroyer and two minesweepers were hit, later one had to be beached to save it from sinking.

During the day's air battles, the Luftwaffe lost 38 aircraft to Fighter Command's 32. These were significantly larger losses for both sides—losses neither air force could sustain if they continued at the same rate over a long period. Goering wanted to inflict substantial damage on Fighter Command and Dowding was trying his best to manage his fighters to avoid or reduce his losses.

Monday, 12 August

The day dawned fine again just as the Luftwaffe meteorologists had predicted.

Today would be the day when the Germans would start to concentrate more of their bombing raids on our radar stations and airfields. As we have seen, both sides had radars, although they were used for quite different purposes. The Germans used theirs for targeting while the RAF used it as a long-range detection system. The Germans did not understand or appreciate the fighter control system that Dowding had spent years developing and refining. We shall see that in the coming days, the other problem the Luftwaffe would face was that, although the radar towers were clearly visible and poorly defended, trying destroy their open, wooden lattice structures would prove to be extremely difficult. It also appears that the Germans did not realize that Dowding had mobile units available to plug any gaps in the overlapping radar cover if any stations were put out of action.

With good weather expected throughout the day, the first raid arrived at 7:30 a.m., with a fighter-sweep heading towards Dover. Predictably, it was designed to try to draw Fighter Command in to the air so that they would be back on the ground when the first of main raids attacked. 11 Group's reaction was to scramble just a single squadron, 610, from Biggin Hill, who lost one aircraft with another four damaged for the loss of two Bf 109s during the ensuing dogfight.

At 8:40 a.m., a group of aircraft were spotted heading for the Kent-Sussex coast from the Calais area, these were the elite experimental squadron EG 210, flying sixteen Bf 110s each equipped with a single 500lb (227kg) bomb. They were flying low enough to avoid radar detection, and as they approached the coast close to Beachy Head and Eastbourne, they split in to four separate groups of four aircraft. Each group then flew towards a specific radar station—the first group headed for Pevensey, the next for Rye, the third for Dover, and the last group made their way past Dover, northwards a few miles to Dunkirk, which is five miles (8km) east of Faversham close to the north Kent coast. The radar station at Pevensey was particularly badly damaged, but the re-enforced concrete transmitting and receiving block survived. Similar damage was inflicted at Rye where they had to use a back-up diesel generator until power was restored. At the Dunkirk radar station, one of the bombs exploded close enough to the concrete transmission block to move it sideways several inches. Although Dover was temporarily put out of action, Pevensey, Rye, and Dover were all operational again within a couple of hours. At around the same time, the town of Dover was hit by the long-range guns stationed on the French coast.

The Luftwaffe exploited the temporary gap in radar cover by sending a formation of Ju 88s to dive-bomb the forward airfield at Lympne on the Dungerness Peninsula in Kent.

At 11:45, a formation of more than fifty aircraft, including Ju 87 dive-bombers, attacked two small convoys, code-named *Agent* and *Arena*, in the Thames Estuary. This force was aided by a further twelve aircraft. Squadrons from Biggin Hill and Hornchurch were scrambled to intercept. During the resulting dogfight 501 Squadron from Biggin Hill lost four Hurricanes and two pilots.

The radar station at Poling in West Sussex, picked up a very large raid that was heading towards Portland, comprising a hundred Ju 88s and one hundred and twenty Bf 110s, with a further twenty Bf 109s acting as top cover. As it approached the coast, some of the formation changed direction, with fifteen Ju 88s making their way towards the radar station at Ventnor on the Isle of Wight. Intense and accurate bombing started a number of fires and demolished most of the buildings on the station. Although a mobile radar unit was bought in to provide some radar cover, the bombing effectively put it out of action until15 September. 609 and 152 Squadrons were scrambled to intercept this raid, and whilst ignoring the high-flying Luftwaffe fighters, they charged in to the bombers and shot two down for the loss of two of their own aircraft. Once the German fighters had reacted to the attack a large-scale dogfight developed, during which they lost a further four Bf 110s and two Bf 109s.

The rest of the attacking formation headed for Portland, Portsmouth, and Southampton, bombing two convoys, *Snail* and *Cable*, on the way. In response, Fighter Command scrambled over fifty aircraft, but the bombers still managed bomb Portland and Portsmouth. In Portsmouth, they hit the docks, shipping, the railway station, and the town, where they killed twenty-three people and injured a further hundred. They also bombed the Spitfire works at Southampton.

Shortly after this, a number of low-flying Bf 110s and high-flying Dornier bombers attacked the airfield at Manston on the northeast corner of Kent. Even though 54 Squadron, who used the airfield as a forward operating base, managed to get airborne to defend it, they could not prevent the bombers from causing sufficient damage to put it out of action for the rest of the day. In fact, 65 Squadron, who were also operating from the airfield as a forward operating base were still taking off as the bombing raid began. By the time the bombers turned for home, their fighter escort had already largely left, leaving them at the mercy of 56 Squadron, who had arrived on the scene from Rochford near Southend.

This was to be the first major attack on a British airfield, with the attack lasted almost two hours, during which around one hundred and fifty bombs were dropped, destroying hangars and workshops and damaging two Blenhiems stationed on the airfield.

Further down the coast, Hawkinge positioned on top of the cliffs above Folkstone, received a comparable amount of damage to that inflicted on Manston from a formation of Ju 88s. They badly damaged two hangars, demolished a number of buildings, and cratered the airfield. In spite of this, the airfield was back in operation the following day. The bombers also attacked Lympne causing significant damage. Thus, in the first major attack on Fighter Command's airfields, the Germans inflicted significant damage to the three most important, forward airfields closest to France.

Unfortunately, for the Luftwaffe, their Intelligence Service began the misjudged and misleading process of writing off all of the aircraft on each airfield they attacked. This process would lead to them drastically underestimating Fighter Command's strength in the days and weeks to come. Due to this faulty intelligence, a significant mismatch developed between what the German aircrews were being told they should encounter during their raids and the actual number of Fighter Command aircraft they faced in the skies over Britain. The Germans claimed that during attacks that day, they had destroyed sixty-nine RAF fighters, whereas Fighter Command had only lost twenty-two. The Luftwaffe had lost thirty-one aircraft.

Equally misleading was the German intelligence about the effects of bombing on the British radar. Their signals service decided that the bombing was relatively ineffectual as most radar stations appeared to be back in operation within a few hours. What they did not know was that some of the mobile units were sending out signals to make it appear that the radar system was still operational when, in fact, it was not. The signals service also decided that the radar station control rooms must be buried deep underground, whereas they were all fairly flimsy buildings on the surface. They concluded that attacking the radar stations was a waste of time and effort that could be better directed at other targets. This proved to be a disastrous interpretation and move.

Tuesday, 13 August

The day began with low cloud, occasional rain, with a blanket of fog over the Channel and the airfields in Northern France, which eventually cleared to reveal another bright sunny day. After a number of delays, *Alder Tag* (*Eagle Day*) began in some confusion.

Wood and Dempster report that planning for this phase of the battle had been conducted in minute detail, using aerial photographic maps that showed airfields, harbors, and other important targets. Unfortunately, they included Fleet Air Arm and Coastal Command airfields in their list of targets, airfields, that, as we shall see, they continued to attack instead of concentrating on Fighter Command actual bases. Poor aerial photographic interpretation had led them to misidentify aircraft at these airfields as front-line fighters—this goes some way to understanding why Luftwaffe Intelligence would get their estimates of Fighter Command's strength so badly wrong during the coming weeks.

Luftwaffe Intelligence had and would continue to severely over-estimate Fighter Command's losses and the damage on Fighter Command airfields.

From the British point of view, Fighter Command were deeply concerned about the attacks on the radar installations. If these continued, there was the possibility that the Germans would be able to knock out enough stations that gaps would start to appear in radar cover that would allow the Luftwaffe through to their targets. From the German point of view, they knew that they either had to destroy the radar stations or fly extremely low, to avoid detection, something that only a few specialist units were experienced in undertaking. They also thought that mass attacks would overwhelm Fighter Command's command system, which presumably they thought was similar to theirs.

At just after five in the morning, Ju 88 and Do 17 bombers began to take off from their bases for what was supposed to be the first planned large-scale raids on Fighter Command's airfields and other targets. As they were taking off, Goering sent out a message delaying the action until later in the day, when their meteorological people had said the weather would improve.

Unfortunately, this revealed a major weakness of the German communications, for, while the sixty Bf 110s from ZC 26 received the message and turned back, the seventy-four Dorniers from KG 2, they were meant to be escorting, did not. To make matters worse, the fighter and bombers used different radio frequencies, which meant that they could communicate with each other. Both formations were flying in cloud, which also meant that when the fighters turned for home the bomber crews did not see them go and continued on the mission.

As the bombers approached the English coast, they split into two formations, one headed for Sheerness in the Thames Estuary and the Coastal Command airfield at Eastchurch, the other made its way past Hastings and on towards the Hampshire airfields of Odiham and Farnborough, neither of which were Fighter Command bases. Both formations had already been detected by radar operators, and four squadrons were scrambles from Tangmere, Kenley, Northolt, and Exeter to attack the second formation. The first fighters to arrive were from 43 Squadron who managed to break-up the bomber formation before they reached their targets. They shot down two bombers for the loss of two Hurricanes, and a further two bombers were shot down as they headed for home.

Meanwhile, the first formation was still heading for the Thames Estuary in low cloud, as 74, 151, and 111 squadrons were scrambled. 74 Squadron were the first to engage the enemy, attacking the rear of the formation just as the bombers at the front were releasing their bombs on the airfield at Eastchurch on the Isle of Sheppey. The bombers managed to damage two hangars, achieving a direct hit on the Operations Room as well as destroying five Blenheims from 35 Squadron, and a Spitfire from 266 Squadron on the ground. They also killed twelve people and injured a further forty. As they headed for home, their vital cloud cover began to disperse, and 111 Squadron's Hurricanes together with those of 151 Squadron attacked the bombers, shooting down four and damaging four others, three of them beyond repair. One of 151 Squadron's aircraft was the only Hurricane in Fighter Command to be fitted with cannons rather than the usual eight browning machine guns, which, for once could be used to great effect. Some cannon-armed Spitfires had also started to reach operational squadrons, but they faced continuous problems with their cannons jamming and occasionally freezing.

What Luftwaffe Intelligence failed to realize was that Eastchurch was a Coastal Command airfield, which meant that for all their efforts, they had inflicted no real damage on Fighter Command—they would however later claim to have destroyed ten Spitfires during the raid. They also decided that the airfield had been put out of action completely, but it actually became operational again within ten hours.

At 11:40 a.m., British radar picked up another raid heading for Portsmouth. This too had left France in some confusion, for it was the Ju 88 bombers this time that had received the orders to turn back, and did so, whilst their escorting Bf 110s did not, and continued on their way. Aircraft from Middle Wallop and Tangmere were scrambled to intercept, shooting down five of the German long-range fighters for the loss of one Hurricane with three other being damaged.

At 1 p.m., radar detected the build-up of another large raid near the coast at Cherbourg. With its intended target uncertain, 10 Group ordered a number of squadrons to standby and informed 11 Group of the raid just in case it flew towards Portsmouth or Southampton. Ten minutes later, it appeared that the aircraft were indeed heading for Portland, so 10 Group bought aircraft at Warmwell, Exeter and Middle Wallop to readiness, 11 Group did the same with 601 Squadron at Tangmere. As the Germans approached the Dorset coast, they turned towards the Isle of Wight and split into two separate formations. One comprising approximately one hundred and twenty Ju 88s escorted by over forty Bf 109s, headed to the west of the island, the other formation, made up of seventy-seven Ju 87s with more than fifty Bf 109s and around thirty Bf 110s providing cover, headed for the east of the island. The fighters from Exeter and Warmwell encountered the western formation first and attacked the fighters, which having flown such a long distance, would be getting low on fuel. The Ju 88s continued northwards, crossing the coast close to Southampton before heading for Middle Wallop, where they were attacked by 609 Squadron that had taken off from the airfield. 609 Squadron were then attacked themselves by some of the covering Bf 109s. The Hurricanes of Exeter's 238 Squadron, having tried to disrupt part of the fighter cover, also attacked some of the Ju 87 dive-bombers that dropped their bombs on the airfield at Andover. Here nine Stukas were lost for the fairly ineffectual bombing of yet another airfield that did not belong to Fighter Command—it was the Headquarters of Maintenance Command.

Some of the Ju 88s bombed Southampton, then they too bombed Andover having mistaken it for Middle Wallop. This time, they inflicted significantly more damage than the Ju 87s. One group of Ju 87s did succeed in bombing Middle Wallop just as 609 Squadron was returning to refuel and rearm.

Another element of the Luftwaffe formation, comprising Ju 88s, headed towards Portland, where, even though they were engaged by Hurricanes and Spitfires from Exeter, Warmwell and Tangmere still inflicted some damage on the harbor and town. They too then headed for Southampton but turned for home when they saw a number of defending fighters in the area.

The last raid of the day began to form up at around 5 p.m. This again comprised two separate formations both with significant fighter cover, one with a large number of Ju 87s that headed for Dungerness, the other, a smaller dive-bomber formation that was apparently heading for Dover. 56 Squadron, who had been scrambled from North Weald, attempted to intercept one group of dive-bombers but were bounced by their fighter cover. The dive-bombers were able to continue towards the Thames Estuary and the Shorts aircraft factory and airfield at Rochester. Unfortunately, they did not find their intended target and turned eastwards, bombing the airfield at Detling, which was a Coastal Command base. Here they inflicted considerable damage, including completely destroying the operations block, most of the hangars, and a fuel dump. They also destroyed a number of Blenheims on the airfield. In spite of the damage, the airfield was back in operation by lunchtime the following day. Those that had not bombed Detling dropped their bombs over a wide area of the Kent countryside on the way home.

In total, the partly stalled *Adler Tag* had cost the Luftwaffe fifty-three aircraft and nearly two hundred aircrew either killed or captured, whilst Fighter Command had lost fifteen aircraft and three pilots. This was also the day that 302, one of the Polish squadrons, became operational at Church Fenton in North Yorkshire.

During the night of 13–14 August, the Luftwaffe bombed Aberdeen, Liverpool, Swansea, the Shorts aircraft factory in Belfast, and the Supermarine factory at Castle Bromwich in the Midlands. These attacks, like the ones before them, added weight to the criticisms that Dowding would face towards the end of the battle that he did not provide sufficient fighter cover at night. This was rather unfair given that, apart from some hastily adapted Blenheims, all of his fighter were designed for daytime operations. Interestingly though, this was also the day that the first newly designed, airborne-interception radar-equipped Bristol Beaufighters were delivered to the Fighter Interception Unit at Tangmere to test out radar guided interceptions that could be used against night-time raiders.

Wednesday, 14 August

The weather was, in general, a repeat of the day before, with cloudy, rainy conditions to begin with, clearing up later. This meant that, yet again the Luftwaffe was unable to launch a day of full-scale attacks.

The Luftwaffe delayed the build-up of their first large formation until shortly before mid-day, by which time the remaining cloud cover had begun to disperse. British radar detected a large number of aircraft over the Calais area, and, in response, Keith Park bought several squadrons at Biggin Hill, Hornchurch, and Kenley to readiness. As the German aircraft crossed the Straits of Dover, they changed direction several times in order to keep Fighter Command guessing about their intended target. They were heading towards the north Kent coast closest to France, an area that was rapidly becoming known as 'Hell Fire Corner.' EG 210, with their Bf 110s, were once again part of the attacking force that was making its way towards Dover. The first British aircraft to arrive were the Spitfires of 65 Squadron, closely followed by the Hurricanes of 32 Squadron from Biggin Hill. With a large-scale dogfight developing overhead, EG 210 slipped in low under radar cover almost undetected and bombed Manston.

For the third day in succession, Manston, the airfield at the heart of 'Hell Fire Corner' was attacked, and with the ground crew refusing to come out from their air raid shelters, the aircrew from 65 Squadron helped refuel and rearm their aircraft. Members of 600 Squadron—a Blenheim-fighter equipped squadron who were taking part in experiments with airborne radar—also helped man the air defense guns around the airfield. The airfield took a hammering and was littered with bomb craters. Four hangars were destroyed as well as three of the squadron's aircraft. Even with the considerable amount of damage that had been inflicted on the airfield, it was operational again the following morning.

Other German aircraft shot down eight barrage balloons at Dover and bombed a lightship marking the Goodwin Sands. With an air-battle involving over two hundred aircraft taking place over the Straits of Dover and North Kent, loses on both sides were to be expected. Unfortunately, Fighter Command lost seven aircraft and two pilots whilst the Luftwaffe only lost two Bf 109s and three Stukas.

At 4:30 in the afternoon, small groups of aircraft from Luftflotte III, set out across the Channel, intending to attack across a wide front—a tactic designed to confuse Fighter Command with regard to their planned destinations—these formations including three He 111 bombers that were heading for Southampton. Flights from two different squadrons were scrambled in response to a number of Ju 88s heading for Middle Wallop. This was the home of 243 Squadron, who were the first to reach the bombers; they were followed by three Spitfires from 609 Squadron. Just as a flight from 601 Squadron were taking off from the airfield, bombs began to fall from the dive-bombing Ju 88s which destroyed one of the hangars and killed three people. 609 Squadron claimed a Ju 88 and a He 111 destroyed. Interestingly, the German pilots reported that they thought they had bombed Netheravon, which was an Army Cooperation Command airfield.

Luftwaffe bombers also bombed RAF Sealand in Cheshire, and RAF Colerne both of which were maintenance units. Middle Wallop, which was a Fighter Command base, was attacked four times in three hours. Another attack caused significant damage to the railway at Southampton.

During the day, Fighter Command lost eight aircraft compared to the Luftwaffe's nineteen shot down by air and ground defenses.

Thursday, 15 August

The weather was once again less than ideal from a German point of view, with overcast conditions, which were predicted to last for most of the day. As a consequence, the Luftwaffe postponed all operations until later in the afternoon. As often happens with the British weather, it actually cleared by mid-morning, but by then it was too late change their plans.

Goering called a conference at Kairnhall with his commanders at which he was about to make one of his many disastrous tactical changes. He informed them that they were not forcing Fighter Command into battle and that they would therefore have to send over larger formations of bombers and fighters. He also responded to complaints from his bomber crews that because the fighters were flying above them they felt that they were leaving the bombers too exposed to British fighters and therefore their losses were too great. To counter this, the commanders were instructed to make their fighters fly in a close air support role. Although this would make the bomber crews feel safer, it would be a disaster for the fighters' ability to effectively engage the British aircraft, because they would lose their invaluable advantage of height, speed, and maneuverability. By having to stay close to the bombers, they would also use up extra fuel, which they were already short of when flying over Southern England. Goering also gave instruction that each Stuka Gruppe (a Gruppe comprised three Staffein [squadrons]) was to be supported by three fighter Gruppes, one flying ahead of the diver-bombers, another providing top cover and the third would be expected to dive with the dive-bombers, a role the Bf 109s were virtually incapable of performing.

He also made a second blunder that day when, responding to the apparent lack of progress on destroying the British radar system, he downgraded their importance as future targets and ordered his aircrews to stop bombing them as primary targets. Fortunately, neither he nor Luftwaffe Intelligence knew how much real damage they were inflicting on this vital element of the Fighter Command's early warning system. Finally, with the significant loss of experienced officers, he ordered that there should only be one officer in any aircrew.

Following the improving weather conditions during the morning, all three Luftflotte would be in action, leading to attacks developing from Norway all the way south and west to Brittany.

Oberst Paul Deichmann, Chief of Staff at II Fliegerkorps, whose aircraft were to lead the day's mass attacks, ordered a raid by Ju 87s armed with either 500lb (227kg) or 250lb (113kg) bombs. He also launched an attack by Do 17 bombers on the airfield at Eastchurch, and sent Bf 110s to attack Manston. With a total of around 1,120 aircraft involved, including a large number of Bf 109s providing fighter support and fighter sweeps, this was planned to be the biggest test for Fighter Command so far.

The first attack to arrive, comprising some forty-nine Stukas escorted by around sixty Bf 109s, was aimed at the airfields of Hawkinge and Lympne on the southeast coast. 54 and 501 Squadrons were first on the scene but were intercepted by the covering Bf 109s just as the Ju 87s were dive-bombing the airfields. They caused sufficient damage to put Lympne out of action for almost three days. Hawkinge fared far better with only one hangar and some buildings being damaged, even so, it would also be unusable for some time. The bombers then went on to bomb the radar stations at Rye, Dover, and Foreness, putting them out of action and effectively cutting all radar cover around 'Hell Fire Corner' for the rest of the day. This gap in radar cover allowed Bf 110s of ZG 76 to fly in and bomb Manston, just after 54

Squadron had taken off. This attack destroyed two Spitfires from 66 Squadron on the ground and killed sixteen people.

As we have seen, Goering and Luftwaffe Intelligence thought that Fighter Command had already been reduced to around five hundred operational fighters, and that they had moved most, if not all of the remaining fighters to the southeast corner of the country, therefore depriving the north and Scotland of any fighter cover. (In fact, only 15% of Fighter Command's Hurricanes and 30% of its Spitfires were stationed in 11 Group.) Consequently, Luftflotte V, expecting no opposition from Fighter Command, launched an attack with sixty-five He 111s from their Norwegian airfields on a number of airfields in northeast England. They were to be escorted by twenty-five Bf 110s equipped with long-range fuel tanks. These Bf 110s, nicknamed 'Dachshunds,' would act as long-range fighter cover for the bombers. The lead Bf 110, flown by the Gruppenkommandeur, had been fitted with a range of equipment designed to pick-up any Fighter Command communications enabling him to discover where defending fighters might be encountered. More than fifty Ju 88s were also sent to attack northern airfields from their bases in Denmark. Before these two formations took off, twenty-five He 115 seaplanes headed towards Firth of Forth as a diversionary raid. Their course was designed to draw any fighters that may still be stationed in the north of the country away from the following main bomber force, thus allowing them to attack their intended targets, airfields which including Usworth, on the outskirts of Sunderland, and Dishforth beside the A1 in North Yorkshire, unopposed.

Just after mid-day, both raids were detected by radar stations along the northeast coast—by June 1940, radar cover had been extended as far as the Orkney Islands. In response, while the main bomber force was still some 90 miles (144km) out to sea, 13 Group scrambled 72 Squadron based at Acklington in Northumberland, which was equipped with Spitfires, sending them to hold at a position over the Farne Islands. Additional Spitfires from 41 Squadron at Catterick in North Yorkshire and the Hurricanes of 605 Squadron based at Drem in Scotland were also called into action.

Unfortunately, due to a navigational error, the He 111s and their escorting Bf 110s were flying too far north. They were on almost the same course as the leading He 115s, who were flying too far south, so that when the latter turned for home, Fighter Command aircraft were already in the area. Realizing their error, as they approached the coast, the He 111s turned south in to the path of 72 Squadron. On spotting the defenders, but expecting no opposition, the escorting Bf 110s immediately formed a defensive circle, while the Heinkels dropped their bombs in the sea and fled back to Norway, but not before they had been engaged by 605 Squadron.

Further south, other elements of the bomber formation approached the coast before heading for the airfields at Acklington, north of Newcastle and Usworth. The bombers heading for Acklington were intercepted by aircraft from 79 and 605 Squadrons, and consequently dropped most of their bombs in the sea before heading home. The bombers heading for the Fighter Command airfield at Usworth were intercepted by 607 and 41 Squadrons. Whilst most bombs were jettisoned in to the sea, a few landed in urban areas in and around Sunderland, causing some damage. In total, Fighter Command shot down thirteen aircraft without loss.

The formation of fifty Ju 88s, having taken off from their airfields in Denmark, were flying northwards towards the Flamborough Head on the North Yorkshire coast between Bridlington and Scarborough. Again, with radar alerting 12 and 13 Groups to the threat, they positioned their fighters to await the arrival of the German aircraft. 73 Squadron's Hurricanes and 616 Squadron's Spitfires were scrambled from 12 Group's airfields at Church Fenton and Leconfield. 264 Squadron's Defiants, who had been moved northwards from 11 Group, were called in to action from Kirton-in-Lindsey together with Blenheims from 219 Squadron stationed at 13 Group's airfield at Catterick. Once engaged, the attackers split in to two different formations, one heading for and bombing Bridlington where they hit a few houses, but not before they had lost six aircraft. The other headed for the Bomber Command airfield at Driffield, where they damaged four hangars and destroyed ten Whitley bombers; they also killed six and wounded another twenty people on the base.

By the time the remaining bombers had returned to their home airfields, the attackers had lost 20% of their aircraft and eighty aircrew—losses that the Luftflotte could not sustain. Consequently, they were withdrawn from the battle and took no further part in daylight raids on the UK.

At approximately the same time, a dozen Bf 109s attacked Manston, destroying two Spitfires and injuring sixteen people.

Three hours later, radar stations along the southeast coast detected the build-up of yet another large formation of enemy aircraft over Calais. This again included the Bf 110s of EG 210, plus Ju 87s, and their escorting Bf 109s. EG 210 headed north of the Thames to attack the airfield at Martlesham Heath where they caused severe damage to two hangars and a number of other buildings. They also destroyed the water mains and telephone lines, putting the station out of action for two days. Three Hurricanes from 17 Squadron, who were operating from the airfield that day, managed to get airborne before the attack, and were joined by Hurricanes from 1 RCAF Squadron, who chased the attackers before being set upon by EG 210s Bf 109s, who shot down three of the defenders.

Just after that raid headed for home, radar detected the build-up of yet another large raid, comprising around one hundred aircraft that was heading for the Dover area. 11 Group, with four squadrons—111, 151, 64—and 1 RCAF already in the air, scrambled three more (17, 32, and 501). Part of the raid, consisting of Ju 88s, Do 17s, and one hundred and thirty Bf 109s crossed the English coast close to Deal. A second formation comprising around one hundred and fifty aircraft, including seventy Bf 109s crossed a little further south between Dover and Folkstone. With six squadrons of Hurricanes from Northolt, Debden, Biggin Hill, North Weald, Croydon, and a squadron of Spitfires from Kenley, 11 Group were in a good position to counter this attack. However, with so many German fighters in attendance, the bombers were able to get through to their intended targets—the Shorts aircraft factory at Rochester and the airfield at Eastchurch, neither of which, as we have already seen, were of direct relevance to Fighter Command. At Rochester, six Stirling bombers were destroyed. Other bombers attacked the radar stations at Dover, Rye, Bawdsey, and Foreness but caused little damage.

At around 5 p.m., another raid, this time directed at targets in Southwest England by aircraft from Luftflotte III, was detected off the south coast, heading towards Portland. This comprised twenty Bf 109s, twenty-five Bf 110s, and forty Ju 87s. The first British fighters in to the air were the two squadrons based at Exeter; they were joined by aircraft from Middle Wallop and Warmwell. In the ensuing dogfight, three Bf 110s were shot down and two others later crashed due to the damage they had sustained, whilst Fighter Command lost eight Hurricanes, with one pilot killed and two were taken prisoner in France.

A second raid also directed at airfields in the southwest crossed the coast just before 6 p.m. This formation, comprising more than sixty Ju 88s and forty Bf 110s was heading for Middle Wallop. As they approached the airfield, a section of the formation broke away to attack the airfield at Worthy Down near Winchester, otherwise known as HMS *Kestrel*—a Fleet Air Arm base—where they caused little damage. The main group arrived over Middle Wallop just as 609 Squadron were taking off. Although the bombers managed to leave a number of craters across the airfield, they left it largely intact. Some of the formation then headed towards Odiham (a Coastal Command base) but bombed Andover instead. Yet again, with only one of their targets, or intended targets being a Fighter Command airfield, the

Germans lost one Ju 88 and four Bf 109s, and a further three Ju 88s were damaged without inflicting too much damage to Fighter Command.

The day was not over yet. At around 6:30 p.m., a number of Dorniers crossed the southeast coast through a gap in the radar cover and headed for Biggin Hill. Both of Biggin Hill's squadrons were scrambled and intercepted the bombers well-before they reached the airfield. They managed to shoot two of the bombers down before their fighter cover reached them; during the resulting dogfight the rest of the bombers continued towards Biggin but bombed West Malling airfield by mistake.

Just as this was happening, EG 210s Bf 110s crossed the coast again supported by eight Bf 109s. As they were making their way towards their target, the airfields at Kenley and Biggin Hill, 32 Squadron, which had just been in action against the Dorniers, was diverted to intercept them. 111 Squadron was also scrambled from Croydon. Both squadrons reached the enemy aircraft just as the escorting Bf 109s had reached their fuel limit and were turning for home. 32 Squadron attacked the fighters as 111 Squadron went for EG 210. In the ensuing fight, they shot down, seven of the fighter-bombers. More important to the Germans and the future course of the battle than the loss of seven aircraft from one of their elite squadrons was the bombing of Croydon airfield and the surrounding area, which killed sixty people and injured a further one hundred and eighty. At the time, Croydon was regarded as London's airport, the town was also considered to be part of London itself. Therefore, although they had not bombed Central London, as far as the British Government were concerned, the Luftwaffe had bombed London. Why should this be so important? Hitler had given specific orders that no bombs were to drop on the capital unless by his specific orders.

Finally, at 7:30 p.m., the last raid of the day, comprising some seventy aircraft, was intercepted by 54 squadron near Dover. By the close of the action, the Luftwaffe had lost seventy-six aircraft and one hundred forty-two aircrew, whilst Fighter Command had lost thirty-four fighters and seventeen pilots. In fact, within the Luftwaffe, Thursday 15 August became known as 'Black Thursday.' The day's attacks had shown that the Luftwaffe could stretch Fighter Command's resources to the limit by sheer weight of numbers. Dowding, in response, would only commit the number of fighters necessary to repel an attack, but, if raids became any larger, more frequent, or were spread over a larger area, 11 Group would have to increasingly call on the services of 10 and 12 Group's, which would reduce their effectiveness in repelling raids in their own areas.

As we have seen, the unexpected mauling that the aircraft from Luftflotte V received at the hands of Fighter Command's northern squadrons, led to significant changes—the cessation of daylight raids conducted by that Luftflotte. In fact, by the end of August, most of their bombers and some of their fighters were transferred to Luftflotte II airfields in Northeastern France to bolster the main attacks.

Friday, 16 August

The day was a near perfect summers day, with bright, clear skies.

Luftwaffe Intelligence reported that, with the intense action of the previous day, combined with losses during the last month, Fighter Command were down to around four hundred and fifty operational aircraft, with maybe another three hundred that could be made serviceable. Goering realized, contrary to his original ideas and plans, that Fighter Command was not going to be defeated in a matter of days. It would take longer to achieve his goal of destroying them, or at least reducing their numbers so that the Luftwaffe could gain air superiority over the invasion area. He realized that attacking convoys to draw Fighter Command in to action had not worked. He also thought that attacking the radar stations had been a failure as they resumed operation shortly afterwards. Attacking the north of England had been too costly in the number of aircraft he had lost, and the Ju 87s, one of his previously most effective weapons, had been too vulnerable when pitted against Spitfires and Hurricanes.

During the late morning, radar operators detected the build-up of a raid heading for the Kent coast, it went on to bomb Manston and West Malling, where the bombers caused sufficient damage on the latter to put the station out of action until 20 August.

An hour later, three separate formations began to fly towards the English coast. The first appeared to be heading for the Thames Estuary, the second was making its way towards the coast between Brighton, and Hastings, and the third forming over Cherbourg, was aimed at the Portsmouth and Southampton area. Aircraft from Hornchurch, North Weald, and Kenley were scrambled to intercept the first raid, which comprised over one hundred Do 17s and Bf 109s. During the ensuing dogfight, a Hurricane and a Spitfire were shot down. 32 Squadron from Biggin Hill, 111 Squadron from Croydon, and 266 Squadron's Spitfires from Hornchurch were scrambled to meet the second, larger formation of around one hundred and fifty aircraft. On seeing the enemy aircraft, all three squadrons headed for the bombers. They were joined by the Spitfires of 64, 65, and 266 Squadrons. In the resulting fight, ten German aircraft were shot down for the loss of a Hurricane and five Spitfires. The bombers managed to drop their bombs on a number of London suburbs, including Wimbledon, Esher, and Malden, as well as attacking Gravesend and Tilbury, in total sixty-six people were killed during these raids.

At 1 p.m., the third raid of the day, comprising one hundred Ju 88s escorted by Bf 110s from Luftflotte III, was heading to the east of the Isle of Wight, when both of Tangmere's squadrons were scrambled. As the raid approached the south coast, it divided into four separate smaller formations. Tangmere appeared to be the intended target of one of these raids, but they also bombed Lee-on-Solent and Gosport where they killed four people and injured a further two. Both of airfields belonged to the Fleet Air Arm. The bombers then flew on towards Tangmere, where, even though the raid only lasted some fifteen minutes, Ju 87s diver-bombers managed to wreak havoc on the airfield, destroying most of the hangars, as well as four of 43 Squadron's Hurricanes and a couple of Blenheims. Ten minutes later, the airfield was also hit by Ju 88s. Between the two raids the Germans had damaged every building on the airfield.

During the afternoon, Churchill and the Chief of Staff, Hastings Ismay, visited 11 Group's Operations Room at Uxbridge. They witnessed the mass of raids which were spread over an area from Hampshire to the Suffolk coast and involved almost all of 11 Group's, most of 10 Group's, and some of 12 Group's aircraft. It was during this visit that Churchill first used the famous phrase 'never in the field of human conflict was so much owed by so many to so few.'

Stuka dive-bombers attacked the Ventnor radar on the Isle of Wight, which had just become operational after the attack on 12 August. This time, they dropped twenty-one bombs causing sufficient damage to put the radar station out of operation until 23 September. However, a mobile unit was set up at Bembridge on the east coast of the island to maintain radar cover and, although this may not have been as effective as an operational station, the signals it sent out led the Luftwaffe signals service to decide that Ventnor radar was still working.

A group of Ju 88s also made their way towards Portsmouth and, in response, 213 Squadron based at Exeter and 249 Squadron at Boscomb Down were scrambled to intercept them. During this encounter, Flight Lieutenant James Nicolson, of 249 Squadron, was attacked by a Bf 110, which set his Hurricane on fire and injured him. In spite of his injuries and the flames engulfing his aircraft, he continued to pursue and shoot down a Bf 110, before he bailed out. For this action, he received the only Victoria Cross awarded to a pilot from Fighter Command during World War Two.

270

Two Ju 88s also bombed Brize Norton in Oxfordshire, which was a Training Command airfield. They injured ten people and managed to destroy forty-six training aircraft as well as eleven Hurricanes that were undergoing repairs on the airfield.

At 5:30 p.m., a formation of He 111s escorted by Bf 110s, crossed the Sussex coast. Spitfires from Biggin Hill together with Hurricanes from Kenley, Biggin Hill, and Northolt were scrambled to intercept them. During the resulting air battle, the Luftwaffe lost four bombers and two fighters, whilst Fighter Command lost five Hurricanes and one Spitfire.

Five minutes later, 234 Squadron's Spitfires from Middle Wallop engaged a number of Bf 109s over Portsmouth. Around the same time, an unarmed Avro Anson rammed into a lone Heinkel bomber flying in the same area, both aircraft crashed.

At 5:50 p.m., 19 Squadron, who were returning home to Duxford from Coltishall in their Spitfires, were directed towards a large formation spotted flying south of Harwich? During the ensuing fight, the squadron claimed a bomber and several fighters were destroyed.

Saturday, 17 August

Although this was to be another clear, sunny summer day, there were no major German operations. Enemy action was confined to a number of reconnaissance fights, three of which were shot down. This break gave the pilots, ground crew, and station personnel at all of Fighter Command's airfields the opportunity to repair their aircraft and airfields, and bring in replacement aircraft and pilots. The Germans were feeling the pressure as well. The bomber pilots in Luftflotten II and III had been asking for a rest, as they had been in almost continued operations for several weeks. Unlike Fighter Command, who gave their pilots some rest and rotated squadrons between 11 Group and other, less pressured groups, the Luftwaffe did not operate such a system. Many of the Luftwaffe aircraft were also in need of vital servicing and repairs.

During the last five days of fighting, Fighter Command had lost 68 pilots, with a further seventy wounded, and only seventy new pilots, most with only the briefest of training, had joined front-line squadrons. Fighter Command had also activated a second (310) Czech squadron that was to be based at Duxford in 12 Group. The rotation of squadrons to and from 10 and 11 Groups' areas continued with 145 Squadron moving northwards to Drem in Scotland, and 602 Squadron relocating to Westhampnett in West Sussex.

Sunday, 18 August

The day started clear and bright but clouded over in the south in the afternoon.

Over the last five days, the Luftwaffe had been specifically targeting what they thought were Fighter Command airfields, many of which, as we have seen were not. Once an airfield had been bombed, Luftwaffe Intelligence assumed that all of the aircraft on the airfield had been destroyed. This meant that they continued to grossly over-estimate the success of their bombing and equally underestimate the number of fighters at Fighter Command's disposal. They could not understand why, given their estimates of the number of Hurricanes and Spitfires Fighter Command should have had, their bomber and fighter pilots kept reporting encounters with large numbers of British fighters. Luftwaffe Intelligence recorded that they had so far destroyed three hundred and seventy-two Spitfires, one hundred and seventy-nine Hurricanes, nine Curtiss Hawks (which did not exist), and twelve Defiants, leading to an estimated strength for Fighter Command of three hundred fighters. In fact, Fighter Command still had almost seven hundred operational fighters in service, with a steady supply of new and repaired aircraft arriving each day.

The large-scale air battles that would take place today would mean that Sunday, 18 August would forever be known as 'the Hardest Day.'

The Luftwaffe knew that Biggin Hill, Kenley, and Hornchurch were key fighter stations around London, but, fortunately, they did not know anything about Fighter Command's control system and the vital role played by these three Sector Stations. They also did not know that on most of the Sector Stations, the all-important sector control rooms were usually above ground and usually only lightly protected by walls and/or earth embankments (although, as we shall see, each station had a reserve control room set up off-station for emergencies).

The intended focus of the day's bombing was the complete destruction of Biggin Hill and Kenley, and, once this had been achieved, the bombers were to direct their attention to Hornchurch and other airfields around London and the southeast.

The Luftwaffe launched its first raid of the day comprising He 111s, Ju 88s, Bf 110s, and Bf 109s around 9 a.m., but just as the Heinkels were taking off, they received a message to say that they were to abort the mission due to haze over Southern England.

Two hours later, reconnaissance flights reported that the haze had lifted, but that cloud was building up over Northern France that would gradually move northwards during the day. It was therefore, not until just before noon that the bombers were given the go ahead to launch their carefully coordinated missions.

The plan, which followed their now established format, was to send between fifty and sixty Bf 109s across the Channel towards London to draw Fighter Command in to the air and, hopefully, away from the following bombers and their intended targets. Today the fighter sweep would be followed, five minutes later, by the bomber force, which consisted of twelve Ju 88s, at least twenty-seven Do 17s, and twenty-five Bf 110s with twenty Bf 109s providing fighter cover. A second force of sixty He 111s with forty Bf 109s was also to take part in the planned mission. However, the weather disrupted the carefully laid plans. The Heinkels took to the sky expecting to rendezvous with their fighter cover. To add to the bomber pilots problems, the Ju 88s and Do 17s forming up in the Paris area were hampered by cloud cover. This led to them having to climb higher than anticipated to clear the clouds to be able to meet up with their fights, which further delayed them setting out for their intended targets. The weather caused even more problems when nine Do 17s that were supposed to fly at low level across the Channel to evade radar detection also had to fly higher than anticipated. Any one of these delays would have disrupted the carefully choreographed raids, which involved different formations of bombers attacking the two airfields in a particular sequence; but with each formation hitting problems, the entire plan began to break down.

The Heinkels and their fighter escort were to head straight for Biggin Hill, followed by the formation of Dorniers mentioned above who would attack at low-level. At Kenley, Ju 88s were to dive bomb the southern side of airfield and, five minutes later, high-level Do 17s were scheduled to bomb the rest of the base. Shortly afterwards, the nine Do 17s, flying without a fighter escort, that were to make landfall close to Beachy Head, would come in at low level and destroy anything that was left standing.

The low-flying Dorniers heading for Kenley managed to avoid detection by radar but were spotted by members of the Observer Corpse, who immediately reported their presence to Fighter Command, who in turn, put all of 11 Group squadrons on standby, and scrambled Kenley and Biggin Hill's fighters. This meant that the bombers would not catch any of the fighters on the ground. Aircraft from Debden, Hornchurch, and North Weald were also scrambled to join 501 Squadron who were already in the air, to intercept the multiple raids. Unfortunately, 501 were bounced by high-flying Bf 109s, losing five aircraft and one pilot.

As the bombers flew across country, Fighter Command was still uncertain of their intended target, but the Station Commander at Kenley, who had already sent 615 Squadron to engage aircraft over Hawkinge, called Croydon to send over 111 Squadron to help defend the airfield. 111 Squadron's Hurricanes arrived at equally low-level behind the bombers just as they were preparing their attack. To add to their woes, the Dorniers were also faced with the airfields ground defenses that included parachute cables (PACs), positioned at 60 feet (18m) intervals, which were fired into their paths. The bombers, using delayed-action bombs, hit some of the hangars, and a number of the buildings, including the mess hall, sick quarters, and station headquarters. The PACs and anti-aircraft guns bought down two of the bombers, and 111 Squadron hit several more. The raid lasted no more than ninety seconds, but in that time, Kenley had taken a pounding. Three minutes later, the main raid comprising the remaining Dorniers, which were now ten minutes late, arrived overhead. As they were preparing to bomb the airfield, 615 and 64 Squadrons intercepted the top cover Bf 109s, and 32 Squadron flew a head-on attack at the bombers. The combined efforts of the defenders managed to break up the bomber formation, causing them to drop most of their bombs on the surrounding area. They also shot down two of the bombers as they broke formation, and inflicted sufficient damage to five others that led to two crashing in the Channel on their way home, and the other three crash-landing in France—only two aircraft from the formation made it home safely. 615 Squadron intercepted another formation, comprising over fifty He 111s and Ju 87s, supported by more than seventy-five Bf 109s, over the Surrey countryside. They managed to break up this formation, with only fifteen bombers getting through to Kenley. Unfortunately, 615 Squadron lost four Hurricanes in the process.

The Ju 88s also managed to bomb the airfield, and at the end of the raid, most of the hangars had been severely damaged, the vital Operations Room had also been badly damaged, and the airfield was littered with bomb craters, so much so, that the returning fighters had to be diverted to other airfields, with 615 going to Croydon. 64 Squadron were originally diverted to Redhill, however, the airfield could not accommodate them, so they had to land back at Kenley on a landing strip laid out between the bomb craters. On the ground, four Hurricanes and a Blenheim had been destroyed, while nine people were killed, and ten others were injured. The Operations Room, which had been hit, was moved to a butchers shop in Caterham High Street, where it became operational again within two hours, but the airfield was effectively put out of action for nearly two and a half days. Wood and Dempster report that so many local fire engines turned up to put out the fires that they blocked the roads around the airfield.

Fighter Command lost four Hurricanes from 32 Squadron and one pilot, and 111 Squadron lost a single Hurricane.

At almost the same time that Kenley was being attacked, German aircraft were heading for Biggin Hill. This formation consisted of Ju 88s, Do 17s, and He 111s, escorted by around forty Bf 109s. 610 Squadron, who had been scrambled from the airfield, attacked to bombers and were joined by 32 Squadron returning from the fight over Kenley. Their actions led to many of the bombers dropping their bombs wide of the airfield. Again, due to delays in forming up the main force of bombers over France, the low flying Dorniers arrived first—expecting the airfield to be covered in smoke and fire from the high-level attack. They were instead met by the fully prepared ground defenses, which shot down one of the bombers. Just as they began their bombing runs, Biggin Hill's Spitfires and Hurricanes arrived to defend the airfield. Shortly afterwards, the high-flying Heinkels appeared over the airfield, but most dropped their bombs short of the perimeter, thus causing little damage. The combined efforts of all of the airfields' defenses resulted in the shooting down of four Ju 88s and six Dorniers.

Enemy action was not confined to the southeast. Shortly after mid-day, a force of some twenty-five Ju 87s and 21 Ju 88s, escorted by sixty-five Bf 109s and fifty-five Bf 110s attacked airfields along the south coast. The Ju 88s attacked the Fleet Air Arm airfield at Gosport, which was still in the process of being cleared following the attack two days earlier. Although Spitfires from 234 Squadron engaged the covering Bf 109s, shooting four of them down, the Stukas who arrived over the airfield unchallenged, bombed four of the hangars and destroyed four aircraft on the ground. Other elements of the Stuka formation attacked the airfields at Thorney Island, and Ford. At Ford, which was only lightly defended by anti-aircraft guns, they bombed hangars and a barracks, killing twenty-eight people, wounding five others, and destroying fourteen aircraft. At Thorney Island, the Stukas hit some of the hangars and a fuel dump. Both of these airfields also belonged to the Fleet Air Arm, so once again, a great deal of effort had been misdirected toward non Fighter Command bases. They also bombed the radar station at Poling, dropping ninety bombs, and causing sufficient damage that a mobile unit had to be brought in to provide cover. Twelve Stukas were shot down by aircraft from 43 and 152 Squadrons sent from Tangmere and Warmwell to intercept them. They were joined by rest of Tangmere's Spitfires and Hurricanes as well as 604 Squadrons Blenheims from Middle Wallop who claimed two more dive-bombers. In total, the Luftwaffe lost sixteen Stukas that day.

At 5 p.m., a large formation of bombers with their fighter escorts were detected heading for the Essex and Kent coasts. Fifty-two Heinkels were to make their way towards Fowlmere—a satellite airfield for Duxford—before turning south towards North Weald. At the same time, forty-eight Dorniers would cross the coast at Deal before heading up and across the Thames towards Hornchurch. With radar giving them plenty of notice, 11 Group bought thirteen squadrons to action stations and asked 12 Group to send four squadrons to provide cover for their two important Sector Stations.

The northern formation comprising Heinkels were intercepted by 56 and 54 Squadrons, who managed to shoot down one of the bombers. They had better luck with their Bf 110s escorts, shooting down seven and damaging several more. They were then joined by 85, 257, 310, and 151 Squadrons.

To the south, whilst trying to find the Dorniers, the Hurricanes of 32 and 610 Squadron's Spitfires were intercepted by their fighter escorts and lost four aircraft. With the bombers now flying in cloud, and little chance of finding their target—the airfield at Hornchurch—they turned for home. On their way back down the Thames, they too ran in to the British fighters called to defend North Weald.

The last attack of the day was targeted towards Croydon and Manston, where two Spitfires were destroyed on the ground, one person was killed, and fifteen others were injured.

During the day's intense fighting, the Luftwaffe lost forty-eight aircraft while Fighter Command lost twenty-seven with ten pilots dead. In the last ten days, the Luftwaffe had lost three hundred and sixty-three aircraft while Fighter Command lost one hundred and eighty-one in the air and thirty on the ground. To counter-balance this, Fighter Command had received one hundred and seventy-one replacement aircraft. A more worrying figure for Dowding and Fighter Command was the loss of one hundred and fifty-four pilots with only sixty-five new pilots entering squadron service. At the time, it is reported that the Flying Training Units were still only working at two-thirds of their capacity.

Wood and Dempster report that during the period from 8–18 August, Fighter Command had lost ninety-four pilots, either killed or missing. However, aircraft production had increased and repair units made sure that any replacement aircraft that were required by the end of a day's fighting were delivered before mid-day the following day. They also report that by this phase of the battle, ground crews were simultaneously refueling and rearming the aircraft and checking the engines, oil and glycol systems, replacing oxygen cylinders, and testing the radio sets within eight to ten minutes of the aircraft landing. They had even dug slit trenches beside the aircraft dispersals so that this work could continue even when the airfields were under direct attack. Due to the amount of destruction sustained by most of the airfields, repair and maintenance was carried out day and night away from the hangars which were usually one of the Germans primary targets.

Monday, 19 August

It is interesting to note that, both sides were holding conferences on 19 August. At Fighter Command, it was made clear that the main priority was to defend 11 Group's airfields from attack. Leigh Mallory was still insisting that the Big Wing strategy should be adopted, even though it would have been impractical given the size of the area over which the Luftwaffe were attacking, i.e., all of 11 Group and much of 10 Groups' territory. Keith Park reiterated that his main targets were the German bombers, and that his pilots should avoid, if possible, getting in to combat with the German fighters. One of their concerns was that by concentrating on the bombers they would be increasingly vulnerable to be bounced by the fighters, and that in response to focusing on the bombers, the Luftwaffe might just increase the size of the fighter escort. Fighter Command also introduced changes to the operation of their airfields, these included a larger number of anti-aircraft guns being located on them and the possibility of moving the operations rooms from the airfields, together with the sick quarters and radio equipment to prevent them from being put out of operation.

On the other side of the Channel, the Luftwaffe conference, held at Karinhall, had different worries. Goering confirmed that due to high losses, particularly those of the previous day, the Ju 87s were to be withdrawn from operations unless specifically required, such as attacks on convoys. He also decided that Luftflotte V, based in Norway would discontinue daylight raids. He confirmed that airfield attacks would continue and that, from now on, Bf 110s would be escorted at close-quarters by Bf 109s. He also moved all of Luftflotte III's single-seat fighters stationed in Northwest France to concentrate them in the Pas-de-Calais area under Luftflotte II's control. Much of the most effective and worst damage caused to our Sector Stations had been inflicted by low-flying bombers, but due to the heavy losses involved in flying these operations the Luftwaffe ceased this type of bombing, switching the bombers to higher-level attacks instead. They also increased their fighter cover to provide better protection from Fighter Command aircraft. Additionally Goering proposed that the same fighters should escort bombers so that they would get to know each other. From the pilots view, they thought being equipped with radios that could enabled them to communicate between their fighters and bombers should be a priority.

Flying activity was limited to isolated raids, mainly conducted by fighters around the Thames Estuary, Kent and Hampshire coasts, with little affect. Shortly after mid-day, a large fighter sweep approached Dover, followed by another raid two hours later. At around the same time, bombers attacked Portsmouth and Southampton causing limited damage. At teatime, bombers crossed the Channel and Southern North Sea to attack the Kent coast and Harwich, again with little effect.

Even though there was only limited activity, the Luftwaffe lost six aircraft and Fighter Command lost three. This break from the heavy bombing that Fighter Command's airfields had been subjected to over the previous days allowed it time to repair some of the damage and resupply its hard-pressed squadrons.

A group of Ju 88s attacked the oil storage depot at Llanreath near Pembroke Docks in Wales where they scored direct hits on two oil storage tanks; a further eight tanks also exploded and the resulting fire burnt for over a week. In all, ten of the fifteen oil tanks were destroyed by the attack and its aftermath.

Tuesday, 20 August

The weather took a turn for the worse, with showers in the west, moving eastwards during the day, followed by sunny skies over the Channel.

Morning activities were restricted to small-scale raids across Gloucestershire and Oxfordshire and an attack on the still burning oil storage tanks at Llanreath. Reconnaissance flights were also dispatched to look at airfields across Cambridgeshire and Bedfordshire.

Due to the prevailing weather conditions, the first sizable raid did not appear until after mid-day, when around sixty Bf 109s approached Dungerness and another forty headed for Dover. As these were fighter sweeps, Park did not react and kept most of his fighters on the ground, only scrambling two squadrons to chase them back across the Channel.

The Luftwaffe employed the same tactics throughout the afternoon, and even though they attacked Manston, Eastchurch, Lympne, West Mailing, and Hawkinge, again Fighter Command only scrambled one squadron in response. Bombers also attacked a convoy code-named *Agent* off the east coast. Fighter Command responded to this raid by sending a number of squadrons, but most failed to find the bombers in the poor weather. EG 210 with their Bf 110s were out-and-about again with a characteristic low-level strike on the airfield at Martlesham Heath, although this time they caused little damage.

He 111s attacked Liverpool and its docks, before returning across the midlands where they dropped a few more bombs on their way home. One of the bombers was shot down over County Durham.

At 2:30 p.m., 602 Squadrons Spitfires were scrambled to intercept a group of Ju 88s approaching the Sussex coast. They shot down one of the bombers for the loss of one of their own aircraft before the rest of the raiders turned for home. 302 Squadron, one of the two operational Polish squadrons, shot down its first enemy aircraft, a Ju 88, during the afternoon. A raid comprising some twenty-seven Dorniers and thirty Bf 109s set out to attack the airfield at Eastchurch but were successfully intercepted by the Hurricanes of 615 and the Spitfires of 65 Squadron.

Half an hour later, the last raid of the day, more Ju 88s attacked Bibury, which was a satellite airfield for Pembrey, killing one person and damaging two Spitfires belonging to 92 Squadron.

The oil storage tanks at Llanreath, that were still on fire from the previous night's bombing were once again subjected to attack.

At almost the same time, Churchill was giving his now famous 'Never in the field of human conflict' speech in parliament, in which he said that:

'The gratitude of every home in our Island, in our Empire, and indeed throughout the world except in the abodes of the guilty, goes out to the British airmen, who, undaunted by odds, unwearied in their constant challenge and mortal danger, are turning the tide of world war by their prowess and by their devotion. Never in the field of human conflict was so much owed by so many to so few. All hearts go out to the fighter pilots, whose brilliant actions we see with our own eyes day after day; but we must never forget that all the time, night after night, month after month, our bomber squadrons travel far into Germany, find their targets in the darkness by the highest navigational skill, aim their attacks often under the heaviest fire, often with serious loss, with deliberate careful discrimination, and inflict shattering blows upon the whole of the technical and war-making structure of the Nazi power. On no part of the Royal Air Force does the weight of the war fall more heavily than on the daylight bombers, who will play an invaluable part in the case of invasion and whose unflinching zeal it has been necessary in the meanwhile on numerous occasions to restrain.'

That night the He 111s of KG 100, that had been specially equipped with the *X-Verfahren* electronic navigation system, were used to target the aircraft factory at Filton near Bristol. They dropped over 16 tonnes of high explosive and five hundred and seventy-six incendiary bombs on the factory killing four people and causing widespread damage.

Wednesday, 21 August

The weather once again played in to Fighter Command's hands, with strong winds, cloud and rain in the north and rain in the south.

Most Luftwaffe attacks were confined to raids by single or small groups of aircraft attacking over a wide area, the types of air activity that Fighter Command found most difficult to detect and intercept. These included targets such as the airfields at Exeter and St. Eval in the southwest, Pembroke in Wales, and Ford in Hampshire. They also bombed Southampton and Bournemouth on the south coast, Grimsby, Newmarket, and RAF Coltishall in the east of the country.

Just after mid-day, radar stations along the Norfolk coast picked up a raid, which turned out to be a group of Do 17s. As they approached the coast, they divided in to two groups, one group headed towards the Humber and the Wash, the other made for Great Yarmouth. Two squadrons of Hurricanes were scrambled to intercept the southern formation—66 and the Polish 302 Squadron—however, a flight from 242 Squadron, led by Douglas Bader managed to reach the bombers first and shot one of them down before the others disappeared in to the clouds.

The more northerly raid was intercepted off the coast near Skegness by 611 Squadron based at Digby who had recently been re-equipped with new Spitfire Mk.IIs. The Spitfires managed to shoot down one of the bombers, while two others collided in mid-air.

To the southwest, Ju 88s attacked a number of 10 Group airfields including Brize Norton and Middle Wallop. 234 Squadron from Middle Wallop and 17 Squadron from Tangmere were scrambled to intercept the raid and shot down one bomber each. Other bombers attacked the airfield at St. Eval in Cornwall, where 238 Squadron had arrived from Middle Wallop for a rest—bombs destroyed a hangar and four fighter-reconnaissance Blenhiems of 236 Squadron.

German bombers also attacked the Bomber Command airfields at Binbrook in Lincolnshire and Watton in Norfolk, and the Armament Camp airfield at Stormy Down in Wales.

Although flying was restricted by the weather, Fighter Command still claimed thirteen Luftwaffe aircraft shot down for the loss of just one of its own aircraft.

Thursday, 22 August

With strong winds, gusting to gale-force and rain, flying was going to be difficult; and consequently, for the third day running Luftwaffe operations were extremely limited.

During the morning, the large guns on the French coast were used for the first time to shell a convoy code-named *Totem* at it sailed through the Straits of Dover. After firing at the convoy, they once again turned their attention to Dover itself. At 12:30 p.m., a formation of EG 210s Bf 110s escorted by Bf 109s were detected heading for the convoy as it made its way through the English Channel. They were intercepted by 54 Squadron from Hornchurch, 610 Squadron from Biggin Hill, and 615 Squadron from Kenley. The fighter-bombers turned back, but Hornchurch's Spitfires managed to shoot down one of the escorts, and one of the fighter-bombers received sufficient damage that it crash-landed in France. During this brief encounter, one of Kenleys Hurricanes was shot down by another member of its own squadron, killing the pilot.

Around 7 p.m., the Luftwaffe sent over waves of Bf 109 to strafe a number of airfields, including Manston. Once again, Dowding and Park were not going to be drawn in to needless fight and consequently only the Spitfires of 616 Squadron from Kenley were sent up to engage them. EG 210 were again in action, flying in at low-level to bomb Manston. As well as cratering the airfield, they also caught the remnants of 600 Squadrons Blenheims on the ground who were in the process of completing their move back to their home base of Hornchurch. The attack left two hangars and a number of other buildings in ruins, and it put the airfield out of action once more.

The balance sheet for the day showed an unusual change of fortunes with Fighter Command losing five aircraft compared to the shooting down of two Luftwaffe aircraft.

During the night, the *X-Verfahren*-equipped He 111s of KG 100 once again attacked the aircraft factory at Filton in Somerset causing yet more damage and injuring four people.

Friday, 23 August

The poor weather continued to play its part in the battle. Cloud and rain showers over Southern Britain meant that yet again the Luftwaffe could not capitalize on the damage they had been inflicting on Fighter Command. Equally, Fighter Command had another day to continue to repair their airfields and infrastructure, replace lost or damaged aircraft, and bring in replacement pilots. Enemy activity was limited to the occasional reconnaissance flight and lone raiders, most of which Fighter Command completely ignored.

This was also the day that 307 (City of Lwow) a Polish Defiant equipped squadron was formed as a night-fighter squadron, and another Polish unit 304 Squadron was established as a Bomber Command squadron at RAF Bramcote in Warwickshire.

Overnight, among other targets, the Luftwaffe had intended to bomb the aircraft factory at Filton outside Bristol. However, in the poor weather, a bomber dropped its bombs on Harrow and Wealdstone in Middlesex by mistake. Unfortunately, this was yet again classed as a raid on London. In the early hours of the morning on 24 August, more than two hundred bombers had attacked the Dunlop factory in Birmingham, which caused significant disruption to tire production.

Saturday, 24 August

With a change in the weather, the day dawned clear and bright in the south, with drizzle in the north. After four days of relatively little action due to bad weather, the day also proved to be relatively quiet allowing both sides to continue to regroup and re-equip.

Goering had reiterated that Fighter Command's airfields should the Luftwaffe's daytime targets, and today was designed to be the start of a sustained period of bombing in which he hoped to overwhelm Fighter Command's resources—by now he and Luftwaffe Intelligence thought that yet again they were down to around three hundred or four hundred fighters.

At 8:30 in the morning, Pevensey and Dover radar stations detected the build-up of a significant raid over the French coast, which comprised over forty Ju 88s and Do 17s, escorted by more than sixty Bf 109s. Fighter Command scrambled 11 squadrons including the Spitfires of Biggin Hill's 610 Squadron to intercept them. They succeeded in scattering the bombers before their fighter escorts could interfere—they also managed to shoot down a fighter and bomber in the process. 54 Squadron then joined in the fight as the enemy formations turned for home shooting down another Messerschmitt.

Two hours later, radar operators again detected a large raid approaching the Kent coast. Hurricanes from North Weald and Gravesend, together with

610 Squadron's Spitfires, who had only just returned to Biggin Hill from the previous attack, were sent to intercept it. They were joined by the Defiants of Hornchurch's 264 Squadron, who were at their forward base at Manston. The Defiants were the first to engage the bombers as they tried to bomb their airfield, shooting down one bomber and damaging another before the escorts set about them. The results were predictable, with three Defiants being shot down and a further two damaged. As Biggin Hill's Spitfires joined the action, the escorting Bf 109s turned for home, and during the chase, a Bf 109 was shot down for the loss of a Spitfire.

At 3 p.m., a large formation was spotted, which was initially thought to be heading for London, before changing course towards the airfields of Hornchurch and North Weald. 11 Group scrambled a large number of fighters in response, including the three squadrons at Hornchurch, both of Biggin Hill's squadrons, 151 from North Weald, 501 from Gravesend, and 615 from Kenley. Keith Park also requested help from Leigh Mallory's 12 Group who tried to provide a three-squadron wing. Unfortunately, it spent so long forming that they did not reach the action until the bombers were on their way home. In fact, only two squadrons were able to join together, the third, 19 Squadron, eventually set out on its own.

Worse was to follow. What was left of 264 Squadron having returned to Hornchurch following their combat over Manston, were scrambled just as the bombers arrived. In the rush to get airborne, two Defiants collided and another one was shot down soon afterwards. Following the day's actions, 264 Squadron had lost twelve Defiants and fourteen pilots in just three days.

During the following ninety minutes, Hornchurch and North Weald were both heavily bombed causing severe damage, but both airfields managed to remain operational. North Weald was attacked by nearly twenty bombers and suffered significant damage with nine people killed and another ten injured. The rest of the bomber formation had been split up by 151 and 111 Squadrons who had raced to the station's defense.

At the same time, Manston was bombed once again, destroying much of what was left of the airfields infrastructure, including all communications with 11 Group Head Quarters at Uxbridge. Even as the bombs were still falling, men were working in one of the bomb craters trying to repair the severed telephone lines. Communications were re-established within two hours, but the airfield had been so badly damaged that Fighter Command had to abandon it apart from using it for emergency landings. During the attack, seventeen people were killed. Part of the raiding force also caused significant damage in nearby town of Ramsgate.

Half an hour later, two raids from Luftflotte III were detected setting out from the Cherbourg Peninsular. Their targets were the airfield at Middle Wallop and Portsmouth. 609 Squadron based at Middle Wallop were scrambled to intercept and were the first of the defenders to reach the enemy bombers. Unfortunately, they arrived too low and made contact just as coastal anti-aircraft guns opened fire. The Ju 88s and Bf 110s managed to drop over two hundred bombs on Portsmouth, causing widespread, large-scale damage, killing more than one hundred people and injuring over three hundred others.

During these air battles, Fighter Command lost twenty aircraft while the Luftwaffe lost thirty-nine.

An incident occurred over night that was to have a major influence on the rest of the Battle. As the night-time bombing of Britain intensified, large formations, again from the Cherbourg Peninsular, headed for the Thames Estuary and for four hours, attacked the oils storage tanks at Rochester and Thameshaven as well as the London docks and the surrounding area. Due to poor navigation, one of the bombers also dropped its bomb-load in the heart of the city at Aldgate and the east end of London; other bombs fell on Oxford Street. This bombing killed nine people and injured another fifty-eight.

As we have seen during previous raids on 15 and 23 August, bombs had been dropped on areas that were considered to be part of London, but this was the first time that bombs had landed in the center of the Capital (see chapter 4). In response, Churchill ordered an immediate raid, within twenty-four hours, to be targeted on Berlin—a target that Goering had assured the German people that the RAF would never be able to attack. Hitler's outrage at this led to a fatally flawed change in Luftwaffe daytime tactics and the start of the Blitz, a change which, as we shall see, effectively decided the outcome of the battle.

Sunday, 25 August

The day began with early-morning mist, which cleared to leave a clear morning with cloud developing later.

Many of the Luftwaffe crews took advantage of early mist to rest during much of the day. Consequently, the first large-scale raid did not take place until 5 p.m., when Luftflotte III dispatched over two hundred bombers from the Cherbourg Peninsular and the French coast close to the Channel Islands. Once again, they made their way towards Portsmouth and Southampton before dividing in to three separate formations. Having been detected by the radar station at Ventnor, aircraft from 10 and 11 Groups were scrambled from Warmwell, Exeter, and Debden to intercept them. During the ensuing fight, a number of the Bf 110s managed to break through the defenses and made their way towards Warmwell, where they damaged a couple of hangars and the sick quarters before turning for home. A second formation, comprising Ju 88s and Bf 110s, headed for Portland. 87 Squadron's Hurricanes attacked the Ju 88s, while the Spitfires of 609 Squadron made for the fighter-bombers.

Less than an hour after this raid, another formation of around one hundred aircraft, including a number of Bf 110s, were spotted heading for Dover. Spitfires and Hurricanes were scrambled from Gravened and Biggin Hill who managed to chase the raiders back across the Channel.

During the day, the Fighter Command shot down twenty enemy aircraft for the loss of sixteen of their own fighters. More worrying for Fighter Command was the loss of nine pilots, with four others missing and another four wounded.

Following on from the formation of a bomber unit at Bramcote five days earlier, a second Polish bomber squadron was formed at the base on 25 August.

During the night, scattered German air raids continued over much of the country, while Bomber Command sent eighty-one bombers to attack Berlin in response to the attack on central and the east end of London the previous night. In fact, only half of the Wellingtons and Hampdens that took part in the raid dropped their bombs due to thick cloud cover. Bombing injured two people in the city. This meant that the raid was fairly ineffectual, but tactically and psychologically, it had a tremendous impact on the people of Berlin, Hitler, and Goering.

Monday, 26 August

The day dawned bright with high cloud, but otherwise flying conditions were good.

The first raid of the day developed at 11:20 a.m. when over one hundred and fifty aircraft were detected congregating over Lille. Six squadrons, including 616 Squadron that had just moved south from Church Fenton to Kenley, were scrambled as were 264 Squadrons remaining Defiants that had moved back to Hornchurch from Kirton-on-Lindsay four days earlier. As was often the case with newly transferred, relatively inexperienced aircrew, as the pilots 616 Squadron were still trying to gain valuable height, they were bounced by a number of Bf 109s who shot down seven of their Spitfires with the loss of two pilots and two others wounded. The unfortunate Defiants also took yet another pounding, resulted in the loss of three aircraft, but not before they had managed to shoot down one Dornier and damage another one. With sufficient warning, the defenders, comprising some seventy fighters, managed to intercept the enemy formation before most of the bombers could reach their targets, the airfields at Biggin Hill and Kenley. Even so, some bombers managed to bomb both airfields before turning for home, fortunately causing little damage this time.

At 2 p.m., radar picked up two large raids, comprising over seventy Dorniers, escorted by one hundred and twenty Bf 109s and Bf 110s that were heading across a wide front from the Thames Estuary to Harwich. As they approached the coast, the enemy formation split in to two, with the southern group apparently heading for London and the airfields at North Weald and Hornchurch; the northern raid were making for Debden. Fighter Command scrambled ten squadrons, including 1 Squadron RCAF from Northolt, and 310 the Czech squadron from Duxford. The Czech pilots, who were on their first operational mission, were the first to reach the Debden-bound raid, followed by 65 Squadron from Hornchurch, and 111 from Croydon. The Canadians joined in when the bombers reached the Clacton-Colchester area. 11 Group requested additional help from 12 Group to cover Debden. As the main group of bombers headed home, 310 Squadron set upon them, shooting down two Dorniers and a Bf 110 but they lost three of their Hurricanes in the process; 56 and 111 Squadrons also lost two aircraft each.

With many of the 11 Group fighters engaged in intercepting the bombers, most of the attackers turned for home, however six broke through the defenses and managed to reach Debden where they attacked the airfield causing considerable damage and killing six people on the ground. 19 Squadron finally arrived shortly after the bombers were heading for the coast.

85 and 615 Squadrons were sent to intercept the southern formation heading for Hornchurch and North Weald, initially engaging them off the north Kent coast west of Margate. With their fighters turning for home due to low fuel levels, the bombers abandoned their mission and also turned back, but not before they unloaded their bombs across a wide area of Kent.

While these attacks were drawing to a conclusion, another equally large raid mounted by Luftflotte III comprising more than fifty He 111s, escorted by over one hundred fighters, was heading for Portsmouth. Fighter Command's southern and southwestern airfields were brought to readiness, with 11 Group scrambling aircraft form Tangmere and Westhampnett and 10 Group sending Spitfires from Middle Wallop and Warmwell and Hurricanes from Exeter. Low cloud over the southern counties prevented many of the defenders from finding the Germans, but those that did managed to break up the raiding formation, causing many of the bombers to drop their bombs in the sea before turning back across the Channel. British fighters managed to shoot down three aircraft and damage another two, bringing the day's tally to forty-one German aircraft for the loss of twenty-seven of their own aircraft and six pilots killed.

With the withdrawal of virtually all of their single-seat fighters, Luftflotte III realized that it could not continue to sustain such heavy losses to its bomber force and would switch to largely night operations for the foreseeable future.

Tuesday, 27 August

Once again, the weather deteriorated with rain during the morning and cloud during the rest of the day. This restricted Luftwaffe activity to only one significant raid, giving both sides time to recover from the previous three days' intense action.

Today would see another significant meeting in which Keith Park and Leigh Mallory clashed over the tactics being used during the battle. Park maintained that the correct policy was to send as many fighters as were necessary to counter each raid so that he could preserve his overall strength. Also, given the limited time, he and his pilots had between raids being detected and being able to identify their targets and get airborne, it meant that he could only send individual squadrons or flights into action. Mallory maintained that assembling a number of squadrons as a wing, or Big Wing, that could engage the enemy in larger numbers, was the best policy. Park pointed out again, that 11 Group did not have sufficient time to bring such a large number of aircraft together, and that by doing so the Germans bombers would reach their targets, which were largely his airfields. Park decided that to prevent any further misunderstandings he informed his controllers that, rather than contacting 12 Group Sector Stations for support they should contact 12 Group Head Quarters instead.

On the continent, the Luftwaffe had moved yet more Bf 109s to the area around Calais so that they could provide their bombers with even more fighter support.

By mid-day, the weather had begun to improve and radar operators detected a raid assembling in the Cherbourg area. 10 Group scrambled two squadrons, which managed to shoot down one of the bombers and damage two others, one of which crash-landed back at its base.

Fighter Command's rotation policy continued with 65 Squadron moving from Hornchurch to Church Fenton. It was replaced by 603 Squadron which was bought down from Turnhouse in Scotland.

During the night, Luftwaffe bombers again ranged far and wide over the UK. Dorniers raided the southwest, and, unusually, fighters scrambled by 10 Group managed to shoot three of them down.

Wednesday, 28 August

Although it was cloudy throughout the day, this time it did not restrict flying.

The first raid of the day, comprising almost fifty Dornier bombers together with a large number of fighters, began to build over Dunkirk. At just before 9 in the morning, 501 Squadron, 85 Squadron from Croydon, and 615 from Kenley were scrambled to meet the raid. They were joined by 79 Squadron, who had moved south from Usworth to Biggin Hill the previous day, replacing 32 Squadron who moved in the opposite direction to Acklington in Northumberland. Also preparing to move northwards to take them out of the fighting, were 264 Squadrons Defiants, who yet again were moving back to Kirton-on-Lindsay. However, before they moved, they were once again called in to the action losing another three aircraft, with three others damaged. The raiders bombed Manston causing only slight damage this time, shortly before Winston Churchill was due to visit the airfield. They also hit Eastchurch where they caused large-scale damage, including the destruction of a number of Fairey Battles; they also bombed the airfield at Rochford on the northern side of the Thames Estuary. 85 Squadron, now based at Croydon, adopted Croydon's 111 Squadrons tactics and flew a head-on attack at the enemy formation, shooting down six Bf 109s.

Just after mid-day, 54 Squadron flying from Hornchurch intercepted Do 17s attacking their airfield for a second time that day, but the bombers did little damage and again the station managed to remain serviceable.

The third raid, consisting of a large number of Bf 109s and Bf 110s crossed the Channel heading for the Kent coast and Thames Estuary. Despite Park's instructions to only scramble fighters to intercept raids, which contained bombers, seven squadrons were scrambled to counter this attack. Consequently, in the ensuing dogfight, Fighter Command shot down six enemy aircraft for the loss of five of its own fighters.

That night, the Germans sent over their first of five consecutive mass raids on the docks at Liverpool and Birkenhead, considered to be second in importance as a target to London docks. Due to poor navigation, and the defenders using *Starfish*—diversionary fires to draw the bombers away—few bombs fell on their targets, with some landing up to 150 miles (241km) away. Enemy bombers also attacked Manchester, Derby, Sheffield, Coventry, and London. To add to the nights activities, Bomber Command attacked Berlin again.

Thursday, 29 August

Rain showers and low cloud again restricted flying during the morning, but with improving conditions during the afternoon, the Luftwaffe sent out large-scale fighter sweeps across the Channel. In response to the first raid, comprising nearly seven hundred fighters and fighter-bombers, that arrived just after 3 p.m., Park scrambled thirteen squadrons, expecting bombers to arrive shortly afterwards. The first to encounter the enemy were 85 Squadron from Croydon who lost three Hurricanes in the attack. These were followed by 610 Squadron from Biggin Hill who lost two Spitfires, before Park realized that the attacking force comprised only fighters and recalled his aircraft. Unlike the previous day, this time most squadrons responded to the call and returned to their bases without becoming entangled in a needless dogfight.

Around teatime, two further fighter sweeps crossed the Channel and were once again largely ignored. One, however, caught 501 Squadron patrolling above Hawkinge, and, with the advantage of height and speed bounced the Hurricanes, but not without losing two of their own aircraft.

During the day's combat's Fighter Command shot down seventeen enemy aircraft for the loss of only seven of its own fighters.

264 Squadron, having moved northward the day before, were replaced at Hornchurch by the Spitfires of 222 Squadron. 615, one of Kenley's squadrons, also moved to Prestwick in Scotland to be replaced by 253 Squadron who came down from Turnhouse in Edinburgh.

Friday, 30 August

In the early hours of the morning, the Luftwaffe bombed Tyneside, Hartlepool, Swansea, Merseyside, and Manchester, with only limited effect.

The morning bought with it clear and bright skies and idea flying conditions. Therefore, the Germans planned to launch a number of large-scale raids comprising over 1,300 aircraft. In response, 11 Group would fly the largest number of sorties of the entire battle and come under enormous pressure. A lucky hit, during the morning, when bombs managed to cut the power cable to the radar stations at Dover, Foreness, Fairlight, Rye,

Pevensey, Whitstable, and Beachy Head, effectively put the 'eyes' of Fighter Command out of action for three crucial hours and only added to the pressure 11 Group would be under.

Shortly after dawn, the Hurricanes of 111 Squadron together with three Spitfires from 54 Squadron intercepted a group of Dorniers, escorted by thirty Bf 110s that had been sighted heading towards Manston.

Just before 10 a.m., the first large raid of the day began to build over the Cape Griz Nez area west of Calais. They comprised a mixture of Heinkels and Dorniers that would set out for their targets at 30-minute intervals led and supported by Bf 109s and Bf 110s. Park held back from engaging the first element of the raid—the now standard fighter sweep—and waited for the following bombers. The second element comprising forty Heinkels and thirty Dorniers, escorted by sixty Bf 109s and thirty Bf 110s, crossed the coast, on a wide front. Shortly after 11 a.m., Park scrambled nine squadrons in two waves from Biggin Hill, Kenley, Croydon, Tangmere, Debden, and Hornchurch to join 85 Squadron who were already in the air patrolling the coast above Dungerness. The first wave of RAF fighters, comprising 43, 79, 253, and 603 Squadrons met the raiders between Deal and Folkstone. The second wave were led by 85 Squadron who undertook a trademark Croydon-based squadron, head-on attack on the bombers. The second bomber formation, a mixture of Heinkels and Dorniers, supported by more than a hundred fighters, appeared to be heading towards London. As they flew in land, they divided into two smaller formations with each one heading for different Sector Stations. The ensuing dogfight covered much of skies above Kent. The third formation, crossing the coast near Brighton, were met by 43 and 253 Squadrons, the latter also having only recently transferred south from Prestwick in Scotland to Kenley.

While these raids were still heading for the southeast coast, Park put a further sixteen squadrons on standby and requested the assistance of two squadrons from 12 Group to provide cover over Biggin Hill and Kenley. Yet again, instead of providing the necessary cover, the 12 Group fighters headed for the attackers and therefore failed to intercept a large number of Ju 88s that bombed Biggin Hill, causing considerable damage to the airfield, including badly damaging two of the hangars, and severing the cables of the telephone system, cutting communications with 11 Group. Bombs also fell on the nearby village of Keston. At the same time, Kenley was being bombed. Park responded by pulling 79 and 74 Squadrons out of the action over Kent and Sussex to cover both airfields in the absence of the 12 Group fighter cover. German bombers also hit Croydon and Detling.

At 1 p.m., Park phoned 12 Group to find out where the additional fighters were that were supposed to protecting his airfields. They responded by telling him that the aircraft could not find the enemy, to which Park politely responded that they were not supposed to be looking for enemy aircraft, they were supposed to be covering his airfields.

Fifteen minutes later, while some of the aircraft from the first raid were heading for home, the next raid crossed the coast in three waves, 10 minutes apart, heading for Hawkinge, Lympne, and Manston, all of which were bombed, together with Kenley, Tangmere, and Shoreham.

At 4 p.m., another raid, comprising over seventy aircraft were spotted heading for the Thames Estuary and possibly the London docks. In response, aircraft from Biggin Hill, Kenley, Hornchurch, North Weald, and Croydon were scrambled. 242 Squadron led by Douglas Bader also came down from Duxford. Once again, the raiders changed direction and headed for 11 Group airfields. Although, as we have seen, Detling was not a Fighter Command station it was also heavily bombed and put out of action. Hornchurch, Croydon, Gravesend, and Duxford were also seriously damaged. An hour later, German bombers flew as far inland as Oxford and Luton to bomb aircraft production related factories. Seven squadrons were scrambled to intercept these raiders all of which had been flying almost continuously since early morning. The Oxford-bound raid was successfully intercepted and turned for home before they could fulfil their mission, but the bombers, escorted by Bf 110s that were heading for Luton succeeded in bombing the Vauxhall car works, killing fifty-three and injuring a further sixty people. However, the car works was not involved in aircraft production—another failure by Luftwaffe Intelligence.

During this raid, 303 Squadron crewed by Polish pilots, who had been on a training flight from Northolt, spotted a number of Dorniers. One of the Pilots broke formation pursued and finally shot down one of the bombers. On returning to Northolt, he received a severe telling off, followed by the decision, based on his squadron commanders recommendation, that the squadron would be declared operational.

At 6 p.m., ten Ju 88s, flying at very low level to avoid detection, flew towards the Thames Estuary before turning south and heading for Biggin Hill. With 79 Squadron on the ground and 610 Squadron patrolling elsewhere, the airfield suffered a devastating attack. One bomb hit a trench killing everyone inside, another bomb exploded close to a WAAF's trench burying its occupants. The stores building, armory, both messes and a third hangar were also hit. By the time the attack had ended, thirty-nine people had been killed and a further twenty-six had been injured. The damage inflicted was enough to lead to control of its aircraft being temporarily transferred to Hornchurch.

During the day, all of 11 Group's twenty-two squadrons had been in action, many of them flying four times in quick succession. They lost thirty-nine aircraft, including eight from 222 Squadron, whilst the Luftwaffe lost forty-one airplanes.

That night a large force of Ju 88s and He 111s bombed Liverpool again, while Dorniers and Heinkel bombers also attacked Manchester, Worcester, Bristol, London, and Portsmouth.

Saturday, 31 August

The month closed with another fine, clear day, which meant that once again the Luftwaffe would be out in force.

By the morning, the radar stations that had put out of action the day before were operational as was Biggin Hill. 610 Squadron, who had been at the airfield since beginning of the battle were preparing to move north to Acklington in Northumberland for a rest, to be replaced by 72 Squadron, who were moving in the opposite direction.

Just before 8 a.m., one formation of German aircraft was heading for Dover whilst three others made their way towards the Thames Estuary. Following the experiences of the previous day, Keith Park scrambled his squadrons early in order that they should be able to gain the valuable height that often made such a difference to the outcome of any dogfight. He scrambled two squadrons towards Margate to intercept the Dover raid, but on realizing that it comprised only Bf 109s, flying at 25,000 feet (7,620m), he recalled them. Unfortunately, although 253 Squadron's Hurricanes received the message, 1 RCAF Squadron did not, and during the ensuing battle, they lost three aircraft. Having found no other aircraft to engage, and, running low on fuel, the German fighters decide to shoot down the barrage balloons protecting the harbor before returning home.

As they were returning, the other three waves consisting of Heinkel and Dornier bombers protected by sixty Bf 110s—two hundred aircraft in total—were approaching the Thames Estuary. Park responded by scrambling thirteen squadrons. When they reached the entrance to the Thames, the Germans divided in to three separate formations, each heading for different Sector Stations. The first group, who were met by 257 Squadron's Hurricanes, inflicted little damage on Hornchurch for the loss of two Bf 110s and two Hurricanes. The formation then headed for North Weald where it was more successful. In the ensuing dogfight near Colchester, 56 Squadron lost four Hurricanes while the bombers continued their mission, causing significant damage to the airfield.

The second group, intending to attack Duxford, took 12 Group by surprise, in fact they called Park at 11 Group for assistance, who sent 111 Squadron from Croydon racing to help. On arrival, they formed up for their usual head-on attack, and managed to shoot down one of the bombers. Fortunately, the bombers were unable to bomb the airfield. The third group, comprising twenty Dorniers and fifty Bf 110s attacked Debden, which, without any fighter cover, was left completely unprotected apart from its ground defenses. It was hit by a hundred bombs, which destroyed four buildings including the sick quarters. They also damaged four Hurricanes on the ground, and injured eighteen people. Shortly after they turned for home, the bombers were engaged by the cannon-armed Spitfires of 19 Squadron, who had been scrambled from Duxford's satellite station at Fowlmere. Unfortunately, not only were the Spitfires bounced by the Bf 110s but many of their cannons jammed leaving unable to return fire. Consequently, four were shot down for the loss of only one Bf 110.

At 9 a.m., two more waves of bombers approached the Thames Estuary intent once again on attacking the two non-Fighter Command airfields of Eastchurch and Detling. One wave comprising twenty Dorniers with their fighter escort dropped around eighty bombs on Eastchurch but did little damage. The other wave, comprising only fighters, strafed Detling, again without inflicting too much damage.

At 1 p.m., waves of Bf 110s and Bf 109s crossed the coast to attack radar stations, including Foreness, Rye, Dungerness, Pevensey, and Beachy Head. They managed to inflict some damage but not sufficient to put them off air. Park decided to leave them alone and wait for the next wave of bombers, who were not far behind.

Fifteen minutes later, the next raid, comprising over one hundred bombers, having crossed the coast near Dungerness, split in to two separate formations to attack Croydon and Biggin Hill. At Croydon, the bombs started to fall just as 85 Squadron were taking off. In their rush to take off, and with the consequent disadvantage of height, 85 Squadron lost three Hurricanes for the downing of two Bf 110s. The same thing happened at Biggin Hill where high-level bombers arrived overhead just after 72 Squadron had scrambled. At Biggin, the Operations Room was hit causing the roof to collapse, and the newly repaired telephone system and power cables were once again put out of operation. To bring the station back on line, yet again telephone engineers continued to repair broken lines during the bombing. With the Operations Room temporarily out of action, the staff moved to a chemist shop in the

High Street, where within twelve hours a fully functional Operations Room had been established. The Officers Mess was hit and a workshop was destroyed, and two of the hangars, which had already been badly damaged two days earlier were hit once again. In fact, the airfield was so badly damaged that her fighters had to be diverted to Croydon and Kenley to land. Unfortunately, as we have seen, Croydon was also bombed, this time they destroyed one of the hangars while other buildings on the airfield were badly damaged.

Another formation of bombers attacked Hornchurch, where 603 Squadron, that had recently transferred south from Scotland were airborne. Unfortunately, 54 Squadron were still in the process of taking off as the Dorniers bombed the airfield destroying three Spitfires. Miraculously, all three pilots received only minor injuries. More than fifty bombs fell across the airfield, cutting the main power cable, killing three people, and wounded a number of others. The gallant work of all the personnel meant that by late afternoon, all of the bomb craters had been filled in and the airfield remained operational.

The final raid of the day arrived around teatime, when Ju 88s and Bf 110s of EG 210 returned to bomb Biggin Hill and Hornchurch. At the latter, they managed to destroy another two Spitfires on the ground. In spite of all the damage inflicted on Biggin Hill and Hornchurch, both airfields would be operational the following morning.

The days almost continuous fighting had led to the loss of thirty-seven Fighter Command aircraft and nine pilots were killed while eighteen others were seriously wounded for the downing of only thirty-nine German aircraft. With Fighter Command's losses very close to those of the Luftwaffe, everyone knew they were in a critical phase of the battle.

German night-time raids were again dominated by widespread single aircraft and small formations of bombers attacking targets that included Manchester, Bristol, Durham, Hereford, Leeds, and York. The main attack targeted, for the fourth night running, Liverpool and Birkenhead.

Following their disastrous losses, the Defiant equipped squadrons received instructions that in future they were only to be used as night-fighters unless daytime bomber-only formations were detected.

During August, Fighter Command had lost two hundred and eleven Hurricanes, with a further forty-four damaged. Eighty-five Hurricane pilots had been killed, with one more missing and sixty-eight wounded. They had also lost one hundred and thirteen Spitfires, with forty others damaged, for the loss of forty-one pilots, three missing, and thirty-eight wounded. Thirteen Blenhiems had been destroyed, ten damaged, and six aircrew killed, with three others missing. As we have seen, the Defiant squadrons had suffered badly, with seven destroyed and three damaged, plus seven crew killed and four wounded.

In total, for the month Fighter Command had lost three hundred and forty-four aircraft, with ninety-seven damaged, one hundred and thirty-nine pilots had been killed, seven were missing, and another one hundred and ten were wounded. The Luftwaffe had suffered far worse, with six hundred and sixty-nine, almost twice as many aircraft lost, and one hundred and eighty-two damaged. But their aircrew statistics tell a more important story, with four hundred sixty-three dead, two hundred and one wounded, and a staggering eight hundred and four missing, many of which were of course prisoners of war having not made it back across the Channel. Goering's change in tactics, to keep his fighters in close support of his bombers, had led to three fifths of his losses being amongst his fighters.

Although the Luftwaffe were causing significant, almost crippling damage to Fighter Command, and in particular 11 Group's airfields, they were themselves suffering very high, unsustainable losses of aircraft and, more importantly aircrew. Unlike, Fighter Command, who as we have seen regularly rotated their squadrons to give them rest and time to replace both pilots and aircraft, the Luftwaffe did not. The only way Luftwaffe aircrew were taken off flying was through capture, injury, or death. Now that most of the Bf 109 units were stationed close to the coast, they were being used in ever-increasing numbers to provide cover for the bombers. The result was that many of the aircrew were exhausted. Goering had told them that it would be a short fight, and Luftwaffe Intelligence had told them that Fighter Command were down to their last few hundred aircraft. The aircrew knew different. They were continuously being met by large numbers of Spitfires and Hurricanes wherever they attacked. However, because Goering was using an increasing number of German fighters to provide protection for his bombers, Fighter Command were finding it increasingly difficult to avoid fighter-versus-fighter combats as they tried to reach the bombers, which meant that consequently, they were suffering increasing losses. Even with this worrying situation, rather than the Luftwaffe calling the shots, Fighter Command were still able to largely control where to engage the enemy and in what numbers, although this meant that on many occasions, all of 11 Group's squadrons were either in the air or on standby for every raid. Their pilots also knew that if they had to bail-out and were not too badly injured, they were on home territory and would probably be flying shortly afterwards. Differences in the planning and approach to providing replacement aircraft between the two sides was also beginning to tell, and although Fighter Command were short of pilots, they were never short of aircraft, whereas the Luftwaffe were facing increasing shortages of replacement aircraft and spares.

One of the biggest problems facing Dowding was the increasing lack of training replacement pilots were receiving before being transferred to operational squadrons. Many of the new pilots were directly out of training, with little flying and no combat experience. Often they were going straight in to the fight where they faced being shot down almost immediately because the experienced pilots on the squadrons did not have the time to provide combat training. This situation also increased the loss of aircraft with new or repaired fighters barely keeping pace with the losses on some days. Although Dowding could turn to Bomber and Coastal Command for replacement pilots, they too lacked the necessary single seat fighter experience he really needed. As we have seen, he had built-up Czech and Polish crewed squadrons and even if there were still problems with communications, their pilots would often fight with a passion verging on recklessness. As a result, Polish pilots accounted for nearly 20% of all 'kills' during the battle, with 303 Squadron having the fourth highest 'kill' tally of all of Fighter Command's squadrons during the war and the highest tally in the Battle of Britain.

12 Group felt that they were being called too late and were missing out on the action, and while Keith Park used his squadrons individually, or maybe two at a time, Leigh-Mallory continued to push for the use of Big Wings. Park pointed out that on 26 August, while 12 Group were forming their Big Wing, the bombers had hit Debden, the closest 11 Group Sector Station to 12 Group. Even if the Big Wing could attack the Germans on their way home, it would obviously be too late to prevent them bombing of his airfields. (In fact, during the battle the Big Wing only engaged the enemy on seven occasions, including, as we shall see in the next chapter, 15 September. Their final encounter during the height of the battle was on 18 September.)

What Fighter Command, Dowding, and Park really needed was either a change in tactics by the Luftwaffe to give 11 Group's airfields and squadrons some relief or a couple of days of bad weather, they were to get neither in the next few days.

As the Battle of Britain Historical Society web site reports:

'Up to the end of August, the whole of Fighter Command had been under extreme pressure. Day after day, the Luftwaffe had targeted the airfields of 11 Group and the radar stations along the south coast while at night they had turned to heavy bombing raids on the larger cities. The last few days of August, and the first days of September were to prove of great concern for both Dowding and Park.'

Sunday, 1 September

The few clouds that littered the sky in the morning soon cleared to leave another bright, sunny, summer's day.

The Luftwaffe raids had now settled in to a pattern that would continue over the next six days. As we have seen, initially, they would send over a large number of Bf 109s to draw Fighter Command in to the air, in the hope of either shooting them down or causing them to return to their bases just as the main, bombing attack arrived over their airfields. Park's usual response to this was to either send one or possibly two squadrons to head them off, or more often to leave them alone. These fighter sweeps were to be followed by waves of bombers with substantial fighter cover that would attack Fighter Command's bases. The waves would be timed so that Fighter Command would have little if any time to turn their fighters around, but as we have seen, squadron and station personnel had developed rearming, refueling etc. to such a fine art that, even today's Formula 1 pit crews would appreciate it. We have also seen that Park would rarely send more than half of his fighters available to him in to battle at any one time to be able to preserve sufficient aircraft to meet this pattern of attack—a tactic that usually meant that he could cope with the now almost continuous flow of enemy aircraft.

As part of his strategy of rotating his squadrons, Dowding dispatched what was left of 151 Squadron's Hurricanes and its pilots from Stapleford to Digby in Yorkshire and replaced them with 46 Squadron's Hurricanes. He also moved 56 Squadron, also flying Hurricanes, from North Weald to Boscombe Down in 10 Group, and replaced them with Hurricanes of 249 Squadron.

Shortly after 10 a.m., the radar stations at Foreness, Dover, and Pevensey detected a raid building up over the French coast that turned out to be the usual, initial fighter sweep. These were followed by over sixty Dorniers and Bf 110s, with a significant fighter escort. As the formations neared the English coast, which, with such large numbers of aircraft was spread between Dungerness and Margate, they followed the now familiar patterns of dividing in to separate groups each one heading for different airfields.

One formation made its way towards Eastchurch and Detling, another headed for Biggin Hill, Kenley, and Croydon, and a third aimed for the northern shore of the Thames Estuary and airfield at Rochford, near Southend and the docks at Tilbury. In response, 11 Group scrambled fourteen squadrons including the Spitfires of 54 Squadron from Hornchurch and 72 Squadron, which, as we have seen transferred south, but had to temporarily moved to Croydon due to the extensive damage inflicted on Biggin Hill. They were joined by 85 Squadron also from Croydon and 1 RCAF Squadron from Northolt. As the others engaged some of the bombers close to Maidstone, 72 Squadron were bounced by some of the covering Bf 109s losing three aircraft in the process. Once again, 79 Squadron who were still at Biggin Hill were caught on the ground before they could get airborne. Bombing resulted in the only partially operational airfield being put out of action again completely for several hours. This meant that 79 Squadron having managed to take off would also have to be diverted to Croydon when they wanted to land. While trying to defend their airfield, the squadron lost three Spitfires in the air and four more on the ground.

The bombers who had targeted Detling and Eastchurch also managed to reach and bomb the docks in East London before attacking Dover on their way home.

At around 1:30 p.m., as the British fighters were still returning to their bases to rearm and refuel, a second large raid of more than one hundred and fifty aircraft were spotted flying towards the Kent coast. This followed a similar pattern to the last raid, with the larger formation splitting up into smaller groups heading for different airfields. Aircraft from 1, 54, 72, 85, 253, and 616 Squadrons were scrambled from Hornchurch, Croydon, and Kenley, meeting the enemy aircraft between Folkstone and Hastings.

Biggin Hill was again one of the main targets for the third day running, with Dorniers coming in at high level and Bf 110s swooping in at low level. They hit the hangars, workshops, and messes causing severe damage for the loss of four aircraft. Fifteen minutes later 85 Squadron were bounced by Bf 109s near Kenley and lost five Hurricanes. Biggin Hill and Kenley were not the only targets for this raid, the Germans also bombed Hornchurch, North Weald, Gravesend, Hawkinge, Lympne, and Detling as well as the London and Tilbury docks.

The third raid of the day followed the same pattern and route as the previous two, with one formation bombing Hawkinge, Lympne, and Detling on the way to Biggin Hill where once again they caused significant damage. Apart from hitting many of the buildings, which were already extensively damaged, they also hit the Operations Room and one of the female trenches. For their work during this and the previous raids, two WAAF's were later awarded the Military Cross. The damage led to the airfield being temporarily declared non-operational again and engineers from the Post Office worked through the raids and the night to re-establish the all-important telephone lines needed to link the station with 11 Group Head Quarters and other essential services. The airfield would be returned to operations by the following morning. A friend of mine records speaking to Les Thompson, who was an airframe rigger at Biggin Hill at the time of this raid. Les recalled that during the raid he hurried to his allotted air-raid shelter but while he was down there the felt a compulsion to get out and risk being disciplined as well as injury from falling bombs, so he ran across to another shelter. One of the bombs fell at an angle and penetrated the ground right underneath the shelter he had just left. Its explosion resulted in the deaths of a large number of personnel, mostly the WAAF's referred to above. He could never account for that compulsion but it saved his life.

While the telephone lines and water mains were being repaired, air force personnel once again used the temporary Operations Room in the chemist shop in Biggin Hill High Street, which would be operational within an hour and fully operational within twelve hours. However, with such extensive damage to the infrastructure on the airfield, it would not be able to handle its full complement of aircraft—four squadrons—hence, once again some aircraft were diverted to Croydon.

For the first time in recent weeks, the Luftwaffe lost less aircraft than Fighter Command, with the day's tally being thirteen and fourteen. Fighter Command also lost another five pilots.

The night bought the usual widespread bombing, involving as many as one hundred and twenty bombers with very little chance of Fighter Command being able to intercept them.

Monday, 2 September

After a foggy start, the skies cleared to reveal another lovely summers day.

At 7:30 a.m., radar detected the first raid of the day building over Calais comprising one group of forty Heinkels and another of thirty Dorniers, supported by over fifty Bf 110s in close support and Bf 109s providing top cover. Their intended targets were once again the airfields at Biggin Hill, Eastchurch, North Weald, and Rochford.

Although 11 Group scrambled eleven squadrons, only 72 and 92 Squadrons found the enemy formation that was heading for Biggin Hill. 222, 603, and 249 Squadrons made contact with the second formation as it made its way along the Thames Estuary, where it bombed the Short Brother's aircraft factory at Rochester before turning northwards towards North Weald and Rochford. Fortunately, 222 and 249 Squadrons managed to break up the bomber formation before it reached the Sector Station of North Weald, but this did not prevent them bombing Eastchurch and Detling. At Eastchurch, bombs destroyed five airplanes on the ground and blew up an ammunition dump.

The mid-day raid, comprising some two hundred and fifty aircraft, was once again timed to approach the Kent coast as the defending fighters were still on the ground refueling and rearming. However, Park tried to scramble his aircraft early enough to catch the raiders before they could divide into their attack formations. 72 Squadron reached a group of Dorniers and their escorts close to Margate, and 603 Squadron encountered over sixty Bf 109s near Sheerness. They were followed by 43 Squadron who had flown up from Tangmere and 253 from Kenley who headed for Dungerness. 111 Squadron, which had temporarily moved to Debden, came down to cover the Thames Estuary, and 613 Squadron made their way towards Rye. As the air battle developed above the Kent countryside, the Germans lost fifteen fighters for the loss of six British aircraft.

This attack was followed by another larger raid; this time the bombers managed to hit Eastchurch, Detling, Kenley, and Hornchurch without causing any significant damage. The same could not be said for a raid targeted at Brooklands, where the bombers were aiming to hit the Hawkers factory, which was busy building much-needed Hurricanes. They missed that factory but hit the Vickers factory, which was also on the airfield, causing significant disruption to the production of Wellington bombers.

The last daylight raid, again comprising some two hundred and fifty aircraft, arrived from the Calais area around teatime. Once again 72, and 111 Squadrons, who had returned to Croydon from Debden would feature in the action together with 46 Squadron from Stapleford, 222 and 603 Squadrons from Hornchurch, 501 from Biggin Hill, and 616 from Kenley. While a large-scale dogfight developed, the bombers hit Detling, which was put out of action for three hours, and Eastchurch where they also inflicted significant damage, including a destruction of a bomb dump, the NAFFI, and other buildings, plus five aircraft. The airfield was bombed again shortly afterwards by another formation, which added further to the destruction, so much so that the sick quarters were moved to the nearby village, and other personnel were moved to buildings in the surrounding area. Having suffered so much damage, operations from the airfield were suspendered. Although it was officially a Coastal Command airfield, fighter aircraft including those belonging to 266 Squadron sometimes used the airfield as a forward airbase.

Fifty bombers also made their way towards Hornchurch, but their bomb runs were disrupted by 603 Squadron who had been sent back to defend their airfield. As the Germans were making their way back down the Thames, the Polish pilots of 303 Squadron caught them with one section of the squadron chasing them all the way back to the French coast.

During the day's raids, almost all of 11 Group's squadrons had been in action, some of them as many as four or five times. They had shot down twenty-two and damaged nine German aircraft for the loss of twenty-five of their own with a further four aircraft damaged. So for a second day running, Fighter Command's losses were higher that the Luftwaffe's—a very worrying situation.

That evening small-scale raids were mounted against targets on the south and east coast, as well as Merseyside, Birmingham and Wolverhampton.

Tuesday, 3 September

The day dawned with clear-blue skies in the south, and low cloud and rain in the north and Scotland.

Dowding continued to rotate squadrons, consequently, 54 Squadron moved northwards from Hornchurch to be replaced by 41 Squadron who came down from Catterick in North Yorkshire. 66 Squadron was also transferred from Coltishall in Norfolk to Kenley.

Bishop reports that:

'Across the Channel, nearly 2000 barges, 1600 escort vessels, 419 tugs and 168 transports had been assembled. On the same day, Fieldmarschall Wilheim Keitel ordered the embarkation of invasion materials to begin in eight days' time, on the 11 September, the date set for Invasion Day minus ten.'

At 8:30 a.m., the usual fighter sweep comprising around forty Bf 109s crosses the Channel followed a short time later by the build-up of more than fifty Dorniers, eighty Bf 110s, and forty Bf 109s. An hour later, this formation reached the Thanes Estuary before turning northwards towards, Hornchurch, North Weald, and Debden. 11 Group scrambled nine squadrons and requested the help of an additional two from 12 Group who sent 310 and 19 Squadrons from Duxford and Fowlmere. Bombing at North Weald caused a significant amount of damage, with two hangars hit, together with the transport depot, the main stores, and the Operations Room, which received a direct hit. Even so, the airfield remained operational throughout the day. When the smoke had cleared, the attack left four people dead and a further twenty injured. During the confusion prior to the attack on North Weald,

Hurricanes from 46 Squadron shot down two Blenhiems heading towards the airfield having mistaken them for Bf 110s.

A similar level of destruction was inflicted on Hornchurch and Debden, while other bombers attacked the docks in east London and Tilbury. 310 Squadron, flying with their usual determination, managed to shoot down three Bf 110s and another two crashed in mid-air, trying to avoid them. On their way home, a number of RAF squadrons caught the Germans over the Thames Estuary. These included aircraft from 46, 303, 257, 310, 222, and 19 Squadrons, with the latter still experiencing problems with the cannons on the Spitfires.

While this action was taking place, Goering held a meeting with his top commanders at The Hague, where he informed them that their attacks on Fighter Command airfields were not heavy enough. He instructed them to use Bf 110s in support of their bombers rather than Bf 109s due to the Bf 110s longer range and therefore ability to stay with, and defend the bombers throughout their entire missions. They should continue to send out initial Bf 109 fighter sweeps to draw Fighter Command in to the air. He informed them that, according to Luftwaffe Intelligence, Fighter Command was down to as little as one hundred operational fighters, but it still had sufficient strength to defend the area around London. Although Kesselring agreed with this estimate, Sperle was somewhat skeptical, given the reports from his pilots, he thought that Fighter Command had around six hundred fighters in the south of the country with another four hundred in the north and west, figures that were far closer to reality. However, as Stephen Bungay comments that following the loss reports from Kesselring's pilots,

'...he and his staff believed he had more or less established air superiority, and the key thing was to attack something within the Bf 109s range that the British would have to come up and defend. They could abandon airfields – they had lots of them. They could not abandon London.'

Kesselring thought that if the bombing of London was successful, the British Government would have to negotiate a peace deal otherwise the Germans would be in a position to invade the country. However, Sperle completely disagreed with these tactics and expressed the opinion that the Luftwaffe should continue its bombardment of the airfields.

Goering and Luftwaffe Intelligence also said that the ring of airfields that provide protection for London were out of action, and that Fighter Command's communications network was in disarray. He pronounced that this phase of the air campaign was nearly complete, and that Fighter Command was 'no longer the great force it used to be.' He thought that his tactics would now force Fighter Command to put whatever aircraft they had left in to the air, where his fighters would be able to shoot them down. This would then allow his bombers a clear passage to London. What he failed to register was that the plan that he predicted would take only two to three weeks to accomplish, had so far lasted two months and was still not complete, and the window of opportunity open for invasion was rapidly closing.

Given Hitler's anger at Bomber Commands attacks on Berlin, Goering thought that at last he might agree to a large-scale bombing campaign on London. However, between June and the start of September, the Luftwaffe had lost over a third of its aircraft, including two-thirds of its Bf 110s and nearly half of its Bf 109s. When the numbers of damaged aircraft are added to these figures, their operational force had been reduced to less than half of its original strength, so providing the all-important, overwhelming fighter protection that the bombers required would be more difficult.

Goering's pilots were feeling the strain as much if not more than those of Fighter Command. His fighters were often pushing their fuel levels to the limit to stay and fight and protect the bombers, with the consequence that many were running out of fuel and crashing in to the Channel on the way home.

On this side of the Channel, Keith Park once again complained that, while 13 Group were sending experienced squadrons to replace his tired units, he felt that 12 Group were exchanging them with inexperienced squadrons who would take time to come up to operational standards. It was time that he did not have, especially with most of his airfields working at reduced capacity due to the pounding they were suffering at the hands of the enemy bombers. If the situation continued, he was not sure how long some of his most important airfields could remain even partially operational.

The next attack was not launched until 2 p.m.; and in response, 11 Group scrambled a large number of their aircraft, and asked 12 Group to cover their northern airfields. However, most of the bombers turned back before reaching the English coastline.

Losses to both sides for the day stood at sixteen aircraft each, but Fighter Command had lost another eight pilots. During the night, Liverpool was again the main target.

Wednesday, 4 September

The weather continued to be fine and clear in the south of the country, and wet and cloudy in the north and Scotland.

Over the last few days, the Luftwaffe had been given or were preparing to add thirty important airplane-related factories to their list of targets, in an effort to stem the flow of both fighters and bombers to the RAF.

Raids in the morning followed the usual, now predictable format, allowing Park to better position his forces in response. Yet again, the early morning fighter sweep was largely ignored, 11 Group only scrambling three squadrons to intercept it. While the Bf 109s were engaging the British fighters, Bf 110s slipped through to bomb Lympne, Dover, and Eastchurch, where they destroyed eight aircraft on the ground.

Just after mid-day, Kent radar stations detected the build-up of a large force of more than fifty Heinkels, thirty Dorniers, and two hundred fighters heading along a broad front that stretched between Folkstone and Beachy Head. In response, Park bought twelve of his and two of 10 Group's squadrons into action and held the rest on standby. Although most of the enemy aircraft were turned back, a small group managed to break through and bombed the Shorts aircraft factory at Rochester, which was in the process of building Stirlings, the RAF's first four-engined, heavy bombers. This raid was followed soon after by a second formation of over three hundred aircraft heading for the Brighton and Worthing area. The formation included EG 210 with their Bf 110s flying their now trademark low-level strike, this time against the radar station at Poling.

At 1 p.m., Park scrambled the aircraft at readiness, comprising 43 and 601 Squadrons at Tangmere, 66 and 253 at Kenley, 79 and 72 at Biggin Hill, the latter still residing at Croydon due to the damage at their home airfield. They were joined by 222 and 603 Squadrons from Hornchurch and 41 Squadron, who had recently moved south from Catterick. North Weald sent 249 Squadron, Stapleford scrambled 46 Squadron, and Debden sent 73 Squadron, which had been transferred down from Church Fenton. These would be joined in the air by 234 from Middle Wallop and 602 from Westhampnett both 10 Group airfields. During the ensuing fight, 66 Squadron, who we have seen had only recently been transferred south, and were relatively inexperienced, lost five Spitfires. The loss of aircraft and pilots during the first few days of action once a squadron had been moved in to 11 Group's area was continuous problem and some aircraft arrived still flying in pre-war three aircraft close 'vic' formations, which often proved lethal for their pilots.

Shortly before 1:30 p.m., as the air battle developed over north Kent, a group of low-flying Bf 110s flew in undetected at low level towards Guildford. 253 Squadron were sent down from Kenley to intercept them and managed to shoot down six aircraft before a couple of them reached their intended target, Brooklands, where, yet again they bombed the Vickers factory instead of the Hawkers factory. Unfortunately, this time they killed eighty-six workers, injured another six hundred and thirty, and disrupted production of Wellington bombers. On the way home, the Germans lost a further nine Bf 110s.

In a day of intense action, the Luftwaffe lost one Bf 109, three Heinkel bombers, and thirteen Bf 110s, while Fighter Command lost nine Spitfires, six Hurricanes, and six pilots.

That night in the Sportpalast in Berlin, Hitler would make a monumental speech to an audience comprising mainly Nazi women that would change the course of the battle and its outcome. In it, he referred to Bomber Commands bombing of Berlin and other targets, stating that:

'...if the British Air Force drops 2,000, 3,000 or 4,000 kilos of bombs, then we will now drop 150,00, 180,000, 230,000, 300,000 or 400,000 kilos, or more in one night. If they declare that they will attack our cities on a large scale, we will erase theirs! We will put a stop to the games of these night-pirates, as God is our witness. The hour will come when one or the other of us will crumble, and that one will not be National Socialist Germany.'

The following day, he issued orders for the start of large-scale attacks on London, code-named *Operation Loge*.

As Bishop points out:

'Bombs had been falling in British civilians for three months. Over a thousand had been killed by the end of August, and as many again injured. But to switch the whole weight of the German bombers against London, rather than the RAF airfields, was a decisive change of strategy by the Luftwaffe.

'London was an obvious strategic target. Heavily populated, it was the hub of national road, rail, and water transport and of the country's commerce, industry, and finance. It was the nation's biggest port and the centre of the government, legislature, and judiciary. Primary targets would still be industrial and commercial, in particular the docks. But the

305

Luftwaffe command was fully aware that many civilians would be killed. It was part of the plan to cause terror and chaos and create pressure from a panic-stricken public on Britain's rulers to seek term with Hitler. The threat of invasion loomed in the background.'

Meanwhile, German bombers set out again that night to attack Bristol, Cardiff, Swansea, Liverpool, Nottingham, Newcastle, and Tilbury.

Thursday, 5 September

The day was clear and bright in the south of the country and improving from the previous day's poor weather in the north.

The Luftwaffe spent much of the day reorganizing the disposition of their bombers, bringing them from the south of Paris to the airfields in the area around Calais, so that they would be ready for the concentrated bombing of London—they also took the opportunity to rest some of their crews.

The first raid of the day followed the usual routes, covering the area from Folkstone to the Thames Estuary, but this time the Luftwaffe sent only small numbers of aircraft rather than the expected large formations. In response, Park scrambled his squadrons, sending 41 Squadron from Hornchurch down to Manston and then out to cover the approaches to the Thames Estuary. The services of 111 Squadron, now back at Croydon were called on, together with aircraft from Gravesend and Kenley. 66 Squadron were back in action, but again they lost another three aircraft. 19 Squadron joined in the fight but this time without their troublesome cannon-armed Spitfires, reverting instead for standard eight machinegun-equipped aircraft.

Bombers attempted to target the airfields at Eastchurch, Lympne, North Weald, Hornchurch, Biggin Hill, and Croydon but most were prevented from reaching their intended targets by fierce defensive action from fourteen of 11 Group's squadrons. At Biggin Hill, effective defensive action by some of its own aircraft led on this occasion, to most of the bombers dropping their bombs wide of the airfield. Even so, Group Captain Grice, the Station Commander, ordered the blowing up of the remnants of the last remaining hangar in the hope that the Luftwaffe might then leave the airfield alone—he was later threatened with a Court Marshal for destroying air force property.

At 1 p.m., the first air raid of the afternoon, comprising over fifty Ju 88s and He 111s supported by around one hundred Bf 109s, headed for the oil storage tanks at Thameshaven. Even though 72, 73, and 43 squadrons were scrambled to intercept the raid, the bombers managed to break through and set fire to the oil tanks. In the ensuing dogfight, four aircraft and one pilot were lost from the newly arrived 73 squadron. Bombers also attacked Biggin Hill and Detling.

An hour after detecting this raid, radar picked another one comprising fifty aircraft that crossed the coast at Dungerness. Many of the defending fighters that had been in action during the previous raid were still on the ground being refueled and rearmed, so 41 and 66 Squadrons were sent to intercept the raid. Another raid, this time comprising Ju 88s flew towards the Essex coast. These were intercepted by 72 and 73 Squadrons Spitfires and Hurricanes. Among the Hurricanes of 46 Squadron that were also in action was the first four cannon-armed Hurricane to fire its guns in anger.

Dowding, having realized that the Luftwaffe were now specifically targeting the vital aircraft factories at Brooklands, Kingston, and Southampton, asked Park to provide specific air cover for them during air raids. 10 Group volunteered to provide three squadrons to support the hard-pressed 11 Group squadrons in these activities. Park called on 12 Group to provide air cover for these targets. He also bought 504 Squadron down from Catterick in North Yorkshire to Hendon to increase the number of fighters around the capital.

At 3 p.m., when aircraft engaged against the previous raid were still disengaging and returning to base, a new raid comprising thirty-five Ju 88s plus their fighter escorts was detected heading towards the Kent coast and Thames Estuary. In response, Park scrambles more aircraft including 41, 73, 111, and 253 Squadrons to intercept them. The Polish pilots of 303 Squadron from Northolt who were originally heading for the south coast in their Hurricanes were diverted to the same area where they succeeded in shooting down three aircraft.

Having previously lost so many aircraft on the return journey across the Channel, the bombers were met by a large contingent of Bf 109s arriving to escort them home.

During the day's air battles, the Luftwaffe had lost twenty-three aircraft and Fighter Command had lost twenty fighters and fifteen pilots.

In France, more bombers were arriving at airfields after being transferred from Luftflotte V ready for the major escalation in the bombing campaign.

During the night, a large bomber force attacked targets in London, Manchester, and Liverpool. Lone bombers also scattered bombs over many other, smaller targets across the country.

Friday, 6 September

The weather was again fine across the entire country, which meant that everybody on the airfields in 11 Group would have no opportunity to rest or undertake anything more than essential repairs.

At 8 a.m., radar picked up the predictable first raid of the day, when lone Bf 109 raiders made for different aircraft factories. Park called 10 Group to ask them to provide cover for the vital Hawker factory at Brooklands; and although they sent 609 Squadron from Warmwell, it made no contact with the enemy. Unfortunately, while the squadron was back at its base refueling and rearming, a number of Bf 110s managed to bomb the factory without causing too much damage.

This raid was followed, just before 9 a.m., by a large raid comprising around three hundred Ju 88s, He 111s, and Do 17s escorted by Bf 109s; this large formation crossed the coast between Dover and Dungerness. It then spread out and headed for Biggin Hill and North Weald, as well as the oil storage facility at Thameshaven, which was still on fire from the previous day's attacks. Park scrambled a number of squadrons to cover possible targets, with 1 and 73 Squadrons being sent to the north Kent coast; 111, 303, and 510 were to cover the vital sector stations of Biggin Hill and Kenley; 249 and 601 Squadrons were sent to the Maidstone area; and Middle Wallop's 234 Squadron were to cover Dover. During the fighting, the valiant Polish pilots of 303 Squadron lost seven aircraft when they were bounced by a formation of Bf 109s. Bombers managed to attack the Hawker works at Brooklands and the Pobjoy aircraft factory at Rochester but fortunately they caused little damage.

During the early afternoon, a smaller raid of two hundred enemy aircraft followed the same route and, even though Biggin Hill was one of their main targets, they also managed to get as far as the airfields at Debden and Hornchurch. They were incepted by 72, 234, 602, 603, and 303 Squadrons.

The final raid of the day, comprising only fifty aircraft, crossed the coast just before 6 p.m. Again, they followed the same route as the pervious raids but the main target this time was the Sector Station at Hornchurch. Only two squadrons of fighters—222 and 111—were sent to intercept them.

The Battle of Britain Historical Society web site records that on 6 September the War Office were ready to implement the order *Invasion Alert No. 1*, that would trigger a full military and civilian response to an imminent invasion. Other sources say this did not happen until 7 September and that they issued *Alert No. 3*, which meant that they were expecting the invasion within three days.

Night-time activity was significantly less than on previous nights, with effectively only nuisance raids spread across the country.

During a meeting between Dowding, Park, and Leigh-Mallory, Dowding decided to classify each of Fighter Command's squadrons as either A, B, or C where:

'A' squadrons were all of those in 11 Group, together with the squadrons in 10 and 12 Group's regarded as being on the front-line.

'B' squadrons comprised those that were not on the front-line, but that were ready to be transferred to the front-line if, and when necessary.

'C' squadrons were ones that had been in the heat of the fighting and had been transferred out from the front-line for rest and an opportunity to bring in much needed replacement pilots and aircraft.

This would allow Dowding, Park, and Leigh-Mallory in particular to be able to prioritize which squadrons needed rest and where their replacements would come from, so that they could maintain operational effectiveness at the front-line airfields.

In the past two weeks, Fighter Command had come under intense and constant pressure. They had lost two hundred and ninety-five aircraft, with another one hundred and seventy-one badly damaged. More worrying, one hundred and thirty pilots had been killed and a further one hundred and twenty-eight had been wounded. Dowding had had to reduce the number of pilots assigned to each squadron from twenty-six to sixteen, which meant that pilots were flying many more flights in a day. 11 Group's airfields had suffered considerable damage during the same period, resulting in the forward airfields of Manston and Lympne being effectively put out of action. In addition, as we have seen, Biggin Hill, the most important Sector Station in the ring around London was reduced to being able to operate only one squadron, and five of the other six sector stations were operating well below their fully capacity. Fortunately, the radar system was almost fully operational, and with the Luftwaffe using the same tactics day after day, Park and his controllers were able to get as much warning as possible allowing them to position their aircraft to provide the best possible defense.

Nonetheless, as Bishop informs us, Dowding had even begun to consider whether he should withdraw some of his aircraft to Northern England so that he could bring them southwards in the event of an invasion. Fortunately, just as the Luftwaffe were close to inflicting major damage to Fighter Command they changed tactics.

British photographic reconnaissance flights had shown that since 31 August, German preparations for the impending invasion had accelerated. As Hough and Richards report, on 28 August, there were no barges in Ostend, but there were eighteen on 31 August; seventy on 2 September; one hundred and fifteen on 5 September; and two hundred and five by 6 September, with a similar pattern developing along the French coast. Reconnaissance flights had also identified the build-up of new gun emplacements along the coast, the concentration of dive-bomber units around Calais, and the redeployment of additional bombers to the same area. As Hough and Richards comment, 'the threat across the Channel for weeks feared but uncertain, was suddenly all too real.'

Phase 3: 7 September–5 October

Following their relentless attacks of Fighter Command's airfields, and with Luftwaffe Intelligence informing Goering and his commanders that Fighter Command were rapidly running out of fighters, they decided to switch their bombing offensive to London in order to draw the remaining fighters into battle. Following Bomber Command's attacks on Berlin the Luftwaffe were, at last, given permission to bomb civilian targets in the capital and other cities; they therefore about to unleashed their Blitzkrieg that had been so effective against cities on the continent. 7 September would be the first of fifty-seven consecutive days of bombing inflicted on London and in particular, the people of the East End around London's vital docks.

Saturday, 7 September

Once again, the day was clear, warm and bright, ideal conditions for the Luftwaffe to continue their pounding of Fighter Command's airfields and Britain's aircraft industry. According to Luftwaffe Intelligence, Fighter Command was down to its last fifty fighters.

Following his arrival at Cap Cris Nez on 6 September in his private train—named Asia—Goering could see the White Cliffs of Dover. He was there to witness the start of a new phase of his campaign. As he said, "I have taken over personal command of the Luftwaffe in its war against England." He then spent the morning visiting a number of the local airfields and the afternoon enjoying a picnic on the cliffs wearing his specially designed, powder-blue uniform.

With information intercepted by the listening service—the *Y Service*—based at Kingsbourne in Kent and *Ultra* at Bletchley Park, both Churchill and Dowding knew that Goering had decided to switch bombing from Fighter

Command's airfields, aircraft manufacture, and other military sites to London on 5 September. Intercepted instructions indicated that once the redeployment of his forces had been completed, Goering was going to launch as many as three hundred bombers on the city during the afternoon of either 7 or 8 September. Of course, this was Ultra Secret information that could not be passed to others in Fighter Command without being able to gain the information from another source. Therefore, at 8:30 in the morning, with everyone in Fighter Command's control rooms and airfields expecting the now familiar early morning raids, only a single Dornier was detected heading across the North Sea. Spitfires from 266 Squadron were dispatched from RAF Wittering to chase it away.

Some three and a half hours later, radar stations along the Kent coast detected a small number of Bf 109s heading across the Channel. Controllers at 11 Group's Head Quarters at Uxbridge sent the Spitfires of 66 Squadron, who were already engaged in a standing patrol in the area, to intercept them. During the brief but fierce dogfight, two of their number were damaged and crash-landed on their return to Kenley.

At 2:30 p.m. in the afternoon, with his grand picnic in full-flow, Goering, together with Bruno Loerzer who was in charge of Fliegerkorps II, and Kesselring watched his 'great armada' building up over Northern France ready to head towards the Kent coast and Thames Estuary. It is said that the airplanes covered an area of something like 500^2 miles (800^2km).

It was almost ninety minutes later that radar stations along the Kent coast first detected the raid building up on their screens. Fifteen minutes after that, when Park was meeting Dowding at Bentley Priory, they were informed of the impending raid. At 4:15 p.m., the Observer Corpse spotted the approaching raid; and confirmed that it comprised some three hundred bombers escorted and protected by around two hundred Bf 110s and six hundred Bf 109s—this really was to be a large raid.

With Park away at Bentley Prior, his deputy John Willoughby de Broke scrambled eleven squadrons from across 11 Group comprising aircraft from Northolt, Kenley, Gravesend, North Weald, Tangmere, Croydon, Hornchurch, Stapleford, and Debden. He called 10 Group for support from 234 and 609 Squadron based at Middle Wallop and Warmwell, and also contacted 12 Group to ask for their support. For the first time Bader's 'much vaunted Big Wing' comprising 17, 242, and 310 Squadrons based at Duxford and Fowlmere would be sent in to action. With Luftwaffe fighters providing close support below, beside and behind the bombers as well as other providing top-cover, Fighter Command's pilots frequently added additional height to that given by their controllers to enable them to arrive into battle above the German formations. This often meant that when they engaged the enemy formations, they were above the bombers, their main targets, and they became involved in fighter-versus-fighter action. Today provided a good example of such action; Bader leading the Duxford Big Wing was directed to fly at 10,000 feet (3,048m), however, he decided that this was too low and took the formation up to 15,000 feet (4,572m). Consequently, it took twenty minutes to get the Wing together and flying at the height Bader thought necessary to go in to combat. As the Wing approached the bombers, they were bounced by the defending fighters losing two Hurricanes in the process.

As each of 11 Group's squadrons took off, they were sent to cover their vital Sector Stations and the important oil storage tanks at Thameshaven.

As the raiders made their way towards the Kent coast, 11 Group controllers realized that they were not heading for their usual targets, namely Fighter Command's airfields. They broke up in to smaller units that continuously changed direction to confuse the defending pilots but steadily made their way towards London. This change of tactics left many of the defenders flying above the Sector Stations in the wrong position to intercept the raid before they arrived over the East End of London. Consequently, only 501 and 249 Squadrons managed to reach the enemy bombers before they started their bombing runs. By this time however, most of the German single-engined fighter escorts were running short of fuel and had already started to turn for home. The first formation of bombers flew in from the Thames Estuary and the second wave approached from the south where it was intercepted by aircraft from 1 and 603 Squadrons.

To add to the defenders problems, many of their fighters were still trying to gain height as bombs began to rain down on Woolwich Arsenal, the Harland and Woolf shipyards, the London docks, their warehouses and the surrounding houses. Bombs fell across a wide area including West and East Ham, Canning Town, Stratford, Wapping, Poplar and Whitechapel. Around 13,000 people in Silvertown were effectively trapped by fires and had to be evacuated via the River Thames. It is reported that the resulting fires produced so much smoke that as it drifted eastwards the airfield at Hornchurch had to be closed.

The Duxford Big Wing finally arrived from the northwest as the first of the bombers were heading home and others—amounting to two hundred and fifty additional bombers—were still making their way towards London guided by the fires and smoke. In spite of their planned, coordinated attack, two of the squadrons in the Wing had still not gained sufficient height to join in any action. The Polish pilots of 303 Squadron headed for the side of the bomber formation in line abreast and fired at the last minute to inflict the maximum damage possible. They claimed that nearly a quarter of the bombers were destroyed or damaged, in reality their tally was closer to five. That night Bader and Leigh Mallory decided that they should increase the number of squadrons in the wing from three to five and moved 611 and 74 Squadrons, who had both recently converted to cannon-armed Spitfires, to Duxford.

When the bombers finally left, more than 300 tons (304 tonnes) of bombs, many of them, delayed-action, had been dropped over a seven-hour period, killing four hundred and ninety civilians and injuring 1,200 more. As Parker points out, these were as many casualties in one night than Fighter Command suffered in the whole of the battle. 'It was now the battle not just of "the Few" but also of the many.'

The Harland and Wolfe shipyard had been almost totally destroyed in the attack and the munitions factory at Woolwich Arsenal suffered a direct hit on one of its gunpowder storage bins. The London docks were badly affected with almost 40 miles (64km) of warehouses ablaze. One of the major problems firefighters faced with tackling this colossal blaze was a lack of water.

Many of the fires were still burning the following morning. As well as the huge amount of damage inflicted on the docks, in the surrounding area complete streets had been flattened in the sustained attack. As the bombing was dying down, Park flew back from Bentley Priory to his headquarters in Uxbridge to survey the damage. The Luftwaffe had lost forty-five aircraft while Fighter Command lost twenty-eight with a further twenty-nine damaged. On their return, the Luftwaffe reported that there had been little opposition, which appeared to confirm Luftwaffe Intelligence's estimates that Fighter Command were running short of aircraft. In fact, as we have seen, this apparent lack of defenders was because most of their fighters were positioned to cover the expected raids on 11 Group's airfields.

With only a short break, at around 8 p.m., the Luftwaffe switched from daylight bombing with Luftflotte II to night bombing, raids with two hundred and forty-seven of Luftflotte III's bombers. This then continued until the early hours of the following morning killing another three hundred and six people and seriously injuring a further 1,337 others; this really was the start of the infamous Blitz. Over six hundred fire engines from as far away as Coventry were involved in controlling the fires in East London, smoke from the fires was still so thick that it prevented 600 Squadron's Blenheims from taking off for their night-fighter operations from their base at Hornchurch. The fires were so large and so extensive that the day became known as 'Red Saturday' by the firemen.

During an evening meeting with his fighter commanders, Goering criticized them for failing to protect the bombers, and accused them of cowardice. He ordered them to fly in closer contract with the bombers, but they argued that this would reduce their fighting capabilities even further. It was during this conversation that Goering asked Adolf Galland what he would like, Galland famously answering that he would like a squadron of Spitfires, to which Goering stomped off. As Galland records in his book, *The First and the Last:*

'The theme of fighter protection was chewed over again and again. Goering clearly represented the point of view of the bombers and demanded close and rigid protection. The bomber, he said, was more important than record bag figures. I tried to point out that the Me109 was superior in the attack and not so suitable for purely defensive purposes as the Spitfire, which, although a little slower, was much more manoeuvrable. He rejected my objection. We received many more harsh words. Finally, as his time ran short, he grew more amiable and asked what were the requirements for our squadrons. Moelders asked for a series of Me109's with more powerful engines. The request was granted. "And you?" Goering turned to me. I did not hesitate long. "I should like an outfit of Spitfires for my group." After blurting this out, I had rather a shock, for it was not really meant that way. Of course, fundamentally I preferred our Me109 to the Spitfire, but I was unbelievably vexed at the lack of understanding and the stubbornness with which the command gave us orders we could not execute—or only incompletely—as a result of many shortcomings for which we were not to blame. Such brazen-faced impudence made even Goering speechless. He stamped off, growling as he went.'

As the switch from daylight to night-time bombing occurred, the code word *'Cromwell'* was issued (indicating that an invasion had started). As Wood and Dempster relate in *The Narrow Margin*, 'church bells rang, road blocks put up and Home Guards roamed the countryside with loaded rifles,' several strategic bridges were blown up and all troops were brought to battle stations. There was confusion within the air force that may well have been caused by changes introduced by the Air Ministry on 27 August. As Overy explains, until then the Air Ministry had used a three-level system for indicating the severity of the treat of invasion:

Level 1: indicated that an attack was improbably;
Level 2: meant that an attack was probably;

Level 3: that it was imminent.

On 27 August, they suddenly reversed the system. This meant that when a Code 1 was issued on 7 September, indicating that they thought an invasion could be expected within the next twelve hours, some airfields reacted to the imminent alert, others were still using the old codes so did not react, and still others did not get the signal at all.

Hough and Richards comment that:

'...for the Luftwaffe, and the citizens of London (especially the working people in the East End), 7 September appeared to be a day and night of German success. For Dowding and Park it was a day of immense relief and growing conviction that Fighter Command would prevail.'

Bungay reports that that night the Air Ministry called Park to tell him to prepare to evacuate his southern, coastal airfields as part of the invasion alert but he ignored the instruction.

The day ended with the Luftwaffe losing fourteen bombers, sixteen Bf 109s, and seven Bf 110s, while Fighter Command lost twenty-three aircraft, six pilots, and a further seven were wounded.

Sunday, 8 September

The day dawned with clouds building up over the south of the country, rain in Northern Scotland and a drop in temperature.

As we have seen, the Luftwaffe had adopted the tactics of sending their aircraft over in three waves over a period of between forty-five and sixty minutes; this was designed to allow bombers to reach their targets while Fighter Command's fighters were on the ground being refueled and rearmed or to swamp them in the air with too many targets. To counter this, Park changed his tactics, he would bring some of his squadrons to readiness in pairs with the Spitfires ready to take on the escorting fighters while the Hurricanes attacked the bombers. Squadrons that were at fifteen minutes readiness notice would then be bought to readiness to take on the second wave. Squadrons held at thirty minutes waiting could then be either sent to protect individual targets, support squadrons already in the air, or be held at readiness to intercept a third wave of attackers. Group controllers would be responsible for deciding which squadrons would pair up over which airfields before directing them towards the enemy formations.

Park also swapped 43 Squadron at Tangmere with 607 Squadron at Usworth. He bought in 92 Squadron from Pembrey in South Wales, and transferred 79 Squadron in the other direction. He also moved 111 Squadron to Drem in Scotland for a chance to rest and regroup after their high-risk, head-on attacks.

The first raid of the day that arrived around 11:30 a.m. in the morning and was small compared to the armada of the previous day, comprising some twenty Dorniers escorted by thirty Bf 109s. These were initially intercepted by the Spitfires of 41 Squadron, which were mounting a standing patrol. They were joined by 46 Squadron from Stapleford, 222 Squadron from Hornchurch, and 605 Squadron from Croydon. During this encounter, the bombers scattered, but not before one of their number had been shot down together with one of their escorts; 11 Group lost five aircraft.

There was no further action for the rest of the day until Luftflotte III took over to mount their night-time raids beginning at 7:30 in the evening. With around two hundred and fifty bombers, they again attacked sites over a large area of east London as well as targeting the City for the first time, killing four hundred and twelve and injuring another seven hundred and forty-seven people. Bombers also managed to put most of the South London train terminals out of action.

To help them navigate to their intended targets, the Luftwaffe had developed a system of two intersecting radio beams—known as *Knickebein* (meaning crocked leg)—that converged over the target. This had been developed from an earlier blind-landing system called *Lorenz*. The German bombers would fly along one of the beams until they picked up the signal from the other beam at which point the system produced a continuous sound so that they knew they were over the intended target. However, once the British had discovered the system—in what became known as the 'Battle of the Beams'—to counter it they used requisitioned hospital X-ray machines to distort the signal by spreading the width of the beam. This interference disrupted the system to such an extent that it was almost useless and consequently bombs were dropped over a far wider area than the bomber crews had intended.

Monday, 9 September

The weather was almost the reverse of the previous day with clear conditions over Scotland, rain over the south of England and thunderstorms in the east. With the absence of an early raid, Park and Dowding realized that Luftwaffe tactics had indeed changed and that they were settling down in to yet another predictable pattern. With the move away from bombing Fighter Command's airfields, Park and his hard-pressed station commanders were able to continue their work in bringing their airfields and squadrons back in to full operation. With enemy raids beginning later in the day, they were also able to move some of the aircraft to their forward airfields ready to intercept the bombers, something they had virtually had to abandon during the height of the bombing campaign against their bases.

The first raid of the day was detected building up in the Calais area by radar at 4:30 in the afternoon. When the information was passed to Park, he is reported as saying to his controller "when will they ever learn…same time, same course and the same target I would say." As the Battle of Britain Historical Society web site says, 'Immediately he called a number of squadrons to "readiness." This time he was going to be ready for them. He knew just how long it would take them to cross the coast, he knew just how long it would take them to manoeuvre to get in to place for their run to the target.' He also knew how long their fighter aircraft would be able to stay with the bombers before they would have to turn back due to a lack of fuel.

Twenty minutes later, the Observer Corps reported the specific number of the enemy aircraft involved in the raid. At 5 p.m., 11 Group scrambled seven squadrons from across their area. At 12 Group, Bader suggested that his Big Wing should be involved. Park positioned his aircraft to meet the threat, with two squadrons covering South London, three over North Kent, one over the east Kent coast, and another two covering the area around Guildford. He also asked 12 Group to position their Big Wing between Hornchurch and North Weald, but Bader decided to ignore these orders and flew to the west of London.

At 5:30 p.m., the two squadrons covering Guildford intercepted a group of bombers and their escorts heading for the aircraft factories at Weybridge and Brooklands. They managed to shoot down one bomber but lost three fighters including two that collided. As this action was taking place, other enemy aircraft were heading for London from the east. These were intercepted by the defenders flying over north Kent and Bader's Big Wing, which flew in from the west. Due to the success of Parks tactics, most of the bombers scattered before they could reach their targets. Following the action, the Big Wing claimed to have shot down twenty-one German aircraft, in fact they only shot one down. Fighter Command lost fourteen aircraft with a further three damaged; six pilots were killed during the day's actions.

Wood and Dempster include the following, which shows the mindset of the Luftwaffe bomber pilots when they comment:

'German aircraft sent out a number of distress signals and radio control stations on the French coast ordered formation leaders to break off the attacks "if the defences are too strong or if fighter protection is too weak." These were heard with great interest by British radio monitoring receivers in Kent.'

At 8 p.m., Luftflotte III began their night-time bombing raids. This time, two hundred and fifty bombers were again used to hit not only East London but also Central London, including the area around St. Pauls and the City of London. They followed clearly define routes both towards and away from their targets in a series of waves. The first would approach London from the south coast and would leave via Essex, the next would come in along the Thames Estuary and return over Beachy Head; the format would then be repeated by the following formation of bombers. By the time the bombers left, four hundred people had been killed, and another 1,400 injured, but the Luftwaffe paid a fairly high price as well, losing twenty-eight aircraft.

Tuesday, 10 September

Heavy rain over the continent, cloud over the North Sea, and rain over most of Britain meant that all daylight Luftwaffe operations were canceled, apart from a few single raiders late in the afternoon. These attacked West Malling, Portsmouth, Biggin Hill, and a number of aircraft factories. Again, this break in large-scale bombing gave 11 Group even more time to prepare themselves for the days ahead.

Coastal Command also reported sighting a number of German Naval ships off the coast of Dieppe that led to another rumor that the anticipated invasion was about to begin.

During the night, one hundred and fifty bombers attacked London, while others bombed Liverpool and South Wales.

Wednesday, 11 September

11 September was originally the scheduled date for the invasion, but because Fighter Command had put up such a strong defense during engagements on 9 September, Hitler postponed this until 24 September in order to give his army, navy and Luftwaffe the ten days' notice they required to prepare.

The bad weather of the previous day gave way to improving conditions across the south of the country while there was still some rain over Scotland.

At 2:45 p.m., radar stations in Kent detected the now familiar plots of a large raid building up over Calais. Almost thirty minutes later the Observer Corps were able to confirm that two raids comprising around one hundred and fifty bombers plus their escorts, were heading for the Thames Estuary. Another raid was detected heading for the Portsmouth/Southampton area. In response, Park transferred control of his aircraft based at Tangmere to 10 Group to help intercept the latter raid, while scrambling fourteen squadrons to intercept the London-bound attack. He also requested 12 Group to position their Big Wing between Hornchurch and North Weald, but yet again, they wanted to be in the action rather than follow his instructions, and headed for the Thames Estuary (this time Bader was resting with his squadron, 242, at Duxford). Even with the Luftwaffe following familiar tactics and routes, many of the defending fighters still struggled to reach the height necessary to give them a tactical advantage to intercept the enemy formations. With their fighter escorts having to turn for home, the defending fighters mauled the bombers; ten were shot down, four more crash-landed in France on their way back, and many of the others were damaged. They also lost a further twenty-one bombers during the Portsmouth/Southampton raid, that included EG 210, who had moved to the Cherbourg Peninsular. They were supposed to bomb one of the Spitfire factories in the area, but hit one that was building Lockheed Hudsons for Coastal Command instead. Fighter Command lost twenty-five aircraft with twelve pilots killed and six wounded.

The Germans, having failed to destroy the radar stations earlier on in the battle, installed jamming equipment on the French coast that caused a significant degree of disruption. This, together with the practice of directing incoming and outgoing raiders close together led to a degree of confusion with the radar operators.

At 5 p.m., a Luftwaffe fighter sweep attacked barrage balloons over Dover harbor; and a convoy in the Channel.

This day of intense action resulted in Fighter Command losing twenty-nine aircraft compared to the Luftwaffe's losses of twenty-five.

With the continuing difficulty in providing effective night-fighters, London's air defenses were strengthened by transferring anti-aircraft guns that had been sent to increase the defenses of Fighter Command's airfields being added to the Inner Artillery Zone. This effectively doubled the existing defenses around the capital. Even with the additional artillery, there was still little chance of bringing down an enemy aircraft, but their fire caused many bombers to drop their bombs away from their main targets, and on residential areas.

That night one hundred and eighty bombers attacked London and Liverpool. During the raids on the capital, Buckingham Palace was bombed, enabling the Queen to famously say, "Now the palace has been bombed, I feel now that I can look at the people of the East End straight in the eye."

During a broadcast to the Nation, Churchill said:

'Therefore, we must regard the next week or so as a very important period in our history. It ranks with the days when the Spanish Armada was approaching the Channel, and Drake was finishing his game of bowls; or when Nelson stood between us and Napoleon's Grand Army at Boulogne. We have read all about this in the history books but what is happening now is on a far greater scale and of far more consequence to the life and future of the world and its civilisation than these brave old days of the past.'

Thursday, 12 September

Again, the weather turned against the Luftwaffe with occasional heavy rain covering most of the country and low cloud over the English Channel. This resulted in almost no flying apart from a couple of lone-raiders that attacked locations in the southwest of the Country. Three small raids bombed the radar station at Fairlight but inflicted very little damage. Another raid dropped bombs on Harrogate, and others attacked Hastings, again causing only minor damage.

With the poor weather conditions restricting Luftwaffe air operations and their attention directed away from their airfields towards London, Fighter Command had been able to bring all but Biggin Hill back in to full operation.

That night's bombing was also limited with only fifty bombers attacking London and others attacking Liverpool.

Friday, 13 September

The bad weather of the previous day continued with rain again in most areas of the country. In the afternoon, low cloud over the Channel began to break-up.

During a lunchtime meeting, Hitler told the Luftwaffe that they had not achieved the air superiority over the Channel necessary for an invasion to take place. He added that, although this had not been achieved to-date, he would continue to assemble the shipping and barges along the French and Belgium coast in anticipation of the Luftwaffe achieving their aims. He also said that the bombing of London would continue in an effort 'to weaken British resolve.'

Although Kesselring thought that Fighter Command was much stronger than Luftwaffe Intelligence had predicted, they still maintained that it was on its last legs with Dowding having to pull all his reserves in to the southeast to defend the capital. The Luftwaffe decided to increase the number of fighters they sent out with the bombers once more to reduce their vulnerability to the defending fighters.

The only sizable actions of the day comprised a small force of bombers that used cloud cover to initiate a raid on London. The first raid by a long-range, Fw 200 Condor, four-engined bomber occurred when a single bomber attacked targets in Northern Ireland. A small force of bombers also hit the airfield at Tangmere. Consequently, losses on both sides for the day were light with Fighter Command losing one aircraft and the Luftwaffe losing five.

Keith Park issued instructions that his squadrons should try to maintain their continuity during attacks, as this would be more effective than engaging as individual aircraft. He also instructed them to implement head-on attacks that had proved to be effective at destroying aircraft and breaking up bomber formations.

During the night, one hundred and fifty bombers attacked London.

Saturday, 14 September

The weather remained unsettled with cloud cover gradually lifting over the Channel but with the possibility of some thunderstorms.

In a meeting with his top military leaders, called at short notice, Hitler bought the day of the invasion forward to 17 September in spite of the requirement for ten days' notice. He was convinced that with four or five days of good weather the Luftwaffe could destroy the rest of Fighter Command's aircraft leaving the way for invasion (something that Goering had also been saying for the past couple of months). He was convinced that only the weather had prevented the Luftwaffe gaining air superiority so far. The Germans had assembled all of the barges they needed for the invasion, with spare capacity if necessary, even though the RAF estimated that Bomber Command had destroyed between 12% and 30% of them during the previous weeks.

During the late morning, raiders attacked the south coast between Eastbourne and Brighton killing sixty people. They also bombed South London in the Croydon-Mitcham area killing another fifty.

The first large-scale raids of the day approached the Thames Estuary and the Deal/Folkstone area in three waves shortly after three in the afternoon. These comprised around one hundred bombers but, as they had been instructed, with a higher than usual proportion of fighter escorts. In response, 11 Group scrambled twenty-two squadrons to intercept the raiders and managed to turn them back before they reached London. 12 Group added a further five squadrons to the defenders, however, Wood and Dempster report that the Luftwaffe thought that Fighter Command's response was 'scrappy and uncoordinated' confirming their opinion that during the previous day's Fighter Command had 'begun to collapse.'

As we will see in the next chapter, this estimate was as far from the real situation as it could possibly be, and to strengthen its position even more, Fighter Command transferred the Hurricanes of 302 Squadron from Leconfield to Duxford to join the Big Wing.

During the first week of bombing on the capital the Luftwaffe lost one hundred and ninety-nine bombers.

Chapter 7
The Big Day

Sunday, 15 September

As Alfred Price observes in his book *Battle of Britain Day: 15 September 1940*, a combination of a change in tactics from the Germans and weather conditions meant that during the previous four days, Fighter Command's controllers had been unable to unleash their fighters on the Luftwaffe. This led those in Luftwaffe Intelligence to grossly underestimate Fighter Command's resources, and Luftwaffe Command to use simple tactics that Fighter Command, and Park in particular, was ready to counter.

Korda records in *With Wings Like Eagles: The Untold History of the Battle of Britain*, that the bombing during the previous night was 'noticeably less strong' than on proceeding nights, 'causing many people in the RAF to wonder if the Germans might be preparing something special for September 15.' He concurs with many other authors, that it would turn out to be, 'the decisive day of the Battle of Britain, and indeed very possibly the decisive day of the war.'

Following predictions of good weather, Luftwaffe High Command planned to mount two very large raids on 15 September. The first raid, to be launched at noon, would focus on the concentration of rail tracks around Battersea that linked Southeast England with the midlands and the north. The second, larger raid, would be aimed at docks either side of the Thames. It was thought that these two raids would force Fighter Command's remaining fighters in to the air enabling the Luftwaffe fighters to finish them off.

In order to accomplish these attacks, the Luftwaffe had over six hundred and fifty single-engined fighters, one hundred and twenty-nine Bf 110s, and nine hundred and forty-eight bombers available. To counter these, Fighter Command had eight hundred and two Hurricanes and Spitfires of which one hundred and twenty-six were ready for operation in 10 Group, three hundred and ten in 11 Group, one hundred and ninety-four in 12 Group, and one hundred and seventy-two in 13 Group.

As dawn broke, the stage was set—without knowing it at the time—for what would become a monumental day in British history. It was also Keith Parks wife's birthday, but he had forgotten it; maybe he had too much on his mind.

At 7 a.m., even before any enemy activity had been detected, Park bought one squadron on each of his airfields to readiness in anticipation of the day's actions. These comprised just a small element of the aircraft he had available to him.

The Luftwaffe's activity began with the now predictable, early-morning German reconnaissance flights, the first of which was picked up by British radar as it arrived off the coast of Devon at 8 a.m. 10 Group responded by scrambling two Hurricanes from Exeter, who managed to shoot it down off the coast from Start Point.

Shortly before 9:30 a.m., two small forces of German aircraft were again detected by British radar stations. One flew across the Channel and headed up the coast past Dover. Park thought that this was probably a formation of Bf 109s designed to entice Fighter Command in to a fight so he ignored them just as he had during the previous weeks. The second formation spread out over an area from Dover to Harwich before turning back.

Two hours later, a large number of Dorniers began to assemble close to Paris in preparation for the first main raid of the day. Bungay notes that relentless flying, damage, and serviceability was having a significant impact on the German bomber force. For example, of the thirty Dorniers in III/KG 76 only nineteen were operational, and one Gruppe could only muster eight aircraft. One of the Dorniers tasked with taking part in this raid carried a battlefield flame-thrower designed to deter Fighter Command's aircraft from coming too close to the bomber. However, as Price explains, when it was used, instead of deterring them, RAF pilots thought that the bomber was about to catch fire and sensing an easy kill they attacked it even more. As Wood and Dempster comment that 'the stupidity of large formations sorting themselves out in full view of British radar was not yet realized by the Luftwaffe.'

As the Luftwaffe were gathering their forces, Keith Park in 11 Group's command centre at Uxbridge had just received news that Churchill was coming to see how things were going—he arrived at 10:30 with his wife Clementine.

At 11:04 a.m., the first of the German formations came within reach of British radar controllers. They quickly identified this as a formation of approximately forty aircraft. These were Bf 109s designated to act as close escorts for the bombers, but due to delays in the assemblage to the bomber force, the fighters were circling on their own using up valuable fuel. When the bombers eventually arrived ten minutes late, they too were detected by radar. The raid now totaled around one hundred and twenty aircraft, stepped up from 15,000 to 26,000 feet (4,572–7,924m), most of which comprised fighters either as close escort, top cover, or those flying in front of the bomber force. In response to this build-up and without knowing the exact make-up of the enemy force (which could only be established once it was either in range of the Observer Corpse or Fighter Command's aircraft), Park began to prepare his defenses.

At 11:20 a.m., the German formation crossed the French coast heading for London and air-raid sirens on the north and east Kent coast sounded their warnings.

As Price notes, by now Park had developed his tactics to a fine art to take advantage of the Luftwaffe's weaknesses, namely the limited amount of flying time their fighters would have over British soil. He therefore deployed his fighters in his usual three waves. The first of these, comprising twenty Spitfires from two squadrons based at Biggin Hill were to try to break-up the bomber formation before it crossed the coastline. It is interesting to note that the pilots of one of these squadrons had been awake since 4:30 a.m. Ten minutes later, Park also scrambled a further nine squadrons from Northolt, Kenley and Debden, with their Hurricanes squadrons flying in pairs, to engage the bombers from different direction as they crossed the Kent countryside or flew up the Thames Estuary. Bishop records that one of these squadrons, 504, took off in only four minutes and fifty seconds just after two U.S. Army Air Corps Generals and a U.S. Navy Rear Admiral had arrived at their base at Hendon to see 'the life of a fighter squadron.'

Finally, for this phase, five minutes after the Hurricane squadrons had been scrambled, a further three squadrons of Hurricanes and Spitfires took to the air from their bases at Hornchurch and North Weald to provide a line of fighters designed to engage the enemy before they reached London. Park knew that by the time the German fighters had reached this point, they would be getting low on fuel. At the same time, he also asked for assistance from neighboring 10 and 12 Groups, with the former scrambling Spitfires to patrol to the west of London and in particular to protect the aircraft factories and airfield at Brooklands. 12 Group scrambled its five-squadron Big Wing to patrol over Gravesend. As Price comments, 'For the first time, the tactics of employing so many fighters en masse against a German formation was to be tested in action.'

As the German bombers crossed the English coast close to Folkstone, over twenty bomb-carrying Bf 109s—known as '*Jacobs*'—with their fighter escorts took off from their airfield near Calais. JG 27 and JG 52—the famous yellow-nosed Messerschmitts—were to patrol in front of the bomber force, JG 53 would provide top cover, and JG 3 were designated to the close escort role. They would be joined by twenty-five Bf 110s of KG 76. With their faster speed, this element of the raid would either arrive at the outskirts of London at approximately the same time as the main force, or would be just before them.

Although everything appeared set for the first of the day's big raids, things were not going according to plan for the Luftwaffe. As Price points out, Luftwaffe meteorologists had failed to either discover or pass on the news that the entire force would be flying in to a 90mph (144kph) headwind that would slow the Dorniers progress by an anticipated 100–90mph (160–144kph). This resulted in them taking almost twice as long (thirty minutes) to reach London from the Kent coast than had been anticipated and, together with the delay in assembling the formation, they would arrive over London nearly forty minutes later than planned. The delays and headwind would also mean that their escorting fighters would use up even more fuel fighting the strong winds, which would mean that they would have even less flying time available to stay with the bombers.

Shortly after 11:30 a.m., Park scrambled his second wave of fighters. In a period of only four minutes, ten additional squadrons, comprising some one hundred and twenty-four aircraft were on their way to join in the action, including the Duxford Big Wing that, for once had taken off in record time. There were now two hundred and fifty-four British fighters climbing and heading for their defensive positions. Meanwhile, Park still had a further four squadrons on the ground ready to take off if necessary. To compound the Luftwaffe problems caused by delays and the headwind, the early fighter-fighter combats had eaten into the German fighters' fuel reserves and one-by-one they turned for home, leaving the bombes to continue on alone.

As the Dorniers passed over Ashford, the two Spitfire squadrons (72 and 92) from Biggin Hill that had been the first to be scrambled, having gained a significant height advantage (they were flying at 25,000 feet (7,620m)), and seeing no enemy fighters above, dived on the bombers. As they dived towards the bombers, the German escorts spotted them and, abandoning their charges and increased speed to try to countered the attack. With a large-scale dogfight underway, 603 Squadron's Spitfire arrived on the scene ready to join in the fight. With their fighter escorts fully engaged, the bombers were then confronted by a shallow-diving, head-on attack by the Hurricanes of 253 and 501 Squadrons from Kenley. Their frontal attack was designed as usual to break up the bomber formation, but it remained intact and as the

Hurricanes tried to reform to mount a second attack, they were set upon by the now fully alert close escort Messerschmitts who managed to shoot two of them down. Even though the Hurricanes of Northolt's 229 and 303 Squadrons joined in the battle they had little effect, with fighters being lost from both sides. The bombers continued to maintain their formation and droned on towards their targets. However, due to the relentless attacks by what appeared to be an ever-increasing number of British fighters, their pilots began to break formation and drop their bombs anywhere they could in order to lighten their aircraft and give themselves a chance of escape. Consequently, bombs were dropped over a wide swathe of South London, with one bomb hitting Buckingham Palace and another hitting Beckenham power station.

By mid-day, some of the first wave of Spitfires and Hurricanes started to return to their airfields to rearm and refuel. At the same time, the '*Jacob*' fighter-bombers passed over the top of the Dorniers close to West Mailing airfield. Three minutes later, as the main force flew close to Sevenoaks, the air battle flared up again with the arrival of four new Hurricane squadrons, but they too were largely prevented from reaching the bombers by the defending Bf 109s.

With Fighter Command's aircraft concentrating on the main bomber force, the fighter-bombers reach their targets—the railway stations at West Norwood, Penge, Dulwich, Streatham, Birkbeck, Battersea, and Lambeth. Then, still largely unopposed and having dropped their bombs, they turned and headed for home.

As the main bomber force, comprising some one hundred and forty-eight aircraft, reached the Lewisham-Penge area, their escorting fighters, who were still engaged in dogfights over the fields of Kent and now running low of fuel, turned for home. The bombers were now alone, and as they continued on the way to their targets, Parks' third wave of fighters appeared on the scene. These comprised five squadrons from 11 Group, one from 10 Group, and 12 Group's Big Wing—one hundred and twenty-seven aircraft in total. As the Hurricanes of 504 and 257 Squadrons pressed home their attack, Duxford's Big Wing appeared the scene. The arrival of fifty-five aircraft produced shockwaves through the German bomber crews but gave heart to their fellow RAF pilots. Having dropped their bombs on their intended target—the rail junction at Battersea—and with so many defenders attacking them, the Dorniers scattered in all directions as they turned for home. When all of the other fighters had finished their attacks, Douglas Bader led his Big Wing in a diving approach towards the three bombers at the rear of the formation. The rest of the wing followed him, flying in their vics of three aircraft. Bungay notes that 'there were now so many British fighters in the sky that they had to queue up to have a go at the Dorniers.'

With the flame-throwing Dornier flying on one engine, others were also in trouble. This included a Dornier that, having collided with a Hurricane had one of its tail fins snap off. This caused its fuselage to break and as the aircraft bucked and somersaulted, it went in to a spin. The resulting g-force and stress caused the outer wings to break off and its bomb-load to smash through the fuselage, landing, luckily without exploding, on Buckingham Palace and its gardens. Having elected to bailout of his now crippled Hurricane the pilot hit the roof of a block of flats, before his parachute snagged leaving him dangling with his feet in an open dustbin. The main part of the bomber hit the ground close to Victoria railway station and the pilot, having bailed out, landed near the Oval cricket ground. Unfortunately, a crowd of incensed locals beat him up so badly that, even though some soldiers rescued him, he died of his injuries in hospital. Two other Dorniers crashed near Sevenoaks as they tried, in vain, to make it home, another crashed near Canterbury. A fifth Dornier cashed near Gillingham, and a sixth crashed into the sea close to Herne Bay.

When the German fighters arrived to escort the bombers home, only fifteen of the twenty-five Dorniers of BG 76 who set out, were still together, and most of those had sustained damage. Four aircraft who were not with the formation struggled back to France on their own.

Kesselring had to bring together bombers from a number of units in order to provide a hundred and fourteen He 111s and Dornier 17s for the afternoon's attack, as these formations assembled over their French airfields their escorting fighters joining them. Goering had intended to launch this raid soon after the mornings raid to try to catch Fighter Command's aircraft on the ground, but their ground crews managed to refuel and rearm their aircraft so quickly that Park had all his fighters ready and waiting. To counter the increased number of defending fighters, the number of escorting Bf 109s was to be increased from a ratio of 2:1 fighters-to-bombers, to 4:1, with most of the fighters now tied to close air support. However, the number of operational Luftwaffe fighters available was steadily decreasing and may have been down to less than four hundred.

At 1:45 p.m., the new enemy formations were detected by radar, and in response a lone Spitfire from 92 Squadron at Biggin Hill, was sent out to confirm the raid and report back on its size. Already, Keith Park was preparing his defenses, following the same pattern he had deployed during the morning's raid. He scrambled the Spitfires of 222 and 603 Squadrons to patrol over Sheerness; the Hurricanes of 17 and 257 Squadrons over

Chelmsford; 501 and 605 Squadrons' Hurricanes were to gain height over their base at Kenley; and 249 and 504 Squadrons' Hurricanes were to cover 222 and 603 Squadrons airfield at Hornchurch. The pilot of the lone observation Spitfire, flying at 20,000 feet (6,096m), reported his sighting and, before turning for home, decided to attack six fighters climbing to intercept him. As he chased one of the Messerschmitts in a steep dive, he temporarily blacked out due to extreme G-forces, only recovering consciousness 9,000 feet (2,743m) later. With the Luftwaffe following the same pattern of attack as the morning's raid, Park ordered his first wave of defenders to concentrate on attacking the German fighters to cause them to use up their precious fuel.

Price reports that each of the five groups of enemy bombers had two Gruppes (each of around thirty fighters) proving close cover as they approaching Dungerness, with a further five groups providing the now familiar large-scale, advanced fighter sweep.

One of the Luftwaffe's main objectives was to deal Fighter Command a decisive blow, and, if they had directed at least some of the bombers to 11 Group's airfields, rather than London an hour or two earlier they might have been able to catch many of Park's aircraft on the ground. However, as Korda notes, this was 'the crucial moment of the battle, perhaps the one point at which victory was almost within Gorings [sic] grasp.' Instead he sent all of them towards London, and as Korda concludes, 'the opportunity for the really damaging blow that Goring [sic] expected his forces to deliver had been missed at noon, and would never recur.'

Just after 2 p.m., having confirmed that the raid comprised three separate columns of bombers, Park began to assemble the second wave of his fighter defenses. He scrambled two squadrons of Spitfires—41 and 92—to join the Hurricanes that had previously scrambled to patrol over Hornchurch, before redirecting them to join 222 Squadron that was already patrolling along the Kent coast. He also, dispatched 1 and 229 Squadrons to patrol above their base at Northolt. Five minutes later, he scrambled two more squadrons from Biggin Hill—66 and 72—to patrol over their airfield. He also scrambled the Hurricanes of 46 Squadron to patrol over the London docks—the main target for the coming attack, and 73 Squadron's Hurricanes to position themselves over Maidstone. Park also called for the support of the neighboring groups, with 10 Group providing 238 Squadrons' Hurricanes to join the Kenley Hurricanes over their airfield, and 12 Group to assemble their Big Wing, again comprising five squadrons but this time with fifty-seven aircraft, to head for the Hornchurch area. Park now had aircraft covering the docks and a line of fighters positioned between Kenley, Biggin Hill, and the Thames estuary with most of the other fighters assembling over north Kent and

London along the path he had anticipated the attacking force would follow. This was the position, as Bungay records, that the Germans called 'the dreaded big turn' over London where the Luftwaffe fighter pilots would start to run low on fuel and the bombers would begin to line up for their bombing runs.

The first of the German bombers crossed the English coast above Dungerness at 2:10 p.m., before banking right to head for East London. As they did so, they ran in to the three squadrons of Spitfires patrolling the Kent coast who immediately set about their fighter escort. The bombers were indeed following the route Park had anticipated and positioned his fighter to cover.

At 2:20 p.m., Park began to assemble his third wave of fighters, these comprised the Polish airmen of 303 Squadron, who were ordered to patrol in their Hurricanes over their airfield at Northolt. The Spitfires of 602 Squadron flying northwards from Tangmere on the south coast, were instructed to cover the area between Gravesend and Kenley. He also requested further support from 10 Group, who responded by provided the Spitfires of 609 Squadron to cover the area between Brooklands and Kenley. Fighter Command now had two hundred and sixty-seven fighters in the air, including all operational aircraft in 11 Group; but as Price records, they still faced a raid over twice their size, including a fighter force that outnumbered them three-to-two. Even so, with so many fighters in the air, Fighter Command thought that they would be in a position to inflict significant damage on the approaching bombers.

With the Spitfires of the first defensive wave already engaging the bombers, the Hurricanes of 607 and 213 Squadrons joined in. Flying in a close-spaced, head-on attack, on the right-hand column of bombers, one Hurricane pilot found his escape route blocked by a fellow pilot, and with the prospect of a collision being unavoidable, he opted to hit the Dornier he had been firing at. On impact, both aircrafts right wings sheared off. The Hurricane pilot managed to escape from his stricken aircraft, but the bomber crew did not, and all on board were killed when the aircraft plunged into the ground close to the village of Kilndown, 12km southwest of Royal Tunbridge Wells (an hour later one of the bombs on board the blazing aircraft exploded killing three bystanders and wounding nine others). As Price notes, because the escorting Luftwaffe fighter pilots were under specific instructions to stay with, and defend the slower bombers, they were unable to use their speed and maneuverability effectively. This allowed Park's Spitfires and Hurricanes the space and opportunity to continue their attacks far longer than they had fought during the air battles of August and early September. As the fighting progressed, the bombers continued to make their way steadily over the Kent countryside, when the Hurricanes of 605 and 501 Squadrons began their attack from the side of the formation. When another Hurricane pilot—his aircraft having been hit by defensive fire coming from the bombers—decided to ram his now doomed aircraft into one of the bombers, it seemed to the German bomber crews that this might be a deliberate change in tactics now being employed by a rather desperate air force.

As the bombers approached the Thames near Chatham, the Spitfires and Hurricanes pulled back from their attacks, and the anti-aircraft guns opened fire, hitting one of Dorniers, causing it to pull out of formation. The guns then continued to fire at the next formation as they came within range which comprised the Heinkels in the centre column of the raid. They managed to hit one of these bombers, and dumping its bombs in open farmland, it too turned for home on one engine.

It was during this phase of the action, at 2:35 p.m., that Churchill, who had remained at 11 Group's Operations Room, famously asked Park, "What other reserves have we?"

With all of his aircraft in the sky, Park replied, "None." Price points out, there were only three other squadrons within 100 miles (160km) of London that could be called into action if the Germans mounted another immediate attack, and it would take them at least an hour to reach the battle zone. He also adds that as Park was such an astute commander, he knew that the fairly low cloud cover that was almost completely blanketing his airfields and London, meant that accurate bombing would be more difficult, so he could afford to commit all of his available fighters into the battle.

Bungay recalls Churchill thoughts some time later, when the Prime Minister wrote, 'What losses might we not suffer if our refueling planes were caught on the ground by further raids of "40 plus" or "50 plus"! The odds were great; our margins small, the stakes infinite.'

Having already been in action, three of the squadrons in Park's first and second waves were ordered to return to their bases at Biggin Hill and Kenley to refuel and rearm; a move that Price suspects may have been made in order to give him a tactical reserve. This left nineteen other squadrons, with a total of one hundred and eighty-five fighters, now in position around the southern and eastern side of London, ready to face the enemy bombers and fighters. The first of these to engage the enemy were 1, 46, 249, 504, and 603 Squadrons, who attacked the right-hand column of bombers. The center column was attacked by 1RCAF, 66, 72, and 229 Squadrons, and the left-hand column faced 73, 253, and 303 Squadrons.

The Dorniers at the head of the right-hand column were attacked from behind by two of the Hurricane squadrons, their close-range and intense fire inflicting sufficient damage to cause three of the bombers to pull out of formation, with one crashing into the Thames. The Heinkels following behind were attacked by a third Hurricane squadron led by one of the best fighter pilots in Fighter Command, Bob Stanford Tuck.

The Heinkels that formed the centre column faced a concerted head-on attack by 66 Squadron's Spitfires, while others attacking from behind and underneath, they were then joined by the Spitfires of 72 Squadron and the Hurricanes of 1RCAF and 229 Squadrons. One Heinkel crashed close to Woolwich Arsenal, and three others turned for home. A Spitfire and a Hurricane were also damaged in this action. Meanwhile, the left-hand column was also coming under attack from three squadrons of Hurricanes, including the Polish pilots of 303 squadron. This time, because there had been no delay in the bombers meeting up with the fighters, some of the covering Bf 109s still had sufficient fuel to be able to join the action. They managed to shoot down two of the Hurricanes and damaging five others. In return, one Heinkel was damaged.

Bungay records that Park was nervous in case Duxford's Big Wing did not arrive, or arrived too late or in the wrong place. Guess what, it did indeed arrive too late and out of position, but this may have been a result of the reduced time available to Park in calling for their help, that was a consequence of the lack of delay on behalf of the Germans. While the Big Wing was still trying to gain height as it approached London it was bounced by a number of German fighters. In response Douglas Bader, called on his Hurricanes to counter the fighters while the wing's Spitfires headed for the bombers. In the ensuing fighter-versus-fighter engagements with Adolf Galland's JG 26, two Hurricanes were lost. Meanwhile, at least two of the Spitfires mounted a head-on attack on the bombers, one of which turned for home having sustained some damage.

As the bombers approached their intended target—the London docks—they were still hampered by low cloud cover. Not being able to see their targets, they saw that the area to the north of the docks around East and West Ham was relatively free of clouds, and headed there instead. As they approached East Ham, they were again attacked by intense anti-aircraft fire even though they were still being set-upon by British fighters. Again, Price's comments are interesting. Apparently, the Germans took this as a sign that the British were getting desperate, whereas, Fighter Command pilots had expected the guns to stop firing when they were engaging the enemy. Price records that afterwards 'there would be stern reprimands for the offending anti-aircraft batteries.'

At 2:45 p.m., bombs began to rain down on West Ham, hitting the gasworks at Bromley-by-Bow and destroying one of the gasholders. Other bombs hit St. Mary's Hospital, Upton Park railway station, and a number of houses in the general area, killing seventeen people and seriously wounding ninety-two, with a further forty suffering only slight injuries.

To the south of London, the approaching bombers of the left-hand column, which included the bombers of BG 2 were also unable to see their intended targets and instead of picking out alternative targets they turned for home, releasing their bombs as they went. Consequently, bombs were scattered over a wide area of the suburbs of Southeast London, including my home town of Orpington. Fortunately, these resulted in few casualties. At one point, they were engaged by a lone Hurricane, flown by Group Captain Stanley Vincent, the Station Commander at Northolt, who had taken off in one of the airfields Hurricanes in order that he could join in the fight with his Polish pilots.

While West Ham and Southeast London was being bombed, the nine bombers that had been damaged during their approach to London were being shot down one-by-one as they headed back over North Kent. One even managed to make an emergency landing at West Mailing airfield.

At 3:15 p.m., as the main bomber force headed for home, they were joined by around fifty German fighters sent out to escort them. Unfortunately, the bombers were still not clear of the British fighters as the aircraft that had been scrambled from the most westerly airfields swooped into action. The Spitfires of 602 and 609 Squadrons headed for the retreating Dorniers that had comprised the left-hand column while the Hurricanes of Middle Wallops 238 Squadron made for the Heinkels of the centre column. During the resulting engagement, a further two Dorniers were shot down before they crossed English coast, and others crash-landed soon after reaching the French coast. In the course of this raid, the Luftwaffe lost twenty-one bombers and twelve fighters, while Fighter Command lost fifteen aircraft with another twenty-one damaged.

By 3:25 p.m., the first of Park's returning squadrons, 213, was rearmed, refueled, and ready for action once more. He now had at least a small tactical reserve to call on again.

Shortly before the bombs began to fall on West Ham, the Luftwaffe launched its third raid of the day. Expecting all of Fighter Command's last remaining fighters to be fully engaged with attack on London. At 5:05 p.m., twenty-seven Heinkels of KG 55 set out from Villa Coublay for an

333

unprotected raid on the naval base at Portland and the Spitfire factory in Southampton. They were detected by British radar ten minutes later. At the same time that this raid had been identified, the Bf 110s and Bf 109s fighter-bombers of EG 210 took off to mount their own raid on the Spitfire works. The radar operators over-estimated the number of aircraft taking part in this raid and consequently seven squadrons were scrambled, three from 10 Group and four from 11 Group. The fighter-bombers missed their intended target and instead their bombs landed on nearby houses killing nine people and seriously injuring another ten. Most of the defending aircraft were unable to find the low-flying, fast moving fighter-bombers. With regard to the bomber attack on Portland, only two Spitfires from Middle Wallop managed to intercept the formation before it got too far back across the Channel, however, the bombers inflicted only slight damage on the harbor.

Price reports that during the day's action, the Luftwaffe lost fifty-six aircraft, of which thirty-five crashed on English soil and twenty-one crashed in the sea; this was the largest loss of aircraft they suffered in a single day. Three more were beyond repair and a further twenty-three had suffered some damage. Eighty-one aircrew had been killed, sixty-three were prisoners, and another thirty-one were wounded. That evening, the RAF and national newspapers claimed to have shot down one hundred and eighty-five aircraft, a figure that Park thought was ridiculous. Fighter Command lost twenty-nine fighters, with twelve pilots being killed, a similar number were wounded; one pilot who decided to follow a bomber across the Channel, against orders, was taken prisoner. Price points out that less than half of Fighter Command's total number of Spitfires and Hurricanes were used during the day, and all of those not in action were situated north and west of London and 11 Group. This meant that even if Park's aircraft had taken a pounding, he could have replaced them by the following day. 12 Group's much-vaunted Big Wing was less effective than thought at the time; its pilots claimed to have shot down twenty-six aircraft, whereas in fact, they only shared in the destruction of six bombers. Their effectiveness in the afternoon's engagements were negated when they were 'bounced' by Luftwaffe fighters, causing the Wing to break up in to small units. Park is said to have been furious that his pilot concentrated on lone or damaged bombers that had already turned for home rather than continuing to break-up and attack the rest of the bomber force. He was also worried that with the losses Fighter Command had experienced during the previous weeks, less experienced leaders were now leading many of the squadrons. The Luftwaffe were facing their own problems, most of their airmen had been in continuous operation since the start of the conflict, they had suffered large numbers of casualties, and the number of serviceable aircraft had significantly reduced.

For the Luftwaffe pilots, the day's action had been significant for all the wrong reasons. As Parker says, they had been repeatedly informed that Fighter Command were down to their last fifty aircraft, but they faced over three hundred fighters that day. Bishop points out that for Fighter Command, everything had gone right from the radar stations detecting the build-up to the raids, to the Observer Corpse detailing numbers and flight paths, to Group and Sector Stations operating and controlling their fighters, and finally to the pilots in their aircraft—everything had worked as it had been designed to do. Even so, he adds that:

'No-one, neither the pilots heading to the pubs in a mood of jubilation and hilarity born of relief, nor the earthbound civilians who had cheered them on, dared yet hope that the ordeal was over. And nor was it, for sometime yet. But on 15 September the moment of greatest danger passed. Though it was far from obvious at the time, the Battle of Britain was won.'

Korda concludes that:

'The invasion would never come, Fighter Command had never lost control of the air for even a single moment, and "the few" had won one of the four most critical victories in British history—the Armada, Trafalgar, Waterloo, and the Battle of Britain.'

Bungay rightly points out that Fighter Command did not win the Battle of Britain on 15 September; it had already done that in the previous three weeks of often-extreme circumstances when it had been able to keep the fully functioning system that Dowding had painstakingly built up operational. This meant that when the big day came, it did not let him down. In the hands of a master tactician, under the watchful eyes of the Prime Minister and a large number of the public across the southeast of England, Fighter Command had proved that it could fight back, maintain air superiority over Britain, and would be a fighting force if Germany tried to launch an invasion.

Chapter 8
The Window Closed

15 September proved to be the turning point in a Battle that had been going on, with increasing intensity for three months. Goering had been confidently predicting that with four or five days good weather he could defeat Fighter Command. However, his pilots and aircrew were taking a pounding from fighters whose numbers never seemed to remotely match the figures they were being told by Luftwaffe Intelligence. The previous day, Fighter Command seemed to be out in huge numbers and were organized, ready to meet them. Could the Luftwaffe continue operations with such a high loss rate?

Monday, 16 September

Even though it was raining, following the events of the day before, everyone at Fighter Command expected the Luftwaffe to continue with the same large-scale air raids, but the enemy stayed away. Their bomber crews were back at their bases 'licking their wounds.'

Fighter Command, the Royal Navy, the British government, and almost the entire nation still expected the invasion to take place. Meanwhile, Goering summoned his Luftwaffe and Fliegerkorps commanders to a meeting on his train at Beauvais to discuss the previous day's actions. It was clear that Luftwaffe Intelligence was wrong, and that Fighter Command was not down its last fifty fighters, even so, Goering was convinced that Fighter Command had only two hundred eighty-eight fighters available on 15 September and that this had dropped to a hundred and seventy-seven by 16 September. He was sure that Fighter Command was drawing-in aircraft from surrounding, non-combat squadrons to bolster defenses in the south and southeast, and that if the Luftwaffe could only have four or five days of good flying weather (just as they had during the Polish and French campaigns), they would wear down Fighter Command's last remaining aircraft. Even though they had suffered significant losses over the last few days, Luftwaffe Intelligence had calculated that Fighter Command had lost seventy-nine fighters the day before when in fact, as we have seen they had only lost twenty-six.

Goering also blamed his fighter pilots for a lack of decisive action during the previous day's combats. Osterkamp, the commander of JG 2 complained about the tactics that they were having to use and the lack of spares available to maintain their aircraft in operational condition.

It was decided that the Germans should once again change their tactics. Luftflotte II would attack British fighters and their airfields as well as London by day, and Luftflotte III would attack Southampton by day and London by night. They also decided, given the large numbers of British fighters, they encountered the previous day, that they would not mount raids comprising large numbers of bombers, except in exceptional circumstances, but should send smaller numbers of bombers escorted by a large numbers of fighters. They would continue with large-scale bomber raids at night, particularly on London, as the RAF did not possess an effective night fighter force. Consequently, that night they would send over another one hundred and seventy bombers to pound the East End and London docks with 200 tons (203 tonnes) of bombs. London however was not their only target that night; they also attacked Liverpool and Bristol.

In his book *The Battle of Britain: Five Months That Changed History May-October 1940*, James Holland makes the point that operationally the Luftwaffe was in a mess. They were short of aircraft and lacked the infrastructure necessary to continue a battle of the intensity of the previous weeks. He comments that Luftwaffe High Command had failed to use either its bombers or its fighters to the best of their capabilities, and had lost sight of what it was supposed to be achieving.

Tuesday, 17 September

The day started with showers and some thunderstorms, but conditions improved during the afternoon, allowing the Luftwaffe to mount fast-moving raids, comprising fifty plus fighters. This was to be used as with previous attempts, to draw Fighter Command in to costly fighter-versus-fighter engagements; Keith Park largely ignored them apart from interceptions by 501 and 41 Squadrons and Duxford's Big Wing, each of which lost five fighters. The Luftwaffe also sent over seven or eight main raids comprising large numbers of fighters each with a small number of bombers to act a bait to draw Fighter Command into a fight. In response, Park scrambled twenty-eight squadrons and managed to turn most of the raiders back before they reached London.

In Berlin, Hitler decided once again to delay plans for the invasion as he thought, unlike Goering, that Fighter Command was still a real threat. He also thought that to the British people the prospect of an invasion was still a very real threat. In Britain, the threat of invasion was viewed as a very real possibility; and even though the Luftwaffe had received a serve shock two days ago, no one, including all those in authority, could be sure that an invasion would not take place if conditions were favorable. Hence, following an open session of parliament, Churchill called a closed session and during a short speech, he included the following:

'These next few weeks are grave and anxious. I said just now in the Public Session that the deployment of the enemy's invasion preparations and the assembly of his ships and barges are steadily proceeding, and that any moment a major assault may be launched upon this island. I now say in secret that upwards of seventeen hundred self-propelled barges and more than two hundred seagoing ships, some very large ships, are already gathering at the many invasion ports in German occupation. If this is all a pretense and stratagem to pin us down here, it has been executed with surprising thoroughness and on a gigantic scale. Some of these ships and barges, when struck by our bombing counterattacks and preventive attack, have blown up with tremendous explosions, showing that they are fully loaded with all the munitions needed for the invading armies and to beat us down and subjugate us utterly.'

That night, two hundred and sixty-eight bombers flew across the Channel to bomb London, Liverpool, and Glasgow. Meanwhile, as we saw in chapter four, Bomber Command was keeping up its attacks on the build-up of invasion barges with considerable affect.

Wednesday, 18 September

Once again, the weather was unsettled, even so, at 9 a.m., a force of fast-moving fighters crossed the Channel, heading for North Kent. This time, Park scrambled fifteen squadrons to meet them, but because they were flying so fast, only five squadrons, from Biggin Hill and Hornchurch, managed to intercept the raiders, five of their aircraft were shot down.

Two hours later, four raids comprising one hundred and fifty aircraft crossed the coast. This time Park delayed scrambling some of his fighters and, unfortunately, between twenty and thirty bombers and some of their fighter escorts managed to bomb Chatham and Rochester before they were intercepted by the Big Wing. In response, most of the German aircraft scattered. The Big Wing claimed to have shot down thirty aircraft, with another six probables and two damaged, whereas in reality they only shot down two bombers and seven escorts.

In response to a further raid that afternoon, Park again scrambled a significant number of fighters. This time 92 and 302 Squadrons intercepted a faint attack over the Thames Estuary and Duxford's Big Wing attacked in an almost vertical dive claiming thirty bombers and fighters shot down (they only bought down four aircraft). In fact, an additional squadron had been added to the Big Wing by the arrival of 616 Squadron that even though it was based at Kirton-in-Lindsey in Lincolnshire, flew down to each day to join the Wing. Park also instigated wings of three squadrons at Northolt and Tangmere designed to attack the second and third waves of bombers.

Dowding had a major success with his fight to get more pilots to operational squadrons. Finally, he had managed to persuade the Air Ministry to combine some of the Fairey Battle light bomber squadrons to release a few of their pilots and asked that two thirds of all the pilots in training over a four-week period be directed to join Fighter Command.

During the day's actions, Fighter Command lost twelve aircraft and three pilots, and the Luftwaffe lost fifteen aircraft, with fifty airmen either dead or taken prisoner.

That night, with the threat of invasion still a possibility, Bomber Command, Coastal Command and some Fleet Air Arm units launched large-scale raids, comprising almost two hundred aircraft on the invasion barges and troop concentrations. Air photographic reconnaissance had shown that there were 1,004 invasion barges in the Channel ports with a further six hundred in the river towards Antwerp. During September, the three commands dropped 1,400 tons (1,422 tonnes) of bombs on the invasion barges and ships, which represented almost 60% of all the bombs dropped during the month's raids.

That night, the Luftwaffe began the intensive night bombing campaign, as outlined on 16 September, on London and Liverpool.

It rained all the following day and consequently there was little in the way of action. Probably in responds to the previous night's raids, Hitler ordered a halt to the build-up of invasion barges and also initiated the dispersal of invasion troops away from the coast.

To counter the latest change in tactics introduced by the Luftwaffe, Park issued revised tactics of his own. He wanted his fighters to intercept the enemy later in order to give them a better chance of gaining the altitude necessary to engage on more even terms. He ordered the Spitfires from

Biggin Hill and Hornchurch to climb to 20–30,000 feet (6,069–9,144m) to attack the highest fighter cover. He also wanted his controllers to improve their ability to determine the size and composition of each raid so that they could deploy their defenses more effectively and asked his pilots to continue their attacks on the enemy formations once they had turned for home.

He employed the same tactics to counter large numbers of fighter and fighter-bombers on 20 September. These raiders crossed the coast at several locations including twenty at Dungeness, thirty over Dover, and twelve at Lympne. This time, Park scrambled four squadrons of fighters, two each from Biggin Hill and Hornchurch to intercept the raids. Biggin Hill's aircraft were the first to engage the enemy formations but the aircraft from Hornchurch were bounced by a second wave of fighters. Consequently, Fighter Command lost seven aircraft to the Luftwaffe's two.

With an improvement in the weather forecast for Saturday, 21 September the Luftwaffe were able to put into practice their revised daytime targeting instructions of 16 September. They mounted a raid on the Hawker aircraft factory at Brooklands. A Ju 88 managed to bomb the airfield, but only one bomb hit the target, and this failed to explode. The unexploded bomb landed in the building that housed the Hurricane production line, where a Canadian engineer named Patton loaded it on to a makeshift sledge and dragged it outside. He dumped it in a crater made by another bomb where it later exploded.

During the evening, a large raid crossed the coast between Dover and Lympne to attack the airfields at Kenley, Biggin Hill, and Hornchurch as well as London. In response, Park scrambled twenty squadrons as well as the Duxford Big Wing and one squadron from 10 Group. During the subsequent fighting, the Luftwaffe lost nine aircraft without loss for Fighter Command.

During the night, German bombers attacked London, Liverpool, Warrington, Nottingham, Bolton, and Colchester.

Unfortunately, for the Luftwaffe the good weather did not continue for the rest of the weekend and although the early morning fog gradually cleared, as far as air operations were concerned, it proved to be the quietest day since 10 July. Only ten individual raiders crossing the Channel, one of which—a Ju 88—was shot down. Even though the day remained quiet, the threat of invasion was still foremost in many people's minds not just in Britain and on the continent but also in America where the President sent a message to Churchill saying that he had received reliable information that the invasion was due to start at 5 p.m. that day.

Improving weather conditions for next five days enabled the Luftwaffe to resume their tactic of launching large-scale fighter and fighter-bomber raids.

The first major attack on Monday, 23 September comprised two hundred aircraft in four large and two small formations that fanned out across the southeast of England. In response, Park scrambled twenty-four squadrons, but as was so often the situation with fast-moving fighters and fighter-bombers, they proved difficult to intercept. In fact, only the aircraft from Biggin Hill and a squadron of Hurricanes from Debden managed to engage the enemy.

In the late evening, another five waves of fighters crossed the Channel and even though Fighter Command scrambled twelve squadrons in four wings, they could not find the enemy aircraft.

Improving weather conditions also enabled the Luftwaffe to launch larger night-time raids than they had been able to do for the previous three nights, with an attack targeted at London comprising two hundred and sixty-one bombers.

On Tuesday, 24 September, an early morning raid of two hundred bombers in five different formations of between five and fifty aircraft, spread out across a 10-mile (16km) front. They had set out for London but were intercepted and turned back at the coast before they could get anywhere near their target.

Just before lunchtime, another large raid comprising some two hundred aircraft again in five formations crossed the Channel. In response, eighteen RAF squadrons were scrambled but yet again only two managed to find and engage the enemy.

Shortly afterwards, one raid that did succeed in fulfilling its mission was the crack unit EG 210. Flying low as usual to avoid being detected by radar, they attacked the Supermarine works at Southampton with their Bf 110s, and although they caused only minor damage to the factory, they managed to kill a hundred people sheltering in an air raid shelter. However, they did not manage to launch the raid completely unscathed because when they went on to attack Portsmouth anti-aircraft guns shot down one aircraft and damaged two others.

The following day, the Luftwaffe deployed a large formation of He 111s and Bf 110s together with a sizable fighter escort and EG 210 that appeared to be heading for the Westland factory at Yeovil. In fact, it changed direction and made for the Bristol works at Filton where they were building Blenheim medium bombers. The bombers dropped 90 tons (91 tonnes) of bombs on the factory, causing extensive damage, badly damaging some of the Blenheims and killing or injuring one hundred and fifty people. The damage inflicted on the factory stopped aircraft production for a week. Although the raiders managed to get through to their target unopposed, aircraft from two 10 Group squadrons intercepted them on their way home and shot down five bombers as they crossed the south coast. To help divert attention away from the main raid, the Luftwaffe also launched a fighter raid on the naval base and harbor at Portland.

In the early evening, a raid by Bf 110s was intercepted off Start Point on the south Devon coast, and three squadrons halted a raid aimed at London. At the conclusion of the day's activities, Fighter Command had lost four aircraft but the Luftwaffe had lost thirteen aircraft.

In response to the previous day's raid, and to prevent future damage, Dowding relocated 504 Squadron based at Hendon to Filton on the outskirts of Bristol to help defend the aircraft factory from further attacks.

During the early evening, another raid comprising seventy-six He 111s and Ju 88s, and escorted by Bf 109s, was launched on the Spitfire works at Southampton. This time they were more successful. They dropped 70 tons (71 tonnes) of bombs on the site and managed to destroy three Spitfires, damage more than twenty others, and temporarily halt aircraft production. They also killed thirty people. Six squadrons were scrambled from 10 and 11 Groups after the raid had been detected, including 303 Squadron at Northolt that was in the middle of an inspection by the King. They managed to intercept the raiders shooting down three bombers for the loss of six aircraft.

Following the raid on Filton two days earlier, the Luftwaffe sent the same units—KG 55, ZG 26, and EG 210—over on Friday, 27 September to repeat their success, but this time 10 Group were ready for them. They scrambled five squadrons who on meeting the raiders over Yeovil broke up the bomber formation. In response, they dropped their bombs before turning for home and meeting up with a covering formation of Bf 110s that were waiting for them off the Dorset coast close to Swanage. The Bf 110s were then attacked by a number of aircraft including those from 609 Squadron. Meanwhile, EG 210 continued to their target at Filton but were also intercepted and lost four aircraft.

Before this raid however, the Luftwaffe launched a large-scale, early-morning fighter and fighter-bomber sweep across a wide front over Southeast England. This comprised Bf 110s escorted by large numbers of Bf 109s who were intercepted by pairs of Fighter Command squadrons that managed to turn the raiders back. The fighter-bombers dropping their bombs to hasten their escape. Some of the fighters hung around to try to meet up with the next raid, comprising fifty-five Ju 88s. However, as they were late forming up, they were consequently intercepted by over one hundred Fighter Command aircraft. This led to the first large-scale dog flight since 15 September, and caused most of the raiders to turn back.

The Germans also launched another fairly large raid on the Bristol factory at Filton, but only the Bf 109s and Bf 110s got through, and they were then intercepted by aircraft from 152, 609, 56, and 504 Squadrons. Crossing the Dorset coast with this raid was another one heading for London but it was intercepted and most of the raiders were turned back although twenty aircraft managed to get through the defenses to attack the city.

In all the day's fighting Fighter Command had lost twenty-eight aircraft while the Luftwaffe had lost fifty-five, including twenty-one bombers.

During one of the raids that flew in over Kent, a Ju 88 flown by Uffz Fritz Ruhlandt was shot down near Faversham and crashed on Graveney Marsh. Some of the soldiers of the 1st London Irish Regiment who were billeted nearby arrived expecting the crew to surrender, but they did not. Following a brief gunfighter, the Germans did indeed surrender and the soldiers then took them to the nearest pub for a drink. The aircraft was subsequently recovered and sent to RAE Farnborough for inspection. This war-time, gun battle—the last one fought on English soil—became known as the 'battle of Graveney Marsh.'

The following day the weather changed once again with cloud over the Channel. After the continuing losses inflicted on their bombers, the Luftwaffe introduced yet another change in tactics, from now on formations would normally comprise faster flying Ju 88s escorted by between two hundred and three hundred fighters unless conditions allowed the use of slower, more vulnerable bombers. In response, Kesselring sent over smaller formations of aircraft to target London and Portsmouth. Both raids were intercepted but during the ensuing fights Fighter Command lost sixteen fighters and nine pilots, while the Luftwaffe only lost three of their aircraft.

Even with a slight improvement in the weather, the following day most activity was confined to the occasional lone raider or reconnaissance flights. In the late afternoon, three formations—comprising fifty, twenty, and twenty aircraft (all fighters)—also tried to reach London. During the evening, the town of Sittingbourne in Kent came under heavy bombing.

Weather conditions continued to improve on the last day of the month allowing the Luftwaffe to launch a series of large-scale fighter and bomber raids aimed at London. The early morning attack, comprising around two hundred aircraft was intercepted by twelve squadrons of Spitfires and Hurricanes in the Maidstone area who managed to force most of the bombers to turn back. The escorting fighters stayed to fight and the resulting dogfights ranged back and forth across and along the Thames Estuary. From late morning to mid-afternoon, further raids were mounted against Weymouth, and London, but again most of the attackers were faced with significant numbers of defending fighters and turned for home before reaching their targets.

Kesselring mounted another raid on aircraft production in the southwest of England. This time He 111s escorted by a large number of fighters tried to reach the Westland factory at Yeovil. However, they were intercepted by four squadrons on the way to their target and a further four on the way back. To affect their escape, the bombers ditched their bombs over a wide area close to the town of Sherborne in Dorset. A force of around one hundred and eighty aircraft also tried to attack the aircraft factories at Weybridge.

During the day's action, Fighter Command lost twenty aircraft and eight pilots while the Luftwaffe lost fifty aircraft.

This proved to be the last of the great air battles, and following the losses they had sustained during the previous months, Kesselring decided to convert almost one third of his Bf 109s into fighter-bombers so that Fighter Command could not continue to ignore his fighter sweeps and lone raiders. He also changed tactics, sending these aircraft over at high altitude where Hurricanes could not reach them and where it would take the Spitfires almost half an hour to climb to their flying altitude to be able to fight. However, these changes had a major impact on his fighter aircraft and their pilots. The additional weight of the bombs reduced their flying time and range, and because the Bf 109s were not built to fly for long durations at 30,000 feet (9,144m), they had neither the heating nor pressurized cockpits to counter the freezing temperatures and thin air. This tactic also added additional burdens on already tired and overstretched pilots and crews. These changes, together with the losses they had already sustained together with the arrival of replacement pilots with little training and no chance to gain additional experience apart from the heat of battle was taking its toll. Added to this is the fact that they were now being asked to take on the role of fighter-bombing for which they had little or no training, it did nothing to raise the spirits of the German pilots.

Kesselring and Sperle also decided to withdraw their bombers from daylight raids and concentrate on night-time bombing instead, unless they had thick cloud cover in which the bombers could hide during daylight. Wood and Dempster comment that after almost three months of continuous fighting the Luftwaffe had lost 1,652 aircraft with little to show for it.

To counter these new tactics, Park established a system whereby a couple of Spitfires from 66 Squadron would maintain a standing patrol at high altitude to act as spotters for incoming raids. This would eventually lead to the formation of No.421 Flight and later on 91 Squadron, one of the most famous photographic reconnaissance squadrons in the world.

According to Bishop, October 1940 became known as 'Messerschmitt month' with fighter-bombers attacking virtually all of the airfields in Southern England as well as London, Portsmouth and Southampton. Consequently, during the first five days on October, the Luftwaffe mounted fighter and fighter-bomber raids in large waves, when conditions allowed, or in small formations or individual aircraft across much of the south and southeast on England. Most of the larger formations were easy to detect and intercept, but the smaller formations and single fighter-bomber raids were much harder to follow and therefore often got through to their intended targets. As well as airfields they attacked the De Havilland aircraft factory at Hatfield where a Ju 88 from KG 77 killed twenty-one people and wounded a further seventy before being shot down by anti-aircraft fire. On 1 October, a small raid was also mounted against targets along the east coast of Scotland.

At night, the Luftwaffe kept up their relentless bombing of the capital, Liverpool, Manchester, Glasgow, Aberdeen and Swansea, sometimes sending as many as three hundred bombers to cause chaos, death, and destruction across the country.

On 4 October, Hitler met Mussolini, who wanted his air force to take part, and therefore share some of the glory of the battle. On this side of the Channel, the day heralded an important milestone in Fighter Command's efforts against the Luftwaffe for it was on this day that it again reached a total of seven hundred operational fighters, including Blenheims, Defiants, and Gladiators something it had not been able to achieve since late September and late August. For most of the battle, there were between two hundred to two hundred and fifty Spitfires and three hundred and fifty to four hundred Hurricanes on operational strength.

Chapter 9
They Think It's All Over

Phase 4: 6 October–31 October

With the heavy losses incurred during their daylights raids over the last twenty-eight days, the realization that the Luftwaffe had failed to gain the vital air superiority over the English Channel and Southern England, and with their bombers and fighters coming up against an increasing number of British fighters, Hitler and Goering switched tactics once more. The bombers would concentrate on night bombing unless weather conditions gave them vital cloud cover and a measure of protection to mount daylight attacks. Under all other weather conditions, they would mount fighter and fighter-bomber sweeps or lone aircraft, or small formations.

The increasingly unpredictable weather associated with autumn in Britain dictated when, where and how many raids the Luftwaffe would be able to mount during October. For much of the time rain restricted flying operations. Most raids comprised fighter and fighter-bomber sweeps were aimed at Fighter Command's airfields south and east of London. On occasions, the Luftwaffe also bombed Fleet Air Arm airfields in the south and southwest. They also targeted the aircraft factory at Yeovil.

When weather conditions improved for instance between 11–13 October, they were able to mount larger attacks on Fighter Command's airfields with more than a hundred aircraft, but the improved conditions that allowed the Luftwaffe to send over larger numbers of aircraft also enabled Park to mount a larger defense. With the Luftwaffe again using predictable tactics, he was also able to change his tactics. With this temporary improvement in the weather and the larger number of aircraft flown by both sides, RAF and Luftwaffe losses were generally fairly close to each other. It was back to a war of attrition aimed, as Goering planned, at weakening Fighter Command. However, although British aircraft production was now able to more than keep pace with losses, the Luftwaffe were not.

Goering also set out a new plan of attack that included gaining complete air control over the Channel and coast, the progressive and complete destruction of British industrial and civil life, the demoralization of the civil population of London, and the progressive weakening of Britain's forces. The first part of this new plan is quite interesting given that all of his previous plans since June were designed to achieve this and the second half had been his aim since August.

On 8 October, Churchill gave a speech in the House of Commons, which updated the MP's on the Luftwaffe bombing over the last month and to make sure that with the worsening weather conditions associated with autumn people did not think that the threat of invasion had completely disappeared or that the fight was over. His speech included the following:

'Meanwhile, what has happened to the invasion which we have been promised every month and almost every week since the beginning of July? Do not let us be lured into supposing that the danger is past. On the contrary, unwearying vigilance and the swift and steady strengthening of our forces by land, sea and air which is in progress must be at all costs maintained. Now that we are in October, however, the weather becomes very uncertain, and there are not many lucid intervals of two or three days together in which river barges can cross the narrow seas and land upon our beaches. Still, those intervals may occur. Fogs may aid the foe. Our armies, which are growing continually in numbers, equipment, mobility and training, must be maintained all through the winter, not only along the beaches but in reserve, as the majority are, like leopards crouching to spring at the invaders throat. The enemy has certainly got prepared enough shipping and barges to throw half a million men in a single night on to salt water—or into it.

'…No one can predict, no one can even imagine, how terrible war against German and Nazi aggression will run its course or how far it will spread or how long it will last. Long, dark months of trials and tribulations lie before us. Not only great dangers, but many more misfortunes, many shortcomings, many mistakes, many disappointments will surely be our lot. Death and sorrow will be the companions of our journey; hardship our garment; constancy and valour our shield.'

Was Churchill specifically using Biblical phraseology and alluding to the armor of God in Ephesians chapter six?

On 12 October, Hitler decided to postpone *Operation Sealion* once again but insisted that preparations for invasion should be continued purely for the purpose of maintaining political and military pressure on Britain over the winter. Although this signaled the end of a possible invasion until the spring or early summer of 1941, as we see from the extract of the speech above, the British Government and military could not be certain that this was true and that therefore that the threat of invasion had passed.

Following a brief period of more settled conditions, autumn returned to a mixture of cloud, fog, and rain showers. Consequently, following three days of increased air activity, the Luftwaffe reverted back to small-scale raids and attacks by single bombers. When they could not penetrate inland, they would attack towns along the Kent and Sussex coast. They also took advantage of the cloud cover to attack convoys in the Channel when suitable targets presented themselves.

To counter a new threat by high-flying, nearly continuous streams of fast-moving, fighter-bombers, Park issued another set of instructions. He wanted his, and some of 10 Group's squadrons, to operate in pairs or wings as long as getting the additional squadrons airborne did not delay the rest of the aircraft from climbing to the required height of between 20–30,000 feet (6,096–9,144m). They were to cover other squadrons that would be climbing to their operational heights and act as spotters for raids once enemy formations had been detected building up over France. He also wanted aircraft to be in the air ready to counter any attacks, and have other squadrons on the ground held at readiness so that they could take off to meet additional threats. Squadrons at readiness were to take off and climb to 30,000 feet (9,144m) and patrol between Maidstone and their sector stations. Additional squadrons were to climb to between 20–27,000 feet (6,096–8,229m). Spitfires were to provide a fighter screen on a line between Hornchurch and Biggin Hill. The Hurricanes were still primarily tasked with attacking the bombers. When a raid comprising more than one hundred and fifty aircraft had been spotted, Park would call for assistance from neighboring groups.

Night-time bombing continued to wreak death and destruction not only on London but also on cities across the country; during the night of the 15–16 October, bombs killed more than four hundred people and wounded a further eight hundred.

Following Mussolini's desire to take part in the battle, a large contingent of Italians had been transferring from their home bases to two airfield in Belgium since the latter part of September. They were to fly joint missions with aircraft from Luftflotte II. After familiarization work and a certain amount of re-equipping, they were declared operational on 22 October, but

General Milch, who was in charge of Luftflotte V considered the Italians to be more of a liability than an asset.

On the night of 24 October, eighteen bombers and their aircrew, belonging to the Italian Air Force, took part in their first action in the battle. Fiat BR.20, twin-engined, medium bombers took off on a mission to bomb Felixstowe and Harwich. Of the bombers that set out, one crashed shortly after take-off and ten bombers managed to locate Harwich and drop their bombs without causing any real damage. On the return flight, two bombers got lost and their crews bailed out, and another bomber crash-landed.

The following day, Heinkels belonging to Luftflotte V took off from their base in Norway to attack the airfield at Montrose in Scotland. Flying in at low level, they caught the defenses off-guard and caused significant damage to some to the airfields building and 111 Squadron's Hurricanes; they also killed five people and wounded another eleven.

On 29 October, the Italians made their second appearance of the battle when, on the insistence of Mussolini, a small number of Italian aircraft took part in the lunch-time raid. Their bombers joined in a raid on Ramsgate while the Luftwaffe attacked Portsmouth and London. Using fifteen Fiat BR 20 bombers escorted by thirty-nine Fiat CR 42 *Falco* biplane and thirty-four Fiat G 50 *Freccia* fighters, their attack was fairly ineffectual and, as with many of the raids since the middle of September, Fighter Command managed to drive many of the raiders back across the Channel before they could reach their targets. There are also reports that they also took part in the slightly more successful raid on the Royal Marine Barracks at Deal, where seven soldiers were killed and another twelve were wounded.

29 October marked the last substantial, daylight activities of the Battle of Britain.

With a return to drizzle and rainy conditions the following day only small-scale fighter and fighter-bomber raids were mounted against London and the southeast. Poor weather continued on the last day of the month, which, turned out to be end of the battle. This also marked the last of fifty-seven days or nights of continuous bombing of London, although the Blitz would not end until 8 May 1941, by which time over 1,000,000 homes were damaged or destroyed, more than 21,000 people had been killed in the Capital, and over 250,000 people had been made homeless.

Even though the most significant periods of the battle had passed in the previous months, Fighter Command lost another one hundred and eighty-five aircraft in October's air battles, and the Luftwaffe lost three hundred and seventy-nine. During the entire four months of the battle, Fighter Command lost a total of 1,087 aircraft, and the Luftwaffe had lost 1,652. Interestingly, both sides thought that the others losses were significantly higher with Fighter Command estimating Luftwaffe losses as 2,698, and the Luftwaffe estimating Fighter Command's losses as 3,058. Although they will be forever known as 'The Few,' 2,367 Fighter Command pilots flew during the battle and 446 of them lost their lives. On the German side, 1,644 aircrew were killed and a further 1,445 are recorded as missing presumed killed. During the battle, British fighter production totaled 2,354 whereas the Luftwaffe received only nine hundred and seventy-five new aircraft.

The Battle of Britain may have finished but night bombing of the capital and other cities continued. Fighter Command may have won the first large-scale battle of the war fought only by aircraft, but as we will see in the next chapter, long-held, deep-seated resentment and opportunism would rear its ugly head to take away, from Dowding and Park—the two men who led us to that victory—the praise, honor and recognition they deserved.

Chapter 10
Scapegoats in the Aftermath

Even though the air fighting still continued but on a smaller scale, and with the ever-increasing night-time Blitz in full swing, Fighter Command had broken the back of the Germans' attempts to gain air superiority over Britain. However, as Holland writes:

'Yet at this moment of great triumph for the RAF and especially Fighter Command, the release from the stranglehold prompted not celebration but acrimony, jealousy and the worst kinds of ugly political jostling.'

This had been on the cards for a very long time. Dowding was known as a man who had strong opinions on how Fighter Command should operate; after all, he had been in charge of it since its formation. He had been willing to protect it from the push by so many high-ranking men in the RAF to put bombers first. However, he was not interested in politics, only what was best for building up and maintaining Fighter Command. Dowding was known to be 'his own man,' stubborn and resolute, who held firmly to his principles. He had ruffled a lot of feathers over the years, and, as we have seen, he had been due for retirement prior to the start and again during the Battle. As Dowding was disliked by many people at the Air Ministry, they had been trying to get rid of him for some time, they had tried unsuccessfully on four occasions so far, but this was their opportunity. One of the other underlying problems was that Keith Park had been put in charge of 11 Group by Dowding over the head of Leigh-Mallory, and Park had Dowding's full support. This meant that if Dowding went Park too would have to go. Politicking was about raise its ugly head.

Back in February 1940, following a meeting held at Bentley Priory, Leigh-Mallory is reported to have said, in front of Keith Park, that he would move heaven and earth to get Dowding removed from Fighter Command.

In his book about Keith Park, Vincent Orange comments that Dowding thought that Leigh-Mallory's reluctance to cover 11 Group's airfield when requested to do so was because he 'found it increasingly difficult to accept his place in the rear, behind the front line.' Leigh-Mallory thought that he was a great leader and was frustrated to find himself in a supporting role. However, with Douglas Bader, a national hero in his group, he had an opportunity to shine. Orange observes that Bader's idea of a Big Wing 'seemed to provide him [Leigh-Mallory] with a way of making a direct contribution to the battle.' We also see from Bader's behavior that he, like Leigh-Malory, was also unhappy to be taking a backseat, supporting role. Brown also includes similar comments about the two of them. Of Bader, he writes that he was aggressive, self-seeking, and ready to challenge existing structures in Fighter Command. He adds that without Bader there would not have been a Big Wing in 12 Group, but if one had already existed, 'Bader would probably have decided to fight with a single squadron but with free range to do what he liked.' Of Leigh-Mallory, he comments that the introduction of the Big Wing by 'an accepted national hero' was Mallory's opportunity to join in such an important battle and be seen as a 'war leader.'

If you add to this Air Vice Marshal, Assistant Chief of the Air Staff Sholto Douglas' support of Big Wings as a way of being able to shoot down as many bombers as possible, you can see why he supported Leigh-Mallory and the idea of the Big Wing. Of course, this ignores the fact that, as we have seen, the time taken to form and maneuver a large group of fighters into a position to be able to attack the bombers meant that most likely they would have already bombed their targets—which during the most critical period of the battle were Park's 11 Group airfields—and be on their way home before the wing arrived.

Leigh-Mallory and Douglas Bader also had the support of the MP for the Isle of Wight, Peter McDonald, who happened to be the Adjutant (administrator) of Bader's 242 Squadron. Leigh-Mallory also had the support of the Under Secretary of State for Air, Harold Balfour, who went to see Churchill about the use of Big Wings. Their actions have been interpreted as using political influence behind the scenes, and behind Dowding's back. As an MP, McDonald was able to report his criticism of Dowding based on Bader's views directly to parliament, thus, further highlighting the political nature of the maneuvers against Dowding. In fact, the Secretary of State for Air Sir Archibald Sinclair went to see Bader's 242 squadron, and the Chief of Air Staff Cyril Newell also wrote a letter of congratulations to them. Interestingly, Dowding had always had Churchill's full support, and when Churchill heard that Newell was proposing to remove Dowding as

Commander-in-Chief of Fighter Command during the battle, he wrote to Newell, saying that Dowding should remain in office as long as the war continued, and that he should even be considered for the role of Chief of Air Staff. Later, when Churchill found out that Newell and Sinclair had still not confirmed Dowding's continued employment in charge of Fighter Command, Holland reports that Churchill 'was incensed.' Even though they had been trying to retire him, they then reluctantly wrote to Dowding, saying that he would remain in post for the near future.

Why was the Big Wing such a point of contention?

Although the Duxford Big Wing was assembled on a number of occasions, it was only used seven times during the main part of the battle. The first time the Big Wing went in to action was on 7 September. It flew again on 9 September when two more squadrons were added to its number and again on 11 September. Its most influential operations were on 15 September, when it flew twice. It then flew again on 17 and 18 September, but its only really effective action took place on 27 September. To say, therefore, that it had limited use and impact is probably not an understatement. However, as we have seen, on 17 September, Leigh-Mallory claimed that the Wing had, to date, destroyed one hundred and five enemy aircraft with a further forty probably destroyed and eighteen damaged for the loss of only six of its own pilots and another five wounded. Orange notes that at the time it was thought that the Big Wing claims were twice as high as most other squadrons, and it was known that other squadrons' claims were already exaggerated due to the confusing nature of aerial combat. Unfortunately, it appears that Sholto Douglas accepted the claims without questioning them, but why did he do that? The main value of the Big Wing lay in the shock it produced in Luftwaffe aircrew due to the sight of so many aircraft flying in to attack them, especially when they had been continuously told that Fighter Command was down to three hundred, two hundred, one hundred, and fifty fighters, particularly on 15 September.

On 24 September, Sholto Douglas, who although he was Deputy Chief of Air Staff was still only an Air Vice Marshal, told Air Vice Marshal Robert Saundby the Assistant Chief of Air Staff (tactics) that he had received a number of criticisms about the tactics that Keith Park had employed during the battle. These included claims that pilots flew into battle with no clear idea of how many other squadrons were in the air at the same time, and that they did not know who they were supposed to cooperate with. It should be noted that during the battle most aircraft were still fitted with radios that only enabled a maximum of two squadrons to operate on the same frequency. This meant that formations comprising more than two squadrons could not directly communicate with each other. The new VHF radios that gave them the capability to talk to large numbers of aircraft were slowly coming in to service, but few aircraft had been fitted with them. Because of Douglas' comments, Saundby ordered a report to be prepared that would look into the tactics Dowding and Park employed during the battle. The report was to be ready for 1 October.

On 29 September, Park wrote a report to Sholto Douglas, which included his observations about the cooperation, or rather lack of it, from 12 Group and noted that they tended to do their own thing, because as far as Leigh-Mallory was concerned, his own tactics were correct. Park also added that as far as he was concerned there was nothing wrong with using wings of aircraft, but given the situation he was in, and the limitations of radios etc., his use of two squadrons operating together was still the best tactic he could have employed at the time. Air Vice Marshal Donald Stevenson was also asked by Sholto Douglas to provide a report on the operation of wings, and his report was effectively based on Leigh-Mallory's report of 17 September in which the exaggerated claims were included.

Sholto Douglas then organized a conference for 3:30 p.m. on 17 October at the Air Ministry. This meeting would later come to be known by a number of authors as 'the meeting of shame.' It was a high-level meeting attended by twelve people, eleven of which were all of Air Vice Marshal or senior rank. They, including Dowding, Park, Leigh Mallory, Quintin Brand (in charge of 10 Group), and two secretaries. Six of the eleven present—Air Vice Marshal Sholto Douglas, Air Marshal Philip Joubert de la Ferte, Air Vice Marshal Trafford Leigh-Mallory, Air Commodore John Slessor, Air Commodore Donald Stevenson, and Group Captain Henry Crowe—were opponents of Dowdings and Park's tactics. It is also worth adding that Slessor, Stevenson, and Crowe all worked for Sholto Douglas; and Joubert, who was responsible for radar, also reported to him. Therefore, according to Ray, apart from Dowding, Park, and Brand, the only other person present who was skeptical about the use of wings was Charles Portal, who was to take over as the Chief of Air Staff on 27 October. Brown comments that as Sholto Douglas had the support of most of the people at the meeting, its purpose was essentially to denigrate Dowding.

The stated purpose of the meeting was to discuss 'major tactics by fighter formations' and the progress being made on the introduction of night interceptors. For the meeting, Stevenson wrote a covering letter in which he said that Parks' report did not specify whether squadrons were vectored into battle singularly, or in pairs, or even in larger formations. He also included the claims made by 12 Group in Leigh-Mallory's report. Park responded to

Stevenson's comments by asking for him to include his last two instructions that he had sent out to his squadrons that were based on his 'five months experience in the employment of using wing formations.'

Unknown to neither Dowding, Park, nor Brand, Leigh-Mallory had brought Douglas Bader with him. This caused astonishment to a number of those who attended the meeting, as Bader was only a Squadron Leader. Neither Brand nor Park had been given the same opportunity to bring along front-line pilots from their own groups. The focus of the meeting was therefore obvious but, as Orange comments, 'in the event, to produce Bader at the meeting proved a masterstroke, establishing the claim that Douglas and his friends to be patrons of bold, new ideas.'

Sholto Douglas was in charge of the meeting in the absence of Newell, the Chief of Air Staff, who was indisposed, although, as Peter Brown points out in his book *Honour Restored*, he was well enough to take part in a meeting of the Chiefs of Staff of all the services the following day. He must have known what the meeting was all about and how it was going to go, because he knew that Sholto Douglas had invited Douglas Bader. Brown also says that protocol at such meetings meant that someone with the rank of Squadron Leader would normally have had to wait in a separate room until invited in to speak. However, Bader was present throughout the time when the others were challenging Dowding and Park over their tactics and, effectively their professionalism. Brown includes the fact that Bader was not invited at a last minute because he had been granted four days leave from 15 October, covering the date of the meeting on 17, which indicates that his presence had been planned.

The meeting was asked to consider three points:
- That enemy formations should be outnumbered when encountered.
- That fighters should go in to battle with a plan of action, so that escorts were engaged by one part of the force and bombers by the rest.
- That fighters should, if possible, have a height advantage.

Since the start of the German night-time bombing campaign, there had been increasing criticism of Fighter Command's inability to intercept the bombers that were causing so much misery, death, and destruction. To combat this, the new Bristol Beaufighter IF—a specialized night-fighter— had entered service in August, but the aircraft and crews were still effectively testing out their equipment and tactics. By the end of September, Beaufighters had re-equipped five squadrons, but they did not manage to make their first 'kill' until November. McKay notes, however, that two years earlier—towards the end of 1938—Dowding had sat in the backseat of a Fairey Battle during a test flight to demonstrate the use of radar for detecting night-time bombers. He adds that Churchill went on a similar flight early the following year.

On 14 September, Beaverbrook had asked John Salmond, a former Chief of Air Staff, to set up a committee to look at night defenses. The committee's report was critical of Dowding's cautious approach and favored Douglas' quick fix ideas, which included using two Hurricane and two Defiant squadrons as night-fighters. Dowding felt that he could not afford to lose two squadrons of Hurricanes to a hit-or-miss approach to combating night-time bombing when the daytime threat was still very real.

Orange notes that 'Douglas's long speech showed no signs of being informed by a reading of Park's report or his numerous instructions in which these and many other matters of anxious, daily concern had been exhaustively analysed.' When Douglas had finished, it was Keith Park's turn to speak, during which he countered and corrected many of Douglas' points.

Leigh-Mallory stated that he could get a wing of five squadrons airborne in six minutes and over Hornchurch airfield at 20,000 feet (6,096m) in twenty-five minutes. However, as Orange observes, it took them seventeen minutes to leave the ground and another twenty minutes before they even set course for Hornchurch on 29 October, and that was after two months of practice and not under the intense pressure at the height of the Battle. Orange adds that during October, the Big Wing was in operation only ten times, during which, because of the time it took to form and reach its patrol height and position, it could only patrol for an average of twenty-four minutes, and it only shot down one fighter. Weather conditions prevented its use the rest of the time, meanwhile Park's paired squadrons remained operational. Ray reports that a German bomber, from taking off in the Calais area, could be over Canterbury in half the time it would take a Spitfire or Hurricane to arrive from Duxford.

It is said that Park looked tired at the meeting, which was hardly surprising given the pressure he had been under for nearly four months, whereas Leigh-Mallory 'looked and sounded impressive.' Maybe Park realized that the outcome of the meeting was a foregone conclusion, especially when he saw Bader was there. Leigh-Mallory criticized Dowding and Parks' cautious tactic of using only the number of aircraft and squadrons necessary to break-up the enemy formations, which meant that the Germans now had the bombers necessary to bomb London; whereas with bold leadership, they could have been smashed.

Following the meeting, on 21 October, Park sent a list of amendments and corrections to points, criticizing his tactics that he wanted Sholto Douglas to add to the final report, but Douglas refused to add them. He also refused to include similar amendments sent by Brand.

Balfour, the Under Secretary of State for Air, visited Duxford to find out what 12 Group's views were about the tactics employed during the battle from which he also produced a report. Dowding then asked Douglas Evill, his Senior Air Staff Officer at Bentley Priory, to look at Balfour's report and write his own report, in which he countered all of Balfour's points. Dowding then used Evill's report as the basis of his own reply to Sholto Douglas on 6 November.

On 25 October, both Park and Dowding were informed that they would be relieved of their commands; the Air Ministry and the air force hierarchy achieved their wish to get rid of 'Stuffy' Dowding. Sholto Douglas took over Dowding's role as Head of Fighter Command on 25 November, and Leigh-Mallory took over command of 11 Group the following month. Dowding was not retired as expected but was packed off to America as an envoy, a role for which he was totally unsuited. Park was moved to Training Command on 18 December where his experience in 11 Group really paid off. Bungay reports that Park discovered that they were operating at only two-third's capacity and were still using peacetime routines. He eventually moved to take command of the air force in Egypt; and then on 14 July, he took command of the defense of Malta, where his tactical abilities famously came to the fore. Ironically, in August 1944, he became Air Commander-in-Chief of Southeast Asia Command after Leigh-Mallory, who was supposed to take up the role, was killed in an air crash on his way to take up the post.

It is worth reading Orange's book, particularly chapter 11, *The Battle of Britain: The Whirligig in Time*, which tells some of the story of the writing of the wrongs done to Park and Dowding. It is also important to add that not everyone agrees with the view of a conspiracy and it is worth reading the chapter titled "Changes in Fighter Command" in John Ray's book *The Battle of Britain: Dowding and the First Victory 1940*, for an alternative view.

As a follow-up to the battle, and to prove the point that his Big Wing tactics were correct, on 29 January 1941, Leigh-Mallory decided to conduct an exercise based on an actual attack on Kenley, Biggin Hill, and Hornchurch on 6 September. During the 'raid,' he completely mishandled the situation, and the bombers managed to 'bomb' all of the airfields without being intercepted—in fact, most of the defending fighters were still on the ground when the 'attacks' took place.

When the air force originally published its official history of the Battle, Dowding's name was not mentioned, even though he had almost single-handedly built-up the infrastructure, centralized control system, advanced fighter aircraft and radar—often under great resistance from people in the Air Ministry—so that when it was called on, it all worked.

The Battle of Britain was over and in May 1941, Germany would turn eastwards to attack Russia, taking a significant proportion of the Luftwaffe in that direction. Battles would continue across North Africa and Europe. The RAF would move from a defensive to offensive role; the Royal Navy would be embroiled in the Battle of the Atlantic and supporting the Russian convoys. Britain would stand alone with support from the commonwealth and, increasingly, from the USA, with the introduction of the lend-lease scheme in March 1941. It joined the war in December of that year following the Japanese attack on Pearl Harbor. If the Luftwaffe had gained air superiority over the Channel and Southern England, would we have been able to continue even if the invasion had not taken place? The Battle of Britain, arguably the Second World War's first great air battle, kept us in the fight and allowed Britain to become a giant aircraft carrier, army, and naval base for the rest of the war.

Figure 1. Supermarine Spitfire MkI, X4590, a Battle of Britain airplane at the RAF Museum, Hendon.

Figure 2. Hawker Hurricane MkI, P2617, a Battle of Britain airplane at the RAF Museum, Hendon.

Figure 3. Boulton Paul Defiant MkI, N1671, a Battle of Britain airplane at the RAF Museum, Cosford.

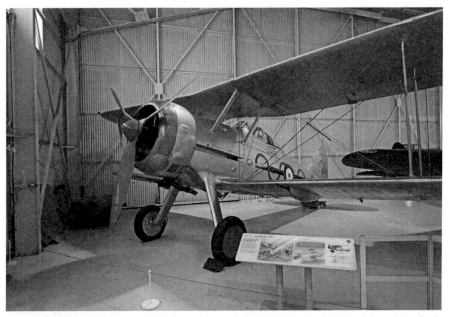

Figure 4. Gloster Gladiator MkI, K8042, built in 1937, at the RAF Museum, Cosford.

Figure 5. Bristol Blenheim MkI, L6739, actually a Canadian Bollingbroke MkIV restored with a Battle of Britain MkI nose. Owned and flown by Aircraft Restoration Company at the Imperial War Museum, Duxford.

Figure 6. Messerschmitt Bf109E, Nr4101, a Battle of Britain airplane at the RAF Museum, Hendon.

Figure 7. Messerschmitt Bf110G, Nr730301, at the RAF Museum, Hendon.

Figure 8. Junkers Ju87G, Nr494083, at the RAF Museum, Hendon.

Figure 9. Junkers Ju88R, Nr360043, at the RAF Museum, Cosford.

Figure 10. Heinkel HeIIIH, Nr701152, at the RAF Museum, Hendon.

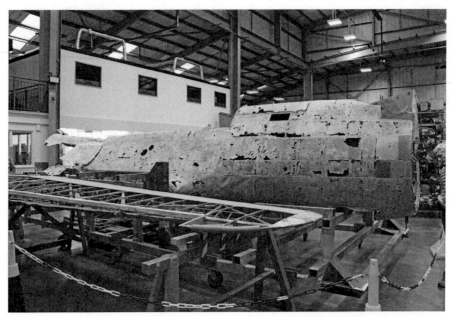

Figure 11. Dornier Do17Z, Nr1160, preserved wreck of the only surviving Do17, a Battle of Britain airplane at the RAF Museum, Cosford.

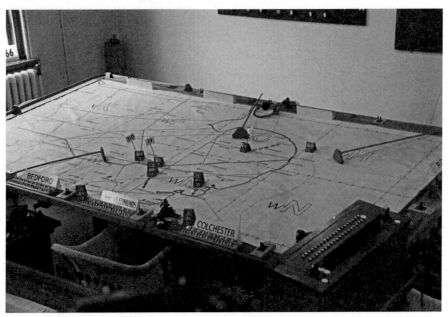

Figure 12. The plotting table in the Sector Station Operations Room at the Imperial War Museum, Duxford.

Figure 13. The Tote boards in the Sector Station Operations Room at the
Imperial War Museum, Duxford.

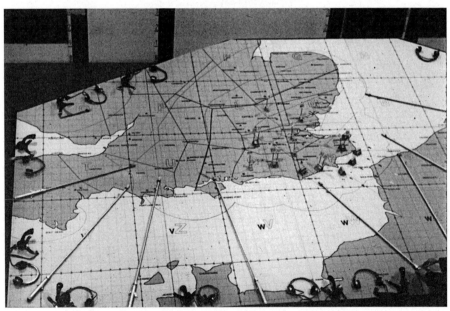

Figure 14. The 11 Group plotting table replica at the RAF Museum, Hendon.

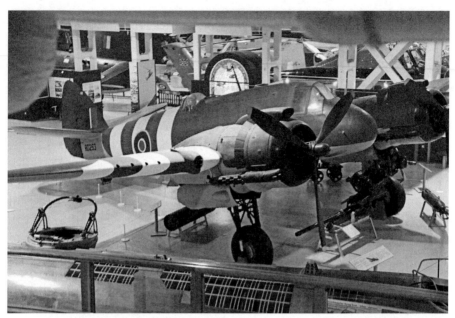

Figure 15. Bristol Beaufighter TFX, RD253, at the RAF Museum, Hendon.

Figure 16. Armada cannons in Victoria Park, Bideford, Devon.

Figure 17. The Culmstock Beacon, an Armada signal station on a hill above the village of Culmstock, Devon.

Figure 18. Baker and Hawkins race-built ship design.

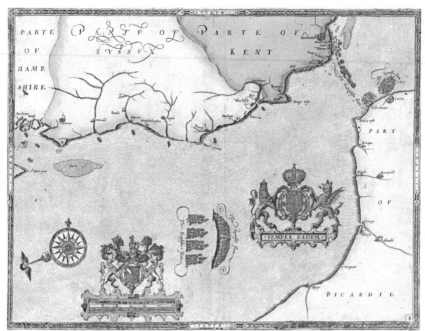

Figure 19. A map published in 1590 showing the English fleet following the Spanish Armada towards Calais.

Figure 20. English and Spanish ships

Figure 21. A Spanish siege gun recovered from the wreck of the
La Trinidad Valencera at the Royal Ulster Museum, Belfast.

Figure 22. The Ark Royal, the English flagship during action against
the Spanish Armada.

Figure 23. The Nuestra Senora del Rosario, the flagship of Don Pedro de Valdes.

Figure 24. English fireships at Calais.

Figure 25. A painting of an English race-built ship.

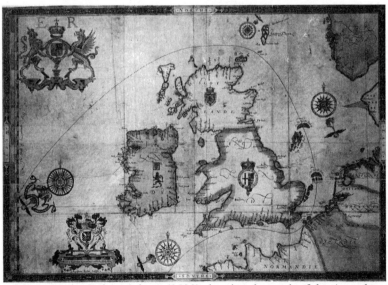

Figure 26. A map by Robert Adams (1590) showing the track of the Armada around Britain and Ireland.

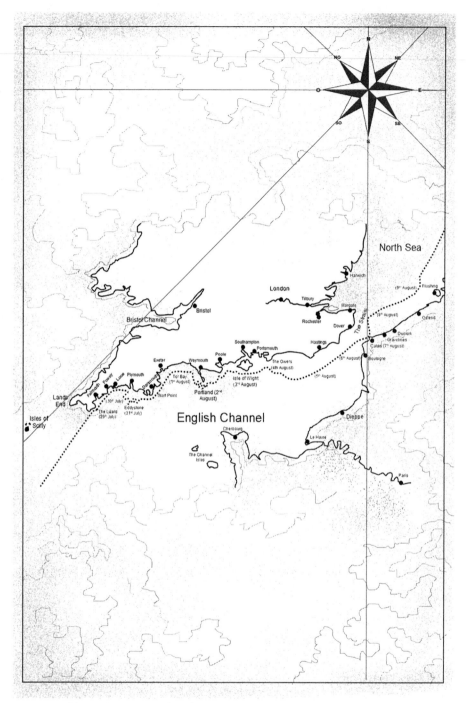

Figure 27. A map showing the progress of the Spanish Armada,
July 29 – August 9, 1588.

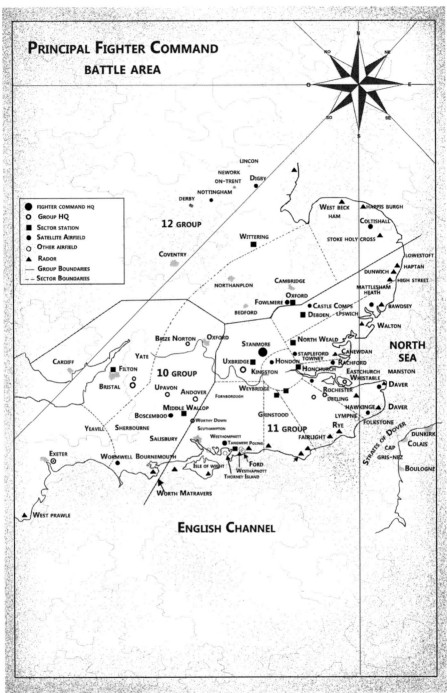

Figure 28. A map showing airfields, radar stations, and Fighter Command's Group and Sector layout in the main battle area during the Battle of Britain.

Bibliography (940)

Barratt, J., 2005, *Armada 1588: The Spanish Assault on England*. Pen & Sword Military, Barnsley. p182.

Bicheno, H., 2012, *Elizabeth's Sea Dogs: How the English Became the Scourge of the Seas*. Conway, London. p399.

Bickers, R. T., 1990, *The Battle of Britain: The Greatest Battle in the History of Air Warfare*. Salamander Books Ltd., London. p208.

Bishop, P., 2009, *Battle of Britain: A Day-by-Day Chronicle 10 July 1940 to 31 October 1940*. Quereus Publishing, London. p392.

Blaxland, G., 1981, *Southeast Britain Eternal Battleground*. Meresborough Books, Rainham, Kent. p160.

Bowyer, C., 1981, *Fighter Command 1936–1968*. Sphere Books Limited, London. p242.

Bowyer, M. J. F., 1979, *2 Group R.A. F.* Faber and Faber, London. p532.

Brown, P., 2005, *Honour Restored: The Battle of Britain, Dowding and the Fight for Freedom*. Spellmount Limited, Staplehurst, Kent. p250.

Brown, P., and Herbert, E. (eds), 2014, *The Secrets of Q Central: How Leighton Buzzard Shortened the Second World War*. Spellmount Limited, Staplehurst, Kent. P318.

Bungay, S., 2000, *The Most Dangerous Enemy: A History of the Battle of Britain*. Ayrum Press Ltd. London. p492.

Churchill, W. S., 2003, *Never Give In! The Best of Winston Churchill's Speeches*. Hyperion, New York. p524.

Collier, B., 1957, *Leader of the Few: The Authorised Biography of Air Chief Marshal the Lord Dowding of Bentley Priory*. Jarrolds, London. p264.

Collier, R., 1966, *Eagle Day: The Battle of Britain*. Hodder and Stoughton Ltd., London. p316.

Korda, M., 2009, *With Wings Like Eagles: The Untold History of the Battle of Britain*. J. R. Books, London. p322.

Deighton, L., 1977, *Fighter: The True Story of the Battle of Britain*. Book Club Associates, London. p303.

Donnelly, L., 2004, *The Other Few: The Contribution Made by Bomber and Costal Aircrew to the Winning of the Battle of Britain.* Red Kite Books. Walton on Thames, Surrey. p288.

Ekin, D., 2015, *The Last Armada: Queen Elizabeth, Juan del Aguila, and Hugh O'Neill: The Story of the 100-Day Spanish Invasion.* Pegasus Books LLC, New York. p413.

Fleming, P., 1975, *Operation Sea Lion.* Pan Books. London. p333.

Harman, N., 1980, *Dunkirk the Necessary Myth.* Coronet Books, Sevenoaks, Kent. p300.

Harris, H. J., 1988, *Drake of Tavistock: The Life and Origins of Sir Fancis Drake.* Devon Books. Exeter, Devon. p92.

Herman, A., 2005, *To Rule the Waves: How the British Navy Shaped the Modern World.* Harper Perennial. New York. p648.

Hewitt, G., 2008. *Hitler's Armada: The Royal Navy & the Defence of Great Britain April–October 1940.* Pen & Sword Maritime. Barnsley, South Yorkshire. p194.

Holland, J, 2010, *The Battle of Britain: Five Months That Changed History May–October 1940.* Bantam Press, London. p677.

Hough, R, and Richards, D., 1990, *The Battle of Britain.* Coronet Books, Hodder and Stoughton, Sevenoaks, Kent. p413.

Hutchinson, R., 2006, *Elizabeth's Spy Master: Francis Walsingham and the Secret War that Saved England.* Phoenix. London. p416.

Hutchinson, R., 2013. *The Spanish Armada.* Phoenix. London. p404.

Johnson, B., 1978, *The Secret War.* Arrow Books Limited, London. p400.

Johnson, J. E., 1985, *The Story of Air Fighting.* Arrow Books, London. p306.

The Kent Aviation Historical Research Society, 1981, *Kent Airfields in the Battle of Britain.* Meresborough Books. Gillingham, Kent. p192.

Levine, J., 2011. *Operation Fortitude: The Story of the Spy Operation That Saved D-Day.* The Bok People, St Helens, Lancashire. p316.

Lewis, B., 1991, *Aircrew: The Story of the Men Who Flew the Bombers.* Cassell Military Paperbacks. London. p188.

Lukacs, John., 1999, *Five Days in London May 1940.* Yale University Press. New Haven and London. p236.

Matthews, R., 2004, *The Spanish Armada: A Campaign in Context,* Spellmount, The History Press, Stroud. p238.

Mattingly, G., 1959, *The Defeat of the Spanish Armada.* Book Club Associates, London. p384.

McDermott, J., 2005, *England and the Spanish Armada: The Necessary Quarrel.* Yale University Press, New Haven and London. p411.

McKay, S., 2012. *The Secret Listeners: The Men and Women Posted Across the World to Intercept the German Codes for Bletchley Park.* Aurum Press Ltd. London. p354.

McKay, S., 2015. *The Secret Life of Fighter Command: The Men and Women Who Beat the Luftwaffe.* Aurum Press Ltd. London. p354.

Milton, G., 2016, *Churchill's Ministry of Ungentlemanly Warfare: The Mavericks Who Platted Hitler's Defeat.* John Murray (Publishers), London. p356.

Moorhouse, G., 2005, *Great Hary's Navy: How Henry VIII Gave England Sea Power.* Phoenix. London. p372.

Munson, K., and Taylor, J. W. R., 1976, *The Battle of Britain.* New English Library, London. p128.

Murray. W., 1988, *Luftwaffe: Strategy for Defeat 1933–45.* Graft Books, London. p477.

Musgrove, D., 2009, *The Great Turning Points in British History: The 20 events that made the nation.* Constable & Robinson Ltd., London. p210.

Nanson, N., 2004, *The Confident Hope of a Miracle: The True Story of the Spanish Armada.* Corgi Books, London. p668.

Ogley, B., 1990, *Biggin on the Bump.* Froglets Publications Limited, Westerham, Kent. p160.

Orange, V., 2001, Park: *The Biography of Air Chief Marshal Sir Keith Park.* Grub Street, London. p301.

Overy, R., 2000, *The Battle of Britain: The Myth and the Reality.* Penguin Books, London. p162.

Parker, M., 2000, *The Battle of Britain July–October 1940: An Oral History of Britain's 'Finest Hour.'* Headline Book Publishing, London. p342.

Ramsey, W. G. (ed.), 1987, *The Battle of Britain Then and Now. After the Battle Publication,* London. p816.

Ray. J., 1994, *The Battle of Britain: Dowding and the First Victory, 1940.* Cassell Military Paperbacks. London. p222.

Read, S., 2006, *The Killing Skies: RAF Bomber Command at War. Spellmount Limited.* Stroud, Gloucestershire. p232.

Reit, S., 1978, *The Hidden War: The Amazing Camouflage Deception of World War II.* Corgi Books, London. p231.

Robinson, D., 2006, *Invasion, 1940.* Constable & Robinson Ltd., London. p317.

Ronald, S., 2007, *The Pirate Queen: Queen Elizabeth I, Her Pirate Adventurers, and the Dawn of Empire.* HarperCollins Publishers. p471.

Schom, A., 1992, *Trafalgar: Countdown to Battle 1803–1805*. Penguin Books, London. p421.

Thomas, D. A., 1988, *The Illustrated Armada Handbook*. Harrap Ltd., London. p218.

Tracy, N., 2010, *The Battle of Quiberon Bay, 1759: Admiral Hawke and the Defeat of the French Invasion*. Pen & Sword Maritime, Barnsley, South Yorkshire. p240.

Tute, W., 2007, *The Deadly Stroke*. Pen & Sword Maritime, Barnsley, South Yorkshire. p221.

Wallace, G., 1957, *R.A.F. Biggin Hill*. Putnam, London. p288.

Ward, A., 1989, *A Nation Alone: The Battle of Britain – 1940*. Osprey Publishing Ltd., London. p208.

Warner, G., 1991, *The Forgotten Bomber: The Story of the Restoration of the World's Only Airworthy Bristol Blenheim*. Patrick Stephens Limited, Yeovil, Somerset. p191.

Wilkinson, J., 1995, *The Pirate and the Prophecy...of the Keigwins of Mousehole and the Spanish Raid on Cornwall*. United Writers Publications Ltd., Penzance, Cornwall. p363.

Winterbotham. F. W., 1974, *The Ultra Secret*. Futura Publications Limited. p239.

Whiting, R., 2004, *The Spanish Armada.* Sutton Publishing Limited. Stroud, Gloucestershire. p212.

Wood, D. and Dempster, D., 1969, *The Narrow Margin: The Definitive Story of the Battle of Britain*. Arrow Books Limited, London. p361.

Wyllie, J. and McKinley, M. 2015, *Code Breakers: The Secret Intelligence Unit that changed the course of the First World War*. Ebury Press, London. p346.